Generous Orthodoxies

Generous Orthodoxies

Essays on the History and Future of Ecumenical Theology

EDITED BY Paul Silas Peterson

FOREWORD BY Brian D. McLaren

☙PICKWICK *Publications* · Eugene, Oregon

GENEROUS ORTHODOXIES
Essays on the History and Future of Ecumenical Theology

Copyright © 2020 Wipf and Stock Publishers. All rights reserved. Except for brief quotations in critical publications or reviews, no part of this book may be reproduced in any manner without prior written permission from the publisher. Write: Permissions, Wipf and Stock Publishers, 199 W. 8th Ave., Suite 3, Eugene, OR 97401.

Pickwick Publications
An Imprint of Wipf and Stock Publishers
199 W. 8th Ave., Suite 3
Eugene, OR 97401

www.wipfandstock.com

PAPERBACK ISBN: 978-1-5326-1888-8
HARDCOVER ISBN: 978-1-4982-4474-9
EBOOK ISBN: 978-1-4982-4473-2

Cataloguing-in-Publication data:

Names: Peterson, Paul Silas, 1979–, editor. | McLaren, Brian D., 1956–, foreword.

Title: Generous orthodoxies : essays on the history and future of ecumenical theology / edited by Paul Silas Peterson ; foreword by Brian D. McLaren.

Description: Eugene, OR : Pickwick Publications, 2020 | Includes bibliographical references.

Identifiers: ISBN 978-1-5326-1888-8 (paperback) | ISBN 978-1-4982-4474-9 (hardcover) | ISBN 978-1-4982-4473-2 (ebook)

Subjects: LCSH: Ecumenical movement—History. | Ecumenical movement. | Christianity—Forecasting.

Classification: BX8.3 .G46 2020 (print) | BX8.3 .G46 (ebook)

Manufactured in the U.S.A.   04/23/20

Contents

Contributors | vii

Foreword | xiii
—Brian D. McLaren

Introduction | xvii
—Paul Silas Peterson

Part One: Ecumenical Reform Theologies

1. Yves Congar: The Birth of "Catholic Ecumenism" | 3
—Andrew Meszaros

2. Edmund Schlink: Ecumenical Theology | 23
—Matthew L. Becker

3. Otto Hermann Pesch: Ecumenical Scholasticism | 42
—Dorothea Sattler

4. George Lindbeck: Ecumenical Unity through Ecclesial Particularity | 57
—Ronald T. Michener

5. John D. Zizioulas: A Pioneer of Ecumenical Dialogue and Christian Unity | 78
—Nikolaos Asproulis

Part Two: Overcoming Liberal-Conservative Polarities

6. Hans Frei: Beyond Liberal and Conservative | 99
—Ben Fulford

7. Wolfhart Pannenberg: Liberal Orthodoxy | 118
—Friederike Nüssel

8. Stanley J. Grenz: The Evangelical Turn to Postliberal Theological Method | 132
—Jay T. Smith

Part Three: Boundary Crossings in Philosophical, Systematic, and Ethical Theology

9. David Tracy: Difference, Unity, and the Analogical Imagination | 153
—William E. Myatt

10. Robert W. Jenson: God's Way and the Ways of the Church | 172
—Christophe Chalamet

11. Stanley Hauerwas: Witnessing Communities of Character | 186
—Victoria Lorrimar

12. Marilyn McCord Adams: Philosophy, Theology, and Prayer | 201
—Christine M. Helmer

Part Four: Ecumenical Theology Today

13. Pentecostalism and Christian Orthodoxy: Revision, Revival, and Renewal | 217
—Wolfgang Vonday

14. Shifting Paradigms—Future Ecumenical Challenges | 233
—Johanna Rahner

15. Theology Today in India: Ecumenical or Interreligious? | 247
—Michael Amaladoss, SJ

16. Next Steps—and Visions? Lutheran Perspectives on Doctrinal Ecumenism | 255
—Bernd Oberdorfer

Contributors

Michael Amaladoss, SJ, is Professor and Director of the Institute of Dialogue with Cultures and Religions, Loyola College, Chennai, India. He has a doctoral degree in systematic theology from the Institut Catholique of Paris. He has taught theology at Vidyajyoti College of Theology, Delhi, India. He has also taught as a guest professor in theological centers in Paris, Bruxelles, Louvain, Washington DC, Berkeley, Cincinnati, and Manila. He has authored 32 books. Some of them have been translated into European and Asian languages. He has also written 470 articles in many languages. His books include *Life in Freedom: Liberation Theologies from Asia* (1997); *The Asian Jesus* (2005); and *Beyond Inculturation* (2005).

Nikolaos Asproulis is Deputy Director of the Volos Academy for Theological Studies, and has written extensively on themes relating to systematic theology, especially in relation to Trinitarian theology, ecclesiology, ecumenical dialogue, theological methodology, political theology, theological education and the history of contemporary Eastern Orthodox theology. He is also the co-editor (with J. Chryssavgis) of *Theology as Doxology and Dialogue: The Essential Writings of Nikos Nissiotis* (2019); (with P. Kalaitzidis) of *Personhood, Eucharist and the Kingdom of God in Orthodox and Ecumenical Perspective: Festschrift in Honour of Metropolitan John Zizioulas of Pergamon* (2016); and (with P. Kalaitzidis, Cyril Hovorun, et. al.) *Orthodox Handbook for Ecumenism: Recourses for Theological Education* (2014) as well as multiple other works and translations.

Matthew L. Becker is Professor of Theology at the Department of Theology of Valparaiso University, and has written extensively on themes relating to modern Christian theology, especially regarding the nineteenth and twentieth centuries. He is the author of the monograph entitled *Johannes von Hofmann, The Self-Giving God and Salvation History* (2004); two chapters for the book, *Twentieth-Century Lutheran Theologians* (2013); and the monograph *Fundamental Theology: A Protestant Perspective* (2015). He is also the editor and translator of *The Collected Works of Edmund Schlink, vol. 1: The Coming Christ and Church and Tradition and After the Council* (2016) and the editor of (and contributor to) *Nineteenth-Century Lutheran Theologians* (2016).

Christophe Chalamet is Professor of Systematic Theology at the University of Geneva. He is the author of multiple works in theology including *A Most Excellent Way: An Essay on Faith, Hope, and Love* (2020) and *Dialectical Theologians: Wilhelm Herrmann, Karl Barth, and Rudolf Bultmann* (2005). He is also the editor (with Marc Vial) of *Recent Developments in Trinitarian Theology* (2014) in which he published "God's 'Liveliness': God in Robert W. Jenson's Trinitarian Thought."

Ben Fulford is Senior Lecturer in Systematic Theology, Theology and Religious Studies Department, University of Chester, and currently working on a monograph on Hans Frei provisionally entitled *God's Patience and our Work: Hans Frei on Freedom and Modern Theology*. He is also the author of *Divine Eloquence and Human Transformation: Rethinking Scripture and History through Gregory of Nazianzus and Hans Frei* (2013) and other articles on the theology of the church fathers.

Christine M. Helmer is Professor of German and Religious Studies at Northwestern University in Evanston, Illinois. She holds an honorary doctorate in theology from the University of Helsinki. She is the editor (and co-editor) of numerous volumes in the areas of biblical theology, systematic theology, Schleiermacher studies, and Luther studies, most recently, *The Medieval Luther* (2020). She is the author of *Theology and the End of Doctrine* (2014), *The Trinity and Martin Luther* (2017), and *How Luther Became the Reformer* (2020).

Victoria Lorrimar is Lecturer in Systematic Theology at Trinity College Queensland (Australian College of Theology). She completed her doctorate in theology at the University of Oxford in 2018, focusing on a theological anthropology for engaging questions around human technological enhancement. She has published various articles in the areas of theology and science, ethics, and ecclesiology.

Brian D. McLaren holds honorary doctorates from Carey Theological Seminary and from Virginia Theological Seminary. He is an author, speaker, activist and public theologian. A former college English teacher and pastor, he is an ecumenical global networker among innovative Christian leaders. His book *A Generous Orthodoxy* (2004) has been called a "manifesto of the emerging church conversation." He is also the author of the highly-praised *A New Kind of Christianity* (2010).

Andrew Meszaros is Lecturer in Systematic Theology at the Pontifical University—St. Patricks College, Maynooth, and completed his doctoral work at the Catholic University of Louvain on doctrinal development. He is the author of *The Prophetic Church: History and Doctrinal Development in John Henry Newman and Yves Congar* (2016). He is currently researching the theological conflicts and disagreements within the *nouvelle théologie*, with special attention to the debate over a theology of history. Other research interests include Christology, soteriology, and ecclesiology.

Ronald T. Michener is Professor and Department Chair of Systematic Theology at the Evangelische Theologische Faculteit, Leuven, and has written on the themes of contemporary theology and ethics in the context of postmodernism. He is the author of *Postliberal Theology: A Guide for the Perplexed* (2013), as well as *The Matrix of Christian Ethics: Integrating Philosophy and Moral Theology in a Postmodern Context* (with Patrick Nullens, 2010) and *Engaging Deconstructive Theology* (2007).

William E. Myatt received his PhD in Constructive Theology from Loyola University Chicago. He has served on the faculty of various colleges and universities, teaching courses in theology and philosophy. Among many articles and reviews, Myatt is the author of "David Tracy: A Critical Theology of Retrieval" in *Theologies of Retrieval* (2019) and "Public Theology and 'The Fragment': Duncan Forrester, David Tracy, and Walter Benjamin" in *The International Journal of Public Theology*. Myatt currently works as Director of Philanthropic Engagement at the Lutheran School of Theology at Chicago, where he oversees the major gift fundraising effort of the seminary.

Friederike Nüssel is Professor of Systematic Theology and Director of the Ecumenical Institute at the Theological Faculty of the University of Heidelberg. She is a member of the International Catholic-Lutheran Commission on Unity, the Ecumenical Working Group of Protestant and Catholic Theologians in Germany, the Vatican Joint Working Group (World Council of Churches) and many other ecumenical working groups and commissions. Nüssel is the author (with Dorothea Sattler) of *Einführung in die ökumenische Theologie* (2008). In addition to many monographs and editorial works, she is also the author of "'Dogmatik als systematische

Theologie'! Zur Aktualität des Dogmatik-Verständnisses bei W. Pannenberg" (2015) and "The Ecclesiology of Wolfhart Pannenberg" in the *Oxford Handbook of Ecclesiology* (2016).

Bernd Oberdorfer is Professor for Systematic Theology at the Department of Theology of the Unviversity of Augsburg. He is the author of multiple essays and articles on ecumenical theology. He is also the editor of (with Peter Gemeinhardt) *Gebundene Freiheit? Bekenntnistradition und theologische Lehre im Luthertum. Historische, systematische und institutionstheoretische Perspektiven* (2008); (with Jörg Lauster) *Der Gott der Vernunft. Protestantismus und vernünftiger Gottesgedanke* (2009); (with Uwe Swarat) *Tradition in den Kirchen. Bindung, Kritik, Erneuerung* (2010); (with Michael Böhnke and Assaad Elias Kattan) *Die Filioque-Kontroverse. Historische, ökumenische und dogmatische Perspektiven 1200 Jahre nach der Aachener Synode (809)* (2011); (with Thomas Söding) *Kontroverse Freiheit. Die Impulse der Ökumene* (2017); (with Oliver Schuegraf) *Sichtbare Einheit der Kirche in lutherischer Perspektive. Eine Studie des Ökumenischen Studienausschusses/Visible Unity of the Church from a Lutheran Perspective. A Study by the Ecumenical Study Committee* (2017).

Paul Silas Peterson teaches theology at the Protestant Faculty of Theology of the University of Tübingen (where he is a Privatdozent) and the Department of Protestant Theology at the Unviersity of Hohenheim (Stuttgart). Previously he taught theology at the Faculty of Theology of the University of Heidelberg. He is the author of *The Early Hans Urs von Balthasar: Historical Contexts and Intellectual Formation* (2015); *Reformation in the Western World* (2017); *The Early Karl Barth: Historical Contexts and Intellectual Formation 1905-1935* (2018); and the editor of *The Decline of Established Christianity in the Western World: Interpretations and Responses* (2017).

Johanna Rahner is Professor for Dogmatics, the history of Dogma and Ecumenical Theology at the Catholic Faculty of Theology of the University of Tübingen. She is the author of *Einführung in die Katholische Dogmatik* (2008); *Einführung in die christliche Eschatologie* (2010); *Wirken Gottes in Wort und Zeichen. Eine Sakramentenlehre* (2016); and *Was ist der Mensch? Grundfragen theologischer Anthropologie* (2017) as well as the editor of multiple volumes, including (with B. J. Hilberath and H. Küng) *Damit alle eins seien, Programmatik und Zukunft der Ökumene* (2015) and (with A. Srübind) *Begegnungen—Entgegnungen Beiträge zur modernen Gottesfrage, kontextuellen Theologie und Ökumene* (2015).

Dorothea Sattler is Professor of Systematic Theology and Director of the Ecumenical Institute of the Catholic Theological Faculty of the University of Münster. She is a member of many ecumenical commissions and working groups and is also the Academic Director (together with Volker Leppin) of the Ecumenical Working Group of Protestant and Catholic Theologians in Germany. Sattler is the author of many works on ecumenical theology, such as (with Friederike Nüssel) *Einführung in die ökumenische Theologie* (2008). She recently edited (together with Volker Leppin) *Reformation 1517–2017: Ökumenische Perspektiven* (2014) and also wrote "In Memory of Otto Hermann Pesch" for *Concilium* (2015).

Jay T. Smith is the President and Bridger Professor of Theology and Ethics at the Yellowstone Theological Institute in Bozeman, Montana. With Stanley J. Grenz he is the author of *Created for Community: Connecting Christian Faith with Christian Living* (2015) and is the co-author of "A Theological Biography," in *Revisioning, Renewing, Rediscovering the Triune Center: Essays in Honor of Stanley J. Grenz*. Smith is also the author of "Baptist Theology: Is There Another Way?," in *Baptist History and Heritage* (2012) and many other publications on Grenz and contemporary theology and church issues.

Wolfgang Vonday is Professor of Christian Theology and Pentecostal Studies at the University of Birmingham. He is the author of multiple monographs, including *Pentecostalism: A Guide for the Perplexed* (2013); *Pentecostalism and Christian Unity* (2013); *The Holy Spirit and the Christian Life* (2014); and *Pentecostal Theology: Living the Full Gospel* (2017).

Foreword

−Brian D. McLaren

THREE STEPS FORWARD, TWO steps back. That, according to the old saying, is how progress comes. Sometimes, it seems like three steps forward, six steps back!

This well-written and well-edited volume offers a thoughtful, comprehensive overview of the amazing, unprecedented steps forward taken by Christian churches around the world over the last several decades in the field of ecumenical theological conversation.

Younger readers might take this progress for granted. But for those of us who remember the days when an inter-faith marriage meant a Presbyterian marrying a Methodist, this collection of essays helps us see just how far we've come.

In the aftermath of two world wars, Mainline Protestants started healing their divides, creating the World Council of Churches and unleashing new ecumenical energies. Theologians of different traditions started reading one another, engaging with one another, seeing one another as conversation partners rather than competitors.

Similarly, Vatican II represented remarkable steps forward. Catholics found new ways to think about and engage with their fellow Christians. While the Cold War intensified in the headlines, this religious detente unfolded, quietly, persistently, powerfully.

Around the same time, the Civil Rights movement showed promising signs that Sunday mornings at 11:00 a.m. might not always be the most segregated hour of the week. Around the world, theologians and church leaders were taking important steps forward in bringing together the descendants of the colonizers and the colonized to begin doing theology in conversation rather than continuing their ad hoc religious apartheid.

Around the time Hans Frei introduced the term "a generous orthodoxy," some liberals and conservatives even dared to hope that they might find common cause and common ground.

Along the way, in some sectors of Christian faith, growing numbers were awakening to the ways that our churches had been ungenerous to the 50 percent plus of Christians who happened to be female, and even less generous to the smaller but still significant percentage who were not heterosexual.

Many of us have spent our lives during a time when the circle of inclusion was expanding, when we rightly felt that a profoundly generous spirit (or Spirit) was on the move. This sense of forward movement infused everything we did. More and more of us could agree that true orthodoxy was inherently generous, and that generosity was truly orthodox.

So much so, in fact, that in 2004, I picked up Frei's term and used it in the title of a book (a book that had an ungainly subtitle that tried to make the same point in another way). Although I was genuinely grateful for my conservative Evangelical background (with a dose of Pentecostalism thrown in), I gradually felt my curiosity leading me to look over the fence, so to speak, so I began to consult people from other traditions for "second opinions." For example, I realized that I needed my more liberal brothers and sisters to help me explore what the Wesleys called Social Holiness and what Walter Rauschenbusch called the Social Gospel.

Similarly, I needed the depth of Roman Catholic Social Teaching, because my tradition's emphasis on personal spirituality, personal holiness, and personal salvation simply didn't match the revolutionary message of the book which my heritage taught me was the Word of God. When I discovered the Catholic Liberation Theologians, I felt like I was given the Gospels afresh.

In addition, I became curious about what the mystical and monastic traditions in both Catholicism and Eastern Orthodoxy had to teach me about theology and spirituality. And I needed insights from my non-white sisters and brothers and my non-straight siblings to help me see my faith beyond the tight limits prescribed by my own birth and privilege.

In these and other ways, my spiritual hunger as a Christian and my spiritual challenges as a pastor conspired to make me eager to open orthodoxy to its maximally generous aperture. For these reasons and more, a generous orthodoxy was not simply interesting to me in an academic sense. It was a matter of spiritual survival.

So in my book called *A Generous Orthodoxy*, I dared to hope that growth in true generosity would make me more orthodox and a deepening in true orthodoxy would make me more generous. That hope, I think, resonated with a wide array of readers around the world, if strong sales (when compared with my other books) are any indication.

You may have sensed a bittersweet flavor of nostalgia as you read the previous paragraphs. I know I felt nostalgic as I wrote them, because in ten or fifteen years, it feels like we have been losing much of the ecumenical ground gained over the last ten or fifteen decades. In many denominations, certain gatekeepers have become chary of doing theology collaboratively and have circled the wagons, tending more toward exclusion than embrace.

Just when bridges need to be built and widened, we find some religious leaders blowing them up and building walls instead. For example, in his historic encyclical, *Laudato Si*, Pope Francis invited people of all faiths to come together to hear the cries of the earth and the cries of the poor. But many of his own bishops have opposed him, with some Catholics even hinting at plans for his removal or for schism.

Similarly, Eastern Orthodoxy faces tensions in its ranks that threaten it with historic schism. The largest of Mainline Protestant denominations in the US, the United Methodists, have been leaning over the precipice of schism as well.

We all recall how the twenty-first century began, not with a rising tide of generosity but with a series of sudden explosions of violent religious fundamentalism in Islam, Christianity, and Judaism, and in Buddhism and Hinduism as well. In the aftermath of September 11, 2001, religious fear, resentment, and supremacy spread around the world like a radioactive cloud, with religious voices calling for violent terrorism in some quarters and violent counter-terrorism in other quarters, mirror images of one another's un-generosity.

So as I read the fascinating, inspiring, and well-written chapters in this well-edited volume, I did indeed feel sadness, sadness that many of our religious communities are undergoing a popular repudiation of the academic work described in this book . . . six steps backward, if you will.

The resurgence of White Christian nationalism represented in the US by the election of Donald J. Trump also feels like a repudiation of the generous initiatives described in these pages.

In a bizarrely ironic way, the most irreligious of American presidents has created greater alignment across the Catholic-Protestant divide than the august figures described in these pages, with Protestants like Franklin Graham and Robert Jeffress lying down with Catholics like Sean Hannity and Steve Bannon to support Trump's ungenerous and unorthodox presidency.

Rather than a lamb-and-lion scenario, we see more of a lion-and-lion scenario . . . an alignment of the ungenerous. We can see similarly strange bedfellows coming together in Brazil, the UK, Russia, and elsewhere, all claiming to be orthodox while demonstrating the very opposite of generosity toward any who don't agree with them.

The ugliness of this ungenerous pseudo-orthodoxy is driving young people away from faith in unprecedented numbers, and it threatens to leave major sectors of organized religion a bastion of regressive and reactionary angry old men, along with the women and young people who defer to them.

That's exactly why this book is so important at this moment. By looking back at an extraordinary convergence of ecumenical experiments in decades past, we can look forward with inspiration and courage to imitate their example in the decades to come. Their work, we now see, began, but was not completed. That remains for us and for our descendants to do.

There is, we must say, no time to waste. In the words of one of the youngest and fiercest moral leaders today (Greta Thunberg), the house is on fire.

The unfolding catastrophe of climate change calls for a pan-religious movement that dares to challenge the global oligarchs and their fossil-fuel-funded global kleptocracy. Who else but communities of faith and moral courage will have the moral vision to challenge humanity to turn from the primacy of profit to the primacy of love? And which single religious body is arrogant or naive enough to think it can turn the tide without collaboration from its religious counterparts?

Not only that, but we live in a time when a tiny super-rich super-elite controls a larger and larger percentage of the world's wealth. As a result, the upper classes hoard luxuries while the masses lack necessities. These same elites function increasingly like mafias to intimidate or buy politicians, creating cartels of corruption. Once again, we need unprecedented alliances across denominations and religions if democracy is to be saved and used to benefit the common good rather than to further enrich the rich and exploit the most vulnerable.

The cries of the planet and the cries of the poor are joined by the cries of those suffering from violence and war. Again, no single religious community can confront the proliferation of weapons alone. But together, a communal David could challenge (nonviolently, of course) the Goliath of the global arms trade, in that most generous of labors, peace-making.

So the issue of ecumenism addressed in this book is truly existential, not merely academic. To make history, it will help us to know history. To become the leaders of tomorrow, it will help us to glean all we can from the leaders of yesterday. So for all these reasons and more, I am honored to commend this volume at this critical moment, in hopes that readers are not merely informed, but more: inspired and fired up for generous, faith-fueled action.

I can say that this volume both informed and inspired me, and for that, I am grateful.

Introduction

—Paul Silas Peterson

THE ESSAYS IN THIS volume address a broad ecumenical sentiment in theology especially as it developed in the second half of the twentieth century. This sentiment was embodied by theologians both inside and outside the official ecumenical movement. Building upon older traditions of ecumenically-minded theology, and following in the wake of the official work of the ecumenical movement in the World Council of Churches (which was founded in 1948), many theologians sought to redraw the confessional lines and integrate new theological sources from other traditions. They also sought to reconcile divisions in Christian belief and practice. This push toward reconciliation was directed both internally and externally: internally between different groups within specific traditions and externally between Christian confessional communities or denominations. Rather than rejecting the concept of "orthodoxy," or the binding status of creedal traditions, many of the key figures in this broad movement sought to reinterpret their respective orthodoxies in light of the conflicts and in order to work toward more unity. Ultimately, they sought to "guard" what had "been entrusted" to them (1 Tim 6:20), and to "hold to the standard of sound teaching" (2 Tim 1:13), yet, simultaneously, they also sought "to maintain the unity of the Spirit" (Eph 4:3). As a result of this reanalysis of their traditional conceptions of the faith in their respective denominational context of theology, many of these theologians effectively redefined (to greater or lesser degrees) their own traditions of Christian faith. This "redefinition" or "revision" can be understood more clearly with the benefit of hindsight. The theologians who advanced these agendas rarely admitted that they were redefining their confessional traditions, although this was what many of them did.

The result of this endeavor ultimately strengthened the sense of commonality among various Christian groups, especially in the second half of the twentieth century. It also provided an opportunity for the deepening of understanding of the respective traditions through the critical and constructive ecumenical engagement. In one sense, this tendency toward a new generosity in theology can be understood as a process whereby various long-held conceptions of orthodoxy ("right teaching") were actually modified. The revision of these various long-held conceptions of orthodoxy in the twentieth century is usually presented as a positive development towards more unity and charity between brothers and sisters of the one faith—and it certainly was this. In its own way, it also ran parallel to the expansion of trends toward liberalism in the twentieth century following the shock of World War II. In this shift towards more liberalism after the war, societies in the Western World became more open and more affirmative towards diversity. The other side of the story, which is sometimes left out of accounts of the history of ecumenical theology, is the story about the many church splits and denominational fractures that followed from the process of doctrinal and ethical revision in the twentieth century. In some cases, the shift towards theological generosity evoked new conservative trends that rejected the revisions. Both the revisions for more unity and the new fragmentation in resistance to reinterpretation are the two sides of the story of doctrinal reform in the twentieth century. They were interlocked with one another in the historical development.

The general ecumenical attitude and the mediating impulse between different Christian groups as it developed in the second half of the twentieth century (building on older traditions) was influenced by cultural and sociopolitical dynamics, but it also reflected a more fundamental impulse within Christianity—one that is much older than the modern ecumenical movement of the nineteenth and twentieth century. This impulse is seen already in the writings of the New Testament which encourage Christians to seek unity and resist discord in the specific congregational contexts. In the early Christian teachings, the discord that was viewed as problematic was, in the first instance, the local conflicts and local divisions within local congregations. Yet, already in the New Testament, there was also a more universal dynamic at play, which ran parallel to the growing realization of the universality of the faith. This growing sense of universality is seen in what we today call the Jerusalem Council (Acts 15; Gal 2) and in the corresponding missionary activities of the apostles. The desire to bring the "good news" (gospel) about Jesus Christ to "the inhabited world" (*oikoumene*) is the fundamental underlying force of "ecumenism." Indeed, this impulse of universality is attributed to Jesus himself in Matthew 28:18–20. It is also found in Acts 1:8: "But you will receive power when the Holy Spirit has come upon you; and you will be my witnesses in Jerusalem, in all Judea and Samaria, and to the ends of the earth." Even in the disputed closing chapter of Mark the message is contained in various forms. In the shorter ending of Mark 16 (which follows verse 8 in some manuscripts), it reads: "And afterward Jesus himself sent out through them, from east to west, the sacred and imperishable proclamation of eternal salvation." Here the concept of universality is clearly reflected with the expression "from east to west." In the longer version of Mark 16:9–20, Jesus is reported to have said in verse 15 "Go into all the world and proclaim the good news to the whole creation." With this follows the summary in verse 20: "And they went out and proclaimed the good news everywhere." These accounts are buttressed by the textually undisputed (in terms of Markian authenticity) ideal temple, epitomized in the words of Jesus as "a house of prayer for all the nations" (Mark 11:17). Indeed, for Mark, it was presumed that Jesus taught that "the good news must first be proclaimed to all nations" (Mark 13:10) before the "Son of Man" (13:26) was to return.

The reconciliation of all with God through Christ implied within itself the reconciliation of all with one another. For the Apostles at the Jerusalem Council the implications of this new reality in Christ was the point of interpretive conflict. While they ultimately embraced a compromise, "with the consent of the whole church" (Acts 15:22), to maintain unity in difference, they already saw it as necessary at that time to address the common core of their faith in the differences of interpretation. In the Petrine appeal for liberality toward the gentile Christians (as Luke reports), Peter explicitly appealed to the foundational, mutually shared, issue of salvation: "We believe that we will be saved through the grace of the Lord Jesus, just as they will" (Acts 15:11).

At a very early period in the Jesus movement, as can been seen in the New Testament, there was a concern for a general sense of collaboration on practical issues (such as financial support of weaker congregations in distant places). Furthermore, there was in the early church an ongoing debate about doctrinal issues that included everyone. The teachings that were articulated to express the sense of unity and being one in Christ were important because they reflected the ultimate realities of their faith. The Christians understood themselves to be unified in Christ, but they actually conflicted with one another on many issues of ultimate concern. As the religious movement spread from city to city and across the countryside from town to town, it had to be decided what these new congregations should be taught. Thus the doctrines of faith, often summarized in a brief "rule of faith," emerged with reference to the earliest apostolic writings, which were later canonized as the supreme (not exclusive) authority in doctrinal disputes. From this very early period up to today, "orthodoxies" (or "right teachings") have been articulated as essential components of the local and universal dimensions of the faith.

The immediate prehistory of the turn to ecumenical theology in the second half of the twentieth century is the emergence of the World Council of Churches (which included the Faith and Order Movement, that focused on doctrinal ecumenism before this). With this, the Second Vatican Council (1962–1965) also offered a major push in the direction of more ecumenical cooperation. As a feature of this general background, the turn to convergence ecumenism in the mid-twentieth century was also very important. More than any other branch of ecumenical theology, the program of convergence ecumenism brought together the desire to overcome the divisions of faith with a real agenda to overcome actual institutional divisions. The work towards an organic unity meant joining churches together into larger Christian communities or uniting churches in broader communions. This program, in turn, raised the question about the status and future of older confessional identities, even church names. Particularly for theologians, the agenda of convergence ecumenism raised major questions about the ongoing status of the various theological traditions. How were the many different accounts of "orthodoxy" to be joined together in the grand convergence? Would they, and should they, be forgotten? From our perspective today, it is clear that the conservative forces won the day. A new approach towards ecumenism formed to preserve these qualities in the 1970s. This new approach turned to the concept of "reconciled diversity." This is one of the central background features in the ecclesial realm which encouraged theologians to expand their own denominational identities. At this time a new reflection about denominational or confessional traditions emerged. In this new turn to the confessional identities, many theologians sought to expand the meaning of these identities to include others, and to revise older understanding of them that emphasized exclusionary characteristics. This led to a kind of generous conception of the "right teachings," as opposed to hardened exclusionary orthodoxies, or the full-scale abandonment of them. In this general approach, one could understand their own tradition in a way that did not necessitate the negation of another tradition. At least this was often times asserted. Yet the challenge of relativism in doctrinal issues was strongly brought against this new generosity. Against this challenge, on the other hand, these revisionary theologians could argue that they indeed did continue to hold to their doctrinal positions as expressed in their respective tradition, but this only in a new way. This is some of the broader framework of the dialectical history of ecumenical theology in the twentieth century, but it did not stop here.

Hans Frei was the first to use the term "generous orthodoxy" to describe this sense of *mediation and openness* ("generous"), on the one hand, and, on the other, to describe the sense of *connection to doctrinal tradition* ("orthodoxy"). This general trend followed from the belief that the diverse expressions of the Christian faith should be in conversation with one another in order to generate a positive relationship of dialog and cooperation. Many of the theologians associated with this sentiment of theology did not attempt to overcome doctrinal positions by eliminating particularity or their specific confessional tradition. They rather undertook the challenging task of making them fit together in a dynamic tension with the various particularities. Something emerged that was neither "my way or the highway," nor "anything goes." This was essentially the theological project to which many of these theologians dedicated themselves. Unfortunately, only a select group of the many theologians could be analyzed in depth here. Perhaps future research will allow for in depth analysis of the many other key figures.

In the first part of this volume ("Ecumenical Reform Theologies"), some of the key figures in this theological program of ecumenical theology are introduced. Andrew Meszaros's essay "Yves Congar: The Birth of 'Catholic Ecumenism'" introduces one of the central figures in Catholic ecumenical theology. Meszaros outlines the exciting biography of the French Dominican friar and shows how he was central to the turn to ecumenical thought in Catholicism, and also one of the driving forces behind the Catholic declaration on ecumenism from the Second Vatican Council. Congar's theology of baptism, which he established from the doctrinal tradition within Roman Catholicism, enabled him to assert that even those who were not Catholics but were baptized Christians were in communion with the Catholic Church, even if this communion was not a perfect communion. This was an important step towards a new ecumenical openness, and Meszaros shows how it emerged in deep conversation with the doctrinal tradition. The expansion of doctrinal heritages is also seen, as Meszaros shows, in Congar's interpretation of the *vestigia ecclesiae* with view to Christians outside the Catholic Church. Congar's creative interpretation of doctrinal tradition is also employed in his account of "catholicity" with view to non-Catholics. In so many ways, as Meszaros demonstrates, Congar promoted a generous interpretation of his doctrinal tradition that opened doors to new understandings of others outside the Catholic tradition. The unique contribution of Meszaros's essay is also seen in his outlining of the academic discourse about this turn in Catholic theology. Meszaros shows how other Catholic theologians view Congar and how his ideas were developed and built upon in the following generations, while also addressing some of the critical voices.

The second essay in the first section addresses an important Protestant ecumenical theologian. Of course, it would have been possible to include an essay at this juncture on the important Protestant theologian, Willem A. Visser 't Hooft. The Dutch theologian and ecumenical leader Visser 't Hooft is correctly highlighted in many works on ecumenical theology, as he was so central to the ecumenical movement and the World Council of Churches. Yet there were also other figures at this time that were promoting an explicitly dogmatic program of ecumenical theology—figures that have received less attention. Matthew L. Becker's essay, titled "Edmund Schlink: Ecumenical Theology," provides an informative presentation, with ample historical background and theological insight, into one of the central German theologians of ecumenical theology. Schlink pioneered a new approach to dogmatic theology that is now just beginning to be studied outside the German context (as his works are now beginning to be translated into English). Becker shows how Schlink turned to an ecumenical understanding of his own dogmatic tradition (Lutheranism) in his early period, leading to his work on the Lutheran confessions from 1940. Schlink contributed a significant amount of work to the ecumenical movement and the WCC. Only later, in 1983, did he publish his *magnum opus* of ecumenical theology: *Ecumenical Dogmatics*. Schlink's ecumenical theology worked to explicate the contemporary significance of the seventh article of the Augsburg Confession from 1530. The unity of the church, in this sense, is based upon a common understanding of the gospel (which is articulated in the preceding articles). Yet, as Becker shows, Schlink also drew attention to the problem of disunity. He wanted to emphasize the point that disunity between Christians was a kind of betrayal of the faith and distortion of the church. Schlink proposed a new theology of renewal in Christ and a new understanding of ecclesial identities as rooted in Christ to overcome the disunity. Becker demonstrates that dogmatic theology and doctrinal positions were not relativized by Schlink but rather reinterpreted. He strove for a new unity in dogma, for example regarding Christology and the sacraments, rather than a unity beyond dogma. The curiosity of this program is its desire to revisit the antitheses between traditions, rather than avoiding them. These antitheses are, in turn, analyzed in light of the Scriptures and the specific contemporary situations in which they are employed in ecclesial traditions and in intellectual traditions. Becker presents Schlink's ecumenical dogmatics especially focusing on the themes of law and gospel, church and ministry and the doctrine of the Trinity. As he demonstrates, Schlink sought to maintain the core dimensions of Protestant theology but he did this with a sense of generosity towards other traditions, seeking to build bridges and open up new avenues of conversation. While Becker also acknowledges a weakness

(Schlink's lack of reference to some specific traditions within Christianity), the groundbreaking methodology that Schlink developed within Lutheran confessional theology remains a challenging and promising methodology for dogmatic theology today.

The third essay in this section is provided by Dorothea Sattler, titled "Otto Hermann Pesch: Ecumenical Scholasticism." In her essay (which also draws upon personal experiences with Pesch), Sattler introduces one of the most significant German Catholic ecumenical theologians of the twentieth century. His work is, however, only partially known in the English-language discourse. Pesch was one of the first Catholic theologians to develop an entirely new evaluation of the Reformation era theologies, and especially a new approach to Martin Luther. His work on Luther sought to provide a new look at the Reformer from a perspective that was not overly determined by confessional paradigms of interpretation. He thus effectively opened the door to a new ecumenical theological approach to Protestantism from a Catholic perspective. As Sattler shows, Pesch was also an ardent supporter of the theological developments of the Second Vatican Council. He promoted these teachings for much of his life and also worked towards a generous conception of theology in his *Catholic Dogmatics from Ecumenical Experience*. Sattler shows how Pesch's theological approach of ecumenism was deeply influenced by a form of scholastic discourse from the Middle Ages that emphasized argumentative exchange, listening and response. While Sattler does raise some questions regarding Pesch's methodology of presenting encyclopedic accounts of theological subjects, Pesch is shown to be a theologian who was active in various discourses and sought to promote a dialogical form of theology that anyone can understand.

Ronald T. Michener's essay for the first section, titled "George Lindbeck: Ecumenical Unity through Ecclesial Particularity," uncovers the biographical and theological world behind Lindbeck's groundbreaking *The Nature of Doctrine: Religion and Theology in a Postliberal Age* (1984) and his conception of a cultural-linguistic approach to theology. Michener draws attention to Lindbeck's international background, including an early period in China, studies in America and Europe, and then later participation in Vatican II and in ecumenical working groups. At an early stage in his theological work, he recognized the need for both an updating of theology and a looking-back. As Michener claims, Lindbeck was deeply influenced by the ecumenical movement and the theological questions that it posed. At the same time, he also draws attention to H. Richard Niebuhr's influence on Lindbeck at Yale, and especially his conception of the cultural dimension of faith, and the work of Hans Frei and David Kelsey. While creatively employing his own theological program, Lindbeck sought to show how doctrinal faith was articulated and lived out in specific languages of faith. These are discourses of interaction and expression that bring the fundamental experiences of faith into a larger language of reflection in which they are interpreted and understood. Understanding doctrines requires a linguistic and cultural assessment of the different languages in their specific grammars and rules of expression. This linguistically embedded framework of religion is essential for understanding the nature of doctrine itself. It is the fundamental framework within which the world is interpreted and religious experiences are understood. As Michener shows, Lindbeck understood the primal narrative of the Christian faith to be essentially linked up with the story of Israel as the people of God. This basic narrative is the framework in which theological articulations in the Christian tradition have their natural home. Michener also outlines how ecumenical challenges drove Lindbeck to reconceptualize the nature of doctrinal conflict itself in different orders of discourse, one ontological in nature, the other regulative. The significance of Lindbeck's thought for interreligious dialog is also presented by Michener, for it is possible to learn from other traditions even if disagreements remain. Michener's essay also includes a discussion of the criticisms that have been brought against the cultural-linguistic method, and many strong counter arguments that provide deeper readings of Lindbeck's work, defending him from the accusations of fideism or relativism. More fundamentally, Michener reminds us of the original intention of Lindbeck's theology: the formation of an ecumenical hospitality in the theological realm. This was central to his concerns regarding the cultural-linguistic method, and the wider philosophical issues and interreligious challenges associated with his theology.

The final essay in the first section is authored by Nikolaos Asproulis. In "John D. Zizioulas: A Pioneer of Ecumenical Dialogue and Christian Unity" Asproulis outlines the biographical and theological background of one of the central figures of twentieth-century Orthodox theology and ecumenism. Zizioulas's shift towards ecumenical theology was driven by tradition itself. He saw the church fathers as working to influence culture and thus he wanted to contribute to the ecumenical work of his time. He saw this work as engaging the contemporary challenges and thus he promoted ecumenism in his ecclesial tradition. As the Secretary of "Faith and Order," Zizioulas sought to promote a theological agenda in ecumenism without trying to transform the WCC into a new church. Later, as Metropolitan of Pergamon, he continued to promote ecumenical theology and ecumenism with a specific emphasis on Trinitarian and eucharistic approaches. Asproulis also documents his contemporary work in ecumenism, leading up to the Holy and Great Pan-Orthodox Synod in Crete in 2016. Although Zizioulas was very influential in the history of Orthodox ecumenism, as Asproulis explains, this recent synod did not follow the theological impulses provided by Zizioulas. In this essay, the theological principles of Zizioulas's ecumenical vision are outlined. The church in this approach is understood as a way of being, a communion, in which the Christian message is actualized in a specific cultural context. In his theology, this religious communion reflects the life of the divine Trinity as an icon. The other aspects of Zizioulas's ecclesiology that Asproulis presents are the eschatological orientation, the emphasis on communion (rooted in the divine being) and the eucharistic identity of the church. Drawing upon these theological themes from the doctrinal tradition of Orthodox Christianity, Zizioulas provided a unique foundation for the ecumenical movement and sought to support Christian unity.

The second section of essays addresses a handful of key theologians from the twentieth century who sought to overcome the liberal-conservative polarities in their respective traditions. Ben Fulford's essay, "Hans Frei: Beyond Liberal and Conservative," introduces the theologian who popularized the term "generous orthodoxy." Fulford provides a brief introduction to Frei's background. As Fulford shows, Frei had a very diverse ecumenical background. He worked as a Baptist pastor and then later as an Episcopalian pastor. He sympathized with both Reformed and Quaker theological and ecclesial tendencies. His theological approach established a middle path between liberalism and evangelicalism. As Fulford explains, Frei sought to understand the enduring and universal principles of the Christian faith across all generations and cultures, while also promoting a theology that would support this. The conception of narrative became central to his theological reflection. He saw this narrative phenomenon already in the New Testament accounts of Jesus. Frei also uncovered the interrelationship between narrativity and normativity. Fulford provides a thorough yet approachable introduction to the central thesis of Frei's famous work, *The Eclipse of Biblical Narrative*. This text was foundational for the emergence of narrative theology in the later twentieth century. It has been widely recognized as articulating the paradigm of narrativity in pre-Enlightenment era theology. Frei showed how the narratives of the Bible created a kind of framework for self-interpretation and an all-encompassing historical reference for Christian theology. One highly informative aspect of Fulford's essay is his analysis of Frei's problematization of the liberal-conservative polarity, especially in his posthumous *Types of Christian Theology*. Fulford also provides an inroad into some central dogmatics subjects, addressing theological method in Frei's approach as well as the identity of Jesus Christ and social ethics. In Frei's work, one encounters a theology that transcends the liberal-conservative divide and upholds the primacy and the non-reducibility of the narratives about Jesus Christ for Christian theology and church life.

The second essay in this section is provided by Friederike Nüssel, titled "Wolfhart Pannenberg: Liberal Orthodoxy." Nüssel's essay draws our attention to a Lutheran theologian from Germany who was both very innovative and, at the same time, in this innovation, very traditional. Nüssel outlines his historical background and sketches out some of the central themes in his theology. In light of challenges from both science and historical research, Pannenberg sought to establish strong arguments for the credibility of the Christian faith. A part of this credibility was related to the issue of ecclesial unity. In his theology, as Nüssel demonstrates, the disunity of the church was not only a central theological problem for Christians among themselves, but also, more generally, a challenge to the credibility of the Christian faith as a whole. In the later 1960s, Pannenberg became deeply engaged in ecumenical theology in Munich. The nature of his approach to ecumenical theology was linked to fundamental theology, or the philosophy of religion, and was closely related to the larger dialogues between the Roman Catholic Church and the Protestant churches in Germany. In the broader scheme of his philosophical theology, Pannenberg developed the idea of an eschatological anchoring point for the contemporary discussion and debate about conflicting theological claims. The purpose of this future orientation had to do with securing the scientific nature of theology. This "proleptic" (anticipatory) conception ultimately situates contemporary hypotheses about the faith in the broader anticipation of their eschatological resolution. The significance of this theoretical framework for ecumenical theological discourse lies in the relativizing and limiting character of the proleptic anchor. What we disagree upon now in doctrinal matters is not a sign of the ultimate contradiction of the faith with itself, but a preliminary conceptual division that will ultimately be resolved in the light of knowledge as fully revealed in the blessedness of divine eternity, or even perhaps before this, as a consequence of the expansion of human learning. At a time when many theologians were moving away from the debates about truth claims in favor of postmodern conceptions of truth, Pannenberg sought to emphasize the necessity of Christian truth claims in discussions of doctrinal difference. His program also entails, as Nüssel shows, a high regard for other Christian traditions of theology. Theologians must wrestle with the competing truth claims in light of the eschatological reference point, in which the conflicts will ultimately be resolved. After presenting his fundamental religious-philosophical approach to theology, Nüssel goes on to outline Pannenberg's ecumenical work on specific dogmatic issues, especially related to the three major divisions in the history of Christianity. She draws attention to his reconceptualization of the condemnations of the Reformation period. She also sketches out his reading of the *filioque* controversy, and the divisive issue regarding the doctrine of justification. Furthermore, Pannenberg's ecumenical understanding of the doctrine of the Lord's Supper and the theological understanding of ordained ministry are presented.

Jay T. Smith contributed the final essay for the second section. His essay is titled "Stanley J. Grenz: The Evangelical Turn to Postliberal Theological Method." Grenz was a unique figure in evangelical theology in the latter part of the twentieth century. He charted out a new path of theology that worked with and also, in some regards, went beyond standard methods of argument in evangelicalism. As Smith shows, Grenz's desire to chart out a new approach in theology was deeply related to his reception of postliberal theology. He was influenced by Lindbeck and Pannenberg, and a more general discourse about the turn to postmodernism in the 1990s. Grenz thought that the theological situation of his day was marked by a polarity between cognitive-doctrinal (or cognitive-propositionalist) and experiential-practical (or experiential-expressive symbolist) approaches. He wanted to develop a new post-foundationalist theological method with the doctrine of the Trinity at the center of the theological enterprise, as a kind of structural framework. To the classic duality of Scripture and tradition, Grenz added a new interplay with culture and the conception of the Spirit working in the present community of a specific locality. As Smith demonstrates, this general theological system was situated on the horizon of eschatology, and here the connection to Pannenberg's theology (as addressed above) becomes apparent. Grenz's emphasis on the cultural dimension of theology, as Smith shows, entailed the plea for theology to hear and respond to the cultural situation. In this he was indebted to both Lindbeck and Paul Tillich. As Smith remarks, Grenz's theological approach, which challenged the fundamental theological propositions of the dominant stream of conservative evangelical theology in the United States in the 1990s, was intensely criticized by leading voices in evangelicalism. Yet this criticism sometimes overlooked the fact that Grenz was, in his own way, advancing the tradition of evangelicalism in a new style of generous articulation. Smith also outlines Grenz's contribution to philosophical theology, specifically his articulation of epistemology in a scheme of coherence theory and pragmatism, as well as his theological Trinitarian anthropology. On the whole, Smith shows how Grenz pioneered a new approach to theology that was both traditional and innovative within evangelicalism. The strength of this approach is its ability to embrace diverse streams of thought while holding to a classic articulation of the central teachings of the Christian faith.

The third section includes four essays that address theologians who were crossing boundaries in philosophical, systematic and ethical theology. William E. Myatt's contribution is titled "David Tracy: Difference, Unity, and the Analogical Imagination." Tracy's theological approach was shaped by a full embrace of the challenge of postmodernism. His thought also reflects the realization of the historicity of beliefs, religious traditions and reason itself. As a Catholic theologian and philosopher of religion, Tracy sought to engage positively the challenge of the fundamental pluralism internal to specific religious traditions. The fundamental question about the nature of truth in theological discourse was thus central to Tracy's development. In his early period, he argued that the two fundamental sources of theology were essentially Christian texts and human experiences. Tracy's theology of religious experience could see in the Protestant theology of Schleiermacher and Tillich an articulation of human experience as a religious phenomenon. He described this religious feeling or experience as the human being's encounter with the limits of existence. This fundamental human experience has a religious dimension which Tracy held to be of central importance for theology. Yet experiences are not the only sources of theology in Tracy's reading. The textual dimension of faith, as Myatt demonstrates, was also a critical aspect of Tracy's theology. He drew upon the thought of his colleague Paul Ricoeur in Chicago, and the religious-philosophical reflection on the nature of hermeneutics itself. The practical dimension of his revisionist approach to theology and the philosophy of religion was explicated in conversation with critical theory. Yet as Myatt argues, Tracy developed this in a specifically theological style. He saw the Christ-event as the central theological category for developing a social critique. Tracy became very popular because of his later work on the concept of an analogical imagination, and the plurality of publics in which theologians are active. This analogical imagination is active in the analysis and interpretation of classical texts as disclosing truth. It is also active in the reconstruction of fragments from the history of the faith. In the creative analogical reconstruction of various fragments, the elements of plurality are joined into a broader conversation about truth, analogous to the truth of art. Thus the challenge of plurality can be embraced without abandoning the concept of truth, but rather with a generous openness to a fuller conception of truth.

The second essay in this section is written by Christophe Chalamet, titled "Robert Jenson: God's Way and the Ways of the Church." Chalamet draws our attention to a unique systematic theological program that emerged in the context of the rise of the ecumenical movement. Jenson's theological understanding was deeply influenced by a view of God as an event. In the movement of divine being all previous conditionality is overcome. Seeking to uncover a new approach to the doctrine of God as an alternative to static conceptions of the divine being, Jenson focused on the trinitarian essence of God and the divine capacity to overcome conditions which were established in the past. More fundamentally, he sought to move away from the language of being and essence and rather focus his God-talk in event language—an event of and within divine relations and an event between God and the world. God thus "happens" rather than being an unmoved mover. Chalamet shows how Jenson's doctrine of God, and his general theological methodology (which seeks to integrate elements from various traditions of the Christian tradition), effectively stretched the Lutheran tradition. This is seen in his view of time and eternity, but also in his ecclesiology. The church is closely linked to this triune view of God, for the Christian community is, as Jenson argued, grounded in this identification of the divine being as act. Thus a view of God is central to the church's own self-understanding, as explicated in the act of prayer. In the final paragraphs of Chalamet's essay, he meticulously analyzes the pros and cons of Jenson's central theological impulses. Drawing out the positive aspects of Jenson's view of God's relation to the world and relation to time, he also returns to the central impulse of universality in Jenson's work. Jenson's theology emphasized the priority of the term "Christian" above confessional identities. This entailed a fundamental universality that remains a challenge for us today.

The third essay in this section is provided by Victoria Lorrimar, titled "Stanley Hauerwas: Witnessing Communities of Character." Lorrimar outlines Hauerwas's specific articulation of Christian pacifist communitarianism. In its own way, this program took on the form of trans-denominational ecumenism. Hauerwas, a self-described "high church Mennonite," welded together intellectual and ecclesial traditions that have rarely been so closely joined. His intellectual development was influenced by the theological ethicists of a past generation. Yet Hauerwas did not simply follow the traditions established before him. He sought to challenge the dominance of Reinhold Niebuhr's influence in American Christianity. His resistance to this approach was also articulated in his criticism of "Constantinian Christianity." In contrast to what he saw as a compromised ethical system of Christianity and Christian engagement with the world, Hauerwas advanced a dual commitment, as Lorrimar argues, to both fundamental Christian teachings and to a radical social ethic. This entailed a deep criticism of liberalism, a criticism of the loss of narrative commitments and a challenge to prevailing conceptions of freedom. The ecclesial self-understanding that emerged from this broader diagnosis of modernity and modern Christianity is essentially one of counter-culturalism. The church is to understand itself as a contrast community to the community of the world. Lorrimar presents the critical terminology in

Hauerwas's system of Christian ethics, focusing on the concepts of narrative, character, kingdom and witness. One of the specific ecclesiological points of emphasis in Hauerwas's system is his understanding of the church and the kingdom of God as a peaceable kingdom. The church follows Jesus in his non-violent life, a life which ultimately led to death in a world enveloped in violence. Lorrimar draws our attention to a fundamental dimension of Hauerwas's ecumenical thinking as well. The rise in levels of secularization, and the new situation in which the church finds itself today, is forcing the universal church to reconsider the nature of unity in terms of a living community. The creative methodology carried out in Hauerwas's approach also has a fundamental ecumenical dimension, one that seeks to draw from various Christian traditions in search of a unified Christian understanding and a new conception of mission today.

The fourth and final essay in this section on boundary crossing is provided by Christine M. Helmer. In "Marilyn McCord Adams: Philosophy, Theology, and Prayer" Helmer shows how McCord Adams sought to reintegrate metaphysical philosophy and theology. The relationship between these fields of inquiry was an issue of major debate in the nineteenth century, as many Protestant theologians sought to keep them separate. McCord Adams drew upon her knowledge of late medieval Christian philosophy, especially William of Ockham, to reestablish this connection at a deep level of interrelationship. McCord Adams was especially concerned with the problem of evil as it is addressed in both philosophy and theology. Going against the majority of Christian theologians (and Anselm of Canterbury's argument in *De Concordia* that evil emerges in the human will and is not the will or the fault of God, nor caused by God), she argued that the principle of the freedom of the will was not sufficient to explain horrendous evils. What or who is then responsible for these evils? Helmer argues that for McCord Adams it is only God—the same God who is responsible for salvation. Helmer analyzes this difficult position and provides an account of the underlying theological and philosophical arguments drawn upon to support it. McCord Adams crossed boundaries in the philosophy of religion and theology, but she also wrote about the importance of prayer. Prayer holds together the fragmentation of human experience and the divine plan of personal redemption. Helmer calls McCord Adams's unique approach a revisionist orthodoxy—a sentiment that bridged the realms of philosophy, theology and ethics.

The final section of essays is titled "Ecumenical Theology Today." It includes four essays that address contemporary issues in ecumenical theology and current challenges in ecclesial movements. Wolfgang Vonday's contribution is titled "Pentecostalism and Christian Orthodoxy: Revision,

Revival, and Renewal." Vonday analyzes a worldwide ecclesial and theological movement, one that continues to grow in importance today. "Orthodoxy" is a complicated concept within Pentecostalism, especially because the concept was often used to condemn the movement. Yet there is also a strong expression of this pattern of thought within Pentecostalism itself, especially when specific teachings about the baptism in the Holy Spirit are made to be orthodox standards to determine boundary markers. Vonday provides historical reference for understanding the emergence of this religious tradition while focusing on the revival and renewal impulses within Pentocostalism, impulses that always push the core to integrate the margins. The strong commitment to the apostolic tradition and the Scriptures within Pentecostalism is connected to an equally strong practical religious orientation. Thus the revival and renewal of the faith is understood in this dual paradigm of teaching and practice. The emphasis on renewal is one of the contributions that Pentecostalism has made to contemporary Christianity. The renewal of the church is never completed, however, for it remains an impulse for the entire life of the church.

The second essay on contemporary issues, which is written by Johanna Rahner, is titled "Shifting Paradigms—Future Ecumenical Challenges." Rahner draws our attention to a central problem in ecumenism today: the simultaneous endorsement of ecclesial and theological diversity alongside the inner-ecclesial theological debate about the unity of the universal church. This tension is described with reference to the concept of reconciled diversity within ecumenism. She asks whether a distinction can be made in this general analysis between a positive form of ecclesial diversity and a problematic form. In this light, Rahner encourages ecumenical theology and ecumenical working groups today to embrace a culture of debate about the truth, for positive momentum is generated in this tension. Only in this deeper engagement at the level of fundamental questions of faith can the true reconciliation of differences be achieved. By contrast, if the ecumenical interrelation remains at the superficial level of mutual affirmation, then true engagement does not happen and a real search for the truth is missed. In addition to this, Rahner addresses the shift toward ethical issues in ecumenism. While these issues are important for the church, they also entail the potential for new divisions. Furthermore, Rahner argues that the church cannot be reduced to an ethical community alone. With this, the modern sense of authenticity is addressed as it relates to ecumenism. Individually oriented spirituality as practiced by many people in the Western world today raises questions about the validity and practical relevance of theology, and more fundamentally about negotiating differences in general. She argues that the contemporary context will nevertheless still need to focus on ecumenism and dialog. This is because the need to work toward social cohesion and tolerance, and beyond this toward a positive view of difference, requires a deeper cooperative approach between religious traditions in their quest for the truth.

The third essay in this section is authored by Michael Amaladoss, titled "Theology Today in India: Ecumenical or Interreligious?" This essay addresses a dynamic seen in many theological contexts in the later twentieth century, a shift from ecumenical theology to interreligious theology. Providing a historical context for the emergence of Asian contextual theology, and the shift from ecumenical movements to interreligious movements, Amaladoss addresses how Christian writers sought in the early twentieth century to show the interrelationship between non-Christian religions in India and Christianity, such as the fulfilment of Hinduism in Christianity. After the Second Vatican Council a variety of theological seminars were also held that sought to address the issues of interreligious relations and ecumenism. In this, however, as Amaladoss addresses, there was a fundamental Western orientation to the theological program. Amaladoss argues that real breakthrough was first made with the emergence of a positive view of other religions: a view of the Kingdom of God as embracing all religions. In this theological approach, the sense of belonging to two traditions at once emerged, such as Hindu-Christians. Amaladoss, who describes himself as a Hindu-Christian, believes that the contemporary challenge today is to return to the question about God—the one God of all, beyond the plurality of the many religions. Amaladoss argues that the various individual experiences of God should not be absolutized in language and in fixed categories. This would lead us away from seeing God as the Absolute. The God of all, as Amaladoss holds, is best viewed through the kaleidoscope of the many experiences of humanity, in continual development and with the appeal of continual beauty.

The final essay in this section on contemporary ecumenical theology, and the final essay of the volume, is offered by Bernd Oberdorfer, titled "Next Steps—and Visions? Lutheran Perspectives on Doctrinal Ecumenism." Oberdorfer addresses the issue of consensus doctrinal ecumenism, the work towards mutual agreement on doctrinal statements by different ecclesial traditions. This form of ecumenical work seeks to achieve a common understanding in the basic outlines of the interpretation of central teachings while allowing for a difference of interpretation in the details. Oberdorfer draws attention especially to the Joint Declaration on the Doctrine of Justification between Lutheran and Roman Catholic churches as an example of this work. This statement of doctrinal consensus on one of the central theological debates of the Reformation period has been celebrated as a groundbreaking achievement. While it has also received recognition in the Methodist and Anglican communions, fundamental theological conflicts between Protestants and Catholics continue to prevent full communion on issues related to the Lord's Supper. Oberdorfer addresses this issue specifically as he outlines some of the issues of doctrinal conflict regarding the understanding of Christ's presence at the Holy Supper, whether both bread and wine are essential conditions, or if celebrating the meal with bread alone without wine is permissible. He also addresses possibilities of agreement in which both teachings regarding the nature of the elements are accepted, allowing for both transubstantiation and consubstantiation. After addressing this potential for agreement regarding the Holy Supper, Oberdorfer moves to the issue of ordained ministry, as especially treated in two recent ecumenical statements ("Declaration on the Way" and "Communion in Growth"). Oberdorfer shows how especially the question regarding the theological status of the office of a bishop is understood in both documents. Regarding the first document, he raises questions about the Roman Catholic exclusion of women from the ministry, and the possibility of achieving a unified conception of ordained ministry given this fundamental disagreement. Regarding the second document, he challenges the ecclesiology as one-sided. He argues that it fails to acknowledge that the office of oversight could be enacted in alternative forms that are not bishops. Furthermore, as he claims, the essential function of the Christian congregation in electing a minister for public preaching and for the administration of the Lord's Supper and baptism is not sufficiently addressed in the second document. Oberdorfer concludes his essay with questions about the nature of ecclesial unity itself. He asks whether it would be possible for one church to embrace a communion with another church, even though the churches disagree about the nature of ordination. As he suggests, the essential question regarding the nature of unity itself requires further research.

The future of ecumenical theology is open. It may indeed build upon the work done in past generations, or it could also seek to follow new paths that have not yet been explored. These essays show how a generation of theologians wrestled with the critical questions facing the church. They show how these theologians struggled with the problem of ecclesial division in theology, understandings of truth in the plurality of traditions and the nature of ecclesial witness in an increasingly secular world. While the great wave of ecumenical ambition in the 1960s and 1970s has now past, the work towards more ecclesial unity still rests upon a more fundamental impulse within the Christian religion, indeed, among other passages in the Bible, the Johannine transmission of Jesus's prayer for unity. The authors in this volume have taken this message to heart, and they seek to show how it can be advanced. Many new questions are also posed, questions which call for further discussion, debate and research. In summary, the arguments in this volume show how the quest for ecclesial unity in face of the division in the church pushed many intellectuals of the church into a deeper conflict, driving them to answer larger questions about the nature of truth itself, the difference between essential and non-essential matters in the conditions for communion and also regarding the future of the faith in a modern world.

Yet there remains a fundamental question about the stability of the generously orthodox approach: can it withstand the criticisms from conservative voices, who claim that it is a heterodox and revisionist betrayal, or from progressive voices, who claim that it is still stuck in dogmatism? Would it not be easier to abandon all fixed dogmatic notions, on the one hand, or rather to embrace them all the more fervently in a radical mode of exclusion? Will the sentiment of generous orthodoxy withstand the test of time? We are still being pulled along, to a certain degree (institutionally at least), from the strong wake of the high period of the ecumenical movement in the mid-twentieth century. It is still too early to know how far the momentum will carry us along. Nevertheless, the great diversification of Christianity with the trends of globalization and immigration will certainly bring new impulses to ecclesial life, and also encourage interreligious and ecumenical dialog. In this sense, there may be a need to rediscover a generous orthodoxy for our situation today—a situation only remotely imagined by past generations of generously orthodox theologians.

Part One
Ecumenical Reform Theologies

1

Yves Congar: The Birth of "Catholic Ecumenism"

—Andrew Meszaros

THE CATHOLIC CHURCH'S EMBRACE of the ecumenical movement can only be adequately explained with reference to the French Dominican friar, Yves Marie-Joseph Congar (1904–1995). Indeed, the first secretary general of the World Council of Churches, Willem Visser 't Hooft (1900–1985), declared Yves Congar to be "the father of Roman Catholic ecumenism."[1]

Congar's Ecumenical Biography

In 1904, Yves Congar was born in Sedan, France, into a devout Catholic family. At age 10, the Great War had begun: German forces had occupied the Ardennes region and his parish church was burned to the ground. For the next six years, Congar would worship in a church that was generously lent to the Catholics of Sedan by the local Calvinist pastor. Far from a homogenous French Catholic town, many of the young Yves's friends were Jews and Protestants. The seeds of his ecumenical vocation were planted already in childhood.

At 17, Congar began his studies for the priesthood in Paris, where he immersed himself in the thought of St. Thomas Aquinas. Four years later, he entered the Dominican novitiate in Amiens, and finally began his core theological studies from 1926 to 1931 at the Saulchoir, at the time a theological powerhouse located in Belgium, known for its academic rigor and historical sensitivity. There he was introduced by his theological instructor, mentor, and confrere, Père Chenu, to the nascent ecumenical movement of *Faith and Order*.[2] Congar completed his "lectorat" thesis in 1928 on the unity in the

---

1. Visser 't Hooft, *Memoirs*, 319.

2. Congar, "Letter from Father Yves Congar, OP," 213–16; *Dialogue between Christians*, 3–4 (hereafter, *DBC*).

Church according to the Tübingen theologian, Johann Adam Möhler (1796–1838).[3] On the eve of his ordination to the priesthood in 1930, he meditated on Jesus' high-priestly prayer in John 17, the experience of which impressed even further upon the young ordinand his vocation to ecumenism: "that they may be one, even as we are one." As he self-describes his vocation, it was at once "ecclesiological and ecumenical [*unionique*]."[4]

From 1931 to 1939, Congar was made Professor of Fundamental theology at the Saulchoir, teaching, among others, a course on ecclesiology. In that period, Congar built up numerous ecumenical contacts and interests. He took classes at the Protestant faculties in France, offered a course on Karl Barth,[5] visited Germany on two separate occasions (1930–31), made multiple visits to England where he met the future archibishop of Canterbury, Dr. Michael Ramsay,[6] and built a relationship with the Orthodox faculty in Paris, the *Insitut Saint-Serge*, where he had regular contact with Georges Florovsky, Sergei Bulgakov, and Leo Zander. It was also during this time that Congar launched *Unam Sanctam*, a scholarly series dedicated to uncovering and presenting a more authentic and vital picture of the Catholic Church. While intending to lead off the series with a French translation of Möhler's *Die Einheit*, the series's first work ended up being Congar's very own: *Chrétiens désunis: Principes d'un "Oecuménisme" catholique* (1937).[7] Offering a positive Catholic vision of ecumenism, the book did much to begin normalizing a suspicious term in Catholic circles, and to articulate an ecumenical program that Catholics could embrace.

With the publication of *Chrétiens désunis*, a dark cloud began to gather over Congar's head. In that same year of 1937, he was denied permission to attend the meeting in Oxford he had worked so hard at preparing. Nearly ten years after the fact, he was told that, when Pius XI refrained from granting such permission, the pope had commented to Congar's religious superior: "The protestants would like that we make all the concessions, and they none."[8]

---

3. See here also Flynn, "Cardinal Congar's Ecumenism," 311–25.

4. Congar, *Journal d'un théologien*, 20.

5. Jossua, *Yves Congar*, 64.

6. Congar made five trips to England before the Council: 1936, 1937, 1939, 1947, and 1956. This last trip especially, however, was less voluntary than "suggested" by his religious superiors.

7. Much of this ecumenical biography can be found in the "Preface" of Congar, *DBC* 1–51.

8. Such is what the pope is alleged to have said according to the then Master of the Dominican Order, Martin Gillet. See Congar, *Journal d'un théologien*, 127.

While the war did much to bring Catholics and Protestants together on a *personal* level, Congar was still amazed at the misunderstandings and prejudices still existing. Five years of captivity in the camps of Colditz and Lübeck also did not make his superiors particularly more understanding of his cause. "From the beginning of 1947 to the end of 1956," wrote Congar, "I knew nothing from that quarter [the Roman curia under Pius XII] but an uninterrupted series of denunciations, warnings, restrictive or discriminatory measures and mistrustful interventions."[9] From 1952 until the Second Vatican Council, all of Congar's writings would be submitted to censors. He was refused permission to publish a Catholic position paper on ecumenism, and to attend the Amsterdam Assembly as an observer.

With the election of John XXIII, Congar's prospects changed. Made a *peritus*, or "theological expert" for the Second Vatican Council, Congar was arguably the most theologically active, not only contributing to numerous discussions, but penning multiple, important texts, including parts of the Dogmatic Constitution on the Church, *Lumen Gentium*, and the preface and conclusion to the Decree on Ecumenism, *Unitatis Redintegratio*.[10] In November of 1994, seven months before Congar was to pass away, John Paul II honored the Dominican's theological contribution to the Church by raising him to the cardinalate.

The Catholic *Status Quo* Vis-à-Vis Ecumenism

At the beginning of the twentieth century, Roman Catholic theology was still in the slow and painful process of ridding itself of counter-Reformation polemic. Its ecclesiology, for example, was one that stressed the visible and institutional aspects of the Church in response to the Reformers who either rejected certain visible elements or diminished them. Its treatises on sacramental theology spent much ink on defending the sacraments' number and efficacy *ex opere operato*. Engagement with non-Catholic positions, even if interpreted generously (which was by no means the norm[11]), was usually relegated to one of the "objections" to which a Catholic refutation and answer would be supplied.[12]

9. Congar, *DBC* 34.

10. For Congar's own summary of his conciliar contributions, see Congar, *My Journal of the Council*, 871.

11. See Congar, "Ecumenical Experience," 74.

12. In most manuals, mentions of Luther, Calvin, or Protestant are almost always in a negative context and await some response, refutation, or dismissal. Peruse, e.g., the otherwise informative and, at the time, popular twelve-volume handbook by Joseph Pohle, *Dogmatic Theology*.

In this charged theological atmosphere, it was difficult, if not practically impossible for Catholic theology to rethink the inherited positions regarding the status of non-Catholic Christians. Echoing the Fathers of the Church, any and all who departed the least bit from orthodox teaching were *extra ecclesiam*. Hence, like heathens and pagans, so too non-Catholics were "outside" the Church. In his encyclical *Satis Cognitum* (1896), Leo XIII taught that non-Catholic Christians have "wandered away from the Spouse." Anyone departing from the Church's teaching or sacraments was "outside Catholic communion" and "alien to the Church"; they were "cut off from Catholic unity."[13] Bishops, even if validly ordained, when not in communion with Peter's successor, had neither the power nor the right to rule, as they were "outside the edifice," "separated from the fold," and "exiled from the kingdom."[14]

Relative to Leo XIII's *Satis Cognitum*, Catholic teaching on non-Catholic Christians developed with Pius XII's *Mystici Corporis* (1943). Pius XII taught that those who do not belong to the "visible Body" have a "certain relationship" [*ordinentur*] with the Mystical Body. Despite this relationship, they are nevertheless "deprived of those many heavenly gifts and helps which can only be enjoyed in the Catholic Church."[15]

Perhaps the most indicative expression of Catholicism's stance towards the ecumenical movement was given by Pius XI in his encyclical, *Mortalium Animos* (1928). Therein, Pius XI explains the Catholic Church's abstention from the *Faith and Order* meeting in Lausanne (1927). The rationale, as expressed by Pius XI, came out of a concern for two fundamental principles which he felt were threatened by the ecumenical movement. The first pertained to the *nature* of unity sought. Unity in faith and government being an absolute necessity for the unity of Christians, any reduction of the visibility of the Church to a loose federation of Christian bodies who may *or may not* be united in faith and government was, for Pius XI, a non-starter.[16] The second principle pertained to the *reality* of the Church's unity: the latent threat in the ecumenical movement was a purely eschatological interpretation of the Church's mark of unity. Accordingly, unity in faith and government was an ideal; it could be hoped for, desired for, and worked for, but was not a reality that was given by God, existing *hic et nunc* in His Church.[17] Lest Catholics give countenance to such a "false Christianity," Pope Pius XI could

---

13. Leo XIII, "*Satis Cognitum*" 9.
14. Leo XIII, "*Satis Cognitum*" 15.
15. Pius XII, "*Mystici Corporis*" 103.
16. Pius XI, "*Mortalium Animos*" 6.
17. Pius XI, "*Mortalium Animos*" 7.

only draw, so it seemed, the following conclusion: "It is clear that the Apostolic See cannot on any terms take part in their assemblies, nor is it anyway lawful for Catholics either to support or to work for such enterprises."[18] What was the solution for Pius XI? "The union of Christians can only be promoted by promoting the return to the one true Church of Christ of those who are separated from it, for in the past they have unhappily left it. To the one true Church of Christ, we say, which is visible to all."[19]

Thusly does Pius XI articulate what is often termed an "ecumenism of return." With the exception perhaps of *Mystici Corporis*, one notes in magisterial teaching of this period not only the lack of any distinction between non-Catholics and non-Christians, but also the lack of any distinction between twentieth-century Lutherans and Martin Luther himself, or twentieth-century Anglicans and Henry VIII. In other words, the ecumenism of "return" is premised on the idea that even those Christians who grew up and received the Gospel outside the visible boundaries of the Catholic Church need to "return" to the Catholic Church, even if they have not "gone" anywhere or "left" anything.

It would be unfair to dismiss out of hand the Catholic critique of the ecumenical movement, especially in the movement's earliest days. From a Catholic perspective, some of the theological principles (or lack thereof) in *Life and Work* and *Faith and Order* during the early years of the twentieth century were, and remain, contrary to Catholic teaching. From a Catholic perspective, any theology that reduces doctrine to a more or less normative expression of religious experience, or subordinates doctrinal truth to rectitude of life, or tries to distil Christianity down to an essence or *Wesen* and finds unity therein whilst dismissing the rest as non-essentials, threatens the plenitude of the deposit of faith. That said, however, it is undeniable that there existed in twentieth-century Catholicism strands of unwillingness and indifference to trying to carry Catholic principles forward into the then-existing ecumenical movement.

In 1946, for example, Congar visited Rome at the invitation of his superior in order to take the temperature of the theological climate there on issues like ecclesiology and ecumenism, the issues dearest to his heart. While he experienced some sure signs of hope,[20] he also encountered suspicion and ignorance. Among the curia, postures towards ecumenism ranged from the aloof

---

18. Pius XI, "*Mortalium Animos*" 8.

19. Pius XI, "*Mortalium Animos*" 10.

20. See Congar's account of his meeting with Mgr. Montini, the future Pope Paul VI, in Congar, *Journal d'un théologien*, 107.

and flippant,[21] to the theoretically open but unenthusiastic.[22] Somewhere in between could be found the echo of a Roman consensus that collaboration with non-Catholics should be reserved for the political (i.e., natural/profane) sphere.[23] The idea of "return" persisted into the Second Vatican Council's discussions and interventions.[24] Indeed, Congar observed in his Council diary that, for some Catholics (who even freely admit it!), ecumenism was tantamount to a "gentle, easy tactic to lead people to the pope."[25]

Congar's Ecumenism

The issue that Congar had to deal with was the following: it was widely thought that, in accord with certain Catholic theological principles, the only viable and appropriate approach for Catholics was to stand back from a deeply flawed ecumenical movement, and continue insisting on the return of those who had left the Catholic Church. Congar's first and most significant contribution, *in nuce*, is to have maintained these same Catholic theological principles whilst simultaneously inferring a very different obligation and course of action: namely, to engage, to be proactive, and to be ready to be enriched.

There are, then three prongs, so to speak, to Congar's ecumenism as it is laid out for the first time in *Chrétiens désunis* in 1937. The first prong has to do with the Church's *unity* and entails the retention of the major Catholic ecclesiological principles laid out in *Mortalium Animos*. These include: (1) that doctrinal agreement is necessary for true unity;[26] (2) that true unity is not an ideal but a reality promised by Christ and given to His Church, visibly;[27] and (3) that this unity is preserved in the Catholic Church (i.e., that the Roman

---

21. See Congar's account of his encounter with Cardinal Tisserant in Congar, *Journal d'un théologien*, 76–79.

22. See Congar's account of his conversation with Charles Boyer, SJ, in Congar, *Journal d'un théologien*, 96–97.

23. See Congar's account of his conversation with Sebastian Tromp in Congar, *Journal d'un théologien*, 100–101.

24. See, e.g., the interventions of Cardinals Spellman and Ruffini as recalled in Congar, *My Journal of the Council*, 213, 428.

25. Congar, *My Journal of the Council*, 484. See also his entry for February 5, 1964: "Worked on the bishops' comments. I counted the number of those for whom ecumenism is just a pleasant way of leading the others to submission to the pope! Wretched ultramontane ecclesiology" (485).

26. Congar, *Divided Christendom*, 108 (hereafter *DC*).

27. Congar, *DC* 80–89, 140.

Catholic Church is the one and unique Church of Christ).[28] Christians may be divided, but the Church is always united.[29] While these principles sound stark when enumerated so, in Congar's book, they are put forward in the context of a fuller discussion of the Church that took as its starting point, not her institutions, hierarchical structure, and sacramental system, but her origin and participation in the life of God. "The oneness of the Church is a communication and extension of the oneness of God Himself."[30] Being clear about Catholic principles, however, is part and parcel of Congar's argument; without it, the subtitle *principes d'un "oecumenisme" catholique* would have been a misnomer, and the book, already controversial at the time, would have been dead on arrival, even at Vatican II.

The second prong of Congar's argument is harnessing the implications of a valid baptism. Congar follows the Catholic theological tradition in his presentation of what baptism *is* and *what makes it valid*. Baptism is the sacrament by which the recipient is incorporated into Christ's body, the Church (which is always one!). What makes a baptism valid is the baptizer's intention to do what the Church does, and his following the proper form of the rite. One is validly baptized, then, even at the hands of a heretic. This was already recognized in the third century by Pope Stephen (d. 257). Congar, consistent with codes 87 and 758 of the then-current *Code of Canon Law*,[31] argues that "valid baptism *ipso facto* incorporates the recipient into the true Church."[32] Where Congar departs from much of past theological precedent, however, is in affirming degrees or grades of ecclesial incorporation *despite* heresy or schism. In other words, separated Christians were more or less connected to the Church, not simply by desire (*in voto*) but really (*in re*), through valid baptism. According to the alternative, heresy or schism frustrates the effects of baptism and cuts someone off completely from the Church, rendering the status of such a person no different from the "heathen" or "pagan" (i.e., non-Christian).[33] For Congar (and later, for the Second Vatican Council), all of those who are baptized within communities

---

28. Congar, *DC* 59, 137–39, 237–38, 258.

29. Congar, *DC* 59. This conviction would hold at the Council too. See, e.g., his remarks in Congar, *My Journal*, 207.

30. Congar, *DC* 48.

31. This is the 1917 *Code*, which would be in effect until it was replaced by the 1983 *Code*. The 1917's Canon 87 pertains to the rights and duties of the baptized; Canon 758 pertains to the various valid and licit forms of baptism. At Vatican II, in the *De Ecclesia* sub-commission, Congar will in fact appeal explicitly to Canon 87 in his input. See Congar, *Quomodo Exponi*, 6.

32. Congar, *DC* 229. See Congar, *DC* 228–34.

33. The American *peritus* Joseph Fenton held this position. See Zuijdwegt, "Salvation and the Church," 164–68.

outside the Catholic Church are, by virtue of their baptism, in communion with the Catholic Church, albeit, imperfectly.[34]

Two things can be observed here. The first is that baptism is the foundation for the Catholic's *ecumenical* engagement. Ecumenical activity is formally different from missionary activity because those being engaged are Christian. After the Second Vatican Council, no Catholic magisterial teaching will address those simply "outside the Church," let alone non-Catholics generally without distinguishing Christians and non-Christians. Baptism is now indexical.

Following from this is the second observation: namely, that baptism, while not the only activity, is an essential activity of the Church. Therefore, bodies or communities who baptize possess an essential element of the Church and, hence, in the words of Walter Kasper, "have a true ecclesial character."[35] This insight, it must be admitted, is not entirely new. According to Augustine, heretical or schismatic sects possessed *vestigia ecclesiae* insofar as, when they were separated from the Catholic Church, they maintained some or all the sacraments and more or less Catholic dogma. Even Catholic apologetics from the Counter-Reform period, when discussing the notes of the Church, rarely if ever were completely oblivious to the ecclesial components of non-Catholic Christians.[36] Congar, however, saw himself as one of the first Catholics to apply the notion of *vestigia ecclesiae* to non-Catholic Christian bodies *as such*, and not merely to the individuals who belong to them. These *vestigia* or *elementa* include the Scriptures, liturgy, sacraments, dogmas, etc.) which various bodies of Christians, to greater or lesser degrees, have maintained. Congar's thesis that there exist *elementa ecclesiae* outside the visible boundaries of the Catholic Church and that these have a "drive" towards their origin, is, in so many words, duplicated at Vatican II. According to Congar, an ecclesial element "calls for integration in the one Body of Christ . . . which is the Catholic Church."[37] Less than thirty years later, the Second Vatican Council would teach: "These elements, as gifts belonging to the Church of Christ, are forces impelling toward catholic unity."[38]

---

34. The crucial conciliar passage here is *Lumen Gentium* 15 (hereafter *LG*), according to which baptized non-Catholics are "joined," "connected," or "linked" [*conjungere/conjunctio*] to the Catholic Church. The "fully incorporated" [*plene incorporantur*] of *LG* 14 implies that there exist gradations of incorporation.

35. Kasper, "Canon Law and Ecumenism," 179.

36. Nichols, *Yves Congar*, 101. Two quite strict examples include Devivier, SJ, *Christian Apologetics*, 331–72; Berry, *Church of Christ*, 159–83.

37. Congar, *DC* 235.

38. *LG* 8; cf. *Unitatis Redintegratio* 15 (hereafter *UR*).

The third and more creative prong of Congar's argument has to do with the Church's catholicity. Moving beyond a merely apologetical and quantitative understanding of catholicity, Congar appeals to the patristic understanding of catholicity that is rooted in Christ's capacity to embrace all humanity, no matter the race, condition, temperament, location, etc. The Church's catholicity, rooted in the catholicity of her Head, is the capacity to embrace and unite all the "material" which she is to incorporate.[39] Her catholicity is her "universal capacity of her unity;" in other words, the strength of the Church's unity is exhibited whenever she is able to honor and embrace in others, "under their diverse forms of experience and expression, the same life of Christ."[40] The Church transcends the particular (i.e., Slav, Italian, etc.) not by eliminating particularity, but by embracing it.[41] Congar calls catholicity the Church's "law of comprehension."[42]

The Church's catholicity, however, while complete and unlimited in terms of its *capacity*, is imperfectly *realized*; it is given as a dynamic capacity, but is manifested only more or less perfectly.[43] Co-relatively, there exist Christian elements which have "in practice received particular emphasis and expression outside the visible body." These "authentic values" have been "embodied in" non-Catholic communities.[44] "What is true in . . . the Lutheran or the Wesleyan experience is, in its Lutheran or Wesleyan setting, a loss to the Catholic Church of today."[45] In order to manifest this catholicity more perfectly, the Church must gather any "genuine Christian aspiration or value,"[46] all authentically Christian insights, that are found outside the Catholic Church. Catholic ecumenism is essentially a matter of the Church, already substantially Catholic (a catholicity not admitting of degrees), becoming more manifestly catholic (a catholicity admitting of degrees).[47]

While this re-integration involves many things, including, for example, prayer, dialogue, and the eradication of prejudice and misunderstanding, the core of Congar's ecumenical agenda for the Catholic Church involves her own reform so as to make her catholicity shine through more. Whether it is her liturgy or theological treatises, the way in which the Catholic Church

---

39. Congar, *DC* 93–102.
40. Congar, *DC* 114.
41. Congar, *DC* 109.
42. Congar, *DC* 111.
43. Congar, *DC* 190–91.
44. Congar, *DC* 256.
45. Congar, *DC* 256.
46. Congar, *DC* 252.
47. Congar, *DC* 254.

lives out her mission will either facilitate and welcome re-integration, or put obstacles in the way.[48] It is the Church's task to reform herself constantly in order to make space for these values.[49] Like someone who, when packing things away, only *seems* to have run out of room in one's house, the Church, whose *capacity for unity is universal*, might need to put her house in order, each thing in its *proper* and *proportional* place so as to give space and breathing room for other authentically Catholic values, as of yet, hidden or squelched, and instead, lived out in other Christian communities. "The most profitable ecumenical work is that which each accomplishes for himself and follows through in his own Church."[50] A helpful summary of his own thought is provided by Congar himself during the time of the Council:

> When I re-read *Chrétiens désunis*, recall my actions and re-examine my past views, I see very little to change. The conclusion I had reached still seems useful to me. I believe more than ever that the essential ecumenical activity of the Catholic Church should be to live its own life more fully and genuinely; to purify itself as far as possible, to grow in faithfulness, in good work, in depth of prayer and in union with God. In being fully herself, in the full strength of her vigour, she will develop her ecumenical power. As I stated in *Chrétiens désunis*, I believe that this presupposes the work of broadening and purification, of reform, if one will, which must begin with the formation of the clergy. If only we really give and radiate God . . . I believe that this plentitude on the part of Catholicism requires that our thought should have absorbed Orthodoxy, the Reform and Anglicanism. Our Catholicism must be of a *post*-Reform nature, that is to say the Reform must really exist for it as a problem which has been faithfully faced in depth and has evoked a living process of assimilation, allowing us to embrace any positive elements the Reform presents and to supply an answer to the questions it really raised.[51]

The influence of Congar's *Chrétiens désunis* on Catholic theology is indisputable. Joseph Famerée rightly states of this "first synthesis" that it "inaugurated an entirely new period of Catholic 'ecumenism.'"[52] Congar also at one point recalled how it helped open up many of the Council Fathers

48. E.g., Congar, *DC* 272.

49. See Famerée, "Aux origins de Vatican II," 126–28.

50. Congar's thought as quoted by his confrere and friend, Jossua, "In Hope of Unity," 171.

51. Congar, *DBC* 31.

52. Famerée, "Aux origins de Vatican II," 124.

to ecumenism.⁵³ Indeed, it is no accident that this program which argued for a *"re-integration"* of ecclesial elements into the Church, and sought to articulate *principes d'un "œcuménisme" catholique* was given a most authoritative *nihil obstat* by the Second Vatican Council's decree on ecumenism entitled *Unitatis Redintegratio* and whose first chapter runs, "Catholic Principles of Ecumenism."⁵⁴

In the eyes of many, however, Congar's ecumenical program as laid out in *Chrétiens désunis* (and even *Unitatis Redintegratio*) is hopelessly outdated. It is difficult for many, including Catholics today, to believe that, at the time, this book merited for Congar a talking-to by his Superior and was what put Congar under a cloud of suspicion for the next two decades.⁵⁵ For Joseph Famerée, *Chrétiens désunis*, for all of its relative historical merits in getting Catholics on the ecumenical bandwagon, is ultimately just a well-thought-out and benevolent articulation of "return" ecumenism.⁵⁶ Famerée's assessment, however, is only partially true because, while there is indeed a dimension of "return," there is also a dimension of reform in Congar's ecumenism. Indeed, Congar's ecumenism involves, as Paul Murray puts it, an "appropriate movement towards communion with Rome, appropriately reformed."⁵⁷ The reform of the Church is precisely what entails a joint-journey among all Christians towards something new—not substantially new, to be sure, but nonetheless new. Moreover, unlike a return model that involves a passive and complacent Catholic Church awaiting others to "make the move," as it were, Congar's ecumenical agenda tasks the Church with purifying and reforming herself. As limited as Congar's initial elaboration is, then, categorizing it as a polite "ecumenism of return" does not seem to do justice to Congar's contribution.

That said, Congar himself admitted the limitations of *Chrétiens désunis* and continued to develop his ecumenical thinking. He published numerous works, both minor and major on the subject. These include, for example, *Aspects de l'oecuménisme* (1962), *Chrétiens en dialogue* (1964), and *L'Église une, sainte, catholique et apostolique* (1970).⁵⁸

---

53. Congar, *DBC* 25. "The book has had its effect. That for which I was once reproached has now been accepted by all ecumenists" (Congar, *DBC* 36).

54. One notices, significantly, that by the time of the Council, "Catholic" modifies *principles* and not *ecumenism*, and that there are no quotation marks—or "scare quotes"—around the word *ecumenism*. For more concrete evidence of Congar's contribution, see his Votum on the Theological subcommmission, *De Oecumenismo*.

55. Congar, *DBC* 35.

56. Famerée, "'Chrétiens désunis' du P. Congar," 681.

57. Murray, "Expanding Catholicity," 292.

58. While this last text is more akin to a brief treatise on the properties of the

Congar's very last major work on ecumenism was *Diversités et communion* (1982). By the 1980s Congar confronts the then-evident ecumenical impasse and limitations of doctrinal convergence strategies. His intention in *Diversités et communion* is to explore ways to unite diverse Christian communities in a Church that has ever exhibited diversity. History gives us abundant examples of how plurality and tension have always existed *within* the Church. Congar, for example, makes much of the controversy over the dating of Easter; the Church was able to stomach differences with respect to something so seminal to the incarnate and historical dimension of Christian worship.[59] Following from this and other examples, Congar argues that intrinsic to unity is plurality.[60] The short volume concludes with a consideration of "fundamental articles" and "reconciled diversity" (*Versöhnte Verschiedenheit*), categories which Congar tacitly accepts, but in a highly qualified manner.

A number of scholars have been engaged in interpreting Congar's later work, assessing its import, and comparing it to his earlier works. While all scholars agree that Congar's thought evolved, the extent to which it evolved and whether this evolution is positive or not, is disputed. Aidan Nichols seems to have offered the most temperate reading of Congar's *Diversity and Communion*. Nichols, for instance, highlights the work's ambiguity which manifests itself in, on the one hand, Congar's apparent enthusiasm for Rahner's radical program of making the Nicene Creed the one "essential" thing, and, on the other, Congar's highly sympathetic treatment of the Orthodox critique of "fundamental articles," a critique Congar seems to make his own.[61] Nichols's cautious reading seems doubly warranted when one considers the style and tenor of the work. *Diversity and Communion* reads more like a casual essay than anything programmatic and systematic. It is ultimately a collation of historical vignettes with ecumenical import interspersed with passing remarks and questions. While Congar's actual position might remain elusive (or perhaps in limbo), asking what Congar was pursuing in this work is still a legitimate question.

Gabriel Flynn, for his part, has clearly traced the development of Congar's ecumenism and has registered a radical shift in Congar's thought. Flynn has been critical of "reconciled diversity" as developed by Congar, and as something, which, for Flynn, when applied to Christian doctrine

---

Church, the note on unity is by far the longest and includes a thorough discussion of the divisions within Christianity.

59. Congar, *Diversity and Communion*, 15–19.

60. For commentary, see Famerée, "'Chrétiens désunis' du P. Congar," 680–81.

61. Nichols, *Yves Congar*, 113; cf. Congar, *Diversity and Communion*, 120.

and Church structure, undermines catholicity, and would result in an unstable, faux unity.[62] He asserts that Congar's earlier *Chrétiens désunis* militated against precisely this "lowest common denominator" approach. Jean-Pierre Jossua, like Flynn, has also recognized a "significant evolution" in Congar's work, but without demur.[63] Paul Murray, in contrast, has defended the continuity of Congar's thought against Flynn, seeing in the early Congar already indications of "Receptive Ecumenism."[64] He argues simultaneously that (1) Congar's notion of catholicity already in 1937 implied diversity, and (2) Congar's version of reconciled diversity precludes any sort of coexistence of separate confessions and instead demands some common doctrinal and sacramental references.[65]

Like Flynn, again, other scholars also register a significant shift in Congar's thought, but do not believe he has gone far enough. On the Protestant side, there is Douglas Koskela, for example, who, whilst discussing Congar's mature thought, suggests—albeit rather obliquely—that what holds back Congar's laudable pneumatological ecclesiology—a later development—from unleashing its ecumenical potential is that Congar ultimately maintains the non-negotiable status of what Catholics understand to be divinely instituted means of salvation. In assessing the ecclesial status of so-called "ecclesial communities," argues Koskela, the grace within these communities should be more determinative than their sacramental system and adherence to the deposit of faith, which, from a Catholic point of view (and from Congar's), might be viewed as deficient.[66]

Also taking Congar's work forward is his confrere, Hervé Legrand, OP. Legrand believes that the program set out in *Diversity and Communion* is continuing through Catholic theology's engagement with the "linguistic turn" and its rethinking of—and perhaps even abandonment of—a propositional truth model of doctrine. For Legrand, the postliberalism of George Lindbeck's *The Nature of Doctrine* is a faithful development of the mature Congar's ecumenical thinking on "reconciled diversity."[67] Whether or not

---

62. Flynn, "Receptive Ecumenism," 399–412; *Yves Congar's Vision of the Church*, 144, 219; "Cardinal Congar's Ecumenism," 321–23.

63. Jossua, "In Hope of Unity," 178–81.

64. For the programme of "Receptive Ecumenism," see Murray, *Receptive Ecumenism*.

65. Murray, "Expanding Catholicity," 288, 299.

66. Koskela, *Ecclesiality and Ecumenism*, esp. 147–65. An extreme example here are the Quakers: no one disputes their spiritual fruits, but their sacramental system is lacking.

67. Legrand, "Yves Congar," 529–54.

Congar would agree to this depends, I suggest, on a host of issues, not least of which is how one interprets Lindbeck.[68]

Moreover, the principle of non-contradiction has to be taken seriously precisely in order for "reconciled diversity" to bear real ecumenical fruit. I would submit, for example, that Congar's assertion that the Greek East and the Latin West's theological (and dogmatic!) elaboration of Trinitarian doctrine are fundamentally—i.e., systematically, philosophically, terminologically—different, and therefore, do not contradict because, while one affirms and the other rejects *filioque*, they do so not *from the same perspective* or *same aspect*. What is a greater challenge, to my mind, is reconciling the "diversity" in, say, Lutheran—Roman Catholic teachings on the number of sacraments, or on justification, a "diversity"—one should note—that arose within the same historical milieu and was instrumental in the division of Christians. Eastern and Western elaborations of the Trinity can be reconciled ostensibly because of different philosophical systems in which *causa* is not the same as *aitia*, nor *principium* the same as *arche*, and in which procession and spiration, furthermore, are understood differently; these diverse systems, moreover, developed culturally and geographically parallel to each other, co-existed for centuries prior to any schism, and did not, in themselves, cause division. By contrast, the different "Denkformen" that exist between Lutheran and Catholic expressions has been attributed to a more personalist-existential mode of speaking on the one hand, and a more speculative-sapiential mode, on the other.[69] But if one believes that the former must bear some relationship to the latter, that *lex orandi lex credendi*, or in Avery Dulles's words, that "performative language cannot be unrelated to informative,"[70] then there is still more work to be done in order to show that the two expressions—Lutheran and Catholic, Augsburg and Trent—are both faithful expressions of the one same Gospel.

---

68. Whether or not the late Congar is an embryonic Lindbeckian depends on how one reads Lindbeck. What is indisputable is that Congar believes that the truth-value of dogma—and doctrine generally—is rooted in its accurate representation of reality (i.e., it carries an "ontological truth value"). Those who believe Lindbeck's cultural linguistic model excludes ontological truth claims would then have to conclude that Congar and Lindbeck are indeed incompatible; others who defend Lindbeck from this charge might be able to perceive a common theological program. For the former opinion, see O'Neill, "Rule Theory of Doctrine," 417–42. For the latter, see Marshall, "Aquinas as Postliberal Theologian," 353–402. Lindbeck provides a short response immediately after Marshall's piece, seconding the latter's reading.

69. E.g., Pesch, "Existential and Sapiential Theology," 61–81.

70. Dulles, "Two Languages of Salvation."

Theology at the Service of Ecumenism

In addition to Congar's works dedicated explicitly to ecumenism, he wrote other major works that put into practice the program set out in *Chrétiens désunis*. This involved, if we recall, the Catholic Church taking upon herself the responsibility to conform herself ever more deeply to Christ. Congar's theological works execute the program of *Chrétiens désunis* by, on a theological and scholarly level, expanding the Church's catholicity, or her capacity to embrace all that is good and true.

In *Vraie et fausse réforme dans l'Église* (1950), for example, Congar discusses the instances and senses according to which the Church can be said to fail, and argues for the necessity of constant purification and reform of the Church. To be sure, he defends what he considers to be *Catholic* principles of reform (and criticizes Luther on multiple fronts), but the very idea of reform was not self-evident in a polemical and defensive style of theology common at the time. The Holy Office's prohibition of a new edition or translation of it is just one indication of the then-*status quo*.[71]

Three years later, Congar published *Jalons pour une théologie du laïcat* (1953). Therein, Congar rediscovers the *tria munera* and discusses anew all the responsibilities—priestly, prophetic, and kingly—of the baptized. In a word, it was a Catholic presentation of the universal priesthood, something taken for granted by protestant Christians, and which was completely underdeveloped in Catholic theology, as indicated by the—at least in retrospect—embarrassing entry for "laien" (i.e., *laymen*) in the *Kirchenlexikon*, which read: s. (-iehe) *Clerus*, and once one turned to *Clerus*, one came across the statement that there is no *real* or *proper* priesthood of believers.[72]

During the years leading up to the Council, Congar was in the midst of writing his two-volume masterpiece, *La Tradition et les traditions* (1960–1963). Therein, Congar put forward a highly nuanced and systematic account of tradition. No doubt, he defended a Catholic and dynamic understanding of tradition that answered certain Protestant allegations about Catholics' identifying their own "tradition" with divine revelation. Nevertheless, in defending the Catholic position, Congar took great pains to put Scripture, Tradition, traditions, and magisterium in their proper relationship. He defended the material sufficiency of Scripture, and criticized theological presentations of tradition which exaggerated the role of the magisterium.

---

71. For more on the drama behind *Vraie et fausse réforme dans l'église*, see Congar, *Journal d'un théologien*, 181–222.

72. Wetzer et al., *Kirchenlexikon*, 7:1323; 3:546.

What is common in all of these works (and others by Congar), is that they are historically sensitive and source-based. History, for Congar, is that "great teacher" which sets records straight. It discovers the principles behind and the meaning of different doctrinal formulations, it puts things in perspective, and it finds useful past precedent. There exists, then, for Congar, a fundamental relationship between history and *ressourcement*, on the one hand, and the ecumenical movement, on the other.[73] A return to the sources inevitably involves a return to the sources that are shared among the different Christian bodies (e.g., Scripture, the Fathers, and even the Medieval scholastics!).

Not only did these (and other) works of Congar's provide argumentation that would ultimately be replicated at Vatican II, but these works arguably have done more for ecumenism in the long run than many a bilateral doctrinal discussion because, from the springs of *ressourcement*, they help rejuvenate in the Catholic's conscience a richer and more catholic understanding of these issues. They proceed "in accordance with a deeper and closer fidelity to our unique source" or "common sources."[74]

Congar contributed his time, energy, and productivity to the ecumenical cause. Beyond his 2,000 writings, he gave hundreds of talks, participated in dozens of meetings and colloquia, preached the Christian unity octave for decades, and collaborated with all the relevant ecumenical centers and their journals for his ecumenical project.[75] He also played a leading role in the Catholic Council for Ecumenical Questions (1952–1963) whose work ultimately gave way to the newly created Pontifical Council for Promoting Christian Unity.[76]

Perhaps Congar's greatest *personal* contribution to the ecumenical movement was his enthusiasm, fortitude, and long-suffering. By his own spiritual conversion to the cause and his conviction of its importance, Congar was able to see himself rehabilitated, and not only to tell others, but also to *show* others what disposition and humility is necessary to engage in ecumenical work. Ecumenism, writes Congar, "asks not less faith, but more. . . . Ecumenism demands a profound moral and even religious conversion. . . . Ecumenism seeks also a reform within ourselves, for we are full of aggressiveness, clannishness and arrogance, of distrust and rivalry. We must be converted by detachment from all this and from ourselves, and acceptance of a humble submissiveness of what the Lord expects of us."[77]

73. Congar, *DBC* 44.
74. Congar, *DBC* 21.
75. Congar, *DBC* 26.
76. Jacobs, "Catholic Conference for Ecumenical Questions," 10.
77. Congar, "Ecumenical Experience," 83–84.

Significantly, the conversion that ecumenism requires, especially of Catholics, is not away from Catholicism but towards it. Congar argued that engaging in ecumenical activity is a profoundly Catholic activity, and that some of the hallmarks of Catholic intellectual life, including Thomas Aquinas and Scholasticism more generally, were timelier than ever: e.g., the necessity of making distinctions; clarity in argument; charitable reading of one's interlocutor; doing one's best to "examine more searchingly" the intention [*scrutemur profundius intentionem*] of someone whose argument we disagree with.[78] All these aspects of the Catholic intellectual tradition behoove and serve ecumenical engagement. Congar did his part to raise Catholic awareness of this.

Conclusion

The story of Catholic ecumenism, in which Congar played a leading role, is a story about how Catholic theology began to recognize all of the implications and consequences that the *vestigia ecclesiae*—especially baptism—had for the *relationship* between the Catholic Church and non-Catholic Christian bodies. Congar realized that Christian reunion would necessitate development and reform on the part of the Catholic Church—a development that is able to reconcile certain doctrines that historically have been alien to it, and a reform that is able to integrate practices that have developed for centuries outside of her.

Any honest assessment of the enduring relevance of Congar's ecumenical thinking will note not only his novel approach and contributions towards ecumenical progress, but also his firm and steadfast maintenance of certain ineluctable Catholic ecumenical principles, principles which have been maintained by the Catholic Church for centuries. They are expressed just as much by Pius XI in *Mortalium Animos* as by the Second Vatican Council. These include the visibility of the Church as an organized society that is united in faith;[79] that the Church of Christ subsists (i.e., *exists* integrally) in the Catholic Church, and by implication, there exist some deficiencies—more or less—in other churches or ecclesial communities, including the lack of the Petrine office;[80] that no amount of damage done by Christians, nor divisions among them, can injure the unity of the Church which remains in the Catholic Church as a gift from God.[81]

78. Congar, "Saint Thomas Aquinas," 196–209.
79. *MA* 6; *LG* 8; *UR* 2.
80. *MA* 10–11; *LG* 8; *UR* 3.
81. *MA* 7; *UR* 3.

In other words, Congar and Catholic theology with him will never acquiesce to what can be termed the "liberal" ecumenism inspired by the theology of Schleiermacher and continuing through this lineage. As Cardinal Kasper has observed with respect to two of Congar's most celebrated—and for our purposes, most relevant—works, *Chrétiens désunis* and *Vraie et fausse réforme*: "This was an ecumenical theology based on the solid terrain of dogma, and not a liberal ecumenism based on subjective experience or on praxis."[82]

It is too early to tell what will come of the newer hermeneutic of "reconciled diversity" that Congar began to explore at the end of his life. I would submit that, from a Catholic perspective, the fruitfulness of reconciled diversity will hinge on the extent to which the Catholic principles maintained by Congar are kept intact. The irony suggested here is that it is precisely those things in Congar which some find dated—and perhaps highly unpopular—that will actually continue to endure and be relevant. It is not just the particular ecclesial realities, sacraments, institutions, etc., which Congar happened to identify as constitutive and perennial components of Christ's Church that some find passé. It is actually the very notion of anything whatever being deemed "constitutive" and "perennial" that appears problematic, if not impossible, to many.

In a contemporary theological climate, however, that finds it increasingly difficult to stomach anything definitive and enduring, there arises a different aspect to Congar's relevance. As sensitive as Congar was to Protestant and Orthodox concerns, as passionate as he was about the ecumenical movement, and as creative and adventurous as he was in his ecclesiological reflections, Congar will, to some, be a constant, sobering, and even sad reminder of the ecumenical limitations inherent in Catholicism itself, and to others, be a pioneer whose principles, patience, and bravery lead to a real progress, the ultimate consequences of which remain unknown.

Bibliography

Berry, E. Sylvester. *The Church of Christ: An Apologetic and Dogmatic Treatise*. St. Louis, MO: B. Herder, 1927.

Congar, Yves. *Chrétiens désunis: principes d'un "œcuménisme" catholique*. Unam Sanctam 1. Paris: Cerf, 1937.

———. *Chrétiens en dialogue: contributions catholiques à l'œcuménisme*. Unam Sanctam 50. Paris, Cerf, 1965.

———. *De Oecumenismo*. October 27, 1961. Congar's Papers, Saulchoir, Archives de la province dominicaine de France.

---

82. Kasper, "La théologie oecuménique," 3.

———. *Dialogue between Christians: Catholic Contributions to Ecumenism.* English Translation of *Chrétiens en dialogue*. London: Geoffrey Chapman, 1966.
———. *Diversités et communion: dossier historique et conclusion théologique.* Cogitatio Fidei 112. Paris: Cerf, 1982.
———. *Diversity and Communion.* English Translation of *Diversités et communion*. London: SCM, 1984.
———. *Divided Christendom.* English Translation of *Chrétiens désunis*. London: Geoffrey Bless, 1939.
———. "Ecumenical Experience and Conversion: A Personal Testimony." In *The Sufficiency of God*, edited by Robert C. Mackie and Charles C. West, 71–87. London: SCM, 1963.
———. *Essais œcuméniques: le mouvement, les hommes, les problèmes.* Paris: Centurion, 1984.
———. *La tradition et les traditions.* 2 vols. Paris: Librairie Arthème Fayard, 1960, 1963.
———. *Le Christ, Marie et l'Église.* Paris: Desclée de Brouwer, 1952.
———. *L'Église une, sainte, catholique et apostolique.* Mysterium Salutis 15. Paris: Cerf, 1970.
———. *Jalons pour une théologie du laïcat.* Unam Sanctam 23. Paris: Cerf, 1953.
———. *Je crois en L'Esprit Saint.* 3 vols. Paris: Cerf, 1979–1980.
———. *Journal d'un théologien (1946–1956).* Edited by Etienne Fouilloux et al. 2nd ed. Paris: Cerf, 2001.
———. "Letter from Father Yves Congar, OP." Translated by Ronald John Zawilla. *Theology Digest* 32 (1985) 213–16.
———. *My Journal of the Council.* Collegeville, MN: Liturgical, 2012.
———. *Quomodo exponi exprimique possit nexus inter homines extra ecclesiam visibilem exstantes et Corpus Mysticum.* May 18, 1961. Congar's Papers, Saulchoir, Archives de la province dominicaine de France.
———. "Saint Thomas Aquinas and the Spirit of Ecumenism." *New Blackfriars* 55 (1974) 196–209.
———. *Vraie et fausse réforme dans l'église.* 2nd ed. Unam Sanctam 72. Paris: Cerf, 1968.
Devivier, Walter. *Christian Apologetics: A Defense of the Catholic Faith.* New York: Benzinger, 1903.
Dulles, Avery. "Two Languages of Salvation: The Lutheran-Catholic Joint Declaration." *First Things*, December 1999. Online. https://www.firstthings.com/article/1999/12/two-languages-of-salvation-the-lutheran-catholic-joint-declaration.
Famerée, Joseph. "Aux origines de Vatican II: La démarche théologique d'Yves Congar." *Ephemerides Theologicae Lovaniensis* 71 (1995) 121–38.
———. "'Chrétiens désunis' du P. Congar 50 ans après." *Nouvelle Revue Théologique* 110 (1998) 666–86.
Flynn, Gabriel. "Cardinal Congar's Ecumenism: An 'Ecumenical Ethics' for Reconciliation?" *Louvain Studies* 28 (2003) 311–25.
———. "Receptive Ecumenism and Catholic Learning—Reflection in Dialogue with Yves Congar and B. C. Butler." In *Receptive Ecumenism and the Call to Catholic Learning: Exploring a Way for Contemporary Ecumenism*, edited by Paul D. Murray, 399–412. Oxford: Oxford University Press, 2008.
———. *Yves Congar's Vision of the Church in a World of Unbelief.* Aldershot: Ashgate, 2004.

Jacobs, Jan. "Catholic Conference for Ecumenical Questions." *L'Osservatore Romano*, July 30, 2003. 10.

Jossua, Jean-Pierre. "In Hope of Unity." In *Yves Congar: Theologian of the Church*, edited by Gabriel Flynn, 167–82. Louvain: Peeters, 2005.

———. *Yves Congar: Theology in the Service of God's People*. Chicago: Priory, 1968.

Kasper, Walter. "Canon Law and Ecumenism." *The Jurist* 69 (2009) 171–89.

———. "La théologie oecuménique d'Yves Congar et la situation actuelle de l'oecuménisme." *Documents Episcopat* 14 (2004) 1–12.

Koskela, Douglas M. *Ecclesiality and Ecumenism: Yves Congar and the Road to Unity*. Milwaukee, WI: Marquette University Press, 2008.

Legrand, Hervé. "Yves Congar (1904–1995): une passion pour l'unité." *Nouvelle revue théologique* 126 (2004) 529–54.

Leo XIII. "*Satis Cognitum*: Encyclical on the Unity of the Church." June 29, 1896. Online. http://w2.vatican.va/content/leo-xiii/en/encyclicals/documents/hf_l-xiii_enc_29061896_satis-cognitum.html.

Marshall, Bruce D. "Aquinas as Postliberal Theologian." *The Thomist* 53 (1989) 353–402.

Murray, Paul. "Expanding Catholicity through Ecumenicity in the Work of Yves Congar: *Ressourcement*, Receptive Ecumenism, and Catholic Reform." *International Journal of Systematic Theology* 13 (2011) 272–302.

———, ed. *Receptive Ecumenism and the Call to Catholic Learning: Exploring a Way for Contemporary Ecumenism*. Oxford: Oxford University Press, 2008.

Nichols, Aidan. *Yves Congar*. London: Geoffrey Chapman, 1989.

O'Neill, Colman. "The Rule Theory of Doctrine and Propositional Truth." *The Thomist* 49 (1985) 417–42.

Pesch, Otto Hermann. "Existential and Sapiential Theology: The Theological Confrontation between Luther and Thomas Aquinas." In *Catholic Scholars Dialogue with Luther*, edited by Jared Wicks, 61–81. Chicago: Loyola University Press, 1970.

Peters, Edward N., ed. *The 1917 Pio-Benedictine Code of Canon Law*. San Francisco: Ignatius, 2001.

Pius XI. "*Mortalium Animos*: Encyclical on Religious Unity." January 6, 1928. Online. http://w2.vatican.va/content/pius-xi/en/encyclicals/documents/hf_p-xi_enc_19280106_mortalium-animos.html.

Pius XII. "*Mystici Corporis Christi*: Encyclical on the Mystical Body of Christ." June 29, 1943. Online. http://w2.vatican.va/content/pius-xii/en/encyclicals/documents/hf_p-xii_enc_29061943_mystici-corporis-christi.html.

Pohle, Joseph, with Arthur Preuss. *Dogmatic Theology*. 12 vols. St. Louis, MO: Herder, 1911–20.

Second Vatican Council. "*Lumen Gentium*: Dogmatic Constitution on the Church." November 21, 1964. Online. http://w2.vatican.va/archive/hist_councils/ii_vatican_council/documents/vat-ii_const_19641121_lumen-gentium_en.html.

———. "*Unitatis Redintegratio*: Decree on Ecumenism." November 21, 1964. Online. http://www.vatican.va/archive/hist_councils/ii_vatican_council/documents/vat-ii_decree_19641121_unitatis-redintegratio_en.html.

Visser 't Hooft, Willem. *Memoirs*. London: SCM, 1973.

Wetzer, Heinrich Joseph, and Benedict Welte, eds. *Kirchenlexikon: oder Encyklopädie der katholischen Theologie und ihrer Hilfswissenschaften*. 13 vols. Freiburg im Breisgau, 1882–1903.

Zuijdwegt, Geertjan. "Salvation and the Church: Feeney, Fenton, and the Making of *Lumen Gentium*." *Louvain Studies* 37 (2013) 147–78.

2

Edmund Schlink: Ecumenical Theology

—Matthew L. Becker

Introduction

IN THE FALL OF 1939, just weeks after Germany's invasion of Poland, a thirty-six-year-old Lutheran minister became an official counselor (*Visitator*) to several congregations in Hesse-Nassau and Westphalia that belonged to the Confessing Church. For the previous four years Edmund Schlink (1903–1984) had been a theology professor at Bethel Seminary, near Bielefeld, where he had offered seminars on Christian dogmatics, the Lutheran Confessions, and ethics. But now that the Gestapo had closed the seminary, due to concerns about the potentially subversive preaching there, Schlink was invited to provide pastoral care to congregations in the region. He was on familiar ground, for he had been born in Darmstadt, the former capital of Hesse, located about twenty kilometers south of Frankfurt. His father had been a professor of mechanics and aeronautical technology at Darmstadt's technical college, which helped to support its reputation as a "city of science" (*Wissenschaftsstadt*).[1] In 1922 young Edmund had followed in his father's footsteps by studying mathematics and the natural sciences at the universities of Tübingen and Munich. Yet he soon shifted his academic focus to the study of human beings, eventually completing a doctorate in religious psychology at the University of Marburg. After experiencing a crisis of faith, however, which led him to drop out of the university for a year and to work on a Silesian farm, he then began his study of Christian theology, initially at the seminary in Bethel and then at the University of Münster, where he completed his second doctorate, this time under the direction

---

1. For a more detailed overview of Schlink's life and work, see Becker, "Edmund Schlink," 15–41. The American edition, *Edmund Schlink Works*, will be abbreviated as ESW. It is based on the five-volume German edition, *Schriften zu Ökumene und Bekenntnis*, which will hereafter be abbreviated as *SÖB*.

of Karl Barth. Like his famous Swiss professor, Schlink also opposed the so-called "*Deutsche Christen*" (DC), who were then seeking to transform Christianity in Germany so as to align it with National Socialism. Schlink thus publicly defended the 1934 Barmen Declaration that condemned the "German Christian" heresy, and he worked to strengthen those congregations that had adopted this declaration as their own. Banned by the Gestapo from speaking in public and opposed by the DC church authorities in Berlin, Schlink nevertheless accepted a call to serve as pastor to the "confessing" congregation of St. Mary's Church in Bielefeld. He carried out this ministry—illegally—through the end of the war. His pastoral experiences during the Nazi period would thereafter shape his theological concerns and the ecumenical vision toward which he worked until his death.

Schlink cared for the Hessen and Westphalian congregations as a confessional Lutheran pastor. Indeed, during these years he carefully studied the principal confessional documents of the Evangelical-Lutheran Church, the fruit of which inquiry was his first major work, *The Theology of the Lutheran Confessions*, initially published in 1940.[2] In his view, these confessions are not "Lutheran," sectarian writings but are instead a normative witness to the orthodox faith of the *una sancta catholica et apostolica ecclesia*. "They therefore make their claim not only with respect to the time in which they arose, but for all time to come, even until Christ's return."[3] As a whole, Schlink's analysis stresses the importance of actively confessing the evangelical faith in the midst of spiritual crises and trials (*Anfechtungen*), when the church itself is undergoing persecution. The book's assertions were tested not only during the so-called "church struggle" (*Kirchenkampf*), when the orthodoxy of the Protestant Church in Germany was at stake, but also within the context of Schlink's own personal life, in the wake of his first wife's death and the challenges of caring for their two young daughters.[4]

After the Second World War, Schlink was called to teach dogmatic and ecumenical theology at the University of Heidelberg. Between 1946 and his death in 1984 this scholarly community would be his intellectual home. Here he sought to bring theology and the church, scholarship and faith, confession and understanding into conversation with one another. Here he also founded the first ecumenical institute in the world, which attracted an assortment of international students who were interested in exploring "the consonance and differences among Christian churches and the numerous

---

2. Schlink, *Theologie der lutherischen Bekenntnisschriften*. The English translation, *Theology of the Lutheran Confessions*, will hereafter be abbreviated as *TLC*.

3. Schlink, *Theologie der lutherischen Bekenntnisschriften* (*SÖB* 4:6 [*TLC* xvii]).

4. In October 1938 Schlink married Irmgard Ostwald (1914–2006), a former student of his who had also previously studied with Barth in her native Basel.

efforts toward Christian unity in our time."[5] Other ecumenical work soon followed. In 1948 he was an official delegate of the Protestant Church in Germany to the inaugural assembly of the World Council of Churches (WCC) at Amsterdam. He later served as a member of its Central Committee. Active for twenty-five years in the WCC's Commission on Faith and Order, he articulated new approaches to such issues as altar fellowship, the eschatological dimension of Christian unity, ecumenical methodology, and conciliarity. He was especially concerned to encourage the participation of the Eastern Orthodox churches in the WCC, and he was instrumental in helping the Russian Orthodox Church to join that ecumenical body in 1961. Between October 1962 and December 1965 he was the German Protestant Church's official observer at the Second Vatican Council and a main speaker for the group of all such observers from the non-Roman churches. Schlink was an obvious choice for this responsibility, given that he had been engaged in structured ecumenical dialogue with Roman Catholic theologians in Germany since 1946.

After his retirement from the university in March 1971, he published shorter works on such ecumenical problems as apostolic succession and the papacy, but he devoted most of his scholarly time and effort to completing his dogmatics, which he had promised to undertake after his study of the Lutheran Confessions. The 804-page *Ökumenische Dogmatik* was published just one year before he died from an embolism (following surgery) on May 20, 1984.

Seeking the Unity of the Church

Particularly strong and influential memories from his involvement in the *Kirchenkampf* shaped Schlink's ecumenical theology. These involved pastoral experiences that had brought him into close contact with Christians from traditions beyond his own. For example, there were the Eastern Orthodox forced-laborers whom he had communed at St. Mary's and the local Roman Catholic priest with whom he had co-officiated at funerals after mass bombings.[6] In trying circumstances he learned first-hand the comfort and strength that the "mutual consolation" of brothers and sisters in Christ can provide. These ecumenical encounters deeply affected his understanding of ecclesiology. "What shines as the truth in extreme situations in the church cannot become false in normal situations, even if it cannot be repeated in

---

5. Schlink, "Der Neubau des Ökumenischen Instituts," 4.
6. Schlink, "Persönlicher Beitrag," in Vogel, *Männer der Ev. Kirche in Deutschland*, 206.

the same way."[7] "Greater than the differences was the power of the name of Jesus Christ we witnessed to together. . . . It became increasingly clear that none of us could speak and act from one's own confessional position without carefully thinking through and really listening to the voices of the brothers and sisters from the other confession.[8]

But Schlink also discovered in the Augsburg Confession itself a theological rationale for seeking such fellowship with Christians beyond the borders of his own church. The seventh article of that confession maintains that the sufficient basis for unity among Christians is agreement in the gospel.[9] This consensus is the *sine qua non* for unity among those who bear the name of Christ.[10] The unity of the church, however, is not merely a "vertical" unity that results from the working of Christ and the Spirit through the gospel and sacraments. This unity also includes a "horizontal" dimension that extends out to the whole of Christendom on earth. The *una sancta* does not consist only of isolated individuals or congregations but of the consensus of all who hear and proclaim the gospel and administer and receive the sacraments, and this consensus, according to the Augsburg Confession, is always two-fold, namely, "a consensus with contemporary, living brothers and sisters in Christ and a consensus with the ancestors in the faith who went before us."[11] Thereby the constitutive factor for church unity is not rites, ceremonies, or a particular form of church order, but solely the *consensus de doctrina evangelii*. This concept of church unity gives rise to the strongest ecumenical impulses, for the *una sancta* is confessed to be a reality on this earth, one that is not only to be confessed but also celebrated and manifested through fellowship in the Lord's Supper. "Separations between believers are distortions of the one, holy, catholic, and apostolic church, a dishonoring of Christ, and a grave

---

7. Schlink, "Persönlicher Beitrag," 206–7. See Eber, "Edmund Schlink" (*SÖB* 1:xiii–xiv). My translation here differs slightly from that by Skibbe, *Quiet Reformer*, 49.

8. Schlink, *Der Ertrag des Kirchenkampfes*, 19–20, 39 (*SÖB* 5:79, 92).

9. "Our churches also teach that one holy church is to continue forever. The church is the assembly of saints in which the gospel is taught purely and the sacraments are administered rightly. It is sufficient for the true unity of the Christian church that the gospel be preached according to a pure understanding of it and that the sacraments be administered in accordance with the divine word. It is not necessary for the true unity of the Christian church that humanly instituted ceremonies should be observed uniformly in all places" (*Augsburg Confession* art. 7 in Kolb and Wengert, *Book of Concord*, 43).

10. Schlink, *Theologie der lutherischen Bekenntnisschriften* (*SÖB* 4:172n17 [*TLC* 207n12]).

11. Schlink, "Die Weite der Kirche," 6 (*SÖB* 1/1:110; *ESW* 1:159).

sin," which should let no Christian or congregation rest in peace.[12] Instead of merely accepting the shame and disgrace of the present divided state of Christendom, the churches should work toward visible unity, seeking visible fellowship, "hastening to meet the coming Christ, who will gather his own into one flock and will hold us all to account."[13]

Schlink held that the basic prerequisite for serious ecumenical dialogue is the ongoing intention to be open to the activity of the risen Christ and the Holy Spirit in the churches beyond one's own. The goal of uniting the separated churches can only be reached if each church repents of its own intransigence and self-importance. He thus called for a "Copernican Revolution" in the consideration of Christendom. Christ and not one's own church body must be the central criterion for recognizing and evaluating the other churches:

> Every church is in danger of understanding itself as the center around which the other churches orbit as planets. This lies so close at hand because all Christians are certain that the church whose message brought them to faith—in which church they were incorporated into Christ through baptism, and through word and sacrament they are again and again nourished anew—is the one, holy, catholic, and apostolic church. But the working of Christ is not restricted to this one church. He works in freedom without being bound by the borders of our churches. We cannot be content to measure other churches in respect to ourselves, but we have to take our starting point with Christ, by whom we are measured along with all churches. He is the sun around whom we, together with other churches, orbit as planets and from whom we receive light. A kind of Copernican revolution is necessary in ecclesiological thinking.[14]

At the very end of his published reflections on the Second Vatican Council Schlink underscores that "none of the churches can remain exactly as it is; in every case a renewal and an unfolding of catholicity, that is, a return to God and a turning toward the other churches, is needed."[15] Distortions and errors in doctrine must be corrected, weak positions strengthened, anathemas canceled. The unification of the churches will not be possible without sacrifices on the part of all of them. No one church can absorb the others, since no church body, including the Roman Church, "can make space for everything

12. Schlink, "Die Weite der Kirche," 7 (SÖB 1/1:111; ESW 1:160).
13. Schlink, "Aufgabe und Gefahr," 2 (SÖB 1/1:14; ESW 1:55).
14. Schlink, Nach dem Konzil, 240 (SÖB 1/2:240; ESW 1:526).
15. Schlink, Nach dem Konzil, 252 (SÖB 1/2:252; ESW 1:535).

that God has done" and is doing "in the others."¹⁶ But where their sacrifices are offered to God, "there is no loss but only the self-sacrifice unto a treasure which is greater than one previously possessed."¹⁷

Schlink hoped that his own work in ecumenical theology would help the separated churches to rediscover the dogmatic foundations that they held in common, foundations that he thought were sufficient to reunite the churches. For him, the purpose of ecumenical theology is to identify the essential content and contours of church teaching (dogma) which grows from the gospel and the church's confession of the triune God. Because "the root of dogma is confession," the church cannot avoid giving voice to dogmatic statements, alongside the other statements of faith (for example, prayer, doxology, witness, teaching).¹⁸ "Where the unity of the church is, there this unity, by its very nature, will also necessarily be voiced in the unity of confession."¹⁹ If the church were only to state its faith in prayer and witness, its response would be incomplete. Downplaying dogmatic statements in ecumenical work is thus basically impossible. Not only do supposedly "undogmatic" church bodies operate according to quasi-dogmatic principles—which have a direct impact on the disunity of the church—but churches that are committed to specific dogmas are in doctrinal disagreement with one another and in need of resolving those differences. "Instead of downplaying dogmatic differences we must take these differences seriously and strive for unity in dogmatic statements, which is essential for the unity of the church, and to do so through new ways of framing issues and new methods for addressing them."²⁰

16. Schlink, *Nach dem Konzil*, 253 (*SÖB* 1/2:253; *ESW* 1:535).

17. Schlink, *Nach dem Konzil*, 253 (*SÖB* 1/2:253; *ESW* 1:535).

18. Schlink, "Die Struktur der dogmatischen Aussage," 302 (*SÖB* 1/1:75; *ESW* 1:120). Schlink begins this essay by noting how "members of the separated churches are able to pray and bear witness together to a far greater extent than they can agree on common dogmatic statements." They are able, to a much greater extent, "to make the prayers of another church their own heart-felt prayer, and to hear the proclamation of the others as pertinent, powerful, and strengthening proclamation for themselves, than they are able to accept the dogmatic statements of others as binding statements" (Schlink, "Die Struktur der dogmatischen Aussage," 251 [*SÖB* 1/1:24; *ESW* 1:67]). His point, of course, is not to avoid articulating dogmatic statements or to ignore the challenges that the differing dogmatic statements create for the separated churches but to interpret these statements anew in light of the whole range of faith statements in the churches and of the transformations that have occurred when the theological content of one form of faith statement (e.g., prayer) is transmitted into another form (e.g., teaching).

19. Schlink, "Die Struktur der dogmatischen Aussage," 302 (*SÖB* 1/1:75; *ESW* 1:120).

20. Schlink, "Die Struktur der dogmatischen Aussage," 303 (*SÖB* 1/1:76; *ESW* 1:120).

The essay from which this last point is taken, an essay that is perhaps his most important shorter work, is a creative attempt to analyze each of the basic statements of faith and to point to their abiding connections to one another. It underscores that within the early church the unity of faith was not premised upon uniformity in dogmatic statements or the use of identical creedal formulas. "Unity in dogmatic statements need not consist in the common acceptance of one and the same formula, but can also consist in the fellowship that gives mutual acknowledgment to different dogmatic formulas."[21] This approach to church unity—which is evident in the New Testament canon that encompasses different witnesses to Jesus Christ and in the variety of differing local creeds that were welcomed and used within the early church—highlights the complex problem of ascertaining and expressing dogmatic unity within the diversity of dogmatic statements and expressions. The key question is: in which of the various dogmatic statements can unity in dogma be recognized and acknowledged? Answering this question led Schlink to develop his *Ecumenical Dogmatics*, wherein he devoted himself to philological and historical analyses of central dogmatic terms and concepts, to the anthropological presuppositions that have shaped dogmatic understandings over the centuries (particularly in the areas of Christology and the sacraments), to the place that the various statements of faith have within the total range of forms of theological statement, and, crucially, to "the *actual* validity which the differing dogmatic statements have had and currently have" among the churches.[22]

Schlink's *Ecumenical Dogmatics*

Convinced that the goal of reuniting the separated churches could only be achieved through careful work in dogmatic theology, Schlink devoted several decades to articulating the essential content of the Christian faith, the acceptance of which he hoped could serve as the basis of unity for all of the churches. The ecumenical significance of Schlink's dogmatics is evident from the prefaces that were written by two non-Lutheran theologians, one a Roman Catholic and the other an Eastern Orthodox, who each affirm the work's basic consistency with the faith taught by their respective churches.[23]

---

21. Schlink, "Die Struktur der dogmatischen Aussage," 303 (SÖB 1/1:76; ESW 1:121).

22. Schlink, "Die Struktur der dogmatischen Aussage," 305 (SÖB 1/1:78; ESW 1:122).

23. See the forewords by Heinrich Fries and Nikos Nissiotis in the first edition of *Ökumenische Dogmatik* (SÖB 2:xvii). Fries confirms that Schlink had presented "the

Divided into five unequal parts, the book seeks to overcome basic dogmatic misunderstandings among the churches and to identify essential convergences in an effort to pave the way toward the visible reunion of broken Christendom.²⁴ The goal of the project is two-fold: on the one hand, dogmatics should be concerned with the unity of faith, with the community of believers, and thereby the unity of the church through the entirety of Christian history. On the other hand, an ecumenical dogmatics is also marked by an orientation to the abiding truths of the Christian faith.

> [The task of such a dogmatics proceeds] not from the outside, namely, not from the dogmatic antitheses that mark the borders of the separated churches, but from the inside, namely, from the dogma that remains common, to scrutinize it, to ground it anew, and to interpret it in the intellectual situation of our time. Thus, here a consensus is not sought out of the traditional confessional antitheses, but just the reverse, the attempt is made from a newly discerned consensus to a new understanding of each antithesis and its weight within the entirety of the Christian faith.²⁵

The task of a truly ecumenical dogmatics is thus not to find elements of doctrine from one's own church that are in the others or to uncover merely what constituted doctrine in the first seven ecumenical councils, nor merely to compare and contrast doctrinal understandings among the contemporary churches or to avoid dogmatic problems altogether by focusing on spiritual experiences and pious feelings. Rather, the task involves careful historical investigation of the multiplicity of biblical statements—as normative, historical statements—that are related to a given dogmatic theme, the analysis of the existing dogmatic disagreements among the churches concerning that theme, and the evaluation of the actual validity of the dogmas within the churches themselves. In addition, an

---

specifically Roman Catholic positions" with "great objectivity, with judicious empathy, and a high degree of understanding" (Schlink, *Ökumenische Dogmatik* [SÖB 2:xviii–xix]), and that a Roman Catholic theologian would only want to insert a few additional dogmatic points, which in themselves should no longer be church-dividing. Nevertheless, one should note that Fries minimizes Schlink's respectful criticism of the more recent Marian and papal dogmas that have created further ecumenical challenges. After identifying eight key teachings that Schlink set forth, which reflect the center of the Orthodox faith, Nissiotis concludes that Schlink's great work could be profitably studied alongside patristic theologians from the Orthodox tradition. In Nissiotis's judgment, Schlink's ecumenical perspective opens up a new horizon on the way toward the reconstruction of the one universal church.

24. Schlink, *Ökumenische Dogmatik* (SÖB 2:51).
25. Schlink, *Ökumenische Dogmatik* (SÖB 2:xiii).

ecumenical dogmatics highlights the complementarity that exists between the contrasting dogmatic emphases among the churches (for example, the importance of the epiphany of Christ, his life and resurrection in Eastern Christology in relation to the stress on the cross and justification in Western Christology). Such a dogmatics keeps open the possibility that existing dogmas could be revised and even corrected in view of new insights, and it seeks novel perspectives on overcoming dogmatic disagreements, for example, by examining how the structure of a theological statement undergoes change when it is translated into other structures of faith that also may serve as faithful responses to the gospel.

After an introductory section on the gospel as "the presupposition of church doctrine" (1–71), the work sets forth the following key doctrines in the four substantive parts: the doctrine of creation (73–210), the doctrine of redemption (211–536), the doctrine of the new creation (537–724), and the doctrine of God (725–91). A concluding section (793–804) explicates God's eternal "decree of love" and the problem of election/predestination, which ends with a "warning to the church" (not to be complacent) and with "an invitation to the world" to trust in the God of love and mercy. Despite its rather traditional structure that marches to the beat of the old method of dogmatic *loci*, there are surprisingly no separate sections on theological anthropology or eschatology, nor does the work begin with the usual questions of prolegomena (for example, regarding the authority of Scripture and issues of hermeneutics). Instead, these matters are treated under various other headings. As in Barth's *Church Dogmatics*, Schlink's text also contains passages in small print that function in most instances as extended footnotes that explore the writings of others that are pertinent to the issue under discussion or, in fewer cases, as longer *excursi* on more complicated peripheral problems.

Given the size of the work, I will here only highlight a few of its important themes:

(1) *Law and Gospel.* Just as in the two central chapters of his book on the Lutheran Confessions, so also in his dogmatics the careful distinction between the law and the gospel is crucial.[26] Not only does the gospel serve as the essential presupposition for Christian dogmatics as a whole but its content is the principal theme of the doctrine of redemption, the largest part of Schlink's *magnum opus*. The "decisive theme" of Christian teaching is sin and grace, law and gospel, judgment and forgiveness, divine wrath and divine mercy. According to Schlink, the second aspect in each of these pairings

26. For a more extensive analysis of this issue in Schlink's theology, see Becker, "Edmund Schlink on Theological Anthropology," 151–82. See also Schilling, *Contemporary Continental Theologians*, 149–51.

takes priority over the first. Grace, gospel, forgiveness, and mercy have the last word, not sin, law, judgment and wrath. To distinguish the law from the gospel is to allow the gospel to silence the law for faith. Ultimately, the gospel alone is God's proper word, for it announces that the sinner is saved by grace alone through faith alone on account of Christ alone.

In Schlink's view this formulation is not a sectarian "Lutheran" one but the essential teaching of the orthodox, catholic faith. As he noted in an earlier essay, the proper distinction between law and gospel "is really of the greatest significance for the whole of Christendom."[27] Nevertheless, this topic has played "only a negligible role in the *dogmas* of the different parts of Christendom viewed as a whole"—the Church of the Augsburg Confession excepted—and in the dogmatic treatment of this issue "considerable differences exist" within Christendom.[28] Thus Schlink called for further reflection on the methodological issues involved in understanding this distinction. For example, one must remember that dogmatic statements, including those that speak of law and the gospel, are only one kind of statement of faith, that they each arose within distinct historical situations, that they contain distinct concepts, that important differences in content may be due to a different structure among the various dogmatic statements, and that they cannot simply be compared with one another as timeless and isolated statements. He hoped that further progress in dogmatic reflection could help to overcome shallow differences and to make "a true comparison between the dogmatic statements" on law and gospel possible.[29] He hoped that those churches which tended to downplay the dogmatic significance of this distinction would rediscover its essential role in Christian teaching and preaching.

This same perspective on law and gospel is set forth more fully in the second part of the *Ecumenical Dogmatics*, a section that comprises seven chapters (313 pages). Following the same pattern in his 1961 essay, this section begins with an analysis of the Old Testament law as both promise and law. Then, after chapters on the humiliation and exaltation of the Son of God, there is a chapter on the New Testament gospel as both gospel and admonition (*Mahnung*). Schlink then treats baptism and the Lord's Supper. In the "summary" of these five chapters he frames the issue in the context of how the relationship between the Old and New Testaments should be articulated. "This question concentrates itself in the question regarding the distinction between law and gospel whereby both a unity and a difference between law and

---

27. Schlink, "Gesetz und Evangelium," 18 (*SÖB* 1/1:143; *ESW* 1:192).
28. Schlink, "Gesetz und Evangelium," 19, 21 (*SÖB* 1/1:143, 146; *ESW* 1:193, 195).
29. Schlink, "Gesetz und Evangelium," 21 (*SÖB* 1/1:146; *ESW* 1:196).

gospel is presupposed."[30] While not all churches have treated this question as a part of dogmatics, in actuality it has been present in all churches through their interpretations of the old covenant, through their preaching of the gospel, and in their fulfillment of the tasks of pastoral care.[31]

The first sub-section of this summary sets forth the problem of the distinction between the law and gospel and outlines the complexities within the relationship. Not only is the distinction the result of a historical sequence in God's acts with humanity but it is the result of how God acts differently in the simultaneity of law and gospel as these are addressed to human beings. With respect to historical sequence, after Moses came Jesus Christ. "Law" is the content of the former covenant through Moses, whereas "gospel" is the message of Jesus Christ, especially the word of the cross and the witness to his resurrection. The additional material in this sub-section, which defines the theological contrast between law and gospel and their respective effects on sinners, is based largely on the essay from the 1956 Barth *Festschrift* (which is not cited) wherein Schlink had identified five basic distinctions between law and gospel.[32] A second brief sub-section acknowledges that there is gospel in the Old Testament law insofar as the latter promises fulfillment in the coming of Jesus Christ and his salvation.[33] Just as the Old Testament does not merely contain law, so the New Testament does not only announce the gospel, since it also contains the warning about the coming Judgment Day. Thus there is also eschatological law in the New Testament gospel, a theme that Schlink had stressed in his address on hope at the Evanston assembly of the WCC and that he had also highlighted in the fifth distinction in his 1956 essay on "law and *paraklesis*."[34] So "the distinction between law and gospel is not only a distinction between the Old and New Testaments," not merely an historical development from the old covenant to the new; it is also a theological distinction that runs through both testaments.[35] But these distinctions should not be understood in such a way as to separate law from gospel, or vice versa. They share a fundamental unity.[36] Almost as long as the first sub-section, this fourth one underscores the origin of both law

---

30. Schlink, *Ökumenische Dogmatik* (*SÖB* 2:518–19).

31. Schlink, *Ökumenische Dogmatik* (*SÖB* 2:519).

32. See Schlink, "Gesetz und Paraklese," in Wolf, *Antwort*, 323–35.

33. Schlink, *Ökumenische Dogmatik* (*SÖB* 2:520).

34. Schlink, *Ökumenische Dogmatik* (*SÖB* 2:520–21); "Christus—die Hoffnung für die Welt," in Lüpsen, *Evanston Dokumente*, 135–44 (*SÖB* 1/1:211–20; *ESW* 1:266–75).

35. Schlink, *Ökumenische Dogmatik* (*SÖB* 2:521).

36. Schlink, *Ökumenische Dogmatik* (*SÖB* 2:521–22).

and gospel in the triune God, "who speaks and acts through both words."[37] Despite their unity in the triune God, however, law and gospel have different purposes and different outcomes. There is a fundamental difference between them: "Through the law God demands everything of us; through the gospel he gifts us with everything. Through the law God demands that we sacrifice ourselves to him; through the gospel God sacrifices himself in Christ for us."[38] And then follows a whole list of contrasts that he had set forth in the earlier essays on this theme. He likewise defends the thesis that "the gospel, not the law, is God's proper word," since God's will is to make alive, not to kill.[39] Thus the dialectic between law and gospel is not a timeless construct that remains constantly in place. Rather, the gospel should always be proclaimed in this world, in every historical situation, so that the word of God's merciful promise and his gracious gifts overcome the divine judgment of the law. This is particularly necessary in times of spiritual crises, when individuals and congregations are suffering the negative effects of the divine working of the law, are persecuted, imprisoned, and killed, and thus when they stand in need of divine comfort.[40] The distinction between law and gospel is thus "learned and retained in *Anfechtung*."[41]

> Through the gospel God reaches out to us, breaks through the doubt, arrogance and indifference in which we have locked ourselves, and opens us access to himself. Through the gospel he sends forgiveness to sinners, confidence to the anxious, freedom to the imprisoned, and life to those fallen in death. It is God's justifying and life-giving power, which does what it says, "the good news . . . through which you are being saved" (1 Cor 15:1–2). Thus, through the gospel God gives himself to be known.[42]

Until the Last Day, when Christ will come to judge the living and the dead, the church is to summon people to repentance and faith. It must do so, Schlink stresses, while there is still time. Whether people know it or not, he warns, the Day of Judgment is coming. He who is the Word of God and the Lord of history will then pronounce two different verdicts: "Come!" or "Depart from me!" Only one of these two commands will apply to each person. Until then, the church must set forth these two alternatives, acquittal by grace through faith or the judgment according to human works. But

---

37. Schlink, *Ökumenische Dogmatik* (*SÖB* 2:521).
38. Schlink, *Ökumenische Dogmatik* (*SÖB* 2:522).
39. Schlink, *Ökumenische Dogmatik* (*SÖB* 2:522–23).
40. Schlink, *Ökumenische Dogmatik* (*SÖB* 2:523–24).
41. Schlink, *Ökumenische Dogmatik* (*SÖB* 2:523).
42. Schlink, *Ökumenische Dogmatik* (*SÖB* 2:3).

the announcement of grace is always to be predominant. Indeed, it is the church's final word, since the gospel, not the law, is God's proper message. The final chapter of the second part of Schlink's dogmatics thus focuses on "the Confession of God the Redeemer," which examines the Chalcedonian dogmatic understanding of the person of Jesus Christ—"the eternal Son of God" who is "true God and truly human"—in service to the gospel.

(2) *The Church and its Ministry*. Schlink identifies the church as the people of God who are called out of the world by Christ and then sent back into it to be "the prophetic-priestly-royal people of God."[43] They are called and sent to announce his lordship over all things. This two-fold movement has its grounding in the worshiping assembly, where the risen Christ is present and active through the actual preaching of law and gospel and the actual administration of the sacraments in accord with their divine institution.[44] In response to Christ's present working in the congregation, the people of God are to offer their praise, confession, prayer, and witness, and they are then called to serve one another and the world in love. Through faithful hearing of the gospel and through the reception of the body and blood of Christ in the Lord's Supper, the baptized believers are built up as the body of Christ, which is growing and will ultimately extend to embrace the entire created universe. In the church, creation comes to its goal under the lordship of Christ. On the way to this goal, the church is the living fellowship of the gifts of grace in whose multiplicity the one grace of Christ actively and repeatedly manifests itself. For Schlink, the church is the "*una sancta*" because the one Christ creates and sustains it. It is "holy" because the one Holy Spirit works in it through the word and sacraments. It is "catholic" because the one Christ, the Lord of heaven and earth, rules it, and it is "apostolic" because its "irremovable basis" is the apostolic teaching that is given in and through the New Testament canon.[45] Only in the apostolic faith that has been once and for all time delivered is the church the one, holy, catholic church in Christ. If the church is the apostolic church in its obedience to the apostolic message of the gospel, then it is thereby the only, holy, catholic church.[46] But this church is also sinful and de-formed. It has frequently departed from apostolic teaching, muddled the apostolic gospel, and undermined its unity through its visible divisions.

---

43. Schlink, *Ökumenische Dogmatik* (*SÖB* 2:569). See also Schlink, "Christus und die Kirche," 209–10 (*SÖB* 1/1:89–90; *ESW* 1:136–37).

44. For further analysis of Schlink's ecclesiology from a post-Vatican II Catholic perspective, see Schwenzer, *Die Grossen Taten Gottes*. While Schwenzer finds much to affirm in the work of Schlink, he raises questions about Schlink's views on priestly ordination, the sacrifice of the mass, the papacy, and the infallibility of the church.

45. Schlink, "Die Weite der Kirche," 4 (*SÖB* 1/1:108; *ESW* 1:158).

46. See Slenczka, "Grund und Norm der Vielfalt," 24–51.

It thus stands under God's judgment. All churches are therefore called to repentance and change. The church as a whole is in need of reform (*ecclesia semper reformanda*) until the Last Day.

According to Schlink, the nature of the church's ministry is shaped and defined by the nature and purpose of the church. He underscores that the church is the people of God who are called and sent by the Spirit through the gospel. This people of God includes both the faithful of the old covenant, who looked forward in hope to the coming Messiah, and those of the new, who have been baptized into the death and resurrection of Christ, sealed by the Holy Spirit, and who await his Second Coming. While all of God's people are sent into the world to carry out their service ministry in accord with the charismata that have been given to them, some are commissioned into a particular ministry and equipped to fulfill it. The apostles of Jesus were the first to be called into such a ministry, which concentrated on missionary outreach and the founding and administering of congregations. All subsequent ministry in the church is grounded on the apostles, whose special authority is unique, non-repeatable, and normative. While the commissioning into later specialized ministries is normally accompanied with the laying-on of hands by bishops (as a valuable sign of continuity with the apostles and the historic church), such "apostolic succession" cannot be separated from that which it signifies, namely, the transmission of apostolic doctrine.[47] Provided the churches remain faithful to the apostolic gospel and exhortations and seek to build up the fellowship of faith in the bond of apostolic unity, there is great room for diversity and breadth in the formulations of confession and church order. Indeed, Schlink notes that there was far greater diversity of church orderings in the early church than was later realized in developments after the the third century.[48] Despite their differences across regions, early Christians acknowledged their unity in the Christ to whom the apostles bore witness and in the multiplicity of spiritual gifts poured out upon the church by the one Spirit.

(3) *The Triune God.* Contrary to the traditional order of the dogmatic *loci*, wherein the locus on God is placed near the beginning, Schlink treats the doctrine of God in the concluding part (just eighty-eight pages, including the appendix on "the loving decree" of God). This placement, which follows the procedure of Schleiermacher in his *Glaubenslehre*, is open to misunderstanding. Schlink was not relegating the doctrine of God to an appendix or merely concluding with some final, peripheral thoughts about

---

47. Schlink, *Ökumenische Dogmatik* (SÖB 2:621). See also Schlink, "Die apostolische Sukzession," 79–114 (SÖB 1/1:160–95; ESW 1:211–48).

48. See Schlink, *Ökumenische Dogmatik* (SÖB 2:599, 610–11, 614).

God. Rather, the fourth part of Schlink's dogmatics underscores and concentrates those doctrinal elements about God's being and actions that Schlink had raised in the earlier chapters but had not fully synthesized. While an ecumenical dogmatics cannot say everything about God, since it is only "one voice in a many-voiced choir" that gives glory to God and teaches about him, such a dogmatics must set forth the basic contours and features of the Christian doctrine of God. In Schlink's view, this can only be done as the conclusion to the dogmatic process as a whole. For him, dogmatics must ultimately be not only about what God has done in and through the crucified and risen Christ and through the ongoing mission of the Holy Spirit but also about who God is as the object of the church's praise. Dogmatics cannot thus avoid engaging the ontology reflected in the authoritative creeds of the ancient church. The basis for the church's doxology of God is the gospel of Jesus Christ and its unfolding in the world through the work of the Spirit, as voiced in the multiplicity of the ancient church's creedal statements, particularly the Niceno-Constantinopolitan and the Chalcedonian Definition, all of which were meant to keep the gospel "good news."[49]

In chapter 26 ("The Triune God") Schlink analyzes the unity of God within the distinctions among the Father, the Son, and the Holy Spirit, and he explicates the distinctions among the Father, the Son, and the Spirit in the unity of God. Both approaches toward understanding the immanent Trinity are juxtaposed in two vertical columns on two pages. The left column presents the first way (unity within the distinctions), while the right column presents the second (the distinctions within the unity), and thus each way is correlated visually to the other. He then proceeds to highlight the key elements in trinitarian dogma as a whole. Here he emphasizes that there is a basic dogmatic consensus between the East and West, even if each has held different premises for its respective understanding of the Trinity. These premises, Schlink maintains, were themselves not revealed but arose in the history of dogma as legitimate attempts to interpret the historical revelation. They were therefore "already deductions from existing traditions."[50] The controversy over the *filioque* clause, which he admits is a difficult ecumenical issue, is nevertheless in his view a disagreement over deductions drawn from deductions, "where the various deductions acting as underlying premises cannot be convincingly derived from the biblical witnesses." These deductions are therefore an insufficient basis for "defining a dogma

---

49. For the importance of the ancient church's confession for Schlink's understanding of church unity, see especially Eber, *Einheit der Kirche*, 199–209.

50. Schlink, *Ökumenische Dogmatik* (*SÖB* 2:758).

that determines the boundary between faith and false teaching."[51] Given that the differences between the Cappadocians and Augustine regarding their respective understandings of the Trinity did not originally have any church-dividing significance—which was also the case with respect to their efforts to relate the authoritative revelation to the eternal God—one cannot hold that these deductions from these differences have any church-dividing significance today. "If we are open to the multiplicity in which the churches praise the perfection of the triune God, then the walls between them will become transparent and finally fall down."[52]

Conclusion

With the publication of the new German edition of Schlink's writings, which is now also being translated into English, his work should undergo renewed attention. While some might be inclined to dismiss his theology as too conservative or too confessional, others may find in his work a helpful resource for articulating what is essential and abiding in the Christian faith. As confidence in Western bourgeois culture undergoes further decline, and more and more people become truly fearful for the future of the planet, Schlink's sober realism about the nature of sin and evil, about God's coming kingdom and eschatological judgment, about the radical promise of divine reconciliation in Jesus Christ, and about the new creation in Christ, may have something to offer this troubled world. Surely Schlink's criticisms of the churches as all-too-human institutions—despite his ultimately hopeful, expansive vision about the future of the one, holy, catholic, and apostolic church—and his summons for the churches to be penitently self-critical, are also apropos, especially in light of the "ecumenical winter" we seem to be experiencing.[53]

To be sure, Schlink's underlying tone is distinctly Lutheran in character, and he unfortunately marginalizes some Christian traditions (e.g.,

---

51. Schlink, *Ökumenische Dogmatik* (SÖB 2:759).

52. Schlink, *Ökumenische Dogmatik* (SÖB 2:791). See Skibbe, *Quiet Reformer*, 125.

53. Schlink's one piece of fiction, the novella *Die Vision des Papstes*, also outlines this basic ecumenical impulse. Initially published under the pseudonym Sebastian Knecht (so as to attract a wider audience, especially among Catholics, than if he had been identified as the author), the story is about a pope who receives three visions of Christ that set him on a new ecumenical initiative: the unification of the Christian Church. For that to work, each church, including the Roman Church, must repent. Each must see itself as subordinate to Christ and the apostolic witness. They must not "harden themselves again toward one another, and fail to do what they are entrusted to do in the midst of a constantly increasing human crisis" (Schlink, *Vision of the Pope*, 79).

the Baptist) while emphasizing others (e.g., the magisterial Reformation churches, the Roman Catholic, and Eastern churches), yet his concern is to take doctrine and dogma seriously, as if they truly matter for the unity of the church. While formally open toward brothers and sisters beyond his own confession, his humble and conciliatory method of ecumenism was undertaken consciously and intentionally from within the perspective of his own confessional tradition and community. Some may see this as a weakness, especially if they are convinced they can understand and respond more appropriately to contemporary issues on some other theological (or confessional) basis. Still, such a commitment was for him not opposed to his call for a "Copernican Revolution" in ecclesial thinking and attitude. Rather, his work demonstrates that one can be both confessional and ecumenical.[54] In particular, his moves toward the Eastern Orthodox Church must be acknowledged as truly ground-breaking. His *Ecumenical Dogmatics* reflects the kind of careful, respectful attention to the Scriptures, the *ecumene*, and the history of church traditions that is necessary for properly understanding church doctrine in such a way as to foster devotion to Christ and his church. While his work certainly emphasizes key and distinctive elements in Lutheran theology—for example, the normative character of Scripture, the centrality of the gospel in distinction from the law, the radical nature of sin, the basis of faith in the living Christ, the sacraments of baptism and the Lord's Supper, and the adiaphoral nature of church order—the tenor of Schlink's theology is one of reconciliation.[55] As with all such dogmatic, academic theologies, however, the challenge is to transfer their insights to local communities, where visible communion remains partial, if not altogether elusive.

Schlink's theology is also properly pastoral in its basic orientation. Even when reading one of his technical essays, one detects the voice of a person who has labored and suffered as a shepherd in Christ's field. Not merely in Schlink's sermons and devotional texts but also in his academic work there is the central emphasis on the living presence of Jesus Christ in the contemporary world. This witness to the crucified and risen Lord clearly took place within a life that was lived "between the sacraments," that is, between the daily return to "the once-for-all baptism" and the going "forward daily to the Lord's table, which is prepared for us again and again."[56] In other words, there is in the work of Schlink a consistent witness to the living, triune God, who calls sinners to repentance and faith, who acts mightily to

---

54. See Smit, "Confessional *and* Ecumenical?," 446–74.
55. Skibbe, *Quiet Reformer*, 107.
56. Schlink, *Theologie der lutherischen Bekenntnisschriften* (SÖB 4:154 [TLC 183]).

save them, and who sends them back into the world to share God's gospel and love in word and deed.

Bibliography

Becker, Matthew. "Christ in the University: The Vision of Schlink." *The Cresset* 80 (2017) 12–21.

———. "Edmund Schlink on Theological Anthropology, the Law, and the Gospel." *Lutheran Quarterly* 24 (2010) 151–82.

Eber, Jochen. "Edmund Schlink 1903–1984: Ein Leben für die Einheit der Kirche." In vol. 1 of *Schriften zu Ökumene und Bekenntnis*, by Edmund Schlink, xi–xxii. Edited by Klaus Engelhardt. Göttingen: Vandenhoeck & Ruprecht, 2004.

———. *Einheit der Kirche als dogmatisches Problem bei Edmund Schlink*. Göttingen: Vandenhoeck & Ruprecht, 1993.

Kolb, Robert, and Timothy Wengert, eds. *The Book of Concord*. Philadelphia: Fortress, 2000.

Lüpsen, F. L., ed. *Evanston Dokumente*. Witten: Luther, 1954.

Schilling, S. Paul. *Contemporary Continental Theologians*. Nashville: Abingdon, 1966.

Schlink, Edmund. "Aufgabe und Gefahr des Weltrates der Kirchen." *Ökumenische Rundschau* 1.1 (1952) 1–13.

———. "Christus und die Kirche." *Kerygma und Dogma* 1.3 (1955) 208–25.

———. *Der Ertrag des Kirchenkampfes*. 2nd ed. Gütersloh: C. Bertelsmann, 1947.

———. "Der Neubau des Ökumenischen Instituts und Studentenwohnheims der Universität Heidelberg." *Ruperto-Carola* 10.23 (1958) 197–200.

———. "Die apostolische Sukzession." *Kerygma und Dogma* 7.2 (1961) 79–114.

———. "Die Struktur der dogmatischen Aussage als ökumenisches Problem." *Kerygma und Dogma* 3.4 (1957) 251–306.

———. *Die Vision des Papstes: Erzählung*. 2nd ed. Göttingen: Vandenhoeck & Ruprecht, 1997.

———. "Die Weite der Kirche Augsburger Konfession." *Lutherische Rundschau* 1.3 (1949) 1–13.

———. *Ecumenical and Confessional Writings (The Coming Christ and Church Traditions and After the Council)*. Vol. 1 of *Edmund Schlink Works*. Edited by Matthew L. Becker. Translated by Matthew L. Becker and Hans G. Spalteholz. Göttingen: Vandenhoeck & Ruprecht, 2017.

———. "Gesetz und Evangelium als kontroverstheologisches Problem." *Kergyma und Dogma* 7.1 (1961) 1–35.

———. *Nach dem Konzil*. Göttingen: Vandenhoeck & Ruprecht, 1966.

———. *Ökumenische Dogmatik: Grundzüge*. 3rd ed. Göttingen: Vandenhoeck & Ruprecht, 2005.

———. *Schriften zu Ökumene und Bekenntnis*. Edited by Klaus Engelhardt et al. 5 vols. Göttingen: Vandenhoeck & Ruprecht, 2004–2010.

———. *Theologie der lutherischen Bekenntnisschriften*. 4th ed. München: Chr. Kaiser, 1954.

———. *Theology of the Lutheran Confessions*. English Translation of *Theologie der lutherischen Bekenntnisschriften*. Translated by Paul F. Koehneke and Herbert J. A. Bouman. 1961. Reprint, St. Louis: Concordia, 2003.

———. *The Vision of the Pope: A Narrative*. English Translation of *Die Vision des Papstes*. Translated by Eugene Skibbe. Minneapolis: Kirk, 2001.

Schwenzer, Gerhard. *Die Grossen Taten Gottes und die Kirche: Zur Ekklesiologie Edmund Schlinks*. Paderborn: Bonifacius, 1969.

Skibbe, Eugene. *A Quiet Reformer: An Introduction to Edmund Schlink's Life and Ecumenical Theology*. Minneapolis: Kirk, 1999.

Slenczka, Notger. "Grund und Norm der Vielfalt: Edmund Schlink (1903–1984)." *Kerygma und Dogma* 49.1 (2003) 24–51.

Smit, D. J. "Confessional *and* Ecumenical? Revisiting Edmund Schlink on the Hermeneutics of Doctrine." *Verbum et Ecclesia* 29.2 (2008) 446–74.

Vogel, Heinrich. *Männer der Ev. Kirche in Deutschland. Eine Festschrift für Kurt Scharf zum 60. Geburtstag*. Berlin und Stuttgart: Lettner, 1962.

Wolf, Ernst, et al., eds. *Antwort: Karl Barth zum Siebzigsten Geburtstag am 10. Mai 1956*. Zürich: Evangelischer, 1956.

3

Otto Hermann Pesch: Ecumenical Scholasticism

—Dorothea Sattler

OTTO HERMANN PESCH (1931–2014) very much would have liked to live to see the year 2017—this I know from many personal conversations with him. Long before this anniversary of the Reformation, 500 years after the publication of Martin Luther's 95 theses on indulgences, he frequently felt challenged, as one of the few present-day Roman Catholic Luther scholars, to address the spiritual heritage of the Reformation in presentations and publications and to describe the lasting importance of this body of thought.

For the 4th edition of *Hinführung zu Luther*[1] by Pesch, which was published posthumously in 2017, the Lutheran church historian Volker Leppin wrote an introduction inviting us to consider Pesch's insights especially on the occasion of the celebration of the Reformation. Leppin gives this advice: "Those who in the course of this anniversary would like to perceive a different Luther than the one of memorials, stamps and logos will in Pesch's introduction, despite the more than thirty years which have passed since its first publication, attain a fresh, different, literally liberating view. Luther is liberated from the confinement of denominational traditions much in the same way as the readers are liberated from own prejudices if they let themselves get involved with the spiritual adventure of this reading matter."[2]

During Pesch's lifetime there were dates which even before 2017 offered him external causes for the adoption of Lutheran ideas: In 1983 the 500th birth anniversary of Martin Luther[3] and in 1996 the 450th anniversary of the reformer's death.[4] Pesch always was hesitant about the prospect

---

1. Pesch, *Hinführung zu Luther*.
2. Leppin, *Belehrte Ökumene*, viii.
3. Pesch, *Neuere Beiträge*.
4. Pesch, *Wat heeft Luther de Katholieken (nog) te zeggen?*.

of still being able to be active in 2017. His scepticism was justified. He died in Munich on September 8, 2014. In the Roman Catholic liturgical calendar that day is the feast of the birth of Mary, mother of Jesus. In the work of his later years, Pesch accepted the challenge to address the biblical tradition of Mary's obedience of faith in an ecumenical perspective in the spirit of Martin Luther.[5] All his life Pesch was a person crossing borders within his own Roman Catholic denomination as well as in the dialogue with the Reformation theologies.

Contexts

No one leads a life unrelated to contemporary history. Each person has a distinctive personal history. The contexts in which Pesch wrote his theological works are a key to understanding his thinking. The theological-historical contexts influenced Pesch like many of his colleagues at other universities; the biographical contexts are unique and can only intuitively be taken into account with respect to the interpretation of his works because sober data do not permit any insight into the individual understanding of life.

Theological and Historical Contexts

It is my perception that the contexts in which Pesch conceptualised his theological works are concentrated on three that can be presented here in chronological order. (1) Roman Catholic theologians who during the time of the Second Vatican Council (1962–1965) distinguished themselves with activities within research and teaching as a rule have a permanent interest in the reception of the documents from that Council. Pesch strongly endeavoured to keep the events of the Council alive in our conscience. (2) After the Second Vatican Council we saw the beginning of an intensive phase of ecumenical dialogues. From the Roman Catholic side on the international level, the dialogues were primarily led bilaterally regarding the respective controversial issues. Pesch mainly helped form these efforts in the German "Ecumenical Working Group of Protestant and Catholic theologians" that was founded in 1946 and in 1980 co-opted him especially because of his high competence in questions of the doctrine of justification; he was not appointed to be a member of ecclesiastical committees.[6] His

---

5. Pesch, *Katholische Dogmatik aus ökumenischer Erfahrung*, 1/1:848–77.

6. In the years from 1980 to 1986 the Ecumenical study group of Lutheran and Catholic theologians was involved in a study with the goal to examine the condemnations formulated in the sixteenth century within the subject areas justification,

methodical approach, which tries to understand the historical genesis of the controversies and then asks about their relevancy for contemporary theological dialogues, has been highly recognized in some subject areas. (3) A leading question that already was discernible in the beginning of Pesch's theological thinking gained strength at the end of his work: How can one rationalize the existence of God under the conditions of the contemporary perception of reality? As he grew older, the question of justification of sinful human beings before God changed to the question of justification of the existence of God in view of the suffering creation. His efforts for an interpretation of the confession of faith easily accessible to human beings is discernible very early in his theological work and makes his concerns appear to be related to those of Martin Luther.[7]

Second Vatican Council

Pesch enjoyed being active in academic teaching. Part of the content he wanted to impart to students from all faculties at the University of Hamburg was knowledge about the Second Vatican Council.[8] In the doctrinal documents from this Council a new definition of the position within the Roman Catholic doctrinal tradition is undertaken in many subject areas which has to be understood as approaching Reformation positions.[9] The encouragement to ecumenism connected with the Second Vatican Council Pesch accepted actively and effectively in his life.

In conformity with the Lutheran conviction of a Church always in need of reform, the Second Vatican Council (1962–1965), too, says that the Church is "at the same time holy and always in need of being purified"; it "always follows the way of penance and renewal."[10] The Second Vatican Council took up other important concerns of the Reformation in the

---

sacraments and ministry with regard to if they—viewed from a contemporary theological perspective—still have schismatic effect. See Lehmann and Pannenberg, *Lehrverurteilungen—kirchentrennend?* Regarding this, Pesch was instrumental in the preparation of the section "Justification" whose content had influence on the "Joint Declaration on the Doctrine of Justification," signed on October 31, 1999, by the Lutheran World Federation and the Pontifical Council for Promoting Christian Unity. See Meyer et al., *Gemeinsame Erklärung zur Rechtfertigungslehre.*

7. Pesch, *Kleines katholisches Glaubensbuch.*

8. Otto Hermann Pesch several times delivered a lecture on the Second Vatican Council for students from all faculties and published the edited manuscript. See Pesch, *Das Zweite Vatikanische Konzil.*

9. For all following references to Council texts, see Rahner and Vorgrimler, *Kleines Konzilskompendium.*

10. Second Vatican Council, *Lumen Gentium* 8.

sixteenth century. In all constitutions, decrees and explanations from this Council, the Christological orientation of the argumentation has priority. At the very beginning, the Church constitution says that *Jesus Christ* is "the light of nations," not the Church as one still could read in the prepared text sources.[11] The priority of the biblically transmitted scripture over church tradition is registered in the constitution on divine revelation: "Sacred Scripture is the word of God," "sacred tradition" (only) hands on the word of God.[12] Regarding many detailed questions within the subject area "scripture and tradition," ecumenical convergences could be reached in the last decades in light of the intensive Roman Catholic reflections on this subject area. Questions about the doctrine of grace and justification thematically were not central for the teaching of the Second Vatican Council. But if one reads the documents one will be surprised at the mentioning of divine action in time and history for the benefit of the individual human being as well as the entire creation especially at the beginning of all Council documents. Ecumenical encounters open a path to salutary self-assurance for all denominational traditions. Long forgotten insights regain importance. In this regard, one should first think of the strengthening of the awareness, expressed in the texts of the Second Vatican Council, of having a share in the common priesthood as baptised in accordance with the biblical tradition (1 Pet 2:9).[13] Also, regarding vernacular liturgy Roman Catholic reform movements before and after the Second Vatican Council have adopted argumentations from the Reformation tradition.

Ecumenical Dialogues

Until the end of his life, Pesch adhered to the instruction of the Second Vatican Council to conduct dialogues with brothers and sisters from other Christian traditions "par cum pari" (among equals). Pesch never refused to enter into a dialogue even though his scepticism towards the guidance of the dialogues grew steadily in view of the lack of ecclesiastical reception. This was especially the case regarding the subject area of eucharistic community for which he diagnosed a refusal of thought in his own tradition.

After the Second Vatican Council, the Roman Catholic Church began an intensive dialogue, which mainly related to the bilateral area (the conversation between two Christian traditions). Pesch especially was involved in

11. Second Vatican Council, *Lumen Gentium* 1.
12. Second Vatican Council, *Dei Verbum* 9.
13. Cf. Second Vatican Council, *Sacrosanctum Concilium* 14, 48; *Lumen Gentium* 9–10; 26; 34; *Ad Gentes* 15; *Apostolicam Actuositatem* 3.

the conversations between the Roman Catholic and the Lutheran theologies. He felt committed to the tendency within ecumenical hermeneutics that is very aware of the oppressive reality of the world, something that requires a common social commitment of all Christians. At the same time, he held sober dialogue to be the call of the hour. It is not always necessary to regard one's own option as an alternative to other justified procedures. Especially because of his knowledge of the history of theology, Pesch was called upon to enter into a scientifically founded discourse in ecumenism.

Today, predominantly in the Reformation tradition, there is a departure from the ecumenism of convergence (or even consensus) and, connected with this, a movement towards the so-called social ecumenism in which the common responsibility for socio-political concerns (justified in a Christian sense) has priority. In my opinion, there sometimes is little awareness that these are two profiled areas of action which in light of the totality of the people involved in the ecumenical movement by no means are alternatives and cannot be realized with good reasons simultaneously as options in one single human life. Many factors—those that are intended or those that are dependent on specific situations—have an impact on the personal choice of a person's ecumenical commitment. The simultaneity of the different forms of action in the common orientation towards the gospel is a strength of ecumenism. Both doctrine and service thus "unite." In my opinion, the aspect of urgency must be given special attention in this connection. There are times and places where it is necessary to act at once and not only just to talk to each other.

Belief in God and Doubt about God

During his lifetime, Pesch believed that the critical question about the existence of God had gained new relevancy again. As he grew older, Pesch regarded the belief in God in the ecumenical community as the matter predominantly in need of justification with arguments—prior to all potentially controversial discussions about the action of that God in relation to the creation qualified as sinners.[14]

Pesch's intuition proved to be correct: Today, all Christian denominations face the challenge of justifying their confession of the existence of God in light of the objections from the "New Atheism." The questions about the assumption of the existence of God which can be identified with representatives of the New Atheism have great affinity with the arguments of the criticism of religion in the late nineteenth and early twentieth centuries.

14. Pesch, *Justification and the Question of God*.

Why does an omnipotent God not prevent suffering? Why does God give humans the gift of freedom if it is in danger of being abused?

Biographical Contexts

An aphorism formulated by Peter Handke states: "Before any meeting: Consider the road the other person has taken."[15] In ecumenism, it is very important to have knowledge about the biographical background of an argument which has influence on a theological judgment. These can be personally justified without being immediately apparent in the argumentation. The following not only applies to Pesch: Theological options are deeply connected with on the one hand one's own decisions and on the other hand the experiences in one's life that are initiated by other people.

Pesch spent his childhood and youth in the turmoil of the time under National Socialist rule. He certainly was not unfamiliar with the scenarios of war in Cologne. His year of birth (1931) was not drafted for military service but his school education was delayed. After (late) graduation from high school in 1952, Pesch entered the Dominican Order and completed his studies in philosophy and theology in Walberberg near Cologne and in Munich. In 1958 he was ordained a priest. In 1965 he received his doctorate with a study—an unusually extensive one for his time—on the doctrine of justification with Martin Luther and Thomas Aquinas.[16] Even at this stage, he sought the dialogue between medieval scholasticism and the Reformation. Teaching activities in Walberberg followed. No one knows which other paths in academic theology would have opened for Pesch if he had not met a woman he married after leaving the order in 1972. Their daughter Anja remained his happiness in life—a consolation after the early death of his wife. In light of his knowledge of Reformation theology and his ecumenical commitment, the Protestant Faculty of the University of Hamburg called the Roman Catholic theologian Pesch to a chair in systematic theology which he held from 1975 to 1998. As a person crossing borders between denominations, Pesch was a respected personality attracting much attention in the theological public—in one way or another: For some, he was a commentator giving critical judgements on his own tradition in life as well as in thought, for others he was a communicator with immense knowledge and numerous personal contacts.

Pesch loved music. In ecumenical services, he liked to play the organ and he proved himself to be very familiar with the Reformation tradition

15. Handke, *Phantasien der Wiederholung*, 42.
16. Pesch, *Theologie der Rechtfertigung*.

regarding song melodies. For the end of his earthly days, Pesch had wished for a quiet time surrounded by his closest family. He spoke openly about having planned everything in case of his death. He did not want long speeches at his grave. It certainly would be in his spirit to preserve his memory by reading his theological writings. In the preface to his *Hinführung zu Luther* he reminded us that Martin Luther towards the end of his days finished his lectures with "Be commanded to God." The possibility to form a free opinion with the blessing of God is a great good—this is not the only matter Pesch and Martin Luther agreed on.

Crossing Borders

From the beginning of his academic activities, Pesch was closely connected with the life and thinking of Martin Luther. Both theologians share the experience of the turning point in one's existence constituted by leaving a community of monks and establishing a family. Talking about the freedom of a Christian has a special relevance in this connection: It is the foundation of an inner attitude with an appreciation of autonomy in relation to the ecclesiastical institution in light of the attachment to Jesus Christ which decisively determines human existence.

Choice of Topics

Long before he left the order himself, Pesch was already intellectually engaged with Martin Luther. Presumably, his academic teacher Heinrich Fries in Munich was involved in Pesch's decision to combine two concerns in his dissertation from 1967: His interest in medieval scholastic theology which had its protagonist in his former brothers in the order of the Dominicans Thomas Aquinas, as well as his passion for the study of the Lutheran world of thought.[17] The focus on the doctrine of justification seems quite obvious in the spirit of Luther—to take heed of this was an insight that is relevant in the ecumenical context to this day. The criteriological function of the doctrine of justification for theology as a whole is also a topic in recent ecumenism.

Pesch was one of the most renowned Luther researchers in Roman Catholic theology after the Second Vatican Council (active in this subject area before him and partly at the same time were Joseph Lortz, Erwin Iserloh and Peter Manns). Pesch's *Hinführung zu Luther*[18] is written with

17. Pesch, *Theologie der Rechtfertigung*.
18. Pesch, *Hinführung zu Luther*.

an attitude I would like to call sympathy remaining sober. A high appreciation of the theological content of Luther's writings is combined with critical questions, especially regarding Luther's conception of the human being and the diastasis of faith and love. In his "Vorwarnung an den Leser" Pesch reveals what is important to him: Firstly, a both specifically theological and generally understandable presentation of Luther's basic concerns, secondly, a presentation of Luther's concerns beyond the denominationally controversial positions. Pesch honoured both concerns. At the very beginning he informs about the state of the research on Luther, and in footnotes, comments and marginal notes he again and again gives insights into his extensive knowledge; what he calls "shop talk," i.e., detailed information important for research, can be found at the end of the book. To the parts based chronologically on Luther's life, Pesch adds chapters with a thematical focus. All questions that are of importance to this day within ecumenical theology in conversation with Luther are addressed, the question of the "freedom of a Christian"; the subject of humans as "just and sinful at the same time"; the teaching of the "two kingdoms"; the relationship between faith and love; the understanding of the proclamation of God's word and the celebration of the sacraments. At the end Pesch's presentation focuses on the doctrine of justification. His concern is to rediscover Luther for Christian ecumenism: He is a common teacher in relation to the Christian teaching. For many Roman Catholic Christians this *Hinführung zu Luther*[19] was very important reading material even before 2017—which it also will be in the future.

Based on the insights from his very extensive dissertation on Martin Luther's and Thomas Aquinas's doctrine of justification, Pesch in his book *Frei sein aus Gnade*[20] faces the challenge to establish a dialogue between the testimonies of tradition and modern approaches to questions of anthropology. Apart from looking back on Luther and Thomas Aquinas, he also introduces the time of Augustine into his train of thought, thus succeeding in having a conversation with theological thinkers from three eras: Antiquity (Augustine), Middle Ages (Thomas Aquinas) and the beginning of modern times (Martin Luther). The tension between the freedom of man and the grace of God suggested in the title is a deliberate choice in light of the aspirations of modern man for autonomy. Pesch shows that the questions formulated in modern times by no means were foreign to the concepts known from traditional history. At the same time, he succeeds in leading his dialogue partners into a (fictitious) ecumenical conversation about the understanding of sin, justification, grace, freedom and assurance of salvation. In this connection,

19. Pesch, *Hinführung zu Luther*.
20. Pesch, *Frei sein aus Gnade*.

the magisterial statements are always present in the background—especially the theological positioning of the Council of Trent. Pesch's book constitutes an important pioneering work with regard to the subsequent ecumenical agreements on fundamental questions of the doctrine of justification because he introduces two coordinates into this controversy in an innovative way—the belief in God and ethics.

In recollections of the history of his publications, Pesch in personal conversations sometimes remembered that he had difficulties with placing his presentation of the history and content of the Second Vatican Council[21] on the book market in the beginning of the 1990s. First, there was no publishing house for this project. However, the publication of the first edition soon was followed by further editions. The basis of this publication are lectures Pesch held in Hamburg. With his book, Pesch in the times that were not yet characterised by the 40th or 50th anniversary of the Council has presented an overview of the chronology and content of the Council which was of great importance for an entire generation: Those who have not experienced the Council themselves can feel the atmosphere of this turning point. At the same time, it becomes clear which challenges the Roman Catholic Church faced in the 1990s, in Pesch's opinion. Quite a few of the problems he formulated still exist to this day—for example the search for adequate forms of collegiality between bishops or answers to the open question of God in dialogues with people who favour an atheistic confession.

It was Pesch's great desire to be able to publish a complete overview of his theological insights before the end of his life. He succeeded in this in his work *Katholische Dogmatik. Aus ökumenischer Erfahrung.*[22] The first volume—with the subtitle "Die Geschichte der Menschen mit Gott" (the history of humanity with God)—could only be published in two volumes, a second volume with the subtitle "Die Geschichte Gottes mit den Menschen" (the history of God with humanity) followed. Pesch follows the path familiar from dogmatics and arranges his thoughts in accordance with tracts: The teaching of the word of God, Christology, anthropology, theology of creation, Trinitarian theology, ecclesiology, sacramental theology and eschatology. Pesch consistently includes anthropological references, biblical sources and testimonies from all denominational traditions into his reflections. Copious literary references characterise this work which for a long time will be regarded as a source of theological insights in ecumenical responsibility.

---

21. Pesch, *Das Zweite Vatikanische Konzil.*
22. Pesch, *Katholische Dogmatik aus ökumenischer Erfahrung.*

Choice of Methods

In his time, Pesch was one of the few remaining theologians who intensively concerned themselves with the thoughts of medieval scholasticism. His participation in the preparation of the Latin—German edition of the writings of Thomas Aquinas occupied him for decades.

For Pesch, the benefit of this intensive education not only was being able to gain a comprehensive knowledge of all tracts of theology, for example by studying *Summa Theologiae* (a comprehensive work Thomas Aquinas wrote as a course book for students), rather, this led to an important methodical shaping: At their places of education, the scholastic theological schools lived off the discussion of open questions which were to be debated in an argumentative discourse. Frequently, students of theology were allowed to question their teachers spontaneously on any topic— "quodlibet": whatever occupied the student's minds. Even today, to me it seems to be an important exercise for teachers (not only) of theology to deepen their own thoughts in conversations with other people and to touch the limits of what can be said.

Pesch received special education in the art of listening to questions that arise, from the way Thomas Aquinas structured his "quaestiones" (questions) in his *Summa Theologiae*. Thomas first indicated that there are questions that arise; then he strengthened the arguments contradicting his own theological position—introduced by "videtur quod"—"it seems justified" to think like this. This is followed by a short reference to tradition ("sed contra"—"but this is contradicted by" a testimony from tradition), and then a detailed argumentation in favour of one's own position ("responsio"—reply) takes place. With Thomas, each treatment of a question ends with the refutation of the other, initially presented opinions which are called individually. In oral disputations it was customary to ask for confirmation of adequate presentation of the opposing argumentation already at the beginning of the presentation of the opposite positions.

From my point of view, it is rather obvious to describe the outlined medieval scholastic methodology as a place of learning for ecumenism which Pesch already explored at a very early stage in his theological work. Every conversation becomes more open when the questions that arise are recognized as questions affecting everyone. Disputes can only be considered to be meaningful if there is a reciprocal listening to the respective arguments and misunderstandings are excluded as much as possible. Any theological positioning requires an argumentation that can make use of testimonies from tradition while these alone on the other hand cannot be viewed as guarantors of truth. Even at the end of the presentation of one's own position it is vital to remind of the opposing opinions in order not to regard the conversations as concluded.

I am in favor of an ecumenical culture of conversation that even today respects the basic rules of scholastic disputation methodology. Pesch was well practised in this approach. In my opinion this is one of the reasons why he received high recognition from people who did not share his opinion but acknowledged that he sought to understand their points of view while presenting arguments for his own opinion.

Denominationally Characterized Catholic Identity

When I met with Pesch in ecumenical contexts I never perceived that he had doubts about the meaningfulness of his membership in the Roman Catholic denomination. Needless to say, he was aware of the "coincidence" which plays a lasting part in one's life in connection with the inclusion in a specific ecclesiastical tradition in the context of infant baptism. From my point of view, such a biographical view on the conditions of one's own confessional existence still is very important in ecumenism today. The realization that one as a rule is a member of a denomination because of conditions in the family and not on the basis of one's own decision can be a conceptual way of opening oneself to ecumenism.

Which understanding of the catholicity of the Church did Pesch have? What was dear and valuable to him in his own denominational tradition? Which queries did he direct at the Reformation theologies? I will answer these questions not with reference to individual parts of his writings but rather in the form of a retrospective that includes personal experiences from meetings with him.

The Ecumenical Understanding of "Catholicity"

Which criteria decide who is "catholic"? In the ecumenical context, we are very familiar with understanding the term "catholic" as a common denominator linking the Christian denominations of all the communities that form the one, sacred and apostolic Church, in the sense of the Niceno-Constantinopolitan Creed of 381. In this early period of Christianity, "catholic" first of all means omnipresent, present everywhere in intention—encompassing all spaces. This definition focusing on *local conditions* is not the only one from tradition and not the only one possible even today. Already in the early Middle Ages, there were disputes concerning the understanding of the term "catholic" *temporally*—no longer locally. Catholic then is what always pertains, forever. Pesch put his life at the service of the search to regain the catholicity of the Church both in local and temporal regards. Because of his extensive studies of Reformation literature, he was very familiar with and agreed with the definition of the term of catholicity in the sense of the Reformation tradition. For Philipp Melanchthon it was very important to label the Church of the Reformation as catholic and the Roman Church as non-catholic.[23] According to Melanchthon, "catholic" is a church forming its life in accordance with the scripture. Hence, catholic is who is *original*—who corresponds to the beginning, the traditional origin.

Appreciation of One's Own Denomination and Queries to the Reformation Tradition

All through his life, Pesch remained mentally very deeply connected with his Roman Catholic origin. Processes within his own denomination he observed critically in the constructive sense and commented on them with alert attention. He showed appreciation for the concerns that are essential for a social institution that sees itself primarily situated in the space of the universal church—a reliable liturgical order, a confession of faith based on tradition, an assignment to serve in leading positions, preceded by an assessment of the suitability of future position holders (both personally and professionally).

Pesch's queries directed mainly at the Reformation traditions must be understood inversely with regard to the familiarity with the idiosyncrasies of the own denomination. In the area of liturgy, Pesch was committed to an order where the personal preferences of individuals assigned with leadership do not have priority. He appreciated listening to the proclaimed word that is sounded unexpectedly and not chosen by one's own discretion. In accordance with this, he also advocated a form of ordination maintaining (in the sense of the Lutheran tradition) the idea that the ordained person acts under the authority of the Spirit of God also in relation to the assembled community of the baptised. On the question of the ordination of women, Pesch did not agree with Martin Luther who considered the service of public preaching of the gospel to be inappropriate for women based on anthropological considerations. On detailed issues of ethics Pesch took a rather reserved stance—possibly strengthened in this by Thomas Aquinas who held decisions based on an individual's conscience in high respect.

From the beginning of his time as a theological teacher and even more so with increasing age Pesch showed his incomprehension at the fact

---

23. Sattler, "'Mit der katholischen Kirche Christi eines Sinnes.'"

that the theological language is so inaccessible to people. Long sentences with many foreign words were an abomination to him. Especially in the thematic area of the doctrine of justification he called for a form of speech that is realistic and based on experience. Regarding the characterisation of every human being as completely corrupted by sin he had serious doubts especially about the receptivity of this message. Images—with personal and relational connotations—of God's willingness to accept man in all his distress—including the distress of guilt—were close to him. He was extremely concerned with the question of how "unbelievers" living without trust in God can regain hope today.

Results and Desiderata

I would like to summarize what in my view characterises the lifework of Pesch in ecumenical respect.

Results

Every human being exists in limitations. Every theology is situated contextually—in space and time. Pesch lived in a cultural environment which highly appreciates historical research. He presented many publications that could not have appeared without intensive source studies. At the same time, he was aware of the challenge to impart the central Christian theological contents to people today in the language of our time.

Pesch wanted to do justice to this idea that initially was foreign to him. His historical research deserves great respect in this context. At the same time, Pesch always argued that a language accessible to many people should be spoken in theology. It was important to him to extrapolate the relevance of the gospel for contemporary life. He liked being invited to conversations at very different localities. He was a wanderer between the worlds.

Desiderata

Looking back at Pesch's theological work I detect three desiderata. I am quite certain that he himself agreed with the hope that these wishes would be fulfilled by theological work in the future. In the present situation of ecumenical discussions, our view of the sixteenth century is no longer—as was the case at the beginning of Pesch's scientific studies—orientated towards the person of Martin Luther and his doctrine of justification. The multilateral conversations between Christians of all denominations were not the primary point of reference in the work of Pesch. Is it still possible today to impart encyclopaedic knowledge in questions of the Christian faith? Pesch endeavoured to do just that. In doing so, he joins a rather large group of theologians of the twentieth and twenty-first century from the area of systematic theology who presented a "sum" of (their) theology. For Pesch, Thomas Aquinas certainly was the guiding light. Again and again, the Christian confession of faith was the reference point in Pesch's theological interpretations. Is this (still) advisable today—or should not more fundamental questions be raised in theology, questions which first of all take the existential needs of the people into consideration? Pesch was aware of his limitations. Only at a late point he discovered the inter-religious context of his actions and his thinking. He was particularly concerned with the question of which significance the Jewish religion has for Christianity. Pesch added a dedication to me to the last of the three partial volumes of his *Katholische Dogmatik*: "From now on Eccl 12:12 applies." There one can read: "There is no end to the crafting of many books, and too much study wearies the body." I also take the next verse to heart: "Let the conclusion of all of these thoughts be heard: Fear God and obey his commandments" (Eccl 12:13).

Bibliography

Handke, Peter. *Phantasien der Wiederholung*. Frankfurt: Suhrkamp, 1983.
Lehmann, Karl, and Wolfhart Pannenberg, eds. *Lehrverurteilungen—kirchentrennend?* 3 vols. Matrix: Dialog der Kirchen 4–6. Freiburg: Herder, 1986–1990.
Leppin, Volker. "Belehrte Ökumene. Otto Hermann Peschs Luther." In *Hinführung zu Luther*, by Otto Hermann Pesch, i–viii. Ostfildern: Schwabenverlag, 2017.
Meyer, Harding, et al., eds. *Gemeinsame Erklärung zur Rechtfertigungslehre*. Vol. 3 of *Dokumente wachsender Übereinstimmung*. Paderborn: Bonifatius, 2003.
Pesch, Otto Hermann. *Das Zweite Vatikanische Konzil: Vorgeschichte, Verlauf, Ergebnisse, Nachgeschichte*. Würzburg: Echter, 1994.
———. *Die Theologie der Rechtfertigung bei Martin Luther und Thomas von Aquin: Versuch eines systematisch-theologischen Dialogs*. Matrix: Walberger Studien 4. Mainz: Matthias-Grünewald, 1967.
———. *Frei sein aus Gnade: Theologische Anthropologie*. Freiburg: Herder, 1983.
———. *Hinführung zu Luther*. Ostfildern: Schwabenverlag, 2017.
———. "Justification and the Question of God." *LWF Studies* 2 (2003) 107–16.
———. *Katholische Dogmatik aus ökumenischer Erfahrung*. 2 vols. Ostfildern: Schwabenverlag, 2008–2010.
———. *Kleines katholisches Glaubensbuch*. Kevelaer: Topos plus VG, 2004.
———. "Neuere Beiträge zur Frage nach Luthers, reformatorischer Wende." *Catholica* 37 (1983) 259–87; 38 (1984) 66–134.

———. "Wat heeft Luther de katholieken (nog) te zeggen?" *Luther-bulletin* 6 (1997) 4–22.

Rahner, Karl, and Herbert Vorgrimler, eds. *Kleines Konzilskompendium.* Freiburg: Herder, 1966.

Sattler, Dorothea. "'. . . Mit der katholischen Kirche Christi eines Sinnes . . .': Melanchthon und die Ökumene." In *Philipp Melanchthon: "Grenzüberschreitungen." Lebenskreise eines Reformators,* edited by Hanna Kasparick, 102–20. Wittenberg: Drei-Kastanien-Verlag, 2010.

———. "Ökumenisch eine katholische Kirche werden? Das Verhältnis zwischen Vielfalt und Einheit aus (einer) römisch-katholischen Sicht." *Beihefte zur Ökumenischen Rundschau* 105 (2016) 67–80.

4

George Lindbeck: Ecumenical Unity through Ecclesial Particularity

—Ronald T. Michener

GEORGE LINDBECK HAS BEEN a leading champion for ecumenical discussion, primarily between Lutherans and Roman Catholics, for most of his academic career. He has zealously modeled an intentional "generous orthodoxy" (a term coined by his Yale colleague and friend, Hans Frei) that favorably acknowledges the diversity of various Christian traditions.[1] He is most known for his part in the so-called, "Yale School" of postliberal theology and his writing of a fairly short, yet provocative book, *The Nature of Doctrine: Religion and Theology in a Postliberal Age* (1984). This book has been so influential that in 2009, its 25th anniversary edition was released, including a new introduction by Bruce Marshall and a new afterword by Lindbeck. It also includes the foreword (by Lindbeck) to the German edition. In addition to German, the book has been translated into French, Italian as well as Chinese and Japanese.[2] Before we discuss the implications of Lindbeck's work and his ecumenical vision, it will be helpful to provide the context for his work that fueled his vision, including his personal history and academic formation.

Personal Background and Ecumenical Context

George Arthur Lindbeck, the son of American Lutheran missionary parents, was born in 1923 in Louyang, China. Lindbeck was often sick as a child, hence his Chinese language skills remained weak. Nonetheless, prior to age 12, his exposure to Chinese culture was significant for the development of his

---

1. Although Lindbeck's primary area of concern was Lutheran/Roman Catholic dialogue, as we will see, he has also had significant interest in interreligious dialogue.

2. Lindbeck, *Nature of Doctrine*, vii.

thought. Lindbeck was enthralled with literature about this ancient imperial city of his birthplace, Louyang, being fascinated by its ruins and tombs. At its peak, Louyang may have reached a population of a million, even larger than Rome during the first two hundred years after Christ. For Lindbeck, it became especially significant to note the radical differences between Louyang's majestic past and its feeble present while observing many continuities of culture. He observed this in particular through some close Chinese Christian friends of his parents, a pastor and his wife.[3] Lindbeck describes this couple as both "warmly Christian" yet "Confucian to the core." This incongruity, Lindbeck claims, "implanted ways of thinking that are still with me, now consciously rather than subliminally."[4] With this experience firmly in mind, Lindbeck maintains the conviction that our community shapes us more than we are shaped by ourselves, and community shaped culture can withstand the trials and devastations of history. Although human beings are more or less similar wherever you go, linguistic differences can make common communication unobtainable. These views of community, culture, and language are what led to Lindbeck's "cultural-linguistic," model of religion.[5]

Bernhard Eckerstorfer submits that Lindbeck's confessional background of growing up in the "Christian diaspora of Asia" was greatly influential for the two primary aspects of his work: (1) Holding to one's community faith as a minority and (2) Religious pluralism and internal divisions among Christians.[6] Lindbeck guarded his Lutheran identity, but sought reconciliation among diverse perspectives. He was "willing to see traces of the Holy Spirit" across boundaries as his standard practice which led to his active engagement with ecumenism.[7] We will return to Lindbeck's ecumenical project shortly.

At age 17, Lindbeck left China to study in the United States at Adolphus College in St. Peter, Minnesota. He then continued his studies at Yale Divinity School, completing a Bachelor of Divinity in 1946. This was followed by a year at the Pontifical Institute of Medieval Studies in Toronto and an additional two years at the École Pratique des Hautes Études in Paris. In 1955, although already teaching, he finished his PhD at Yale on John Duns Scotus. Yale would remain his academic and career "home" until his retirement in 1993. Lindbeck's widely diverse background of study no

---

3. Lindbeck, "Interview," 28; Michener, *Postliberal Theology*, 63; Eckerstorfer, "One Church in the Postmodern World," 401

4. Lindbeck, "Interview," 28.

5. Lindbeck, "Interview," 28; cf. Michener, *Postliberal Theology*, 63–64.

6. Eckerstorfer, "One Church," 401, 403, 400.

7. Eckerstorfer, "One Church," 400.

doubt further developed his ecumenical ambitions. He was appointed by the Lutheran World Federation to function as an official ecumenical observer at the Second Vatican Council, living in Rome throughout this time (1962–1964) with his wife and daughter.[8]

In an interview, Lindbeck was asked his most sharp memory of his experience at Vatican II. He referred to a speech by Archbishop Léon-Arthur Elchinger of Strasbourg at St. Peter's on the debt of Catholics to non-Catholics. Elchinger claimed that if Catholics were discovering anew the doctrine of justification by faith, exemplified in the book of Acts and Galatians, then this is because it has been kept alive by those outside the Roman Catholic church communities, stemming from the Reformation. Lindbeck said this speech brought tears to his eyes. He did not imagine that an archbishop would make such a public proclamation in order to renew the church.[9] Lindbeck enthusiastically supported *aggiornamento*, a significant Italian word during Vatican II that refered to "updating" the Roman Catholic church in view of contemporary concerns. This process of bringing the church up to date was advocated alongside of and connected to *ressourcement* theology—looking back and drawing from the ancient biblical and patristic sources of the Christian faith. But for Lindbeck, if *aggiornamento* loses its integral connection to *ressourcement*, then theological liberalism will be the result—guided more by modernist tendencies than faith. Both "updating" and "looking back" were essential for generating the ecumenical hope of bringing Catholics and Protestants together, and would be critical for Lindbeck's work throughout his career.[10]

Eckerstorfer remarks that Lindbeck's service at Vatican II became the "seed-bed" for his ongoing commitments to Catholic–Lutheran dialogue. Lindbeck became a member of the Joint Commission between the Lutheran World Federation and the Vatican from 1968 to 1987, while also co-chairing the commission for ten years. His various ecumenical activities during this time appear to have been more important to the development of his thought than his academic work in teaching and research.[11] As Lindbeck put it: "It is the ecumenical movement even more than my teaching at Yale . . . that has been the context of my thinking."[12] Nonetheless, in spite of this state-

---

8. Lindbeck, "Interview," 28; Eckerstorfer, "One Church," 401; Michener, *Postliberal Theology*, 64.
9. Lindbeck, "Interview," 30–31.
10. Marshall, "Introduction," ix, x.
11. Eckerstorfer, "One Church," 401–2.
12. Lindbeck quoted in Eckerstorfer, *One Church*, 402.

ment, Lindbeck's theological development was shaped in and among his colleagues at Yale. It is to this which we now turn.

The "Yale School"

Lindbeck was highly influenced by H. Richard Niebuhr at Yale, a theologian greatly interested in the Christian faith in view of culture, also an important aspect of Lindbeck's thought. At Yale, with its emphasis in historical theology, students were expected to examine the depths of their particular ecclesiological traditions, rather than looking at religion with vague universalist tendencies. With these emphases at Yale, Lindbeck could focus on the Lutheran confession, while still thinking of the broader culture.[13] Lindbeck's theological work developed on the coattails of his colleagues (such as Hans Frei and David Kelsey) who formulated key features of his approach, along with much help from other theologians, philosophers and cultural theorists. When discussing his book, *The Nature of Doctrine* in his Foreword to the German Edition, Lindbeck gives generous credit to those from whom he learned and borrowed:

> The only fresh aspect of the book, I had supposed, was its ecumenical focus. The ingredients were borrowed. My Yale colleagues, Hans Frei and David Kelsey, supplied the narrative hermeneutic (admittedly different in character from what usually passes under that name) which the book favors, while its grammatical or regulative understanding of doctrine has patristic roots retrieved with the help of such authors as, among theologians, the German Lutheran, Edmund Schlink, and the Canadian Jesuit, Bernard Lonergan, and, among philosophers, Ludwig Wittgenstein. (They are not responsible, to repeat the usual disclaimer, for the use I have made of their work.) Similarly, the "cultural-linguistic" theory of religion is, except for its name, adapted from Clifford Geertz, and amounts, the way I use it, to little more than a semiotic version of that mélange of ideas from Weber, Durkheim, Hegel and Marx used by everyone who talks about religion in our day (and which I know chiefly at second hand, not least as transmitted through Peter Berger).[14]

Although the "Yale School" is a misnomer, as there has never been such official "school" as such, the term does express the commonalities of thought that Lindbeck shared with his colleagues such the aforementioned Yale

13. Eckerstorfer, "One Church," 402.
14. Lindbeck, *Nature of Doctrine*, xxx.

scholars along with William Christian, Paul Holmer, and Brevard Childs. Among all his influencers, perhaps the greatest was Hans Frei, especially Frei's appropriation of Karl Barth's hermeneutical perspectives.[15] This breadth of influence, joined with his ecumenically driven background, comes together in his most renowned work, *The Nature of Doctrine: Religion and Theology in a Postliberal Age*, where Lindbeck makes his case for a cultural-linguistic theology.

A Postliberal Cultural-Linguistic Theology

As noted above, Lindbeck's ecumenical hopes combined with his awareness of the destructive ramifications of theological liberalism, together produced his theological perspective astutely expressed in *The Nature of Doctrine*. Bruce Marshall says: "The Nature of Doctrine offers the promise that church and theology need not flee the world but can meet the world on its own terms without accommodating themselves to it."[16] Hence, Lindbeck is advocating a postliberal theology that is "profoundly rooted in Scripture and the Christian tradition and at the same time deeply responsive to the genuine needs of the time, which the Christian sources themselves help us identify."[17]

In order to lay out his proposal of a cultural-linguistic theology, Lindbeck summarizes what he considers to be the three most well-known theories of religion: the cognitive-propositional, the experiential-expressive, and another that combines the two.[18] The cognitive-propositional approach has "affinities" to Anglo-American analytic philosophy that is preoccupied with the factual content of religious statements. Doctrines are fundamentally about truth claims that correspond to objective realities.[19] For the cognitive-propositionalist, the "aesthetic and nondiscursvely symbolic dimensions of a religion—for example, its poetry, music, art, and rituals," are reduced to "external decorations designed to make the hard core of explicitly stable

---

15. Eckerstorfer, "One Church," 403. It should be noted that Lindbeck was also greatly influenced by Thomas Aquinas, although not without criticism. See Marshall, "Introduction," xviii–xix. Some certainly see the legitimacy of Lindbeck's appropriation of Thomas. Outside of Christian faith, Thomas argued, "the human mind 'totally fails to attain' to God, so that the non-Christian philosopher who has demonstration of God's existence nonetheless fails 'to have a [true] belief that God exists'" (Marshall, "Introduction," xix, citing Aquinas, *ST* II-II, q2, a2, ad 3).

16. Marshall, "Introduction," xii.

17. Marshall, "Introduction," xi.

18. Lindbeck, *Nature of Doctrine*, 2; cf. 49–50.

19. Lindbeck, *Nature of Doctrine*, 2, 10.

beliefs and precepts more appealing to the masses."[20] The second approach to religion Lindbeck identifies as "experiential-expressive." This perspective is especially relevant for theological liberalism (beginning with Schleiermacher), and emphasizes the common experiential or aesthetic dimensions among various faiths. A third perspective that is predominant among ecumenical Roman Catholics, attempts to combine the cognitive-propostional with the experiential-expressive, suggesting both are significant for the Christian religion. For instance, this approach would be noted in scholars such as Karl Rahner and Bernard Lonergan.[21]

Lindbeck finds it difficult to imagine doctrinal reconciliation among the above approaches. For the cognitive-propositionalist, either one accepts or rejects the truth statements of doctrine. If one accepts that doctrinal truth statements point to reality, then one cannot affirm the experiential expressivist position that religions are "diverse expressions or objectifications of a common core experience."[22] However, if one takes a symbolist position among experiential-expressivism, it would be possible to argue that a doctrine may remain constant, although it will create different experiences among different persons. In this way, doctrines function as symbols that may or may not point to divine reality. Although Lindbeck claims that such combined approaches attempt to be more conciliatory and ecumenical, he believes that ultimately the "complicated intellectual gymnastics" that must take place to harmonize the two perspectives are not persuasive.[23] Instead, Lindbeck proposes a new model: The cultural-linguistic approach.

The cultural-linguistic approach views religion as an entire organizing, interpretive framework for reality containing its own particular, internal logic and grammar. Drawing upon Wittgenstein's "language games" Lindbeck finds that religious traditions, like language, are intrinsically related to a way of life that includes both intellect (cognition) and behavior. Our language in our community context shapes and conditions our experience.[24] This perspective has its roots in other disciplines, such as anthropology, sociology, and philosophy, as Lindbeck readily acknowledges.[25] This is clearly evident in the sources from which Lindbeck draws to support his position (e.g., Geertz, Kuhn, Wittgenstein, among others). In a similar fashion,

---

20. Lindbeck, *Nature of Doctrine*, 21–22; cf. Eckerstorfer, "One Church," 409.

21. Lindbeck, *Nature of Doctrine*, 2.

22. Lindbeck, *Nature of Doctrine*, 2, 17. Lindbeck submits this as a thesis of Bernard Lonergan's theory of religion.

23. Lindbeck, *Nature of Doctrine*, 3.

24. Lindbeck, *Nature of Doctrine*, 19, 23–24.

25. Lindbeck, *Nature of Doctrine*, 18.

Lindbeck argues, to be religious means we acquire the skills of a certain religious language. As Christians, for instance, we must learn and internalize the story of Israel and Jesus so that we interpret the world from this faith story.[26] This idea is basic to Lindbeck's postliberal agenda—the grammar of our faith is intratextual, it "redescribes reality within the scriptural framework rather than translating Scripture into extrascriptural categories. It is the text, so to speak, which absorbs the world, rather than the world the text."[27] Rather than allowing outside stories and interpretive frameworks for understanding reality determine the direction of our own Christian story, our own Christian story with its particular grammar of faith, governs our entire interpretive fabric.

It is important to note that the cultural-linguistic perspective does not deny the importance of propositions or experiential aspects of religion. In Christian theology truth claims are important, but they cannot be separated from their own internal grammar. This reflection, likewise moves us to consider aspects of our humanity (in the vein of the experiential-expressivist) that ordinarily we would not. This internal grammar of Christian faith is not reduced to propositions, but is internally embedded in one's entire life that comes from habitual practice and skill development.[28] As Lindbeck explains:

> Sometimes explicitly formulated statements of the beliefs or behavioral norms of a religion may be helpful in the learning process, but by no means always. Ritual, prayer, and example are normally much more important. Thus—insofar as the experiential-expressive contrast between experience and knowledge is comparable to that between "knowing how" and "knowing that"—cultural-linguistic models, no less than expressive ones, emphasize the experiential or existential side of religion, though in a different way.[29]

Lindbeck goes on to say that for the Christian, proclaiming the gospel is first about telling the story, and only after that does the story "gain power and meaning insofar as it is embodied in the total gestalt of community life and action."[30] Thus, in the cultural-linguistic approach, experience and expres-

---

26. Lindbeck, *Nature of Doctrine*, 20.
27. Lindbeck, *Nature of Doctrine*, 104.
28. Lindbeck, *Nature of Doctrine*, 20, 21.
29. Lindbeck, *Nature of Doctrine*, 21.
30. Lindbeck, *Nature of Doctrine*, 22.

sion are still vital, but language is the "preexperiential" foundation that gives shape to the experience and expression.[31]

In order to learn the language and grammar of Christian faith with skill, as mentioned above, for Lindbeck it is important to be saturated in the story of Israel and Jesus. Lindbeck becomes more emphatic about this in his "Foreword to the German Edition" (2003). He insists that dogmatics must begin with ecclesiology and "Israel-ology." As he puts it, "Israel and the Church are one elect people, and rethinking their relation is fundamental to ecumenism."[32] The first Christians were Jews who followed a risen Messiah. As God's people, the story of Israel was their personal story and history, and the Hebrew Bible was their Bible. This is the background narrative of the Christian church.[33] Unfortunately, as Lindbeck recounts, the church eventually became almost entirely Gentile—hence creating a division, at least in thought, between the old and new people of God. Some started to think of Israel as a type of Christ and the church rather than it being the basis and condition of the church, in continuity with Israel's story.[34]

With its emphasis on the internal grammar of the faith, intratextuality, internalizing the story of Israel and Jesus, and absorbing of the world into the narrative of the Bible, it seems apparent how a cultural-linguistic theology is certainly postliberal in its outlook. What may seem less obvious, however is how it is overtly ecumenical in its approach. Or further still, what ways does such an approach provide avenues for interfaith dialogue?

Ecumenical Particularism

Lindbeck's primary goal has always been ecumenism—especially between Lutherans and Roman Catholics in order to have "doctrinal reconciliation without capitulation."[35] In fact, more recently he said that *The Nature of Doctrine* "was, and still is, peripheral to my main concerns."[36] Lindbeck's cultural-linguistic approach highlights the significance of a community embedded grammar that governs the practices of religious communities.

---

31. Lindbeck, *Nature of Doctrine*, 23. Not all agree with Lindbeck here. For example, C. John Sommerville argues that "numinous experience precedes any religious expectations and creates the need for a religious language" (Sommerville, "Is Religion A Language Game?," 595).

32. Lindbeck, *Nature of Doctrine*, xxxii.

33. Lindbeck, *Church in a Postliberal Age*, 149–50.

34. Lindbeck, *Church in a Postliberal Age*, 152–53, 157.

35. Lindbeck, *Nature of Doctrine*, xxii, cited in Marshall, "Introduction," xxii; cf. Lindbeck, *Nature of Doctrine*, 4.

36. Lindbeck, "Ecumenisms in Conflict," 212, cited in Marshall, "Introduction," xxi.

Whether Roman Catholic or Lutheran, once such embeddedness is understood, then further understanding may ensue. Although practices will remain different, they may reveal adherence "to the same doctrine."[37] The cultural-linguistic approach seeks to show this common characteristic of community identity commitment to a grammar of faith with a vocabulary that varies. Lindbeck says, for instance

> In the light of the generic resemblances between religions and cultures when these are linguistically understood, doctrinal reconciliation without capitulation is conceivable to the extent that oppositions between church doctrines can be construed as lexical rather than grammatical or, in more complicated cases, as regulative rather than propositional—that is, as contextually valid second-order rules of first-order discourse rather than as first-order ontological truth claims.[38]

Although this affirmation does not go undebated, a document in Lindbeck's favor—in which he was involved—is the Joint Declaration on the Doctrine of Justification of the Lutheran World Federation and the Vatican from 1999. But this too is met with objections by some, according to Lindbeck, especially in Germany. However, we will not expound on this further here.[39]

In our view, the cultural-linguistic approach to doctrine does not compromise particularity for ecumenism, but sees the acknowledgement and articulation of a community's particularity (in a denomination, for instance) as the best avenue for authentic, honest ecumenical progress. When a community's particular grammar is recognized, specific differences between denominational doctrinal expressions and practices will emerge. But through this forthright understanding of differences, spaces will also emerge for ecumenical reconciliation.

---

37. Marshall, "Introduction," xxiii.
38. Lindbeck, *Nature of Doctrine*, 128.
39. See Lindbeck, *Nature of Doctrine*, 127. Lindbeck does not agree with those protesting the document, but he does see aspects of confusion in the "Declaration." At the same time, he says that he has sympathy with them, "because they are reacting against a novelty so unprecedented that it is simply an impossibility in terms of the usual categories for thinking about religion in general and Christianity in particular" (Lindbeck, *Nature of Doctrine*, 127). See also insights from Wainwright, "Ecumenical Dimensions of Lindbeck's 'Nature of Doctrine,'" 129.

Interreligious Dialogue

Another greatly significant issue for Lindbeck's cultural-linguistic perspective, one which he himself recognizes, is that of interreligious dialogue. If the world of the Bible is to "absorb" the world, then is it possible to have any type of meaningful, cooperative interaction with other faiths? The cultural-linguistic approach recognizes the possibility of "incommensurable notions of truth" among diverse religions.[40] But this does not mean that dialogue is impossible—in spite of the fact that it does not concede to reducing common ground to shared experiences (as in the liberal, experience-expressivist approach). In fact, since non-Christian religions are distinct from Christianity, engagement with them provides the occasion to recognize positions that have particular insights from which Christians may learn.[41] Just because the Christian faith is affirming uniquely salvific claims does not preclude other religions from speaking truth to Christians "of which Christianity as yet knows nothing and by which it could be greatly enriched."[42] Learning, listening, and engaging others does not require agreement on substantive issues between particular religions.

In Lindbeck's new "Afterword" in the 25th edition of *The Nature of Doctrine*, he returns (for purposes of clarification) back to the question of interreligious dialogue, which he addressed in chapter 3. Lindbeck refuses the pluralist model of John Hick, or Karl Rahner's "anonymous Christian" version of experiential-expressivism that levels communication out to common, universal experiences.[43] Instead, Lindbeck affirms, as is the case in ecumenical relations, the importance of recognizing particular differences among religions to promote healthy communication. For ecumenical relations, however, there is a common overarching story, which is not the case in interreligious communication.[44] In fact, for Lindbeck, certain "alien" beliefs may indeed be false, but may still be justified in their particular context. This is why it is important to recognize the difference between justified and true beliefs as "an important condition for mutual respect between religions." This practice "not only has philosophical but also biblical warrants in the principle of charity and in honor Scripture accords the righteous heathen."[45]

---

40. Lindbeck, *Nature of Doctrine*, 35; cf. Thompson, "Question of Posture," 275.

41. Thompson, "Question of Posture," 275.

42. Lindbeck, *Nature of Doctrine*, 35. See also Thompson, "Question of Posture," 275.

43. Lindbeck, *Nature of Doctrine*, 129.

44. Fletcher, "As Long as We Wonder," 535.

45. Lindbeck, *Nature of Doctrine*, 133.

Honoring the other's context and mode of justification are essential ingredients for manifesting such charity.

Lindbeck provides an example of this perspective by making a distinction between the particularist and universalist dimensions among religions. Usually the particularist dimensions are stressed and the universal dimensions are neglected. The universal aspects of a religion arise in view of their grand interpretive motifs for understanding and organizing reality. Buddhists for example have radically different particular beliefs than Christians, but things such as "Deeds, thoughts, and mindfulness" are understood in similar senses between both religions.[46] It is with such elements in mind that effective interreligious communication may ensue.

All of this above is not to say that interreligious dialogue is simple. As Jeannine Fletcher insightfully writes:

> The practical incommensurability of Lindbeck's cultural-linguistic approach to religious difference is indeed a challenge to any facile notion of dialogue that would claim easy understanding across religious traditions. But the difficulty does not preclude learning the language of the other and, through life-long study, acquiring the rare bilingualism that Lindbeck allows.[47]

Lindbeck made this clear in an earlier essay when he said that the "gravest objection" to the cultural-linguistic approach in this respect "makes interreligious dialogue more difficult."[48] Simply reducing productive interreligious relations to conversation may result in frustration. However, with an intentional understanding about differences, "when each religion considers its relation to other in terms of its emic categories, its native tongue, instead of contorting and distorting its heritage to fit the constraints of a purportedly universalizable etic idiom of salvation."[49] Here we recognize Lindbeck's appropriation of Wittgenstein's "language games." In order to understand other religions, it is important to understand the "language-game"—the context, culture, and practices—of the one with whom we are in dialogue.[50] In spite of the hard work required, Lindbeck's motives are not merely pragmatic, but also servant oriented: "The church is called to serve other religions for the sake of the neighbor, for the sake of humanity, for

---

46. Lindbeck, *Nature of Doctrine*, 132.
47. Fletcher, "As Long as We Wonder," 544.
48. Lindbeck, "Gospel's Uniqueness," 426–27.
49. Lindbeck, "Gospel's Uniqueness," 427.
50. Fletcher, "As Long as We Wonder," 536. Fletcher recognizes that Lindbeck admits that his appropriation of Wittgenstein may not be approved by all Wittegenstein scholars. See Lindbeck, *Nature of Doctrine*, 10; cf. 19.

the sake of God's promise to Abraham that through his seed all nations will be blessed."[51] With these considerations, the cultural-linguistic model for seeking interreligious understanding holds the most promise.

Criticisms and Concerns: Relativism, Fideism, and Truth

In addition to the concern of incommensurability and communication with respect to ecumenism and interreligious relations already noted above, additional primary criticisms that arise for Lindbeck's cultural-linguistic approach include those of relativism, fideism and truth. These criticisms stem from Lindbeck's intratextualism, a characteristic that is critical for cultural-linguistic model. It is indeed "relative" in the sense that its truth is not measured by external sources or general rational principles of common logic. The truth of a particular faith is derived internally. It is also fideistic in that it does not permit outside sources to judge its own veracity. It is rather internally shaped within the context of its community language and practices.

Lindbeck believes that those accusing the cultural-linguistic approach as leading to relativism, are simply mistaken. Those making the accusation see "the theological 'that' and 'what' articulations of a religion's grammar in theology and doctrine" as more secure than the "how" of those skilled religious followers. Referencing Stanley Hauerwas, Lindbeck claims "Dorothy Day and Mother Teresa have done more to sustain continuity with Jesus and the apostles than have theologians with their ever-changing explications of the faith."[52] This of course leads to the question as to the status of the nature of truth *ontologically* for the cultural-linguistic model.

The main worry with those concerned about the relativism of Lindbeck's approach, concerns the notion of truth. If truth is lost or compromised, then we have no access to reality and morals have no anchor. Unfortunately, this worry seems to confuse "arbitrariness" ("what may be right or true for you is not necessarily right or true for me") with a committed relativism to a particular set of beliefs and practices relative to a particular community.[53] In this nuanced sense, Lindbeck may be rightly called a "relativist" but he certainly is not advocating an arbitrary notion of beliefs that simply accommodates to one's whims.

---

51. Lindbeck, "Gospel's Uniqueness," 424.
52. Lindbeck, "Interview," 29.
53. This is the overall argument that Smith makes in *Who's Afraid of Relativism?*

In fact, the meaning of "truth" is highly significant for Lindbeck's general perspective. He describes three functions of "truth" that help clarify his understanding. Propositional oriented truth is about claims of factual judgment. Experiential-expressivist truth is concerned with correspondence to one's symbolic experience. The cultural-linguistic understanding of truth, or "categorical" truth, looks to the internal grammar or "rules" that govern the internal community in which claims of "truth" are made.[54] Since this approach does not in itself propose a notion of truth compatible with the propositional or experiential approach, many misunderstandings arise with respect to the question of "relativism."

Lindbeck, however, does not deny the importance of propositional claims of truth. For instance, Christians affirm that "Jesus Christ is Lord." This is not only a cultural-linguistic truth within a community of faith, but also refers to a propositional and symbolic truth that reflects Christian experience and faith.[55] For both Paul and Luther, according to Lindbeck, the statement "Jesus is Lord" was true regardless of experiences or lack of belief. But it was not a mere assertion. To assert this propositional truth also entailed a commitment to practice the Christian life.[56] One was not absent from the other.

In addition to his description of functions of truth, Lindbeck later describes various kinds of truth statements, which correspond to his proposed functions of truth, with additional nuances. Lindbeck differentiates between what he calls "intrasystematic" (coherence) and "ontological" (correspondence) truth. For "epistemological realists," a truth must be intrasystematic if it is ontologically true, but it is not necessarily ontologically true if it is intrasystematic. In other words, it must point to reality itself, in order to be true.[57] In his more recent "Afterword" to the *Nature of Doctrine*, Lindbeck submits that when "categorical truth" is added to "intrasystematic truth" there are then two necessary (although not sufficient) conditions for ontological truth.[58] Lindbeck nowhere denies the importance of ontological truth, but he recognizes that the notion of truth has various aspects of usage. Unfortunatley with Lindbeck's heavy emphasis on the intrinsic connection between belief and practice along with his unclear nuancing between meaning and warrant, it often creates confusion.[59]

54. Lindbeck, *Nature of Doctrine*, 33–34; cf. 139n10.
55. Lindbeck, *Nature of Doctrine*, 49–50.
56. Lindbeck, *Nature of Doctrine*, 52.
57. Lindbeck, *Nature of Doctrine*, 50–51.
58. Lindbeck, *Nature of Doctrine*, 139n10.
59. This insight is clearly made by Marshall, "Introduction," xvii.

Does Lindbeck's perspective simply resort to fideism? If we take his position on ontological truth seriously, it does not appear to be absent of rational discourse. However, this is not to say that rational discourse itself can set the terms for the truth or falsity of various religious beliefs in question. The Christian is not required to accept non-Christian standards of truth for adjudicating her beliefs.[60] This is not "epistemic isolationism" or a denial of God's grace in creation, but rather an acknowledgement that seeking ultimate common ground with non-Christian worldviews is not the primary task for Christians. Meaningful dialogue may occur even without ultimately common views of truth standards with those outside the Christian faith.[61]

Some, such as Geoffrey Wainwright, understand Lindbeck's theory of truth as insufficient, viewing it as a consensus theory "without a veridical God."[62] But as we have seen, Lindbeck does not compromise on truth simply for the sake of the culturally shaped grammar of the faith community. Faith implies that certain beliefs are held true. But the meaning of "truth" is more complex and varied than a simple acknowledgement of statements matching matters of fact.[63]

Advancing Lindbeck's Proposals Today

In Bruce Marshall's insightful introduction to the 25th edition of *The Nature of Doctrine*, he writes "On both sides of the Atlantic, The Nature of Doctrine has seemed to promise a way forward for Christian theology, Catholic as well as Protestant."[64] This statement, then, prompts the following questions: What *is* the way forward? What can we continue to learn from Lindbeck's theological approach?

In 2002, Lindbeck expressed optimism about our current historical condition since "Ideologies rooted in Enlightenment rationalism are collapsing." Modernity was characterized by radical individualism, rationalism and totalitarian thought. This is "being replaced," for Lindbeck, "by an understanding of knowledge and belief as socially and linguistically constituted."[65] And in view of modernity's demise, Lindbeck later adds: "We are now better placed than perhaps ever before to retrieve, critically

---

60. Marshall, "Introduction," xiii.
61. Marshall, "Introduction," xiii–xiv.
62. Wainwright, "Ecumenical Dimensions," 124, 125.
63. See Thuesen, "George Lindbeck on Truth," 55. Thuesen's article provides a quite lengthy critical analysis of Lindbeck's use of truth and the justification of truth claims.
64. Marshall, "Introduction," viii.
65. Lindbeck, *Church in a Postliberal Age*, 7.

and repentantly, the heritage in the Hebrew scriptures, apostolic writings and early tradition. This retrieval is also more urgent than ever if the churches are to become the kind of global and ecumenical community that the new age needs."[66] Lindbeck's cultural-linguistic theology points us outward from the modern, independent, rational, isolated self, and reminds us that we are always linked to our community. Our community and context shape us whether we like it or not. Indeed, Lindbeck's cultural-linguistic, ecumenical project has been largely descriptive in this regard, but it has many prescriptive implications for providing a climate of generous orthodoxy in our self-saturated societies. We will highlight several of these in the following paragraphs.

Postliberal Intratextuality

As noted above, Lindbeck's cultural-linguistic model is rooted within its own grammar, culture, and language. Rather than seeking to accommodate its program and knowledge claims to the modern expectations that stem from Enlightenment rationality and science, it understands the world in view of its own narrative of the Bible. Lindbeck's perspective is truly "postliberal" in that it does not allow Enlightenment ideals to govern its truth claims, set its agenda, or impose its own terms of reasonability. It does not condescend to outside structures or authorities, but finds its own internal authority within the structure of the community of faith.

Consequently, it eschews the need for a multitude of complex rational and empirical apologetic arguments to defend the Christian faith in view of modernist attacks on its legitimacy. An intratextual approach is self-sustaining within its own narrative.[67] If the Christian narrative allows outsiders to determine its legitimacy, then it is inauthentic, compromising its own integrity.

This emphasis on intratextuality calls us back to the text of the Bible, but not simply as a text to be analyzed and probed, as if it were an

---

66. Lindbeck, *Church in a Postliberal Age*, 9.

67. See Michener, *Postliberal Theology*, 6; Phillips and Okholm, *Nature of Confession*, 12. A criticism of Lindbeck (which he himself recognizes as a weakness) is that he draws upon many and varied outside sources and concepts from anthropology and philosophy to defend his cultural-linguistic approach. He claims that this is "the major structural problem in the book" (Lindbeck, "'I Pray That They Might Be One,'" 71). However, in Lindbeck's defense, using sources outside the narrative to articulate and support a theological approach, is fundamentally different than using the sources to rationally justify the narrative itself or to demonstrate what may be known about the narrative.

encyclopedia of moral lessons and life principles. Rather the text is the story of God working in and through His people, rescuing his people and redeeming all creation. When we allow the biblical story to shape and provide context to our story, we see the overall purpose for theology more clearly. Instead of prioritizing the individual, this story moves the individual into community, opening up avenues for conciliation across traditions and opportunities for rich ecumenical dialogue.

Community and Historical Identity

The notion of Christian community to which we are referring the context of this essay consists of one's particular local faith community as well as the broader tie to the community of faith through history. Lindbeck put it this way: "The ability of the church to foster a sense of community and of personal identity depends on the preservation and enrichment of shared memories of all the communal and individual ways of being Christian which have developed in two thousand years of history."[68] In this sense, community is also about identity—not only with our particular denomination and tradition, but also with the larger history of the Christian faith, and beyond that, to Israel.

To truly internalize our faith story, we must re-connect the Christian gospel with the Jewishness of its roots. N. T. Wright has brought this important point front and center in his theological writings. Jesus Christ was the "embodiment of Israel's returning God" hence his story "enables us to understand the original, historical reality for which those dogmas are later, often dehistoricized, abstract summaries."[69] Much more could be said on the theological thread from Israel to Jesus to the church (including our particular denominational expressions). But for purposes of this essay, Lindbeck's challenge for us to immerse ourselves within the broad story of our faith, provides an important condition for building not only ecumenical unity, but unity within our particular Christian traditions, all of which are tied to this broad theological history.

Lindbeck's perspective on community not only challenges us to recognize our theological unity, but also beckons us to build Christian community in view of this recognition. Rather than being focused on personal ambitions for ministry, personal self-help spirituality courses, or personal interpretations of the Bible, we must intentionally seek out and develop

68. Lindbeck, *Infallibility*, 10, cited in Eckerstorfer, "One Church," 407.

69. Wright, *Simply Jesus*, 175, 176. This issue is pronounced throughout many of Wright's books.

our engagement through, with, and in our local church community. This will not be intuitive for many, and may seem abnormal for others. As Lindbeck aptly states:

> This focus on building Christian community will seem outrageous to some in view of the world's needs, but it is a strength for those who see the weakening of communal commitments and loyalties as modernity's fundamental disease. Perhaps no greater contribution to peace, justice and the environment is possible than that provided by the existence of intercontinental and interconfessional communal networks such as the churches already are to some extent, and can become more fully, if God wills.[70]

The church has always been about "body" (corporate) and community related gifts and practices; Lindbeck's emphasis this direction provides a helpful corrective and reminder in an age where the "I" often takes center stage.

Ecumenical Hospitality

In Lindbeck's grand scheme, both community and ecumenical hospitality are related, prescriptive features that stem from his overall proposal. Some tend to miss that the entire point behind *The Nature of Doctrine* is about "intra-Christian theological and ecumenical issues."[71]

Lindbeck's example of seeking mediation among diverse perspectives is crucial to our work as Christians. Differences are to be embraced, not shunned. But this does not require soft commitments or the reduction of our beliefs to some sort of world Spirit or inclusivism advocated by John Hick. Remaining committed and immersed in our Christian traditions, we must learn from the other, manifesting respect and theological hospitality, showing a willingness to learn from those who maintain different faith practices, yet who share the broad history of faith, as mentioned above. This is the John chapter 17 type of unity that Jesus calls Christians to display in his prayer.

---

70. Lindbeck, *Church in a Postliberal Age*, 8–9.

71. Lindbeck, "'I Pray That They Might Be One,'" 70. Lindbeck suggests that this may be due to the fact that he states his purpose in the introduction, but does not return to it throughout the book. Mike Higton's article "Reconstructing *The Nature of Doctrine*" provides a penetrating analysis of Lindbeck's fundamental ecumenical intentions. Higton submits that Lindbeck's "proposal of a regulative theory of doctrine is, in effect, a proposed sorting and decluttering of the toolbox of practices of ecumenical reasoning—and he suggests that it is to be judged by its ability to make ecumenical reasoning practice a more fruitful pursuit of the basic ecumenical aim" (Higton, "Reconstructing *The Nature of Doctrine*," 23).

This does not mean, however, that we soft-pedal our convictions and particular denominational practices, but we intentionally learn from those who see things differently. If I am Reformed and baptize infants, I want to deeply understand why Baptists only baptize professing Christians, and vice-versa. Transubstantiation is often radically misunderstood by Protestants. Protestants must engage Roman Catholics on this issue to get to the heart of their differences. Seeking fuller understanding does not require agreement, but it does help us get to the essential matters of Christian faith as expressed, for instance, in the early creeds.

In a published conversation in 2012, Lindbeck responded to a question regarding the future of ecumenism. In his view, just as in the past century, we will continue to be plagued by world problems evoking despair and disunity among human beings. In the last century, it was World War Two that cast its dark shadow on hope; today we have ongoing environmental and economic problems. As devastating world issues in the past moved the church to take steps for "visible unity" so our current predicaments will do the same, despite the waning interest in such things now. Nonetheless, Lindbeck is not swayed from his steadfast hope in seeking ecumenical unity in days to come.[72]

Inter-faith Relationships

We also learn from Lindbeck about the importance of learning from persons of other faiths, seeking to understand them without giving up our own ecclesiastical identities. In fact, Lindbeck's "cultural-linguistic model establishes grounds for real receptivity to the rest of the world."[73] We will not rehearse again all the positive aspects of this approach mentioned above, except to emphasize that if we are secure and well-grounded in our particular church community (or denomination) and its theological convictions, we can confidently yet humbly articulate what we perceive to be substantive differences with those of other faiths. If we attempt to boil things down to common ground while avoiding differences, it will only heighten the possibility of tension and avoidance of dialogue. Rather than ignoring doctrinal positions, Lindbeck's position should then motivate us to study well our own faith "grammar" and doctrinal positions within our

---

72. Lindbeck, "'I Pray That They Might Be One,'" 73–74.

73. Thompson, "Question of Posture," 277. Although Thompson appreciates Lindbeck's proposal, he believes any "truths and realities" apart from the church and "related to the grace of Christ" will "likely be dilettante rather than serious" (Thompson, "Question of Posture," 277).

particular traditions. However, this must be done with epistemic humility. This hospitable posturing gleaned from Lindbeck towards other faiths is aptly affirmed by Jeannine Fletcher:

> In the process of encountering people of other faiths in our lived contexts (and even in the more structured setting of interreligious dialogues), it is important to be willing to admit all that we do not know. The encounter with otherness that gives rise to incomprehension is, to follow the thought of Lindbeck, an experience rooted in the reality of diverse cultural-linguistic schemes. Unless one is part of a tradition and shares in its unsubstitutable memories and community-shaping practices, one cannot understand the discrete elements of the faith as one encounters them.[74]

The challenge nevertheless remains to deeply understand and interiorize one's faith tradition, and at the same time manifest epistemic humility and a willingness to acknowledge before the other before us *when* we do not know.

It is best to openly discuss the distinctives of our faith with others in an honest, direct, yet hospitable and amiable manner. In this, we will be acting as charitable representatives of Christ to the world. Of course, this is not an easy task, as many perspectives among religions may be "untranslatable."[75] The Christian understanding of God will not translate into the Hindu understanding since Hindus employ completely different categories of meaning.[76] Nevertheless, this obstacle must not hinder us from seeking conversational opportunities to discuss "untranslatable" concepts and religious practices, and by this manifesting a charitable, service-oriented witness to the Christian faith. After all, if all humans are created in the image of God, then it seems reasonable to suppose that we can learn from various expressions of non-Christian faiths as we think about our own.

Conclusion

George Lindbeck is not simply advocating a "theory" or a perspective on theology. He has devoted his life efforts to a vision of a more unified church. He has sacrificed years of careful research and dialogue to this task—a task that is far from finished. Many have questioned the strength of Lindbeck's proposals,

74. Fletcher, "As Long as We Wonder," 547.
75. See, for instance, Lindbeck, *Church in a Postliberal Age*, 225. This concept of "untranslatability" appears in multiple places in Lindbeck's writings.
76. Moyaert, "Postliberalism, Religious Diversity," 70.

suggesting they are too sectarian to promote either ecumenism or interreligious dialogue. However, as we have seen, this is not the case, especially considering Lindbeck's life's application of the cultural-linguistic approach he is advocating. Certainly, there remains much more to learn from his mediating practices and proposals as we continue to promote a generous orthodoxy from the particularity of our Christian faith traditions.

Bibliography

Eckerstorfer, Bernhard A. "The One Church in the Postmodern World: Reflections on the Life and Thought of George Lindbeck." *Pro Ecclesia* 8.4 (2004) 399–423.

Fletcher, Jeannine Hill. "As Long as We Wonder: Possibilities in the Impossibility of Interreligious Dialogue." *Theological Studies* 68 (2007) 531–54.

Higton, Mike. "Reconstructing the Nature of Doctrine." *Modern Theology* 30.1 (2014) 1–31.

Lindbeck, George. "An Interview with George Lindbeck: Performing the Faith." *Christian Century*, November 28, 2006. 28–35.

———. "Ecumenisms in Conflict: Where Does Hauerwas Stand?" In *God, Truth, and Witness: Engaging Stanley Hauerwas*, edited by L. Gregory Jones, Reinhard Hütter, and C. Roslee Velloso Ewell, 212–28. Grand Rapids: Brazos, 2005.

———. "'I Pray That They Might Be One as We Are One': An Interview with George Lindbeck." In *Postliberal Theology and the Church Catholic: Conversations with George Lindbeck, David Burrell, and Stanley Hauerwas*, edited by John Wright, 55–76. Grand Rapids: Baker Academic, 2012.

———. *Infallibility*. Milwaukee: Marquette University Press, 1972

———. *The Church in a Postliberal Age*. Edited by James Buckley. London: SCM, 2002.

———. "The Gospel's Uniqueness: Election and Untranslatability." *Modern Theology* 13.4 (1997) 423–50.

———. *The Nature of Doctrine: Religion and Theology in a Postliberal Age*. 25th anniversary ed. Louisville: Westminster John Knox, 2009.

Marshall, Bruce D. "Introduction: The Nature of Doctrine After 25 Years." In *The Nature of Doctrine: Religion and Theology in a Postliberal Age*, by George A. Lindbeck, vii–xxviii. 25th anniversary ed. Louisville: Westminster John Knox, 2009.

Michener, Ronald T. *Postliberal Theology: A Guide for the Perplexed*. London: Bloomsbury T&T Clark, 2013.

Moyaert, Marianne. "Postliberalism, Religious Diversity, and Interreligious Dialogue: A Critical Analysis of George Lindbeck's Fiduciary Interests." *Journal of Ecumenical Studies* 47.1 (2012) 64–86.

Phillips, Timothy R., and Dennis L. Okholm, eds. *The Nature of Confession: Evangelicals & Postliberals in Conversation*. Downers Grove, IL: InterVarsity, 1996.

Smith, James K. A. *Who's Afraid of Relativism? Community, Contingency, and Creaturehood*. Grand Rapids: Baker Academic, 2014.

Sommerville, C. John. "Is Religion a Language Game? A Real World Critique of the Cultural-Linguistic Theory." *Theology Today* 51.4 (1995) 594–99.

Thompson, Geoff. "A Question of Posture: Engaging the World with Justin Martyr, George Lindbeck, and Hans Frei." *Pacifica* 13.3 (2000) 267–87.

Thuesen, Peter J. "George Lindbeck on Truth." *Lutheran Quarterly* 10.1 (1996) 47–58.
Wainwright, Geoffrey. "Ecumenical Dimensions of Lindbeck's 'Nature of Doctrine.'" *Modern Theology* 4.2 (1988) 121–32.
Wright, N. T. *Simply Jesus: A New Vision of Who He Was, What He Did, and Why He Matters*. New York: HarperCollins, 2011.

5

John D. Zizioulas: A Pioneer of Ecumenical Dialogue and Christian Unity

—Nikolaos Asproulis

JOHN D. ZIZIOULAS (B. 1931, now Metropolitan of Pergamon, Ecumenical Patriarchate) is widely recognized as the most authoritative thinker and creative spokesman of the Orthodox Church today. A lay theologian, teaching for many years at Glasgow, London and Thessaloniki universities, he became a titular bishop, serving in this way for almost thirty years the constant vision of the Ecumenical Patriarchate towards Christian unity.

Introduction

In 1902[1] Patriarch Ioachim III (1834–1912) encouraged the Christian communities to make every possible effort towards unity. This was an important gesture followed by the famous Patriarchal Encyclical in 1920 calling for the foundation of an ecumenical body, one similar to the League of Nations. After many discussions and reservations, these developments would lead to the foundation in 1948 of the World Council of Churches, joined immediately by many Orthodox churches. After two quite bloody World Wars and the emergence of totalitarian regimes and ideologies in diverse parts of Eastern Europe, certain churches expressed their deep desire to constantly cooperate on the grounds of common concerns. Although the establishment of such an official body, one to deal explicitly with ecumenical dialogue and Christian unity, was initially met with suspicion and hostility by most of the Orthodox churches, the Ecumenical Patriarchate and the majority of Greek-speaking Orthodoxy of that time undertook important

1. Tsetsis, "Ecumenical Dialogue," 321–26.

initiatives in order to theologically justify the need of the Orthodox Church to participate in this movement.[2]

Inspired mainly by certain Greek Fathers (such as the Cappadocians, Maximus the Confessor, and others) but also shaped by the various intellectual and cultural movements of his era, Zizioulas would greatly contribute to the further deepening of such an ecumenically oriented vision, on the ground of his personalistic ontology and eucharistic theology. Expressing both the traditional *ethos* of dialogue encapsulated in the vision and initiatives of the Ecumenical Patriarchate during the previous years, and attempting to address the various fundamentalist trends dynamically increasing within the body of the traditional Orthodox Churches,[3] Zizioulas would note that "I happen to belong to a tradition shaped by the Greek Fathers, and I cannot overlook the fact that the theology of these Fathers transformed the culture of their time. This makes me feel deeply sorry and disappointed when I come across my contemporary fellow-Orthodox who, usually in the name of the faithfulness to the Fathers (!), refuse to open up theology to the challenges of our culture."[4]

If one would like to anticipate Zizioulas's general contribution to the inter-Christian theological and ecumenical scene, one needs to firstly overview both the phases of his involvement in the official ecumenical dialogue and then describe his basic theological insights in order to provide a robust evaluation of his significant ecumenical contribution.

"Faith and Order" Commission, the Bilateral dialogues, and the Holy and Great Synod of Crete (2016)

After his master and doctoral studies at Harvard University (United States) from around 1955 to 1965, which were supported by a scholarship from the World Council of Church (hereafter WCC), and which were completed under the professorial guidance of the German-American Protestant Paul Tillich (1886–1965) and the Russian Orthodox émigré Georges Florovsky (1893–1979), and latter in Athens under the late Greek Orthodox Professor Gerasimos Konidaris (1905–1987), Zizioulas, a young and quite promising Greek theologian of his time, would be appointed by the WCC General Committee to become the Secretary of the "Faith and Order" Commission in 1967, where he stayed up to 1970. This event was of great importance

---

2. Zizioulas, "Self-Understanding," 321.

3. For an overview of the fundamentalist trends in especially Greek speaking Orthodoxy, see Asproulis, "Orthodoxy or Death."

4. Zizioulas, "Faith and Order," 383.

for him, due to the fact that he gained precious ecumenical and theological experience, working at the very center of the ecumenical inter-Christian dialogue. During his three years of responsibility as Secretary, Zizioulas would organize some major events, conferences, and meetings, focusing on issues like: the Christological debate of the Chalcedon Council (451) and the dialogue between the Oriental Orthodox and Eastern Orthodox Churches; the doctrine of the Eucharist and the sacraments of the diverse Christian churches and its relevance for church life; the theological differences between Christianity and Judaism; the meaning of catholicity and apostolicity of the church; the concept of apostolic succession and ordination and many others. In this inter-confessional context, Zizioulas had the opportunity to enrich and deepen his general theological vision in matters closely related to dogmatic and comparative theology (symbolics) with the variety and the richness of the Christian traditions and to further broaden his ecumenical perspective and sensitivity toward the Christian other. Hence, it is not surprising that for him "the Orthodox Church cannot drop out of the ecumenical movement without betraying its own fundamental ecclesiological principles,"[5] something that cannot be easily accepted by the majority of the "Orthodox traditionalists."[6]

According to Zizioulas himself,[7] as Secretary of "Faith and Order" he sought to guide the Commission through a critical situation with a view to the future of the Commission. Although it was widely assumed at that time that the main task of "Faith and Order" was to foster theological dialogue and Christian unity, this was not the case with the WCC itself which was mainly oriented to social issues. Given this ambiguity, one was obliged to ask about the future role and relevance of the Commission within the emerging new priorities of the Council. In the midst of this critical period (1968–1970) two major challenges were raised: on the one hand the demand for restructuring the WCC and the need for "Faith and Order" to be incorporated into the central WCC Organization at the expense of its absorption, and on the other hand the difficult combination in "an organic way" of the Commission's strictly theological agenda (issues strictly related to the dogmatic and doctrinal foundation of the churches) with "horizontalism," the given orientation of the central WCC Organization to social issues. Notwithstanding the challenges of this period, the subsequent developments decisively marked the work of the Commission. This was the case especially regarding the strong support on the part of the Eastern Orthodox

---

5. Zizioulas, "Orthodox Ecclesiology," 309.
6. See, for instance, Demacopoulos, "Innovation in the Guise of Tradition."
7. Zizioulas, "Faith and Order," 380.

for its work against the "enemy of 'horizontalism'" and the full membership of the Roman Catholic Church, which started in the aftermath of the creative developments of Vatican II (1962–1965).[8]

At the same time, however, Zizioulas, being deeply reluctant to any strong reliance of the church's life and theology on mere social issues, would not hesitate to sharply criticize the alleged "ecclesial" character of the WCC, based on non theological or doctrinal grounds, since he shared the opinion that the Council "cannot be turned into a Church, but it must acquire an ecclesial vision shared by all its member churches."[9] In the meantime, however, it could serve as the place of a creative and healthy encounter between Orthodox and Western Christian churches and traditions.

In one occasional paper, entitled "Faith and Order, today and tomorrow,"[10] Zizioulas would provide a general appreciation of the Commission's work, its new challenges and future tasks. He considers the decisive advances of the Commission,[11] since its foundation, as for instance, the focus on the local church by the Nairobi document; the ecumenical document, widely known as the Lima document, dealing with the fundamental sacraments of the church, namely baptism, the Eucharist and ministry; the project of the creedal confession of apostolic faith, supported significantly by Lutheran theologians; and certainly the concept of *koinonia/communion*, as a key concept in ecumenical theology, "as it were, the *heritage* bequeathed"[12] to the subsequent theological generations. It was by the latter development of the incorporation of the *koinonia* concept to its agenda, that Zizioulas understood the openness of the Commission to the entire world, overcoming thus a certain tendency in earlier years towards indifference to the needs and "existential concerns" of the surrounding world. With this move, while remaining faithful to the priority given to theological issues, he sought to overcome any sort of dualism that would separate theology from actual life. One would certainly identify here the method of "correlation,"[13] as developed by the late Paul Tillich, which aims at bringing theology and Christian doctrine into a deep dialogue with the various practical matters and existential concerns of each era.

8. Zizioulas, "Faith and Order," 380.

9. Zizioulas, "Self-Understanding," 327.

10. Zizioulas, "Faith and Order," 379–87.

11. For a systematic introduction to the documents and process of "Faith and Order," see Hovorun, "Official Texts on Ecumenism," 13–19.

12. Zizioulas, "Faith and Order," 381.

13. Tillich, "Problem of Theological Method II," 16–26; Loomer, "Tillich's Theology of Correlation," 150–56.

At the same time, Zizioulas would stress the future task of "Faith and Order." In his view, following the patristic *ethos* of doing theology, the church should open up the frontiers "of theology to other sciences and cultural concerns."[14] In doing so theology should be ready to respond to the gradually emerging and previously unforeseen new scientific and technological challenges, by being based on a culturally relevant hermeneutics of the common tradition. Although he himself did not explicitly put a particular emphasis on hermeneutics in his early work, it appears that in his most recent work the concern for hermeneutics[15] occupies a more central place in his program, to the extent that without hermeneutics of tradition Christian theology would be irrelevant in the midst of a world that seeks to abandon any authoritarian worldview of the past. One could credit this development to his deep involvement in "Faith and Order," which he praised for its "welcome sign that hermeneutics has become part" of its work, applied not only to "biblical . . . but to all tradition as well."[16] However, in order for this goal to be fulfilled, "Faith and Order," in Zizioulas's understanding, must primarily remain a "theological enterprise," focusing on the church's unity in the direction of a common interpretation of the apostolic faith and hermeneutical re-reception of tradition.[17]

Since 1986, when Zizioulas was finally elected as Metropolitan of Pergamon (Ecumenical Patriarchate), he deeply engaged in various ecclesiastical activities related to the bilateral official dialogues of the Orthodox Church with the Anglican and the Roman Catholic churches.

On the one hand, as Chairman of the bilateral dialogue with the Anglican Church (1988), Zizioulas would orientate the discussion towards a more theological agenda, focusing on ecclesiology and its relation to the doctrine of the Holy Trinity, and the relationship between Christology and Pneumatology. The official documents that were produced from these dialogues, such as the *Moscow Agreed Statement* (1976), the *Dublin Agreed Statement* (1984), culminating to the *Cyprus Agreed Statement* (2006), have been more or less marked by Zizioulas's ecclesiological vision and particularly his understanding of primacy and synodality in a Trinitarian and eucharistic perspective.[18]

---

14. Zizioulas, "Faith and Order," 383.
15. Zizioulas, "'La fin est notre point de depart,'" 305–24.
16. Zizioulas, "Faith and Order," 383.
17. Zizioulas, "Faith and Order," 385–86.
18. Martzelos, "Ecclesiological Thought of Metropolitan of Pergamon," 142–43; Asproulis, "*Primacy* and *Conciliarity*," 719–43.

On the other hand, after a long period—since the medieval efforts of the Ferrara/Florence Synod (1438-1445)—of mutual dispute and hostility, the two major Christian traditions, the Roman Catholic and Eastern Orthodox churches met again together in 1980[19] on the Greek island of Rhodes. Because of the problem of Uniatism, it was, however, only in 1982, in Munich, that the official bilateral dialogue between Roman Catholic and Orthodox churches began, being subsequently the place where Zizioulas's contribution has been of indelible influence. Since its very beginning, Zizioulas has been an active orthodox member of the Joint Committee and he worked towards an articulation of its basic tenets, the methodology and the general agenda upon which the dialogue would be based. Particularly, in the first phase of the dialogue (1980-2000), Zizioulas would be chiefly engaged in drafting the common theological documents that would be later approved by the general assembly of the Committee. This was the case with the extremely important key documents (in Munich, 1982; in Bari, 1987; and in New Valamo, 1988), which, by virtue of a more or less common understanding of the eucharistic nature of the church and a common interpretation of the tradition of the undivided church of the first millennium, rendered possible the profound mutual understanding and rapprochement of the "Sister Churches."[20]

Notwithstanding this creative period, the ensuing development of the dialogue would not be as fruitful as it was in the former period. This was due to the political changes which occurred in Central and Eastern Europe with the fall of communism (1989-1990), followed by a tense relationship between the two churches, where Uniatism became the central focus, or rather the alibi for the temporal deadlock of the dialogue, as it was anticipated by the *Balamand Document* (1993). After this impasse for over a decade, the joint commission continued its work in a second phase, from 2006 to today. Now Zizioulas would serve as the co-president of the Joint Committee accompanied by Cardinals Walter Kasper and more recently by Kurt Koch. Although this second phase of the revival of the bilateral dialogue would not be as productive as the initial one, an important text, the *Ravenna Document* (2007), dealing with the "ecclesiological and canonical consequences of the sacramental nature of the Church," would lead to an important revival of the official dialogue. This was, of course, destined to cause serious intra-Orthodox debate.[21] The *Ravenna Document* would be again clearly marked

---

19. For an overview, see Savvatos, "Orthodox Dialogue," 487-90; Asproulis, "*Primacy* and *Conciliarity*," 719-43.

20. Cohen, *Concept of "Sister Churches."*

21. Asproulis, "*Primacy* and *Conciliarity*," 737-43.

by Zizioulas's eucharistic ecclesiology. In this approach, the threefold (regional, local, universal) actualization of conciliarity and primacy was understood as implied in the theo-logic of the early church, as the outcome of the application of the main contours of eucharistic ecclesiology to the approach of the church's nature.

A study of the basic arguments and theological rationale of these documents shows that Zizioulas's ecclesiological thought decisively contributed to the mutual rapprochement of the churches. Beginning with the *Munich Document*, and culminating especially to the *Ravenna Document* (2007), the central place that the Eucharist occupies as the heart of the church in relation to its very being and unity, the importance of the bishop and of the synodical institution for the constitution of the church in various levels (local, regional, universal), the decisive value of the locality as the principle by which the universal church manifests itself in the world and history, and a stark and careful theological interpretation of the issue of primacy are some of the examples of the result of Zizioulas's own contribution to the basis of a common understanding of eucharistic ecclesiology. The great deal of debate that the *Ravenna Document* triggered between the Orthodox representatives led the dialogue to an uncharted path. It obscured its previous quite important achievements towards Christian unity, despite the recent unanimous approval of the *Chieti Document* (2016), which could be considered a real advance of the previous achievements. This increasing unpleasant situation within the Orthodox circles was certainly one of the factors which led Zizioulas to resign the presidency of the Joint Committee in 2015. As it has been aptly reported, "it was precisely his theological authority that inspired unease and underlying hostility in some representatives of the Orthodox Churches."[22]

Furthermore, one would also refer to his direct or indirect contribution to the recently convened (June 2016) Holy and Great Pan-Orthodox Synod in Crete (Greece). It was in 1961, at the Rhodes pan-Orthodox conference, where the goal of the Great and Holy Synod was first announced. Since then a series of pan-Orthodox conferences (in the 1960s), pre-conciliar meetings (1976, 1982, 1986), smaller events leading up to the final pre-conciliar meeting in 2009, and a series of Primates' meetings, took place in order to finally decide the convention of the Synod (2014) and to approve the organization and working procedure of the Synod (January 2016), to set up and finalize the agenda of the issues under discussion in the forthcoming Synod, as well as to overcome various shortcomings.[23]

22. Valente, "Orthodox and Catholics."
23. Gallaher, "Orthodox Moment."

In January 2016, a previously unexpected and completely unforeseen event took place at Phanar in Istanbul.[24] A select group of Orthodox scholars from all around the world was invited to participate with the Ecumenical Patriarch and Zizioulas in an extraordinary meeting on the Future of Orthodoxy and the coming Council. Zizioulas's intervention was indeed tremendous in this regard, since he spent more than three hours discussing the long procedure of the pre-conciliar period, the contemporary challenges, the outdated character of the agenda, as well as the various political factors that put the convention of the Synod itself in danger. A very frank and honest discussion took place, where all the participants had the chance to comment and debate various aspects of the coming Synod. By giving credit to the group of theologians, he called for their responsibility to promote the Council, and to encourage unity. He then ended up by saying that "you (the theologians) all need to write, write, write." This positive attitude towards the role of theologians with regard to the Synod was followed by gestures from the other participants that both undervalued the initially promising contribution of the lay theologians, as well as Zizioulas's own theological legacy. Notwithstanding the positive reception by Zizioulas of the contribution of the select group of scholars at the Phanar meeting, their request to serve as a sort of group of *periti* during the Synod has not been accepted, highlighting the background tendency of Zizioulas's hierarchical perception of ecclesiology.[25] At the same time, while his eucharistic ecclesiology, along with his theology of personhood, have boldly influenced a great deal of his contemporary counterparts from different traditions, such as the late Reformed Colin Gunton (1943–2001) or the Catholic Yves Congar, OP, (1904–1995) to name only a few, the Synod was influenced very little, if at all, by his theological vision. Quite relevant to this direction is the debate between Metropolitan Hierotheos of Naypaktos (Vlachos) and John Zizioulas concerned which Greek words are more proper to refer to humans: human persons (Zizioulas) or human beings (Hierotheos),[26] a case that boldly reveals that the Conciliar fathers in Crete remained mostly uninfluenced by or rather indifferent to the developments in contemporary Orthodox theology, as exemplified by the "neo-patristic synthesis"[27] during the twentieth century, not to mention the tectonic changes and advances in

24. See Ecumenical Patriarchate of Constantinople, "Scholars' Meeting at the Phanar."

25. Gallaher, "Orthodox Moment."

26. For an excellent discussion of the debate at hand, see Ladouceur, "Human Beings or Human Persons?"

27. For the still dominant trend in contemporary Orthodox theology, see Gavrilyuk, *Georges Florovsky and Russian Religious Renaissance*.

various corners of Western theology. This unexpected, I dare to say, defeat of Zizioulas's theology during the proceedings of the Synod manifests the incapacity of the Conciliar fathers to overcome the scholastic way of theologizing, which is still dominant in various circles, and their hostility in view of the challenges posed by the rapidly changing world.

A similar case could be made with the finally approved document "Relations of the Orthodox Church with the Rest of the Christian World," especially with regard to attributing the term "church" to the non-Orthodox traditions, which caused again a debate between the two aforementioned Hierarchs. Zizioulas took the advantage to show that in the patristic literature it was common for the Orthodox Church to always refer to the bodies of those Christians who are not Orthodox as "churches."[28] This became a *causa belli* for those "Orthodox traditionalists" including Metropolitan Hierotheos, who refused to recognize any sort of "ecclesiality" in the non-Orthodox traditions. The result was a really obscured text which tried to keep the balance between the two positions: "In accordance with the ontological nature of the Church, her unity can never be perturbed. In spite of this, the Orthodox Church accepts the historical name of other non-Orthodox Christian Churches and Confessions that are not in communion with her."[29]

The Theological Principles of Zizioulas's Ecumenical Vision

Despite the constructive debate or the often naive criticism addressed against his entire program,[30] Zizioulas still remains a fertile ecumenical thinker, whose ecclesiological thought continues to be of decisive importance for the contemporary witness of Orthodoxy within the ecumenical environment. Following both of his teachers at Harvard University, Florovsky and Tillich, he attempted to develop an ecumenical vision on the ground of the "neo-patristic synthesis" of the former and the existential "correlation" method of the latter, being thus, "capable of leading the West and the East nearer to their common roots, in the context of the existential quest of the modern man."[31] In doing so, his theological program becomes inherently ecumeni-

---

28. A similar discussion is already found in his 1995 article, Zizioulas, "Self-Understanding," 323–24.

29. Holy and Great Council, "Relations of the Orthodox Church," para. 6.

30. For an almost complete list of the primary sources and secondary literature on Zizioulas work, see Asproulis, "Metropolitan John of Pergamon (Zizioulas)," 31–78.

31. Zizioulas, "Introduction," 26.

cal both in scope and method, seeking the visible unity of the *Una Sancta*. Let us turn now to the "first things" of his ecumenical vision:

The Importance of Methodology and Hermeneutics

For anyone familiar with Zizioulas's work, his close reference to the *existential concern* deeply determines his methodological account. By this one especially refers to the questions related to life and death issues, a concern deeply rooted in the very existence of the human being throughout the centuries. In this light, the main task of theology is not just to quote or repeat the sayings and the writings of the Fathers of the Church, a sort of "theology of repetition," but most importantly to seek for the existential relevance of the common Christian tradition, in order to soteriologically address the needs of humanity in our time. In his effort to provide a "dogmatic hermeneutics" and following the existential character[32] and dialogical *ethos* of patristic theology, as it has been brought to the fore by Georges Florovsky, Zizioulas would pose the following critical question: "What would the Fathers say to us today in response to our own concerns, as these are shaped by our Western culture?"[33] During an ecumenical ecclesiological colloquium in Chevetogne (Belgium), in 1986, Zizioulas would openly express his reservation with regards to a profound difficulty in reflecting on the issue of ecclesiology from a specific "orthodox point of view." What lay in the background of his mind was the strong assumption that there is no such orthodox point of view, but only different theological interpretations of the common tradition (Bible, Fathers). Based on such a clear commitment to hermeneutics, Zizioulas would stress that what really matters within the ecumenical movement is primarily the theological presuppositions and not any concrete theses.[34] Towards this end, Zizioulas always makes use of ecclesiology, and especially of the Eucharist, which expresses the nature of the church itself, as the starting point and framework of dealing with Christian doctrine. Since *Ecclesia* is not mainly an institution but more importantly "a way of being,"[35] that is, a way of relating to God, other people and creation in its entirety, dogmatic theology, in the sense of "dogmatic hermeneutics," should certainly be at the center of the ecumenical discussion. This is how his insistence on the primarily theological character of "Faith and Order" should be understood. This plea, however, for a "dogmatic hermeneutics" is

32. Florovsky, "St. Gregory Palamas," 108–9.
33. Zizioulas, *Lectures*, x.
34. Zizioulas, "Mystery of the Church," 136.
35. Zizioulas, "Introduction," 15.

closely linked to the following necessary second step. Drawing on a careful and deep interpretation of the tradition of the Church, the Greek theologian aims at "correlating" the Gospel and the salvific message of the church to the quests of contemporary humanity, which lives in an age completely different from the bygone pre-modern age of the Fathers. This should not be considered as an accommodation of the Good News to the modern *Zeitgeist*, but rather as a vivid interpretation or rather re-incarnation of Christian truth in the language and the life of the contemporary world.[36] This is a necessary goal to be accomplished since, according to Zizioulas himself, "after a rather long experience in ecumenical discussions, I have come to the conclusion that instead of trying to agree on concrete theological theses we should try to agree on theological principles."[37]

Trinitarian Theology

Trinitarian theology constitutes one of the backbones of Zizioulas's entire theological project.[38] In various occasional articles,[39] dealing with Trinitarian theology and mainly based on the legacy of the so-called Cappadocian Fathers (fourth century), Zizioulas wishes to distance himself from the western tendency which closely links the immanent Trinity (God *ad extra*) with the transcendent Trinity (God *ad intra*). By virtue of the central role the eucharistic experience as displayed in the primitive Church, Zizioulas develops a genuine perception of the church not only as community but mainly as an icon, reflecting the communion of the Trinitarian persons (*imago Trinitatis*). The profound Trinitarian roots of his ecclesiology provide the proper means for overcoming the still present problems, often caused by a distorted relationship between Christology and Pneumatology in the field of ecclesiology. As in the intra-Trinitarian life, God the Father, the One, is both the cause and the foundation of the personal otherness of the other two persons (Son and Holy Spirit), in a context of mutual love and communion (the Many). In a similar vein on the level of the church life, the bishop (the one), who presides over the local eucharistic community, is the cause of the unity and the otherness of all the multiple charismata (many), while at the same time he (the bishop) is clearly conditioned by them. The Trinitarian *taxis* of personal relationship and otherness is now transmitted

---

36. Kalaitzidis, "From the Return of the Fathers."
37. Zizioulas, "Mystery of the Church," 137.
38. In this respect, see also Weinandy, "Zizioulas."
39. For instance, Zizioulas, "Father as Cause"; "Trinity and Personhood"; "Pneumatology and the Importance of the Person."

through the eucharistic channel and is realized in the visible structure of the church. Relying on a theological interpretation of the so-called Apostolic Canon 34,[40] and in the light of his Trinitarian ecclesiology, Zizioulas highlights, not uncritically, the decisive importance of primacy (not only on the regional and local, but also on the universal level) always within the context of conciliarity. This is understood as a means of successfully overcoming the impasse concerning the Orthodox understanding of papal primacy, which is regarded as the most serious dividing issue between the Roman Catholic and the Orthodox Church. The debate caused by the *Ravenna Document* as well as all the problems related to the recently convened Synod in Crete are clearly concerned with the strong objections of certain Orthodox churches (primarily the Russian Orthodox Church)[41] and theologians,[42] as expressed with regard to the application of primacy at the universal level. This issue evidently implies a different understanding of ecclesiology.

Eschatology

Zizioulas's emphasis on eschatology[43] in general and on the *eschatological identity* of the church in particular is certainly of utmost ecumenical importance.[44] Following the so-called "eschatological revolution,"[45] namely the overall retrieval of the eschatological vision in the context of Western theology during the early 1920s, he considers eschatology not as the last chapter of the dogmatic textbook, but a kind of "outlook,"[46] a sort of method which needs to inform the entire theological enterprise. According to this eschatological view, where the end, the future, is considered as the cause of the past, the beginning, the church, the proper context of any theological endeavor, is considered not merely as an icon of the Trinity but also or primarily as an icon of the Kingdom of God. This eschatological vision must be constantly

40. Zizioulas, "Primacy in the Church," 269.

41. See Moscow Patriarchate, "Position of the Moscow Patriarchate."

42. See Shishkov, "Primacy in the Church," 32–41. For a discussion, see Asproulis, "Primacy and Conciliarity."

43. Zizioulas has authored many articles dealing with eschatology, such as "Deplacement de la perspective eschatologique," 459–73; "Eschatology and History," 126–35; "Eucharist and the Kingdom of God," 39–82; "Eschatologie et Societe," 475–93; "Towards an Eschatological Ontology,"; "Église et *Eschata*," 12–17; "Eschatology and Existence," 43–72; "'La fin est notre point de depart,'" 305–24.

44. Hays, *When the Son of God Didn't Come*. For an overview of the Orthodox understanding of eschatology, see Begzos, "'L' eschatologie dans l' orthodoxie," 311–28.

45. See Moltmann, *Das Kommen Gottes*.

46. Zizioulas, "Early Christian Community," 147.

reflected into the entire structure and life of the church which is notably revolved around the eucharistic *synaxis*. Appropriating such a genuine eschatological orientation, Zizioulas boldly challenges the ecumenical movement to resist the constant temptation to slide into an "ephemeral secular affair." Thus he reminds his ecumenical counterparts and "sister Churches" that the church is but "a prophetic sign of the Kingdom."[47]

Koinonia

As mentioned above, Zizioulas influenced the recent developments in "Faith and Order." Following a shift made possible between Edinburg and Montreal with regard to ecclesiology, as well as the important developments in Vatican II,[48] *koinonia*, or communion (a deeply biblical and patristic category), became a key concept in the official theological language of the Commission.[49] In this light, he contends that "*koinonia* derives not from sociological experience . . . but because we believe in a God who is in His very being *koinonia*."[50] Based on his interpretation of the Trinitarian being of God and his eschatological ontology, Zizioulas highlights the deeply relational character of the identity, the structure, the authority and the mission of the church, developing thus a robust communion ecclesiology: "Ecclesiology must be based on Trinitarian theology if it is to be an ecclesiology of communion."[51] By his continuous ecumenical efforts, he aspires to render such a relational understanding of ecclesiology, the common ground of an inter-Christian understanding of the identity of the church. In doing so, the quest for a constant re-habilitation and re-reception of the common tradition of the church would provide the ecumenical movement with all the proper means in its struggle against the various challenges and shortcomings of modernity.

Eucharistic Identity of the Church

Because of his emphasis on the eucharistic identity of the church, it is not by accident that Zizioulas praises the *BEM Document* as "a good beginning"[52]

---

47. Zizioulas, "Self-Understanding," 324–25.
48. Zizioulas, "Church as Communion," 50.
49. Zizioulas, "Church as Communion," 49.
50. Zizioulas, "Church as Communion," 51.
51. Zizioulas, "Church as Communion," 51.
52. Zizioulas, "Self-Undestanding," 326.

in keeping the theological and non-secular character of the WCC. For him, the *sacramental* nature of the church is not something secondary in its definition; otherwise the church will become a mere authoritative institution (a typical Roman Catholic tendency), or an activist community (a Protestant tendency) or an archaeological monument (a certain Orthodox tendency). In all these instances, the church is understood as a historical reality, deeply engaged with social and cultural affairs. On the other hand, the church as a sacramental entity, constantly reconstituted by the innovative breath of the Holy Spirit, "asks to receive from God what she has already received historically in Christ as if she had not received it at all."[53] This *epicletic* dimension of the church's life could become the pneumatological input of the Orthodox tradition, interpreted in accordance to the *phronema* of the Fathers, where the church in its nature and life is deeply determined by divine liturgy. Although this perspective is often understood as implying a flight away from history, Zizioulas points out the need to work on a balanced interpretation of the relation between Christology and Pneumatology, so as to overcome the always present tensions.[54] Furthermore, it appears that the sacramental character of the church preserves the dialectic of history and the *eschaton*, of church and the world. Zizioulas frequently recalls that the church is "in the world but not of this world" (e.g., John 15:19), wishing to avoid any kind of conflation or identification of the church with authoritative and oppressive earthly institutions. At this point, however, one should be cautious not to undermine the historical, incarnational dimension of the church in favour of an overemphasis on its eschatological identity, a temptation often evident in various Orthodox accounts of ecclesiology. The priority attributed by Zizioulas to the theological premises, as it is evidenced by his multifaceted engagement in the ecumenical dialogue, should be conceived as a very decisive aspect of his entire program, to the degree that it helps to realize that the final word always remains with God.

Conclusion

Although it is true that Zizioulas himself sometimes boldly criticizes various forms of western theology (for instance, his almost complete devaluation of Augustine,[55] and Aquinas, or his acute division between Eastern personalism

---

53. Zizioulas, "Apostolic Continuity and Succession," 185.
54. Zizioulas, "Christ, Spirit, and the Church." See also McPartlan, *Eucharist Makes the Church*; Berger, "Does the Eucharist Make the Church?," 23–70.
55. Cohen, "Augustine and John Zizioulas."

and Western essentialism, after de Regnon's model),[56] his overall theological enterprise aims at recovering the common tradition as the basis for church unity. Following again Georges Florovsky, he recognizes that "ecumenism in time" should precede and be conceived as the very ground of any kind of "ecumenism in space."[57] Moreover, considering individualism, that is, ecclesiastical *provincialism* and confessionalism,[58] as the basic problems and a real tragedy for the Orthodox Church, he makes a plea for the churches to rediscover the primitive eucharistic and conciliar self-understanding as the proper way of overcoming the obstacles towards Christian unity.

Bibliography

Asproulis, Nikolaos. "Metropolitan John of Pergamon (Zizioulas): Primary Works and Secondary Litterature." In vol. 1 of *Metropolitan of Pergamon John Zizioulas, Ecclesiological Studies, Collected Works*, edited by Stavros Yangazoglou, 31–78. Athens: Domos, 2016.

———. "'Orthodoxy or Death': Aspects of the Greek Religious Fundamentalism During the Twentieth and Twenty-First Century and a Possible Way Out." In *Tradition, Secularization, and Fundamentalism*, edited by Georges Demacopoulos and Aristotle Papanikolaou, 180–203. New York: Fordham University Press, 2019.

———. "*Primacy* and *Conciliarity* in Selected Official Documents of the Inter-Christian Dialogue: An Overview and Critical Assessment with Special Reference to the Ravenna Document." In vol. 2 of *Primacy in the Church: The Office of Primate and the Authority of Councils*, edited by John Chryssavgis, 719–43. Yonkers, NY: St. Vladimir's Seminary, 2016.

Barnes, Rene Michel. "De Regnon Reconsidered." *Augustinian Studies* 26 (1995) 51–79.

Begzos, Marios. "L'eschatologie dans l'orthodoxie du XXe siècle." In *Temps et Eschatologie. Données biblique et problematiques contemporaines*, edited by J.-L. Leuba, 311–28. Paris: Les Éditions du Cerf, 1994.

Berger, Calinic. "Does the Eucharist Make the Church? An Ecclesiological Comparison of Staniloae and Zizioulas." *SVTQ* 51.1 (2007) 23–70.

Cohen, Will. "Augustine and John Zizioulas." In *The T&T Clark Companion to Augustine and Modern Theology*, edited by C. C. Pecknold and T. Toom, 223–38. London: T&T Clark, 2013.

———. *The Concept of "Sister Churches" in Catholic-Orthodox Relations since Vatican II*. Studia Oecumenica Friburgensia 67. Münster: Aschendorff, 2016.

Demacopoulos, George. "Innovation in the Guise of Tradition: Anti-Ecumenist Efforts to Derail the Great and Holy Synod." *Public Orthodoxy*, March 22, 2016. Online. https://publicorthodoxy.org/2016/03/22/innovation-in-the-guise-of-tradition-anti-ecumenist-efforts-to-derail-the-great-and-holy-council.

---

56. See, for instance, Barnes, "De Regnon Reconsidered," 51–79.
57. Zizioulas, "Uniformity, Diversity, and the Unity of the Church," 345.
58. Zizioulas, "Response," 372.

Ecumenical Patriarchate of Constantinople. "Scholars' Meeting at the Phanar." January 7, 2016. Online. https://www.patriarchate.org/el/-/scholars-meeting-at-the-phanar.

Florovsky, Georges. "St. Gregory Palamas and the Tradition of the Fathers." In vol. 1 of *Bible, Church, Tradition, Collected Works*, by Georges Florovsky, 105–20. Belmont: Nordland, 1972.

Gallaher, Brandon. "The Orthodox Moment: The Holy and Great Synod in Crete and Orthodoxy's Encounter with the West: On Learning to Love the Church." *Sobornost* 39.2 (2017) 26–71.

Gavrilyuk, Paul. *Georges Florovsky and the Russian Religious Renaissance*. Changing Paradigms in Historical and Systematic Theology. Oxford: Oxford University Press, 2013.

Hays, Christopher M., et al. *When the Son of God Didn't Come: A Constructive Proposal of the Delay of Parousia*. Minneapolis: Fortress, 2016.

Holy and Great Council of the Orthodox Church. "Relations of the Orthodox Church with the Rest of the Christian World." June 2017. Online. https://www.holycouncil.org/-/rest-of-christian-world?inheritRedirect=true&redirect=%2F&_101_INSTANCE_M8gWCQe69nZW_languageId=en_US.

Hovorun, Cyril. "Official Texts on Ecumenism—A Systematic Introduction." In *Orthodox Handbook on Ecumenism: Resources for Theological Education*, edited by Pantelis Kalaitzidis et al., 13–19. Volos: Volos Academy; WCC; Regnum, 2014.

Kalaitzidis, Pantelis. "From the 'Return to the Fathers' to the Need for a Modern Orthodox Theology." *SVTQ* 54.1 (2010) 5–36.

Ladouceur, Paul. "Human Beings or Human Persons?" *Public Orthodoxy*, June 6, 2017. Online. https://publicorthodoxy.org/2017/06/06/human-beings-or-persons.

Loomer B. "Tillich's Theology of Correlation." *Journal of Religion* 36.3 (1956) 150–56.

Martzelos, George. "The Ecclesiological Thought of Metropolitan of Pergamon in the Framework of the Ecumenical Inter-Christian Dialogue." In *Personhood, Eucharist, and the Kingdom of God in Orthodox and Ecumenical Perspective*, edited by Pantelis Kalaitzidis-Nikolaos Asproulis, 139–52. Volos: Volos Academy, 2016.

McPartlan, Paul. *The Eucharist Makes the Church: Henri de Lubac and John Zizioulas in Dialogue*. Edinburgh: T&T Clark, 1993.

Moltmann, Jürgen. *Das Kommen Gottes. Christliche Eschatologie*. München: Gütersloher, 1995.

Moscow Patriarchate. "Position of the Moscow Patriarchate on the Problem of Primacy in the Universal Church." *Greek Orthodox Theological Review* 59.1–4 (2014) 285–95. Online. https://mospat.ru/en/2013/12/26/news96344.

Shishkov, Andrey. "Primacy in the Church in the Theology of Metropolitan John Zizioulas." Вестник Русской христианской гуманитарной 15.1 (2014) 32–41.

Tillich, Paul. "The Problem of Theological Method II." *The Journal of Religion* 27.1 (1947) 16–26.

Tsetsis, Georges. "Ecumenical Dialogue in the perspective of the Ecumenical Patriarchate." In *Orthodox Handbook on Ecumenism: Resources for Theological Education*, edited by Pantelis Kalaitzidis et al., 321–26. Volos: Volos Academy; WCC; Regnum, 2014.

Valente, Gianni. "Orthodox and Catholics agree on document on Primacy and Synodality." *La Stampa*, September 22, 2016. Online. http://www.lastampa.

it/2016/09/22/vaticaninsider/eng/world-news/orthodox-and-catholics-agree-on-document-on-primacy-and-synodality-38rd8bTllhZ1QyPrPHN3rJ/pagina.html.

Weinandy, Thomas. "Zizioulas: The Trinity and Ecumenism." *New Blackfriars* 83.979 (2002) 407–15.

Zizioulas, John. "Apostolic Continuity and Succession." In *Being as Communion: Studies in Personhood and the Church*, by John Zizioulas, 171–208. Crestwood, NY: St. Vladimir's Seminary, 1985.

———. "Deplacement de la perspective eschatologique." In *L'Église et ses Institutions*, by Jean Zizioulas, 459–73. Paris: Les Éditions du Cerf, 2011.

———. "Early Christian Community." In *The One and the Many: Studies on God, Man, the Church, and the World Today*, by John Zizioulas, 147–69. Alhambra: Sebastian, 2010.

———. "Église et *Eschata*." *Unité de Chrétiens* 184 (2016) 12–17.

———. "Eschatologie et société." In *L'Église et ses Institutions*, by Jean Zizioulas, 475–93. Paris: Les Éditions du Cerf, 2011.

———. "Eschatology and Existence: An Ontological Approach to the Problem of Eschaton." *Synaxis* 121 (2012) 43–72.

———. "Eschatology and History." In *The One and the Many: Studies on God, Man, the Church, and the World Today*, by John Zizioulas, 126–35. Alhambra: Sebastian, 2010.

———. "The Eucharist and the Kingdom of God." In *The Eucharistic Communion and the World*, edited by Luke Ben Tallon, 39–82. London: T&T Clark, 2011.

———. "Faith and Order: Yesterday, Today, and Tomorrow." In *The One and the Many: Studies on God, Man, the Church, and the World Today*, by John Zizioulas, 379–87. Alhambra: Sebastian, 2010.

———. "The Father as Cause." In *Communion and Otherness: Further Studies in Personhood and the Church*, edited by Rowan Williams, 113–54. London: T&T Clark, 2006.

———. "Introduction." In *Being as Communion: Studies in Personhood and the Church*, by John Zizioulas, 15–26. Crestwood, NY: St. Vladimir's Seminary, 1985.

———. "'La fin est notre point de depart.' Pour une ontologie eschatologique." *Revue de Theologie de Philosophie* 147.4 (2015) 305–24.

———. *Lectures in Christian Dogmatics*. Edited by Douglas H. Knight and Katerina Nikolopulu. London: T&T Clark, 2009.

———. "The Mystery of the Church in Orthodox Tradition." In *The One and the Many: Studies on God, Man, the Church, and the World Today*, by John Zizioulas, 136–46. Alhambra: Sebastian, 2010.

———. "Orthodox Ecclesiology and the Ecumenical Movement." In *The One and the Many: Studies on God, Man, the Church, and the World Today*, by John Zizioulas, 309–20. Alhambra: Sebastian, 2010.

———. "Pneumatology and the Importance of the Person." In *Communion and Otherness: Further Studies in Personhood and the Church*, edited by Rowan Williams, 178–205. T&T Clark, 2006.

———. "Primacy in the Church: An Orthodox Approach." In *The One and the Many: Studies on God, Man, the Church, and the World Today*, by John Zizioulas, 262–73. Alhambra: Sebastian, 2010.

———."The Response of the Orthodox Observer." In *The One and the Many: Studies on God, Man, the Church, and the World Today,* by John Zizioulas, 365–72. Alhambra: Sebastian, 2010.

———. "The Self-Understanding of the Orthodox and Their Participation in the Ecumenical Movement." In *The One and the Many: Studies on God, Man, the Church, and the World Today,* by John Zizioulas, 321–32. Alhambra: Sebastian, 2010.

———. "Towards an Eschatological Ontology." Unpublished lecture delivered at King's College, London, 1999, accessed from Zizioulas's private archive.

———. "The Trinity and Personhood." In *Communion and Otherness: Further Studies in Personhood and the Church,* edited by Rowan Williams, 155–77. London: T&T Clark, 2006.

———."Uniformity, Diversity, and the Unity of the Church." In *The One and the Many: Studies on God, Man, the Church, and the World Today,* by John Zizioulas, 333–48. Alhambra: Sebastian, 2010.

Part Two

Overcoming Liberal-Conservative Polarities

6

Hans Frei: Beyond Liberal and Conservative

—Ben Fulford

AT FIRST GLANCE, HANS W. Frei does not fit the profile of an ecumenical theologian. Unlike his colleague, George Lindbeck, he does not appear to have taken a close interest in the ecumenical movement or particular ecumenical dialogues or reconciliation, as Lindbeck did in his *The Nature of Doctrine*. Yet he did seek a way beyond entrenched polarities in modern western Christian theology that run through many ecclesial traditions. In a manner overlooked by the literature on Frei (and for a time obscured by polemics that associated him with a Yale School postliberalism over against a (liberal) Chicago revisionism), he framed his project in terms which sought explicitly to transcend and relativise the conservative-liberal polarity.[1] Beyond that firmly institutionalized division in modern western theology, Frei sought a "generous orthodoxy," a term associated with him but whose meaning in his thought has not received adequate attention.[2] What

---

1. Of the several excellent extended treatments of Frei's work available, none focuses on this important aspect of his analyses. See Campbell, *Preaching Jesus*; Demson, *Hans Frei and Karl Barth*; Dawson, *Christian Figural Reading and the Fashioning of Identity*; Higton, *Christ, Providence, and History*; DeHart, *Trial of Witnesses*; Springs, *Toward a Generous Orthodoxy*; Fulford, *Divine Eloquence and Human Transformation*; Boniface, *Jesus, Transcendence, and Generosity*; Shin, *Theology and the Public*. See DeHart, *Trial of Witnesses*, 30–42, for the history of this polemical framing of Frei as a postliberal.

2. See, e.g., Hunsinger, "Hans Frei as Theologian," 123; Springs, *Toward a Generous Orthodoxy*, 17, 23; Boniface, *Jesus, Transcendence, and Generosity*, xii. They rightly find Frei exemplifying a combination of liberal scholarly values and doctrinal orthodoxy (Hunsinger); the interplay of Christ-oriented traditions and innovation in engagement with nontheological voices (Springs); and a way between closed and open religion grounded in the union of historical particularity and divine transcendence in Jesus Christ, but they miss the ethical and political dimension of Frei's concept and project. Mike Higton sees this connection and goes some way to displaying it in his discussion of the Frei's figural reading of history and political theology in Higton, *Christ, Providence and History*, esp. 4, 167–73.

Frei was after was an approach to Christian theology in the context of the University that took and tailored appropriate theoretical concepts in order to elucidate the meanings and rationality of Christian belief and practice in light of the primary norm instantiated in that practice—the irreducibly particular yet universally significant public identity of Jesus Christ in New Testament narratives. It was at the same time a search for a way of doing theology that would fostered a profoundly humanistic cultural vocation and careful, progressive political engagement for Christianity as a minority religion in western societies.

Frei's Background and Context

Hans Frei came from a family of secularised German Jews.[3] His family were patriotic with a long history in Germany on both sides. The worsening atmosphere toward Jews in Nazi Germany convinced Frei's parents first to send him away to school in England, in 1935, and eventually to emigrate to New York, in 1938. It was at a Quaker school in Saffron Waldon that Frei had some kind of conversion experience focused on a picture of Jesus Christ.[4] In the US, Frei won a scholarship to study textile engineering at North Carolina State University, where he heard H. Richard Niebuhr speak. He went on to study theology at Yale Divinity School and subsequently to pursue a doctorate on Karl Barth's break with liberalism under Niebuhr's supervision. He returned to Yale in 1957 after spells teaching elsewhere and taught there till his death in 1988.

Frei was deeply involved in the life of Yale University, not least during the transformational presidency of Kingman Brewster (1963–1977), when Frei took on significant institutional responsibilities (especially the role of Master of Ezra Stiles, one of Yale's residential colleges, in 1972). Some of Frei's writings from this time touch on Vietnam, the Civil Rights movement, the rise of black consciousness in the US, campaigns for nuclear disarmament, and US foreign policy (especially in Latin America and Libya).[5]

Hans Frei never really found an enduring ecclesial "home." His parents had him baptised as a child in the Protestant State Church of Prussia.[6]

---

3. The sources for most of this paragraph are Woolverton, "Hans W. Frei in Context"; Higton, *Christ, Providence and History*, 15–20.

4. Frei, Untitled autobiographical notes, 1.

5. See Frei, *Theology and Narrative*, 172, 213–33; *Identity of Jesus Christ*, 162–63; *Writings from the Archives*, 170–72. I hope to tell the story of Frei's own politics in my forthcoming *God's Patience and our Work*.

6. Woolverton, "Hans W. Frei in Context," 375.

He had some connexion with the Quakers in Berlin, and later of course was converted in a Quaker school.[7] When he went to North Carolina State University to study textiles, however, he joined a Baptist young people's fellowship. After studying theology at Yale Divinity School, he became a Baptist pastor in New Hampshire, but was drawn to Anglicanism and what he described as its "generous (liberal) orthodoxy."[8] He was ordained priest in the Episcopalian Church in 1952.[9] He taught at the Episcopal Seminary of the Southwest, in Austin, Texas from 1953 until his appointment to Yale in 1957. Yet it was from this time in Austin that Frei would later date the beginnings of doubts about being an Anglican. His heart, he wrote to his friend John Woolverton in 1980, was not in its worship or ethos. He found Quaker meetings "glorious" but recognised that it would not do and did not have much to do with his theological convictions.[10] He believed theology should be written in an ecclesial context, but that context was not Anglican and he was not sure what it was. Yet Frei would seem to have remained an Anglican in some measure. David F. Ford recalls asking Frei about his church practice when Frei was in Birmingham (UK) for the Cadbury lectures in 1987, and describes Frei's Anglican spirituality as prayer-book, consisting in Morning and Evening Prayer.[11] In any case, Frei's theological writings belong less in an overtly Anglican tradition and rather, as Woolverton pointed out, in the broad context of Reformed theology and especially John Calvin, the New England puritans, Jonathan Edwards and Karl Barth, and looking back to Augustine and Anselm.[12]

Generous Orthodoxy: A Voice between Liberalism and Evangelicalism

If Frei sought to make an ecumenical contribution it was not at the level of doctrinal reconciliation between denominations or Churches. As he explained in a response to a paper on Narrative Theology by the evangelical theologian Carl F. H. Henry, he saw Christians in the United States split not so much along denominational lines as into "schools of thought."[13] What

7. Frei mentions Quakers in Berlin in his Untitled autobiographical notes, 1.
8. Frei, Untitled autobiographical notes, 1. Frei also uses this term in the notes (1) to describe the outlook of Robert L. Calhoun, one of his teachers at Yale.
9. Campbell, "Hans W. Frei," 151.
10. Frei, "Letter to John Woolverton."
11. Ford interview with the author, University of Nottingham, April 14, 2015.
12. Woolverton, "Hans W. Frei in Context," 393.
13. Frei, *Theology and Narrative*, 208.

was needed, he suggested, was a kind of "generous orthodoxy which would have in it an element of liberalism . . . and an element of evangelicalism."[14] He sought a voice between *Christian Century*—the periodical of progressive mainstream liberal Christianity in the US in the twentieth century—and the evangelical voice of *Christianity Today*, which was founded to express an informed, evangelical outlook on contemporary affairs (whose first editor was Carl Henry).[15] In fact, the rest of his response to Henry implies that Frei saw his own work, including the argument of *The Eclipse of Biblical Narrative* and the project on which he was then engaged, in these terms.[16] The passage suggests a combination of self-critical, politically progressive openness with a deep commitment to a normative heart to Christianity but its meaning is best understood in the context of Frei's search for the essence of Christianity and for a kind of theology would best attend to and nurture that essence.

In a lecture at Harvard University in 1967, he argued that the question of the essence of Christianity should be re-opened, and that to answer that question one should begin with the realistic narratives of the synoptic Gospels and their character as narratives, whose narrative qualities make possible normative interpretations that do not depend on the perspective of the interpreter.[17] Later, he began to explore the thesis that that essence or identity was bound up with basic minimal norms of practice instantiated in the use of certain biblical narratives in Christian communities, and to ask about the theological conditions under which that characteristic usage waned or flourished.

Liberals and Conservatives in *The Eclipse of Biblical Narrative*

Basic to the argument of *Eclipse* is Frei's identification of something very like the essence he had first proposed in his Harvard lecture as a characteristic of pre-modern Western Christianity. Before the rise of historical criticism in the eighteenth century, Western Christians read the biblical stories in the canon most important to Christianity both literally and historically, that is to say they took the subject of these stories to be their meaning and they assumed that such stories depicted actual historical occurrences. By seeing

14. Frei, *Theology and Narrative*, 208.

15. Paul DeHart sees this quest as a response to the bifurcation between "conservative repristinators . . . and radical progressives" in the 1960s and 70s (DeHart, *Trial of Witnesses*, 13–14).

16. Frei, *Theology and Narrative*, 208, 211.

17. Frei, *Theology and Narrative*, 31–32.

earlier stories as prefiguring events in later tales, these readers construed the unity of the canon in terms of a single composite narrative referring to a single history. They took this history to be the history of the world, embracing their own times and circumstances. The story shifted and changed as it was variously construed and employed in the interpretation of experience, but it performed the same function until the onset of modernity. As the world began to be construed in terms independent of that story, however, questions arose about the relationship between the texts and the events they depicted and to the world of the reader. As exegetes, theologians and hermeneutical theorists sought to address these questions, often in order to commend the rationality of Christianity, they conceived of the meaning of biblical narratives as consisting in its referring to or describing some putative reality beyond the text. That referent or subject matter might be historical (such as Jesus' miracles or the origins of the world), or it might be a set of rational ideas or universal features of human existence.

Insofar as these thinkers found the biblical stories raising questions of historical factuality, they acknowledged a key feature of the texts which had been to the fore in pre-modern readings: their realistic narrative character. This quality Frei understood to denote the kind of story in which characters are "firmly and significantly set in the context of the external environment, natural but more particularly social," so that both characters and circumstances are rendered cumulatively by their interaction in a chronological sequence.[18] Yet, primarily because of their understanding of meaning in these narratives as being about (or referring to) something beyond the text, these thinkers were unable to attend to these narratives as realistic narratives, that is, to the particular way in which they render character and circumstances in chronological sequence. Frei had in mind primarily the realistic narrative components of Genesis and the Gospels. It is not difficult to infer that his chief concern lies with the Gospels and the impact of the eclipse he identifies on Christology: with the way that the character of Jesus rendered in the Gospels is elided or falls out of focus under these procedures.[19] What is significant for my argument here is that Frei traced this development both in English and German theologians and biblical interpreters whom he labelled as liberals and in those he labelled as conservatives, whom he sees not as polar opposites but as disagreeing (along with radicals) within a common outlook which differentiated them significantly from pre-modern theologians.

18. Frei, *Eclipse of Biblical Narrative*, 13–14.

19. Hence Frei's constructive proposals on theological hermeneutics contemporary with *Eclipse* focus on the narrative meaning of the Synoptic Gospels (and especially their more realistic sections) as rendering the character of Jesus Christ.

The core issue here concerned the "miracle-tinged" New Testament stories claiming a unique revelatory status for Jesus as the Messiah. Were these stories to be taken literally? If so, were they reliable, historically? And was this historical revelation essential to human salvation?

On Frei's account, the debate on this question ranged between the extremes not of liberal and conservative, but of orthodox dogmatism and radical scepticism. The former asserted revelation as uniquely salvific and miraculous, locating their positivity—the direct intervention of God in the finite realm—firmly in the narrated events literally understood.[20] The latter denied positivity altogether: revelation was not to be found in unique historical events warranted by miracles, but in a theistic natural religion. Between these options were the mediating theologians, and their dilemma between positive revelation and natural religion represented "a typical instance of the ancient recurrent puzzle whether the liberal . . . has a position with an integrity of its own."[21] The German Neologians illustrated this liberal instability, for Frei. They located historical positivity in Jesus' personal bearing and character, and made an exception for the events in which these were manifested, from the historical conditioning they found in other elements of the stories, such as miracles. Although the stories are time-bound, their real meaning somehow is not, and their authors manage to transcend historical relativity just where it is most evident.

Frei did not find the same instability in conservative positions, but did find in them the effects of the profound shift he explores in *Eclipse*, as exemplified in another eighteenth-century constituency, whom Frei labels the Supernaturalists. They argued for the literal truth, inspiration and factual reliability of Scripture by appeal to "general, rational canons of meaning and general criteria for factual probability."[22] A host of argument supported claims to the reliability of biblical narratives and hence the historical factuality of their reports of miracles and fulfilment of prophecy: the apostolic origin of the New Testament writings, the evangelists' integrity, the congruence of miracles with rational religion, the simplicity and life-likeness of the reports, and the way the shape of events narrated by the New Testament fulfilled Old Testament anticipations. The strategy of these "conservatives" represented a shift away from orthodox and pietist appeals to "the immediately inspired text that it had been to orthodox and pietist commentators."[23] What is more, the supernaturalist approach also mirrored liberal assumptions

20. This definition of positivity comes from Frei, *Eclipse of Biblical Narrative*, 58.
21. Frei, *Eclipse of Biblical Narrative*, 62.
22. Frei, *Eclipse of Biblical Narrative*, 86–87.
23. Frei, *Eclipse of Biblical Narrative*, 87.

about textual meaning, that "historical explanation governs explication of the text" in the case of these narratives.[24] Hence conservatives and liberals both focused increasingly on the "identity of explicative meaning with the historical or ostensive reference of the texts."[25]

Frei also finds eighteenth-century conservatives and liberals—and their nineteenth- and twentieth-century heirs—disagreeing in relation to a shared apologetic agenda of commending "the religious and moral meaningfulness of [Christianity's] chief beliefs."[26] Eighteenth-century liberals and conservatives wrote in dialogue with the adherents of natural religion, disagreeing with them and with one another over the significance of historical revelation in Christ. Conservatives held that the religious truths of the Bible depended entirely for their meaning on the historical events through which they were revealed and urged the rationality of their literal meaning. Rationalists held that the real religious meaning of the Bible, judged by external criteria, was non-literal and hence independent of positivity. Liberals affirmed both the indispensability of belief in the events the Bible reported (historically reconstructed), but related the ideal religious meaning or truth they communicated to a context of religion and morality broader than the Bible. All therefore shared the assumption that the biblical stories were still religiously meaningful, and this assumption shaped their interpretation of them. Here positive, historical faith in Jesus as Messiah, which faith is meaningful only as an indispensable solution to a universally experienced moral lack or dilemma.[27] Conservatives, radicals, and liberals were all, on Frei's analysis, playing a similar game, and all at once recognizing and failing to attend to the realistic meaning of biblical (and especially its christological) narratives. Insofar as Frei gestures in the book toward the possibility of doing theology in a way that attended to that meaning, he gestured to a path that lay beyond the terms in which modern western theologians disagreed with one another, a path which attends primarily to the narrated figure of Jesus and tailors its mode of reading and hermeneutical tools accordingly, and which grounds the possibility of a figural vision of history and a constructive engagement in secular politics with and for the sake of one's fellow humans.[28]

---

24. Frei, *Eclipse of Biblical Narrative*, 87.
25. Frei, *Eclipse of Biblical Narrative*, 87.
26. Frei, *Eclipse of Biblical Narrative*, 117.
27. Frei, *Eclipse of Biblical Narrative*, 125.
28. See "Karl Barth: Theologian," in Frei, *Theology and Narrative*, esp. 172–73

Liberals and Conservatives in the Later Frei

One also finds a similar bringing together of conservatives and liberals in the analysis of the later lectures and papers gathered his posthumous *Types of Christian Theology*. Frei's main concern in these and some other contemporary pieces is to inquire into what relationship between the Christian community's self-description and other forms of academic inquiry is most hospitable to the basic Christian practice of literal reading of Christian Scriptures.

Frei identifies literal reading as a stable tradition in terms of a set of minimal, flexible rules identifiable from broad areas of agreement in the uses of the text in Christian community and which hold through various shifts in the practice and its conceptualisation over history.[29] The most important of those rules is what Frei elsewhere called the literal ascription of the gospel narratives to the character of Jesus of Nazareth, that is: that the stories were taken to concern *him* primarily. This literal reading of these stories then took precedence over other meanings and in the reading of the Old and New Testaments as a unity (another regulative consensus in Christian tradition). Finally, the consensus covered a sense both of the adequacy of the enactment of authorial intentions in the text (so that the text is the focus of interpretive activity) and of the harmony between the meaning of the text and the subject matter it depicted, so that the text depicted that subject matter adequately. In effect, Frei thus re-worked his account of the essence of Christianity advanced in *Eclipse*.[30] He then asked how such literal reading fared in different ways of relating Christian theology as the Christian community's conceptual self-description of Christian beliefs and practices to concepts drawn from other disciplines native to theology's context as an academic subject, such as philosophy. It is important to note that part of his argument is that there should be a positive relationship here because Christian beliefs and belief-ful practices have content, and raise questions of truthfulness.[31] This inquiry produces a five-fold typology ranging between two poles which resolve the ambiguities of Christian theology (as something for the church and as an academic discipline) by subordinating it to a general philosophy or by eschewing any relationship

---

29. Frei gives accounts of the rules comprising literal reading or the *sensus literalis* in Frei, *Theology and Narrative*, 101–4, 110–13, 120–23; *Types of Christian Theology*, 15–16, 56–57, 137–43.

30. For accounts of the development of Frei's thought, see DeHart, *Trial of Witnesses*, 2–40.

31. Frei, *Theology and Narrative*, 95–96.

with philosophy (broadly defined) on philosophical grounds. Both are inimical to literal reading as defined by Frei.

For my purposes here, it is significant that Frei locates liberals and conservatives at neither extreme of his typology. Rather, "the typology cuts right across the ordinary lines of liberal and conservative."[32] They can be found together in Type Five (theology eschewing conceptual re-description in favour of the primacy of biblical language).[33] Liberals and conservatives may also be found together in Type Two (where theologians systematic correlate Christian meanings to general criteria of meaning and truth taken from a philosophical account).[34] Frei takes the liberal Roman Catholic David Tracy and the conservative evangelical Carl F. H. Henry to be similar in this way.[35] Most strikingly, Frei places the archetypal "liberal," Friedrich Schleiermacher, and the archetypal "postliberal," Karl Barth, in close proximity within the typology (Types Three and Four respectively) on account of the way their theologies draw on philosophical conceptual schemes and historical critical insights and procedures in order to articulate the meanings of Christianity without subordinating Jesus Christ systematically to them (more successfully in Barth's more thoroughly *ad hoc* approach to appropriating philosophical concepts and historical inquiry).[36]

I have not space to examine how far Frei's problematization of the liberal-conservative polarity does justice to those Frei examines or the range of thinkers to whom either label might be applied, but I hope I have done enough to indicate both the potential of his approach to disrupt habits of thought about these categories and how far this disruption was part of his project. For Frei in this period of his thought, where Christian theology's public character is mediated through its tensed relationship with the modern university, the real question is not liberal versus conservative. It is rather whether it is better to safeguard the primacy and integrity of the narrated figure of Jesus Christ in Christian practice and the claims he makes upon human beings by having that figure govern Christian

32. Frei, *Theology and Narrative*, 24. People who "give priority to either Christian self-description or Christian theology as a member of a class of disciplines . . . can show up as liberal or conservative" (Frei, *Theology and Narrative*, 27).

33. Frei, *Theology and Narrative*, 4.

34. Frei, *Theology and Narrative*, 4; *Types of Christian Theology*, 24.

35. Later in *Types of Christian Theology*, Frei contrasts Barth to liberals like Kaufman and Tracy and conservatives like Henry who claim there is a general context-invariant criteriology (Frei, *Types of Christian Theology*, 45). He also casts liberals and fundamentalists as "siblings under the skin" in confusing literal reading of the text as being about Jesus with knowing a historical reality (the category mistake analyzed in *Eclipse*) (Frei, *Types of Christian Theology*, 84).

36. Frei, *Types of Christian Theology*, 70–91.

theologians' *ad hoc* use of concepts and historical-critical procedures at the risk of impairing the public intelligibility of that usage (Barth), or whether it is better to augment that intelligibility by respecting the integrity of the conceptual schemes or historical-critical procedures they use, at the risk of diminished conceptual flexibility and practical orientation and the potential subversion of literal reading should the scheme come to determine textual interpretation (Schleiermacher).[37] One had to cut one's losses one way or another, and in the end Frei came down on the side of the first option, but not without a deep appreciation of the judgment involved in affirming the second option—and indeed the motivations of all the ideal positions represented in his typology.[38] Here again Frei's concern for a flexible, resilient essence of Christianity—a generous orthodoxy—was coupled with the social engagement of Christianity. For his sense was that its flourishing was essential to any future contribution which Christian communities might make to a post-Christian western culture, including its political life and search for justice, as a liberally humanistic, and where society polarizes, a reconciling presence.[39]

Toward a Generous Orthodoxy

Theological Method

Frei sought an alternative that would not only transcend the liberal/conservative divide but also be more faithful to what he saw as the heart of Christian identity. Having identified an essence to Christianity (in its prioritising of certain realistic narratives, especially those concerning Jesus Christ), he argued for an approach to theology would best support the critical self-description of Christian belief and practice normed by the analysis of those texts' rendering of the identities of God, Jesus and human creatures. This norm is a narrative picture of Jesus to which Christian tradition gave priority, warranted by its beliefs in the Incarnation and the presence of Christ.[40] In embodying this norm in its varied reading practices and theological discourse, Frei thought, the Christian tradition has prioritised a feature of the text that is relatively robustly distinguishable from readers' perspectives.[41]

37. Frei, *Theology and Narrative*, 197.
38. Frei, *Types of Chrtistian Theology*, 90.
39. Frei, *Theology and Narrative*, 149; "Epilogue," 281.
40. Frei, *Theology and Narrative*, 32.
41. See Frei, *Types of Christian Theology*, 86–87 and the accounts of Frei's position in Higton, "Hans Frei," 231; Springs, *Toward a Generous Orthodoxy*, 148–65; Fulford, *Divine Eloquence*, 261.

For Frei its meaning takes priority over all doctrinal and confessional articulations of Christian doctrine: "The meaning of the doctrine is the story" and not the other way around; a condition of ecumenical generosity.[42] In Frei's work culminating in *Identity* and his later writings, he argues for an approach to theological method which upholds the primacy of these stories.

First, Frei advocated that theology should be dogmatic, rather than apologetic. Apologetic theologies, liberal and conservatives, sought to make Christian claims meaningful by arguing for the possibility for Christocentric faith in human existence.[43] With Karl Barth, Frei asserted that the possibility of the Incarnation, the human need for Christ and the possibility of faith in Christ all follow from follows from the actuality of Christian truth. Because God became human in Christ, we know that God's transcendence does not preclude this immanence, we know that we need this Incarnate Reconciliation, and that it is possible to believe in the Redeemer.[44] The data of human experience and behaviour is far too ambiguous to support a plausible apologetic approach to theology.[45] We need, instead, to distinguish the logic of belief—the rationality of the content of Christian faith normed by the Scriptural identification of God, Christ and human creatures in the stories about Jesus Christ (taken as the culmination of the story of God and Israel)—from the logic of coming to belief: the various motives and reasons by which people come to affirm this content.[46] The two are quite distinct.

The task of theology is, instead, a dogmatic one: to explicate the rational structure of Christian faith as normed by the scriptural narrative identification of God, Christ and us. This stance, however, is more basically founded on Frei's commitment to the priority of the scriptural narrative identification of Jesus Christ, the verbal icon of the Word incarnate, in theological method. Here we find—as Frei's argument in *Identity* exemplifies—the rational pattern of Christian belief set forth normatively in the form of a story. That pattern sets forth the identity of Israel's God, the creator, as both transcendent yet active in and through history in an unparalleled way, fully manifest in the person of the risen Jesus of Nazareth; it sets forth the unique identity of Jesus as entirely human yet (as shown in his resurrection) inseparable from that of this God and full of divine life. To follow and accept the logic of Christian faith—the pattern of

---

42. Frei, *Types of Christian Theology*, 90.
43. Frei, *Theology and Narrative*, 29–30.
44. Frei, *Theology and Narrative*, 30, 171.
45. Frei, *Theology and Narrative*, 171.
46. Frei, *Identity of Jesus Christ*, xii.

Christ's identity—is to believe him to be present.[47] Theology is an exercise in rational doxology inhabited by Christ's presence.[48]

To this irreducibly specific, strange and unique logic, none of our concepts are adequate, in the end.[49] Theology cannot aspire to explain its subject matter, by accounting for how this identity is possible in terms conforming to a general theory of things. Nor can there be any systematic correlation between the gospel and any conceptual scheme without distorting the gospel. Rather, our concepts must be chosen carefully so as not to overwhelm the logic of the story, they must be adopted *ad hoc* and subordinated to the story.[50] For the logic of the story escapes capture by our concepts, and we do best to scramble methods in subordination to it.[51] Its subject matter is abidingly mysterious, as Frei repeatedly emphasizes.[52] Hence there is something fragmentary about this kind of descriptive theological reasoning.[53] The coherence of its conceptual usage lies in its subject, Jesus Christ; the adequacy of it depends upon his making himself present in and through it.[54] The manner by which we thereby signify him "remains unknown in this life and to this life's reason."[55] In such analogical use, the overlap between theological and ordinary usage does not over-determine the former but makes the rational character of the latter intelligible and open to conversation with external discourses and to external challenge.[56]

In articulating this approach, Frei made *ad hoc* use of a variety of philosophical and social science conceptualities, and shows a degree of affinity with reactions to philosophical idealism, and with linguistic pragmatism in philosophy after Wittgenstein.[57] However, he does not advance nor really depend upon the overall coherence or cogency of any general philosophy

---

47. Frei, *Identity of Jesus Christ*, 146, 149, 151–52.
48. Frei, *Identity of Jesus Christ*, 5.
49. Frei, *Identity of Jesus Christ*, 125.
50. Frei, *Types of Christian Theology*, 85–86.
51. Frei, *Theology and Narrative*, 40–41.
52. Frei, *Identity of Jesus Christ*, 74–75, 105, 140, 155–63; *Types of Christian Theology*, 90.
53. Frei, *Types of Christian Theology*, 90.
54. Frei, *Identity of Jesus Christ*, 25; *Types of Christian Theology*, 78–9.
55. Frei, *Types of Christian Theology*, 91.
56. Frei, *Theology and Narrative*, 209. See also Adonis Vidu's discussion in Vidu, *Postliberal Theological Method*, 147–50, 153–54.
57. See also DeHart, *Trial of the Witnesses*, 103. Jason A. Springs brings out Frei's pragmatic tendencies in his *Toward a Generous Orthodoxy*, helpfully defending and illuminating Frei's position, esp. in 121–66.

of personal identity nor of linguistic meaning.[58] His stance is driven by his basic theological commitment to the priority of the Jesus Christ rendered in the stories of Scripture and he appropriates a bricolage of philosophical insights which illuminate but do not overwhelm the scriptural storied pattern of Christological meaning prioritized in Christian tradition. It is an approach which eschewed apologetic strategies without forsaking the making public of the peculiar rationality of Christian belief.

The Identity of Jesus Christ and Social Ethics

This approach to theology, Frei claims, allows us to attend analytically and existentially to the identity of Christ in order to understand his presence with us, which Christians of all traditions and confessions affirm. Frei's analysis there of Christ's presence by way of his identity leads to the heart of the former's generous orthodoxy: a high Christology that entails a humanistic theological imagination and a progressive social ethics.

Frei's describes Jesus as someone with "unsubstitutable individuality and universal saving scope," a figure who is too concretely individual to be mythical but whose uniquely singular identity makes a claim upon every reader.[59] He does so by attending to the renderings of Jesus' identity in the synoptic gospels (taking Johannine and Pauline texts as commentary on the story they variously tell).[60] Frei looks both for Jesus' characteristic actions in particular episodes, as revealing his typical "stance," and the continuous enactment and embodiment of selfhood through changes.

Frei finds Jesus' characteristic intention to be obedience for God in love for human beings, enacted in his redemptive, vicarious identification with them in their guilt and helplessness, an intention most clearly articulated in the Lukan stories of Jesus' temptation (Luke 4:1–13; cf. Matt 4:11), the commencement of his ministry (Luke 4:14–44), and the final Lukan passion prediction (Luke 22:37), but above all the Garden of Gethsemane episode in the passion narrative.[61] This intention is enacted in the whole passion-resurrection sequence, where Jesus' intentions coincide with his divinely ordained circumstances and he undergoes a transition from power

58. In contrast, see Knight, *Liberalism versus Postliberalism*, 9–12, 138–40, 161–62, 198–201, 206–24.

59. Frei, *Identity of Jesus Christ*, 74.

60. Frei tends to treat the synoptics as telling a common story in different ways, which have sufficient overlap in terms of the identity they render to be treated together. See Frei, *Theology and Narrative*, 43, 77.

61. Frei, *Identity of Jesus Christ*, 108–11.

to powerlessness in which he retains saving power of divine magnitude.[62] This same transition involves an increasing emphasis on the agency of God, which climaxes in the resurrection accounts where God alone is active, yet in a veiled manner, and where the presence of divine action is marked only by the risen Christ.[63] This sequence also completes the full manifestation of Jesus as an irreducible individual in the story who has come thereby to define his titles.[64] The force of this cumulative identification of Jesus forces the question of his reality, for he is identified as one whose identity involves his living presence, one who cannot be thought not to live.[65] For his identity is inseparable yet distinct from the identity of God, since Jesus is manifest in his resurrection as the embodiment of God's unmediated presence.

For this same reason Frei's much misunderstood account of Christ's resurrection affirms his bodily resurrection as the logical conclusion to his story.[66] If Jesus is who the story says he is, then he must be alive and bodily risen, since he lives with God's own life.[67] While the discovery of a corpse would refute such a claim, the claim is without historical analogue and impossible to argue from evidence or rational possibility. As such is also an awkward fit for the (historically contingent) concept of historical fact. Hence the textual gesture to an extratextual reality is not like ordinary linguistic referencing; the reference holds because Christ is really present in a unique way and willing to be identified and recognised by way of this story. Its truthfulness also cannot be captured simply in terms of correspondence, for it also involves a claim upon the dispositions of the believer toward God and neighbor. Indeed, for the believer, it involves a recasting one's historical imagination and requires a rethinking of the category of history.[68]

Such is the character of Frei's orthodoxy but it also has generous implications. First, Frei argues in later writings that Jesus Christ's particular identity is both representative and inclusive of all humanity, and he remains

---

62. Frei, *Identity of Jesus Christ*, 112–15. He tells us that Jesus' followers in the early church "did not doubt that the work of saving men was the work of omnipotence" (Frei, *Theology and Narrative*, 49). I owe this reference to Hunsinger, "Hans Frei as Theologian," 118.

63. Frei, *Identity of Jesus Christ*, 116–25.

64. Frei, *Identity of Jesus Christ*, 135–38.

65. Frei, *Identity of Jesus Christ*, 141–48.

66. See, for example, Watson, *Text, Church, and World*, 25–29. Much better is Hunsinger, "Daybreak of the New Creation," 176–78.

67. On this and the following points, see Frei, *Identity of Jesus Christ*, 150–51; *Theology and Narrative*, 108, 164, 200–206, 210–12; cf. 143–44.

68. As I argue in Fulford, *Divine Eloquence*, 191–230. See also Higton, "Hans Frei," 225–28; *Christ, Providence and History*, 114–18, 155–67.

in perpetual solidarity with us, both victimizers and victims, in a way that both undercuts all pretensions to and whose emphasis falls upon his identification with the poor and the oppressed.[69]

Second, Frei's account of Christ's presence in *Identity* gives grounds for hopeful engagement in progressive politics.[70] Here Frei seems in effect to seek to interpret Christian belief in Christ's presence in light of his analysis of Christ's identity, and so understands Christ's presence in Word and Sacrament, and in Christian community, as forms of his self-manifestation grounded in his transcendent freedom as the Living One who lives to God.[71] His account of Christian community, however, sees it in historical terms, where the church's history is constituted by its interaction with the world at large, and goes on to assert the presence of Christ in worldly events.[72] The history of the church and the world is subject, Frei adds, to a providential ordering in Jesus Christ, yet to be recapitulated in his future presence: a summation in which the stories of all aspects of our history will find their intelligibility and fulfilment.[73] In the meantime, that providential governance is mysterious and opaque, yet may be partially and provisionally legible in certain fragments of historical sequence.[74] These are parables of Christ's presence which adumbrate figures of his reconciliation, redemption and resurrection, such as the US Civil War and Civil Rights struggle. On such terms, it seems, Frei affirmed an affinity between the gospel of God's universal governing glory and a "carefully circumscribed progressive politics."[75]

In his writings he ties belief in the resurrection together with the shaping of life patterned after him. Christ's abiding solidarity with human beings in their sin and helplessness (especially the oppressed) and his singular identity as representative and inclusive of all humanity grounds an appeal to ordinary kindness, natural gentleness, enjoyment of one's neighbors of all sorts in their particularity, reconciliation, and neighbor-love.[76] His theology of providence also informed such affirmations and his hopes for the civil

---

69. Frei, *Theology and Narrative*, 205–6; *Types of Christian Theology*, 136.

70. As David Ford notes, Frei "arrived eventually at the beginnings of a first-order political theology" (Ford, "Hans Frei and the Future of Theology," 208). See also Higton, *Christ, Providence and History*, 167–73, and my forthcoming *God's Patience and our Work*.

71. Frei, *Identity of Jesus Christ*, 154–58, 172.

72. Frei, *Identity of Jesus Christ*, 158–59.

73. Frei, *Identity of Jesus Christ*, 159–61, 163.

74. Frei, *Identity of Jesus Christ*, 161–63.

75. Frei, "H. Richard Niebuhr on History, Church, and Nation," 232.

76. Frei, *Theology and Narrative*, 136–37.

rights movement, for peace in Vietnam and his appeal for a more modest global role for the United States marked not by anxiety about decline but "a humanitarianism modified by Christian hope."[77] In one of his later writings he gestured toward an account of divine patience which framed human responsibility toward others as recipients of divine gifts of space and time, and held forth a vision of a global missionary church as a paradigm or parable of the Kingdom of God, of the eschatological realisation of justice, mercy and human equality promised in Jesus Christ's first coming, enacted in the hopeful, realistic, contextually flexible, pursuit of social justice without being in a position to anticipate how the Kingdom will come or therefore advance programme for universal liberation.[78]

The Significance of Frei's Generous Orthodoxy for Today

Frei's death in September 1988 cut short his project on Jesus Christ in the history of modern Christianity and his writing and speaking on social ethics and public theology.[79] The constructive theology he left is mainly fragmentary, exploratory and indicative, not least in setting out his ontological commitments. Frei's enduring significance for Christian theology has to do with the only partially realised potential of the directions he mapped.[80] His Christocentric account of providence is a potent contributions both to that neglected doctrine and to addressing modern theology's troubled relationship with historical consciousness.[81] The directions he indicates in the theology of Scripture and in social ethics likewise deserve closer attention.[82] Pneumatology is perhaps the greatest weakness in his constructive work (it is assimilated to Christ's presence), yet even in this area his approach to dogmatic theology can guide fresh thinking, as in Eugene Rogers's *After the Spirit*. The fruitfulness of his approach for interfaith relations has been

---

77. Frei, "H. Richard Niebuhr on History, Church, and Nation," 231.

78. Frei, *Writings from the Archives*, 168–72.

79. See Frei, *Writings from the Archives*, 161–75, 176–82; *Theology and Narrative*, 213–33.

80. David Ford describes him as a Moses figure in Ford, "Hans Frei's Achievement," 54.

81. See Higton, *Christ, Providence and History*, 25–38, 93–176; Fulford, *Divine Eloquence*, 191–230.

82. See Fulford, *Divine Eloquence*, 231–71; *God's Patience and our Work*; Higton, "Hans Frei."

taken up by the founders of the practice of Scriptural Reasoning.[83] Above all, it is the questions Frei asks about the way we do our theology, and the orientation to the presence of Jesus Christ identified in the gospels within and beyond the church, in thought and a "carefully circumscribed progressive politics," that remains most pertinent to theology today across Christian traditions, and beyond.[84]

That pertinence raises equally a set of counter-questions with which I will close.[85] If we accept the priority of the literal identification of Jesus Christ, and the move from that identity to a reconfigured Christian imagination, then how far are the following possible? First, to make good on Frei's programme of the re-description of Christian meanings as normed by scriptural narrative, with *ad hoc* overlaps with other discourses (a) on the basis of realistic biblical narratives alone and (b) in such a way as to indicate with conceptual depth and reach the specific rationality of Christian discourse shaped around the particular, the Lord Jesus Christ?[86] Perhaps, as David Kelsey's *Eccentric Existence* argues, we need to attend to the distinct narrative logics of a plurality of biblical stories in order to do so.

Second, how adequate and flexible can that practice of re-description be for attending illuminatingly (not comprehensively or finally) to the welter of realities Christians and their neighbors experience across the world—especially ordinary Christians, including victims and the oppressed; to all the ways in which they are formed by their circumstances and their responses to them; to their uses of Scriptures, their ways of making sense of themselves and their circumstances? The flexibility of Frei's approach is promising here, so long as one thinks the story centred on Jesus is worth living and thinking with.[87]

Third, how responsive can this kind of theology be to the insights and challenges for Christian theology and its literal reading that are raised by those experiences without forsaking that priority? There seems to be

83. See Ford, "Hans Frei's Achievement," 63; "Interfaith Wisdom," 347–48.

84. Frei, *Theology and Narrative*, 149. Note the Jewish philosopher Peter Ochs's constructive engagement with Frei in Ochs, *Return to Scripture*. Frei's significance for Roman Catholic theology has yet to be examined to my knowledge.

85. For other stimulating sets of similar questions focused on Frei's *Types of Christian Theology*, see Ford, "Hans Frei's Achievement," 64–65; "Hans Frei and the Future of Theology," 211–12.

86. Frei himself tended to point to Barth here. George Hunsinger's *How to Read Karl Barth* exemplifies the sort of reading of Barth that seeks to display his achievement in this respect. Bruce Marshall's *Trinity and Truth* offers a detailed proposal of a Christian account of truth consistent with Frei's approach.

87. Serene Jones's *Feminist Theory and Christian Theology* exemplifies an answer in respect of one field of discourse and one set of women's stories.

considerable potential for critical reflexivity within the primacy literal reading, so long as the story is worth thinking with.[88] These questions can only really be answered in the receptions of attempts to follow in Frei's footsteps. I would suggest that the enduring vitality and significance of the approach to Frei advocated is bound up with those questions and those answers.

Bibliography

Boniface, Tim. *Jesus, Transcendence, and Generosity: Christology and Transcendence in Hans Frei and Dietrich Bonhoeffer*. Lanham, MD: Lexington; Fortress Academic, 2018.

Campbell, Charles L. "Hans W. Frei." In *A New Handbook of Christian Theologians*, edited by Donald W. Musser and Joseph L. Price, 151–57. Nashville: Abingdon, 1996.

———. *Preaching Jesus: New Directions for Homiletics in Hans Frei's Postliberal Theology*. Grand Rapids: Eerdmans, 1997.

Coffman, Elesha. *The Christian Century and the Rise of the Protestant Mainline*. New York: Oxford University Press, 2013.

Dawson, John David. *Christian Figural Reading and the Fashioning of Identity*. Berkeley: University of California Press, 2001.

DeHart, Paul J. *The Trial of Witnesses: The Rise and Decline of Postliberal Theology*. Malden, MA: Blackwell, 2006.

Demson, David E. *Hans Frei and Karl Barth: Different Ways of Reading Scripture*. Grand Rapids: Eerdmans, 1997.

Dorrien, Gary. *Social Ethics in the Making: Interpreting an American Tradition*. Chichester: Wiley-Blackwell, 2009.

Ford, David F. "Hans Frei and the Future of Theology." *Modern Theology* 8.2 (1992) 203–14.

———. "Hans Frei's Achievement: On Being Theological Hospitable to Jesus Christ." In *Ten Year Commemoration to the Life of Hans Frei (1922–1988)*, edited by G. Olegovich, 54–65. New York: Semenenko Foundation, 1999.

———. "An Interfaith Wisdom: Scriptural Reasoning Between Jews, Christians, and Muslims." *Modern Theology* 22.3 (2006) 345–66.

Frei, Hans W. "Epilogue: George Lindbeck and *The Nature of Doctrine*." In *Theology and Dialogue: Essays in Conversation with George Lindbeck*, edited by Bruce D. Marshall, 275–82. Notre Dame: University of Notre Dame Press, 1990.

———. "Letter to John Woolverton, January 23, 1980." Archival document. Yale Divinity School, Record Group 76, Box 5, Folder 98.

———. *Theology and Narrative: Selected Essays*. Edited by George Hunsinger and William C. Placher. New York: Oxford University Press, 1993.

———. *Types of Christian Theology*. New Haven: Yale University Press, 1990.

———. Untitled autobiographical notes. Archival document. Yale Divinity School, Record Group 76, Box 27, Folder 335.

---

88. Kendall Soulen's *The God of Israel and Christian Theology* and Wille James Jennings's *The Christian Imagination* come to mind as two examples of works which take this brief forward in respect of supersessionism and race respectively.

———. *Writings from the Archives: Theology and Hermeneutics.* Vol. 1 of *Reading Faithfully.* Edited by Mike Higton and Mark A. Bowald. Eugene, OR: Cascade, 2015.

Fulford, Ben. *Divine Eloquence and Human Transformation: Rethinking Scripture and History through Gregory of Nazianzus and Hans Frei.* Minneapolis: Fortress, 2013.

———. *God's Patience and Our Work: Hans Frei on Theology and Social Ethics.* Forthcoming.

Higton, Mike. *Christ, Providence and History.* London: T&T Clark, 2004.

———. "Hans Frei." In *Christian Theologies of Scripture: A Comparative Introduction,* edited by Justin S. Holcomb, 220–39. New York: New York University Press, 2006.

Hunsinger, G. "The Daybreak of the New Creation: Christ's Resurrection in Recent Theology." *Scottish Journal of Theology* 57.2 (2004) 163–81.

———. "Hans Frei as Theologian: The Quest for a Generous Orthodoxy." *Modern Theology* 8.2 (1992) 103–28.

———. *How to Read Karl Barth: The Shape of His Theology.* New York: Oxford University Press, 1991.

Jennings, Willie James. *The Christian Imagination: Theology and the Origins of Race.* New Haven: Yale University Press, 2011.

Jones, Serene. *Feminist Theory and Christian Theology: Cartographies of Grace.* Minneapolis: Fortress, 2000.

Kelsey, David H. *Eccentric Existence: A Theological Anthropology.* 2 vols. Louisville: Westminster John Knox, 2009.

Knight, James Allen. *Liberalism Versus Postliberalism: The Great Divide in Twentieth-Century Theology.* New York: Oxford University Press, 2013.

Lindbeck, George A. *The Nature of Doctrine: Religion and Theology in a Postliberal Age.* Louisville: Westminster John Knox, 1984.

Marshall, Bruce D. *Trinity and Truth.* Cambridge: Cambridge University Press, 1999.

Rogers, Eugene F. *After the Spirit: A Constructive Pneumatology from Resources Outside the Modern West.* London: SCM, 2006.

Rowe, C. Kavin. *Early Narrative Christology: The Lord in the Gospel of Luke.* Grand Rapids: Baker Academic, 2009.

Shin, Daniel D. *Theology and the Public: Reflections on Hans W. Frei on Hermeneutics, Christology, and Theological Method.* Lanham, MD: Lexington, 2019.

Soulen, Kendall. *The God of Israel and Christian Theology.* Minneapolis: Augsburg Fortress, 1996.

Springs, Jason A. *Toward A Generous Orthodoxy: Prospects for Hans Frei's Postliberal Theology.* New York: Oxford University Press, 2010.

Vidu, Adonis. *Postliberal Theological Method: A Critical Study.* Bletchley: Paternoster, 2005.

Watson, Francis. *Text, Church and World.* Edinburgh: T&T Clark, 1994.

7

Wolfhart Pannenberg: Liberal Orthodoxy

—Friederike Nüssel

ONE OF THE LEADING contributions to dogmatic ecumenical conversation was offered by the Lutheran theologian Wolfhart Pannenberg. His ecumenical theology follows from his general approach to systematic theology in which he explores the truth claims of the Christian faith in relation to the challenges of modern philosophy, anthropology, natural sciences and denominational developments. Pannenberg considered the divisions and mutual exclusions of Christian churches to be a contradiction to the Christian confession of the unity of the church which affects the credibility of Christian faith and witness. This essay will explore how Pannenberg's theological concerns and goals were shaped through his biography and intellectual development and how his ecumenical contribution is part of his wider systematic dialogue. With regard to ecumenism, it will be shown that Pannenberg used the methodological achievements of modern liberal theology in order to develop an orthodox perspective on those dogmatic issues and controversies which led to the major schisms in the history of Christianity.

Pannenberg's Background and Intellectual Pilgrimage

Wolfhart Pannenberg was born in Stettin, Germany, on October 2, 1928, and grew up in a secular context. In an autobiographical speech he says that he had been baptized as a child, yet, as he continues: I "did not receive a religious education, since in my early years my parents left the church. My adolescence was that of a young atheist during World War II and shortly thereafter."[1] In 1944, the fifteen-year-old young man, who loved music, came across the book *The birth of tragedy from the spirit of music* by Friedrich Nietzsche. Pannenberg was fascinated by this work and continued to read all of Nietzsche's works in the year 1944. Nietzsche's radical criticism of Christianity was the first intellectual account of Christianity that Pannenberg encountered. While soon after Pannenberg had a visionary experience that left him with the urgent question about the meaning of life, it was his high school teacher Dr. Lange who in his personality offered a counter-image to Nietzsche's picture of Christians as guilt-driven neurotics. In this constellation of intellectual and personal challenges, Pannenberg became curious about the real nature of Christianity and decided to study not only philosophy, but also theology at the university of Berlin in 1947. The connection between philosophy and theology was constitutive for the development of his whole theological thinking. During his time in Berlin, Pannenberg studied theology with Heinrich Vogel, a Barthian scholar, and began to read the philosophical work of Nicolai Hartmann. In 1948 he went to Göttingen to attend Hartmann's courses. Hartmann impressed Pannenberg not only with his ideas, but also in the way he explored any philosophical problem in light of the entire history of philosophy.

In 1949, Pannenberg went to Basel where he continued to study philosophy with Karl Jaspers, but also studied with Karl Barth to whom he was recommended by his German teachers. Barth's consequent focus on the divine revelation as the one and only source of true knowledge of God and his exploration of a Trinitarian theology[2] together with his critique of anthropocentrism and subjectivism were convincing to Pannenberg and shaped his own theological approach. But only after he went to Heidelberg was Pannenberg able to put Barth in a broader context and to discover weaknesses in Barth regarding philosophical and exegetical argument. In Heidelberg, Pannenberg began to study biblical exegesis in greater depth. It was the Old Testament scholar Gerhard von Rad who fascinated Pannenberg with his thesis that "the Ancient God of Israel was a God of history showing himself to be the 'God who acts' as Ernest Wright in America expressed it at the same time."[3] Pannenberg could combine von Rad's exegetical approach with Karl Löwith's courses in Heidelberg on the philosophy of the meaning of history and Nicolai Hartmann's method of integrating a history of ideas into philosophical argument. He also began to study the philosophy of Georg Wilhelm Friedrich Hegel which he "learned to regard as representing the top level of

1. Pannenberg, "Intellectual Pilgrimage," 149.
2. Pannenberg, "Intellectual Pilgrimage," 151.
3. Pannenberg, "Intellectual Pilgrimage," 153.

sophistication in modern philosophy and also as unsurpassed in its philosophical theology."[4] These philosophical approaches to history helped him to develop an understanding of history that could serve to explain the historical character of divine revelation. While he deepened his exegetical studies with the New Testament scholar Günter Bornkamm, the Patristic scholar Hans von Campenhausen influenced Pannenberg's exegetical approach by his innovative evaluation of the historicity of the Easter tradition and the empty tomb[5] that inspired Pannenberg's understanding of the resurrection as part of the divine revelation as a historical event.

The university of Heidelberg became Pannenberg's alma mater. Building on an extended essay he had written on the notion of free will in Duns Scotus already in Göttingen, he wrote his theological dissertation on the doctrine of predestination in Duns Scotus with Edmund Schlink and received his doctorate in 1953. Schlink encouraged him to continue with a second dissertation on the concept of analogy which Pannenberg presented for his habilitation and received the *venia legendi* in Systematic Theology in 1955. He worked with Edmund Schlink at the Ecumenical Institute of Heidelberg University that Schlink had founded in 1946. Through Schlink, Pannenberg was introduced to ecumenism and the issues of interdenominational conversations. In 1956 Pannenberg was ordained, and in 1958 he was appointed to his first teaching position at the Theological Seminary of Wuppertal, where he became a colleague of Jürgen Moltmann, who would become one of his most important theological conversation partners and a friend throughout his life.

In 1961 Pannenberg was offered a professorial position at the University of Mainz which he accepted. The year 1961 became a decisive year in Pannenberg's career as a theologian. Already in Heidelberg he was a member of a theological conversation circle ("der Heidelberger Kreis") with Rolf Rendtorff, Ulrich Wilckens, and Trutz Rendtorff. In 1961 they published a small book with essays that dated back to their Heidelberg conversations. The book was titled *Revelation as History*.[6] While the essays in this book were only intended to offer exegetical foundation to the concepts of revelation and the word of God in the leading theological approaches of Karl Barth and in the existential kerygma-theology of Rudolf Bultmann, the theological audience received this book as a critical manifesto. The young group of theologians unexpectedly found themselves in the center of theological discussion and controversy of the time. In order to provide the historical argument in

---

4. Pannenberg, "Intellectual Pilgrimage," 151.
5. Pannenberg, "Intellectual Pilgrimage," 153–54.
6. Pannenberg, *Revelation as History*.

detail that would support his approach of "Dogmatic Theses on the Doctrine of Revelation" as part of *Revelation as history*, Pannenberg developed his Christology in *Jesus—God and Man* (*Grundzüge der Christologie*), published in 1964. Here he tried to reconstruct "Christology from the apostolic time through the patristic period in terms of implication and explication"[7] and in this way developed Christology "from below" that would explain the historical ground for the church's faith in the man Jesus as the son of God. Pannenberg's approach to revelation as history and to Christology also received attention in the United States. In 1963 he was invited to Chicago to lecture on Christology, where he met Paul Tillich. He also taught as a visiting professor at Harvard in 1966 and at Claremont where he received a call from the newly founded Faculty of Protestant Theology at the University of Munich, which he accepted and then assumed in 1967.[8]

During his years in Mainz, Pannenberg gave several lectures on the theology of the church in which he addressed the issue of church and state and the relevance of Christian churches for democracy and civil society in dialogue with contemporary approaches in the sociology of the church. While in this first approach to ecclesiology, ecumenism did not yet play a significant role, Pannenberg did see the need for interdenominational conversation and ecumenical theology. On his initiation and following his negotiations with the University of Munich, he founded the Institute for Ecumenism and Fundamental Theology as a counterpart to the Ecumenical Research Institute at the Roman Catholic Theological Faculty in Munich that had been founded by Heinrich Fries in 1964.[9] Fries and Pannenberg agreed to give regularly seminars on ecumenical topics, starting with a seminar on the understanding of ordained ministry in Catholic and Protestant perspective in the winter semester of 1969/1970.[10] Thus, ecumenism became one of the major topics of Pannenberg's work.

But, as the name of the Institute for Ecumenism and Fundamental Theology indicates, Pannenberg saw a strong interdependence between ecumenism and a philosophically informed theological argument for the rationality of the Christian faith and the scholarly character of theology as an academic discipline. Thus, in Munich, Pannenberg not only transcended the denominational boundaries between the theological faculties, but engaged in constant dialogue with philosophers such as Dieter Henrich, and with the

---

7. Pannenberg, "Intellectual Pilgrimage," 156.
8. For more details, see Pannenberg, "Intellectual Pilgrimage," 156–57.
9. Kleinschwärzer-Meister, "Geschichte des Ökumenischen Forschungszentrums."
10. See the list of Pannenberg's taught courses in Pannenberg, "Liste der Lehrveranstaltungen von 1959–1994."

sciences, especially physics. In 1973 he published his book on *Theology and the philosophy of science* (1973) in which he responded to both the reform movement of German universities and the challenges from philosophy, especially logical positivism, to the truth claim of Christian religious language and the academic profile of theology. In his next major monograph *Anthropology in Theological Perspective* (1983) he aimed to provide an argument for the anthropological relevance of religion and its societal impact in the horizon of growing secularity. All these monographs take important argumentative steps on the way to his *Systematic Theology*, which Pannenberg published in three volumes between 1988 and 1993.

Pannenberg taught in Munich until his retirement in 1993 and lived in Gräfelfing, a suburb of Munich, together with his wife Hilke Pannenberg until he died on September 4, 2014. During his lifetime he saw World War II, the post-war society of the Federal Republic of Germany and the miraculous economic growth in the 1950s and 1960s, the student's revolution in 1968 and its consequences for university education and growing secularization, the development of defense- and disarmament-politics, the fall of the Berlin wall, the reunion of the two Germanies in 1989/1990 and the development of the European Union. While he shared his political opinions with colleagues and friends, he did not see the task of theology as a political "office of oversight" (*Wächteramt*). In his ecclesiology he argued that it is essential for the church to distinguish itself from the state and from politics on the one hand, and from the future kingdom of God on the other hand. Only if the church would observe this twofold self-distinction would it be able fulfil its mission to be a sign and foretaste of the future kingdom. In his view the most adequate and effective way in which the church could actually support democracy and civil society was to live a communal life in line with the divine promise and command that would at least in a provisional way give witness to the divine destination of a new humanity.

Overcoming Boundaries in Exploring the Christian Truth Claim

Coming from a secular background himself, Pannenberg had a strong sense for the phenomenon of secularization or de-churchification and for the situation in which the existence of God and an explanation of the world in terms of a divine revelation is not evident, but controversial and debatable (he uses the German word "strittig").[11] As a matter of fact, he regarded the

---

11. Pannenberg, *Systematic Theology*, 1:49 (hereafter *ST*): "The fact that the reality and revelation of God are debatable is part of the reality of the world which dogmatics has to consider as God's world."

challenge for theology to arise from the fact that it "is not self-evident that human talk about God can ever be more than that, that it can be genuinely theological and express divine reality. The deep ambiguity of theological discourse lies precisely in the fact that it could all quite easily be no more than human talk and hence not truly theological."[12] The question for theology, therefore, is whether and in what way it can show that Christian teachings "are not merely human inventions and traditions but an expression of divine revelation."[13] In his monograph *Theology and the Philosophy of Science* (1973) Pannenberg discusses the conditions for meaningful theological statements in light of the contemporary philosophical debate, especially logical positivism, but also hermeneutics, and defines the task of theological disciplines. Since the theme of Systematic Theology is the truth of Christian doctrine,[14] and its task is to examine the truth-claim included in this doctrine, Pannenberg analyzes three types and conditions of truth—consensus, correspondence, coherence—that have been important in theological teaching throughout history. In contrast to most approaches in the history of theology, though, he argues that all justified claims of correspondence depend on the criterion of coherence. Coherence is the condition for claiming correspondence between theological propositions and the divine reality, to which all Christian language refers. For a truth-claim, in terms of correspondence, theological reflection on doctrine has to take into account that according to Biblical witness divine revelation will be completed only at the end of history with the advent of the kingdom of God. Therefore, dogmatic propositions are proleptic in the sense that they claim a correspondence with divine reality that can only be verified by the fulfilment of the divine promise in the future. Thus, Pannenberg agrees with Karl Barth that dogma "is 'an eschatological concept.'"[15]

Since the coherence of Christian doctrine is a necessary condition for a rational claim of the truth of the Christian faith and hope and the Christian worldview, the core task of systematic theology as a discipline is to argue for "the truth of Christian doctrine by investigation and presentation of its coherence as regards both the interrelations of the parts and the relations to other knowledge."[16] The goal of Pannenberg's approach in his *Systematic Theology* is to develop a coherent explanation of the divine revelation

12. *ST* 1:7.

13. *ST* 1:9.

14. See the title of chapter 1 in *ST* 1. For a summary and reflection on the relevance, see Nüssel, "Dogmatik als Systematische Theologie!"

15. *ST* 1:16.

16. *ST* 1:21–22.

in Jesus Christ that includes a rational interpretation of the world and of human life. But while the coherence is a necessary condition for defending the rationality of the Christian truth claim, doctrinal propositions have the status of hypotheses and assertions,[17] because they anticipate a future verification through the final revelation in the advent of the kingdom. This is important not only for the status of theological propositions, but also for understanding the teaching authority of theologians and ministers, and for interdenominational conversation. Pannenberg argues:

> When we say that the truth is at stake in the systematic presentation of Christian doctrine, this cannot mean that dogmaticians themselves decide what is true. Attempts to find in the coherence of Christian doctrine and the unity of the world, its history, and its future consummation an expression of the unity of God simply repeat and anticipate the coherence of divine truth itself. They rest on anticipations which repeat the prolepsis of the eschaton in the history of Jesus Christ. Decision regarding their truth rests with God himself. It will be finally made with the fulfilment of the kingdom of God in God's creation. It is provisionally made in human hearts by the convicting ministry of the Spirit of God.[18]

While this statement points to the limitations of the authority of dogmatic theologians, the request for what may be called dogmatic modesty corresponds with the request of a general openness to different accounts of Christian doctrine in different traditions. Theologians cannot make a truth-claim for their own tradition without reflecting on the coherence of their doctrinal position in light of other traditions. It would be just another form of illegitimate transgression of dogmatic competence to deny the truth claim of other doctrinal traditions on a prejudice without reflection and dialogue. Thus, Pannenberg's understanding of the genuine task of systematic theology entails a general respect for other traditions, which may be seen as an important principle of a generous-orthodoxy approach.

The quest for a coherent account of Christian doctrine entails reflection in light of other knowledge and findings. Systematic theology in Pannenberg's view needs to transgress the boundaries of theology as a discipline and engage in interdisciplinary discourse. The reason is not simply that only this kind of conversation permits a reflection on the reasons for the debatability of God. Rather, the reason is genuinely theological. Pannenberg's argument here is that according to a most basic understanding God

17. See *ST* 1:56.
18. *ST* 1:56.

is the all determining reality[19]—a concept that was already used by Rudolf Bultmann.[20] This notion corresponds with the Christian concept of God the creator and of creation being dependent on divine creativeness and preservation.[21] As a consequence, creatures must somehow reflect the divine origin in their very being. With regard to humans, one may take the human endeavor to understand and investigate human nature, the phenomena of the world, and the cosmos, as an expression of their relation to the divine origin. From this perspective it appears reasonable for theology to take interest in non-theological research and findings that enrich the understanding of creation. To cross boundaries in discourses with other disciplines is one genuine task of systematic theology. But this is not the only direction in which systematic theology has to transgress boundaries.

Another demanding challenge for systematic theology arises from the fact that Christian churches across the globe are divided in different denominations that exclude one another and over centuries have mutually condemned one another's teachings. This contradicts the idea of the church as the one body of Christ in the New Testament and with the confession to the one church in the Apostle's Creed and the Nicene Creed. As Pannenberg puts it in the foreword of the third volume of his Systematic Theology: "Hardly any other factor obscures the truth of the gospel of Jesus so much as the fact of church division and its accompanying phenomena, especially the combination in leading ministers of a pursuit of power with a limited outlook."[22] While the "church is called to attest the truth of the gospel to the world,"[23] the division and disunity between churches works as a counter witness to what the church of Jesus Christ should be according to Christ's mission. It seriously affects the credibility of the witness to the one gospel that all churches want to offer. Doctrinal condemnations not only cement divisions but are counterintuitive to any attempt to argue for the truth-claim of Christian doctrine as they present contradicting, mutual exclusive truth-claims. Hence, Pannenberg sees the need for systematic theology to address condemnations between churches and to overcome contradicting presentations and interpretations of Christian doctrine in his *Systematic Theology*.

---

19. See ST 1:159; Pannenberg, *Theology and the Philosophy of Science*, 301–3.

20. Bultmann, "Welchen Sinn hat es, von Gott zu reden?"

21. For further details on Pannenberg's understanding of creation, see Nüssel, "Challenges of a Consistent Language."

22. ST 3:xiv–xv.

23. ST 3:xv.

Reconciling Doctrinal Differences and Condemnations

The history of Christianity is marked by three major schisms about doctrinal questions to which Pannenberg responds in his *Systematic Theology*: the schism about the Christological dogma of Chalcedon that divided churches located in the Byzantine empire and a number of oriental churches into Chalcedonian orthodox churches and pre-Chalcedonian orthodox churches; the schism between Byzantine Eastern orthodox churches and the Roman church about the doctrine of Trinity and origin of the Holy Spirit and the authority of the authentic text of the Nicene Creed; and the schism in the West about the nature of divine grace and human sin and the practice and order of the church between adherents of the Reformation movement and the Roman magisterium.

While Pannenberg does not address the Christological schism as a core issue in his Christological chapters (chapters 9 and 10) of the *Systematic Theology*, his methodological approach to Christology in the dialectics of "from below" and "from above" attempts to overcome the problems of the doctrine of the two natures of Jesus Christ which had been a major issue not only in the early schism but also in Enlightenment theology and modern theology. Pannenberg no longer speaks of two natures, but he takes up the idea that Jesus is the Son of God in his eternal relationship with God the Father, and his truly human life. Jesus is the Son of God in his proclamation and suffering by which he fulfills the will of God. While his mission seems to fail with the trial and crucifixion, his mission is vindicated by God the Father and the Holy Spirit who resurrects Jesus from the dead. In light of the resurrection, the relation between Jesus and his God and Father is revealed as an eternal relation, and this is captured in the notion of the preexistence of the Son. Thus, the Son is truly divine in this eternal relationship with the Father, and in this way he is truly God. Yet at the same time he is truly man in and through his life and realizes the human destination to be the image of God. Pannenberg therefore overcomes the two-natures-Christology and reconciles the theological concerns that were at stake in the patristic debates, which were to understand Jesus Christ as God's revelation through whom humans receive access to God, to avoid Docetism, to emphasize the reality of the human life and suffering of Jesus, and to confirm the unity of the personhood of Jesus Christ as the Son of God.

The issue of the second schism between East and West regarding the origin of the Holy Spirit and the monarchy of God the Father is addressed by Pannenberg explicitly in his doctrine of the Trinity. In agreement with the Eastern Orthodox teaching, he states that the Holy Spirit proceeds from the Father, but not from the Son.[24] He also challenges the Western medieval tradition, including the Reformation theologies[25] for adding the *filioque* to the text of the ecumenical agreement in the Nicene Creed. The theological reason for his critique of the *filioque* follows from his systematic reconstruction of the doctrine of the Trinity. According to his exegetical analysis of the Gospel-reports on the life, suffering and resurrection of Jesus, Pannenberg exhibits the Spirit-mediated relationship between Jesus and the Father as the source and principle of divine self-revelation in and through which God has made himself known as the one God who is Father, Son and Holy Spirit. It is this self-revelation of God in Jesus Christ through the power of the Holy Spirit that was later summarized in the Trinitarian dogma in order to contradict the accusation of tri-theism on the one hand, and modalism and subordination on the other hand.[26] While Pannenberg affirms Augustine's insight that the Trinitarian persons are distinct persons through their mutual relations, he critiques the Western explanation of those relations in terms of causal relations of origin (the genesis of the Son and the spiration of the Holy Spirit). Instead, Pannenberg highlights the fact that according to the Gospel of John, Jesus *receives* the Spirit, and according to Paul is resurrected from the dead by the Spirit. Thus, the Son is not perceived as the source of the Spirit, but rather depends on the Spirit's activity in his life and sonship. The way in which Pannenberg discusses the *filioque* problem shows how he employs Scriptural exegesis to solve dogmatic questions and controversies. In his view, it would not suffice to refer only to John 15:26 as a proof against the *filioque*. Since God has revealed his essence in the life, proclamation activity, suffering and resurrection of Jesus Christ, the Biblical report as a whole has to be taken as the source to discover the eternal relationship between Father, Son, and Holy Spirit.

The doctrinal issues of the third schism in the West that resulted from disagreement about the adequate reform of the Western catholic church—implicitly or explicitly—addressed in various parts of Pannenberg's *Systematic Theology*, but especially in the ecclesiological chapters 12 and 13. The first controversial topic of Reformation theology is the doctrine of justification which Pannenberg explores in the ecclesiological part on the issue of individual salvation. The primary issues in the Reformation debates as well as in modern Catholic-Protestant dialogues were the forensic and effective

24. See *ST* 1:317–20.

25. In an ecumenical statement, the United Lutheran Churches in Germany (VELKD) did not see the need for cancelling the *filioque* in liturgical material but pointed to a way to solve the problem by overcoming causal-relation-thinking in the doctrine of Trinity. See VELKD, *Ökumenisch den einen Glauben bekennen*, 3–4.

26. See chapter 5, *ST* 1:259–61.

character of justification, the Lutheran understanding of the believer as *simul iustus et peccator* and the relation of faith and works. In line with Luther and other theologians of the Reformation, Pannenberg emphasizes the forensic character of justification, but he critiques the late Melanchthonian and gnesio-Lutheran explanation of the forensic character in terms of the imputation of Christ's righteousness. According to Pannenberg's exegesis, this is not found in Paul and was rightly criticized as morally inconsistent and problematic in the time of the Enlightenment. Instead, Pannenberg argues that the forensic character of justification consists in God's declaring the believer to be just in and through his faith in which the believer trusts God's love and mercy revealed in Jesus Christ. Through this the human being becomes a new creature in the union with Christ. Faith *is* just or righteous because it is the right relationship towards God who has revealed his unconditioned love, mercy and forgiveness of sin in the mission, death and resurrection of Jesus Christ. Since faith is naturally combined with love and hope and involves good works like a good tree that bears good fruits, justification and sanctification cannot be separated nor should they be understood as a sequence. Luther's phrase *simul iustus et peccator* is problematic if it were to say that a baptized believer is still a sinner in his or her personhood. In Pannenberg's eyes such an understanding cannot be drawn from Paul, and it would be an inconsistent account of the new life and the Christian identity granted in baptism and adopted in faith.[27]

The second dividing topic in the Reformation was the doctrine of the Eucharist. As Pannenberg recalls in his exploration, the major issues between Catholics and Protestants were concerned with the sacrificial character of mass, the real and bodily presence of Christ in the Eucharist, and the issue regarding communion in both bread and wine. While Pannenberg addresses all three topics in his detailed reflection on the Lord's Supper,[28] the most important and comprehensive topic is the presence of Christ. On this issue, Pannenberg reflects not only about the debate on transubstantiation between Roman Catholic theologians and Reformation theologians, but also on the controversies about the real presence of Jesus Christ between Luther, Zwingli, and later Calvin. He revisits the Catholic doctrine of transubstantiation by drawing on the new interpretations of transignification and transfinalization that emphasize the role of the word and overcome a magical misunderstanding of consecration. Yet he also revisits the Lutheran understanding of real presence. He rejects the idea of a material presence and inclusion of body and blood in the elements and points to the role of

27. See Pannenberg's doctrine of baptism in *ST* 3:239–83.
28. See *ST* 3:283–336.

the Spirit in making the person of Jesus Christ present as the crucified and risen Lord who has offered himself for the proclamation of the kingdom and the testimony of God's love. Moreover, Pannenberg critiques the idea that consecration is reduced to the moment in which the words of institution are spoken. Instead, the Eucharistic liturgy as a whole is the event in which Christ is made present through the Spirit and can be experienced as the one who assembles his church and gives a foretaste of the future community in the kingdom of God. With this emphasis on the liturgy as a whole, and the eschatological significance of the Lord's Supper, Pannenberg also sought to engage theological concerns of the Eastern Orthodox tradition.

The third dividing topic and most pressing ecumenical issue today is the question of ministry and the relationship between the priesthood of all baptized believers and ordained ministers. In a subtle way, Pannenberg responds to the Second Vatican Council's dogmatic constitution on the Church, *Lumen Gentium,* and its ecclesiological definition of the church as "sign and instrument both of a very closely knit union with God and of the unity of the whole human race."[29] He uses "sign and instrument" to characterize the office of ordained ministers to serve the unity of the church.[30] Drawing on the elements that constitute the unity of the church according to the seventh article of the Augsburg Confession, Pannenberg argues that the major responsibility of ordained ministry is to proclaim the gospel purely and to administer the sacraments rightly. While he emphasizes the call of all baptized Christians to be priests and to witness to the gospel, the specific task of ordained ministers is to serve the church in *public* proclamation and carry special responsibility for the unity of the church. In the leadership in worship, in public proclamation, and in responsible leadership in service of the unity of the church, the ministry of ordained pastors can be understood as a sign and instrument of the unity of the church. Pannenberg does not deny the definition of the church in *Lumen Gentium* 1 as sign and instrument, but in his view this definition is only adequate if the church distinguishes itself from Jesus as the head and Lord of the church and from the future kingdom of God that Jesus proclaimed. The church's mission is to be a foretaste of this kingdom; and the church is an instrument of salvation only as a sign that points to the future kingdom. The church, however, is not the giver of salvation or the subject in the act of granting salvation.

---

29. Second Vatican Council, *Lumen Gentium* 1.

30. The chapter on ministry is titled, "The Ministry as Sign and Instrument of the Unity of the Church"; cf. *ST* 3:370.

Conclusions

In this essay I could only very briefly sketch out how Pannenberg addresses the major conflicts behind the three major schisms of the church. This illustrates how he revisits dogmatic controversy by examining the coherence of different doctrines in light of the New Testament teachings and of theological concerns and problems in the history of theology. In sum, the following points are characteristic for his approach: (1) Pannenberg understands the history of the church and the history of theology as the "Wirkungsgeschichte" (impact-history) of the divine revelation in the life of Jesus Christ that left a lasting mark on his disciples. Since all Christian dogma is somehow part of this historical process, all dogma is the object of further reflection and evaluation. (2) In reflecting the explanatory capacity of denominational doctrines, Pannenberg is equally critical toward all traditions. His intention clearly is to avoid denominational bias. (3) While Pannenberg's goal is to present a coherent account of Christian doctrine, he does not summarize his account in dogmatic sentences as one can find them in the old Protestant dogmatic systems, in Friedrich Schleiermacher's *Glaubenslehre* and in Karl Barth's *Kirchliche Dogmatik*. Since systematic reflection on the divine revelation is a continuing and open process, he chooses a style that reflects this openness and invites further critical thinking. (4) Pannenberg explores Christian dogma in light of non-theological academic discourse, the findings of natural sciences, historical method and inquiry, and the development of philosophical inquiry, because only in such a comprehensive approach it is possible to explain the divine essence as the all determining reality. In this way he adopts the principles of the modern liberal tradition in theology.[31] (5) Although Pannenberg does not use the term "orthodox" to formulate a criterion for adequate dogmatic teaching, his approach is nevertheless orthodox in the sense that he examines all *dogmata* in terms of their coherence with Scriptural exegesis. Moreover, he takes the decisions of the ecumenical councils of the ancient church and the patristic argumentation on which they rest as the fundamental part of the "Wirkungsgeschichte" that cannot be abandoned but must be revisited in modern systematic theology.

In the arena of academic theology, Pannenberg's orthodoxy is rarely questioned. Not only his doctrine of ministry, but also his ethical approach and especially his opinion about homosexuality made and still make his theology attractive to "conservative" theologians of different denominations. The potential of his theology, however, lies in the reconciling dynamics and commitments of his systematic approach, in which he employs

---

31. See Ottati, *Theology for Liberal Protestants*, 8–12. See also my review in Nüssel, "Douglas F. Ottati's *Theology for Liberal Protestants*."

liberal methodology to contribute to pure (=orthodox) preaching and teaching of and in the church.

Bibliography

Bultmann, Rudolf. "Welchen Sinn hat es, von Gott zu reden? (1925)." In vol. 1 of *Glauben und Verstehen: Gesammelte Aufsätze*, by Rudolf Bultmann, 26–37. Tübingen: Mohr, 1933.

Kleinschwärzer-Meister, Birgitta. "Geschichte des Ökumenischen Forschungszentrums." *Katholisch-Theologische Fakultät (Ludwig-Maximilians-Universität München)*, October 1, 2017. Online. http://www.kaththeol.uni-muenchen.de/lehre/stud_for_einh/oefi/oefi_geschichte/index.html.

Nüssel, Friederike. "Challenges of a Consistent Language on the Spirit in Creation and New Creation." In *The Spirit in Creation and New Creation: Science and Theology in Western and Orthodox Realms*, edited by Michael Welker, 120–33. Grand Rapids: Eerdmans, 2012.

———. "'Dogmatik als Systematische Theologie!' Zur Aktualität des Dogmatik-Verständnisses bei W. Pannenberg." In *"Eine neue Menschheit darstellen": Religionsphilosophie als Weltverantwortung und Weltgestaltung*, edited by Gunther Wenz, 57–74. Vol. 1 of *Pannenberg-Studien*. Göttingen: Vandenhoeck & Ruprecht, 2015.

———. "Douglas F. Ottati's *Theology for Liberal Protestants*." *International Journal of Systematic Theology* 19.1 (2017) 73–91.

Ottati, Douglas F. *Theology for Liberal Protestants: God the Creator*. Grand Rapids: Eerdmans, 2013.

Pannenberg, Wolfhart. "An Intellectual Pilgrimage." *Kerygma und Dogma* 54.3 (2008) 149–58.

———. "Liste der Lehrveranstaltungen von 1959–1994." In *"Eine neue Menschheit darstellen": Religionsphilosophie als Weltverantwortung und Weltgestaltung*, edited by Gunther Wenz, 251–62. Vol. 1 of *Pannenberg-Studien*. Göttingen: Vandenhoeck & Ruprecht, 2015.

———, ed. *Revelation as History*. Translated by David Granskoo. New York: Macmillan 1968.

———. *Systematic Theology*. Translated by Geoffrey Bromiley. 3 vols. Grand Rapids: Eerdmans; Edinburgh: T&T Clark, 1991–1998.

———. *Theology and the Philosophy of Science*. Translated by Francis McDonagh. Philadelphia: Westminster, 1976.

Vereinigte Evangelisch-Lutherische Kirche Deutschlands (VELKD), ed. *Ökumenisch den Glauben bekennen: Das Nicaeno-Constantinopolitanum von 381 als verbindendes Glaubensbekenntnis*. Texte aus der VELKD 139. Hannover: Vereinigte Evangelisch-Lutherische Kirche Deutschlands, 2007.

Wenz, Gunther, ed. *"Eine neue Menschheit darstellen": Religionsphilosophie als Weltverantwortung und Weltgestaltung*. Vol. 1 of *Pannenberg-Studien*. Göttingen: Vandenhoeck & Ruprecht, 2015.

8

Stanley J. Grenz: The Evangelical Turn to Postliberal Theological Method

—Jay T. Smith

STANLEY GRENZ (D. 2005) was a progressive evangelical theologian and a prolific evangelical writer. Respected by scholars across the theological spectrum, Grenz's theological perspective effectively created a fresh, innovative approach to a theological method that for some had become overly scholastic, and "Biblicist" in its orientation. Grenz's adaptation of particular aspects of George Lindbeck's cultural-linguistic approach to doctrinal construction had a profound impact on what was later to be dubbed, "the Post-Conservative"[1] approach to evangelical theology, and continues to influence the "post-Evangelical" understanding of Christian theology today.[2]

This chapter addresses Grenz's appropriation and use of Lindbeck's cultural-linguistic approach to doctrinal construction as it is understood within an evangelical theological matrix.[3] First, the chapter outlines Grenz's concern for the direction of evangelical theological method, especially with its nineteenth-century turn towards "Biblicism."[4] Second, the chapter addresses the manner in which Grenz combines Lindbeck's approach with Wolfhart Pannenberg's theological method, and its focus on Trinity and history. It notes the contribution of Steven Knowles to studies on Grenz's

---

1. For an explanation of this nomenclature, see Olson, *Reformed and Always Reforming*. Not all evangelical theologians accept this distinction. See Work, "Reformed and Always Reforming," 79–80.

2. See Tomlinson, *Post-Evangelical*.

3. The cornerstone contribution to the evangelical-postliberal engagement is found in Phillips and Okholm, *Nature of Confession*. Grenz's engagement with Lindbeck occurs earlier than the engagements in this volume. Grenz's *Revisioning Evangelical Theology* was published by InterVarsity in 1993. It is surprising that his engagement is not discussed in *Nature of Confession*.

4. See Grenz, *Renewing the Center*, 69–84.

theological method and his appropriation of Lindbeck's concepts. Third, the chapter tracks the influence of Grenz's usage on other contemporary evangelical theologians. Finally, the chapter concludes with an outline of Grenz's theological project after his encounter with Lindbeck's postliberal theological method.

Grenz, Evangelicalism, and the Problem of Method

Stanley Grenz believed that evangelical theological method in the late twentieth century had become problematic for the mission of the church. As outlined by the Princeton theologians in the late nineteenth century, and later refined by twentieth-century evangelicals,[5] Grenz ascertained that evangelical theology, over time, had become increasingly scholastic and Biblicist in its construction.[6] In response to the liberal-fundamentalist divide of the 1920s, and after the formation of the National Association of Evangelicals in 1942, Grenz noted an increasing divide in how North American evangelicals understood and embraced the theological task. He observed the "New Evangelicalism" fathered by Carl Henry was dividing into two different trajectories, the cognitive-doctrinal and the experiential-practical.[7] Note the similarity to Lindbeck's own contrasting categorization, with the cognitive-propositionalist and the experiential-expressive symbolist divisions.[8]

In Grenz's version of Lindbeck's cognitive-doctrinal position, he uses Carl Henry, Millard Erickson, and Wayne Grudem as examples. In each of these scholars, Grenz notes a theological methodology that highlights a rationalist and Biblicist approach to the theological task. For Henry, theological method involved a tapestry of revelation and rationality, with a sure foundation of revelation as deposited in the Christian scriptures.[9] Indeed, Henry understood the Christian faith to be rationally compelling primarily because its basis was in scripture which he understood to be the rational word of the living God. For Erickson, a student of Bernard Ramm, the rational project of Henry had great appeal. Erickson believed that the primary means of understanding the revelation of God is in scriptural revelation and that philosophy was relegated to a supportive role.[10] Additionally, Erickson

---

5. Carl Henry, Millard Erickson, and Wayne Grudem. Grenz, *Renewing the Center*, 86–87.
6. Grenz, *Renewing the Center*, 67–68.
7. Grenz, *Renewing the Center*, 84.
8. Lindbeck, *Nature of Doctrine*, 16–17.
9. Grenz, *Renewing the Center*, 93–94.
10. Grenz, *Renewing the Center*, 121.

believed that the New Evangelicalism of Henry had not gone far enough, and had not engaged in contemporary scientific advances in a meaningful fashion, as well as in the systematic presentation of orthodox doctrine.[11] Grenz notes that Erickson's theology is a "systematic statement of the beliefs and emphases that had characterized the neo-evangelical movement from its beginnings in fundamentalism."[12] Overall, Grenz appreciates the intention of Erickson's project, but ultimately finds it wanting. Grenz's concern lies with Erickson's focus on the propositional dimension of revelation and thus his commitment to Warfield's doctrine of biblical inerrancy.[13] The final example of Grenz's cognitive-doctrinal position is Wayne Grudem. Grudem further refined the heritage of both Henry and Erickson, and exemplified the late twentieth-century emphasis on biblical inerrancy and the consequent development of a third-wave charismatic sympathy.[14] Grudem's view of theology is summarized in his monumental systematic when he states, "systematic theology is any study that answers the question, 'What does the whole Bible teach us today?' about any given topic?"[15] It is in this fashion that Grudem maintains the propositionalist approach to theology, which has as its end result, the extrapolation of correct doctrine.[16]

In Grenz's experiential-practical category, one finds Bernard Ramm, Clark Pinnock and John Sanders. Ramm, shared many of the same presuppositions as his contemporary Henry, but for one important fact: he did not believe that divine revelation was in competition with modern learning, and indeed believed that the two "coalesced."[17] This allowed Ramm a much broader engagement with both modern scientific thought and theologies of the greater Christian tradition. Following Ramm was Clark Pinnock, a protégé of Carl Henry. Pinnock began his career as a conservative neo-evangelical apologist, a Calvinist, first defending the doctrine of biblical infallibility, then biblical inerrancy.[18] Later in his career, Pinnock changed direction, suggesting that evangelical theology should engage other theological perspectives. Pinnock had come to doubt the Calvinistic doctrine of

---

11. Grenz, *Renewing the Center*, 123.
12. Grenz, *Renewing the Center*, 125.
13. Grenz, *Renewing the Center*, 127–28.
14. Grenz, *Renewing the Center*, 155. The "consequent development of a third-wave charismatic sympathy" may not be an automatic consequence of biblical inerrancy, but the possibility of such a development exists and is evidenced in Grudem's work.
15. Grudem, *Systematic Theology*, 21.
16. Grenz, *Renewing the Center*, 156.
17. Grenz, *Renewing the Center*, 115.
18. Grenz, *Renewing the Center*, 136–37. Pinnock, *Defense of Biblical Infallibility*; for Pinnock's about face, see Pinnock, "Evangelicals and Inerrancy," 65–69.

perseverance and became a fully immersed Arminian. He began to rethink not only Calvinism, but also inerrancy.[19] Ultimately, according to Grenz, Pinnock turned toward an "experience chastened reason," and embraced the Wesleyan quadrilateral, which meant that experience and intuition played an important role in his theological construction.[20] This turn allowed Pinnock to anticipate a future, postmodern paradigm for evangelical theology, which embraced biblical narrative, a robust understanding of the Holy Spirit's Trinitarian role, and pietistic renewal.[21] Pinnock's exploration of the issues of God's sovereignty in the "open theism" movement was part of this renewal. The final example of the experiential-practical category is John Sanders. Sanders, with Pinnock, was one of the original authors of the *Openness of God* (1994). The link to Pinnock extends to an early work of Sanders, *No Other Name* (1992), where he found sympathy with Pinnock's methodological concerns. However, Sanders expanded upon the premise of "the openness of God" in other aspects of his work, most notably the volume, *The God Who Risks* (1994). For Grenz's purposes, the most important aspects of Sander's work is his method. According to Grenz, "Sanders proposes three criteria for evaluating any particular Christian theological model: consonance with tradition, conceptual intelligibility, and adequacy for the demands of life."[22] In Sanders we see both an appreciation of scripture and yet a prioritization of experience and practice.

In the conclusion to his analysis, Grenz asserts that evangelical theology has come to a crossroads. Citing the publication of Francis Schaeffer's *The Great Evangelical Disaster* (1984) and David Wells's *No Place for Truth, Or Whatever Happened to Evangelical Theology* (1993), Grenz concludes, citing Dave Tomlinson, that theology has entered a "post-evangelical" era.[23] He makes several interesting generalizations in his conclusion. For Grenz and Tomlinson, evangelicals must re-think their doctrine of scripture, and begin to take the modern-postmodern shift seriously. This includes the move from a realist to a constructionist view of truth; the move from metanarrative to local stories; the question of evangelical boundaries, and an understanding of evangelicalism as a mosaic of local theologies.[24] This growing dissatisfaction with "traditional evangelical"[25] theology from both

19. Pinnock, "Evangelicals and Inerrancy," 139–42.
20. Pinnock, "Evangelicals and Inerrancy," 146.
21. Pinnock, "Evangelicals and Inerrancy," 147–50.
22. Grenz, *Renewing the Center*, 161.
23. Tomlinson, *Post-Evangelical*.
24. Grenz, *Renewing the Center*, 166–83.
25. "Traditional Evangelicalism" refers to the established National Association of

academy and local church impelled Grenz not to develop an apologetic for traditional evangelicalism, but rather to forge a new path for the essence of evangelical theology. This leads us to Grenz's proposal for a third way, based upon his encounter with Pannenberg, his reading of Lindbeck and his evangelical sentiments.

Grenz and Lindbeck's Postliberal Approach to Doctrine

Lindbeck's influence is apparent in Grenz's categorization of the evangelical divide. Indeed, his reading of Lindbeck essentially informs the constructive proposal of *Renewing the Center*. Steven Knowles has identified aspects of Lindbeck's cultural-linguistic understanding of doctrinal construction that has so highly influenced Grenz's project.[26] Outlining the cognitive-propositional, the expressive-experientialist and the cultural-linguistic approaches to doctrinal construction, Knowles tackles Lindbeck's detractors, and ultimately validates Grenz's usage of the paradigm. The primary weakness that Knowles identifies in Lindbeck's model is an "inadequate theory of 'truth.'"[27] For Knowles, Lindbeck's assertion that the cultural-linguistic model can "contain ontologically true affirmations . . . but they are not necessary, as long as there is coherence in the intrasystematic scheme of things" betrays a questionable reliance upon Wittgenstein's theory of language games.[28] For Knowles, this reliance upon Wittgenstein in Lindbeck's model leaves the external influence of Christian revelation in a place of ambiguity. Grenz, however, seems to find a solution for this challenge.

Trinity, Community, and Eschatology: Grenz's Theological Motifs. At the heart of Grenz's theological method is the doctrine of the Trinity. Originating from his study with Wolfhart Pannenberg, and predisposed by his pietistic heritage, Grenz prioritizes the Trinity epistemologically, ontologically and structurally in his theology.[29] This is the "evangelical" center of Grenz's thought. Contrary to Lindbeck's ambiguity towards externally originating truth concepts, Grenz's understanding of the Trinity functions both externally and internally. The Trinity functions as one of three "motifs" in his theology.

Evangelicalism positions that affirm inerrancy and a propositionalist approach to theology and doctrine. This is an unavoidable generalization.

26. Knowles, *Beyond Evangelicalism*, 49–63.

27. Knowles, *Beyond Evangelicalism*, 63.

28. Knowles, *Beyond Evangelicalism*, 63.

29. Pannenberg, *Systematic Theology* 1:1–257; Taylor, *Pannenberg on the Triune God*.

The concept of "motifs" is derived from the need to organize his source material in a fashion that allow the complexity of the cultural-linguistic model to speak clearly to the church.[30] Grenz describes his approach:

> The demise of foundationalism indicative of the postmodern situation opens the way for a post-foundationalist theological method that views constructive theology as an ongoing conversation involving the interplay of Scripture, tradition and culture. The overarching goal of this conversation is to hear the Spirit's voice speaking to the faith community today, one important dimension of which is the task of determining, delineating, articulating and reflecting upon the Christian belief-mosaic. This perspective, in turn, leads to the conclusion that ultimately all theology is—as the "postmodern condition" suggests—"local" or "specific." That is, it is the conversation involving, and the resultant articulation authored by, a particular group in a particular moment of the ongoing existence in the world. Despite the specificity of all theology, these various local theologies share in common "a similar patter, shape or 'style'" that comprises them as Christian theology. A postmodern local theology shares in the designation *Christian*, then, insofar as it reflects the uniquely Christian "style." And this style entails being trinitarian in content, communitarian in focus, and eschatological in orientation.[31]

First, then, Grenz assigns to the doctrine of the Trinity the role of the "structural motif." The Trinity is the beginning and end of history; eschatologically reaching into the present; holding all truth within the Godhead, and allowing all persons to participate in that truth in Christ, through the Holy Spirit. For Grenz, the Trinity is the center of reality, and whatever "Truth" scripture contains propositionally, narratively, or existentially is derived from the active inspiration of the Holy Spirit in space and time. Indeed, he states, "because Christian theology is committed to finding its basis in the being and action of the triune God, it should be ordered and structured in a manner that reflects the primacy of this fundamental Christian confession."[32]

Second, Grenz assigns the concept of community as his "integrative" motif. As early as his *Revisioning Evangelical Theology*, Grenz was contemplating the viability of the "Kingdom of God" as the integrative motif in

---

30. For a succinct account of his understanding of motif, see Grenz, "Conversing in Christian Style," 82–103.

31. Grenz, "Conversing in Christian Style," 93–94. Grenz draws his understanding of "motif" as "style" from Kroeber, *Style and Civilizations*, 76.

32. Grenz, "Conversing in Christian Style," 95.

evangelical theology, concluding that although the Kingdom of God is appropriate, it is incomplete—being eschatologically qualified, our experience of the Kingdom is thus only partial.[33] Grenz concludes that the broader concept of "community" is appropriate as the integrating motif. Understanding that the Kingdom of God is the essential "community," Grenz then turns to the social sciences and contemporary communitarian philosophy to solidify his understanding of the communitarian turn in a radically individualistic Western culture. Grenz states, "Community" is important as an integrative motif for theology not only because it fits with contemporary thinking concerning the nature of the world and the human phenomenon but, more important, because it is central to the message of the Bible."[34] Utilization of the "community" motif is an excellent example of Grenz's understanding and utilization of Lindbeck's conceptualization of the cultural-linguistic model. He has drawn from philosophy (on figures such as Plantinga, Wolterstorff, and Royce), the social sciences (Bellah and others), and theology to cast the importance of community for local, postmodern, doctrinal construction.[35]

Finally, Grenz casts eschatology in the role of the "orienting" motif. Although this is a thoroughly theological appropriation, it is crucial to how Grenz understands the construction of doctrine. Grenz believes that theology proceeds from a unique perspective on the future orientation of the Christian hope.[36] This future consciousness of the Christian community allows for a constructive understanding of the world, an "already-but-not-yet" view, that enables the community to "articulate the Christian belief-mosaic in accordance with the actual (i.e., future) world God is fashioning, and to do so for the sake of the church's mission."[37] These theological "motifs" constitute the Christian "style" for Grenz—the canvas on which his theological sources (norms) weave together to produce a coherent, local doctrine for the postmodern church.

The Sources for Theological Construction. Grenz posits three sources, or in his casting, "norms," for theological-doctrinal construction. First is the "norming-norm" or scripture. Scripture, according to Grenz, derives its authority from the Trinity in general, but through the Holy Spirit in particular. God, the Holy Spirit, addresses humankind through the instrumentality of the Spirit. Grenz, in a more traditional evangelical fashion agrees that the scriptures are authored and inspired by God-the-Holy-Spirit. Indeed,

---

33. Grenz, *Revisioning Evangelical Theology*, 137–62.
34. Grenz, *Revisioning Evangelical Theology*, 156.
35. Grenz, "Conversing in Christian Style," 96–98.
36. Grenz, "Conversing in Christian Style," 99.
37. Grenz, "Conversing in Christian Style," 100.

he concurs that 2 Timothy 3:16 stands as the appropriate understanding of the nature of scripture, in that "the Spirit teaches, reproves, corrects and instructs" through scripture.[38] Yet Grenz proceeds to another affirmation. In that the Spirit speaks through scriptures, it is performing a particular "perlocutionary" act, seeking to inform, instruct and reprove with the effect of specific results. Drawing from the speech-act theory of J. L. Austin and John Searle, Grenz can confidently affirm his Trinitarian centrality with the work of the Spirit of Christ:

> Through the Bible, the Spirit orients our present on the basis of the past and in accordance with a vision of the future. The Spirit leads the contemporary hearers to view themselves and their situation in the light of God's past and future, and to open themselves and their present to the power of that future, which is already at work in the world.[39]

In his use of the Biblical scriptures as his "norming norm," Grenz continues his appropriation of Lindbeck, and in the process, produces a coherent doctrine of scripture that speaks to a postmodern world.

Grenz's second, or better, "secondary" norm is the "theological heritage of the church."[40] John Franke, Grenz's co-author in *Beyond Foundationalism*, explains that the secondary norm functions as "theology's hermeneutical trajectory."[41] In other words, the theo-historical trajectory of the church serves as an informative hermeneutic for the contemporary church. Franke states: "To understand the tradition of the church as providing a hermeneutical trajectory is to acknowledge the importance of tradition without elevating it to a position of final authority because of the ongoing life of the church as it moves toward its eschatological consummation."[42]

Franke notes that the hermeneutical function of tradition is not simply a means of interpreting the faith for the contemporary church, but also "to assist the Christian community in the its vocation to live as the people of God in the particular social-historical context in which they are situated."[43] Franke uses the analogy of a conductor interpreting a Mozart symphony. The tradition of interpretation is important, especially as it pertains to classic performance, although every interpretation is secondary to the actual score.[44] Citing the

38. Grenz, "Conversing in Christian Style," 89.
39. Grenz, "Conversing in Christian Style," 89.
40. Grenz and Smith, *Created for Community*, xxv–xxvi.
41. Grenz and Franke, *Beyond Foundationalism*, 93–94.
42. Grenz and Franke, *Beyond Foundationalism*, 126.
43. Grenz and Franke, *Beyond Foundationalism*, 127.
44. Grenz and Franke, *Beyond Foundationalism*, 127.

work of Frances Young and N. T. Wright, Franke concludes with the assertion, "The Christian tradition provides a historically extended, socially embodied context in which to inherit, apply, and live out the communally formative narratives contained in the canonical text."[45]

Grenz's third, or "tertiary norm" is contained in the thought forms of contemporary culture. Of all of Grenz's norms, this "tertiary norm" is a crucial component to his theological-doctrinal construction, and the one most dependent upon Lindbeck's cultural-linguistic program. Grenz realizes that bringing "culture" into an evangelical theological program would bring criticism, yet he is set upon clarifying this relationship.[46] In the chapter on culture in *Beyond Foundationalism*, Grenz gives his most thorough understanding of the place of culture to date in his program. After exploring the nature of culture anthropologically and sociologically, Grenz posits a general interpretation of culture:

> [We] inhabit socially constructed worlds to which our personal identities are intricately bound. The construction of these worlds, as well as the formation of personal identity, is an ongoing, dynamic, and fluid process, in which the forming and reforming of shared cultural meanings play a crucial role. Culture includes the symbols—the language, material objects, images, and rituals—that provide the shared meaning by means of which we understand ourselves, pinpoint our deepest aspirations and longings, and construct the worlds we inhabit.[47]

From this assessment, Grenz characterizes a theological engagement with culture, consisting of an address of the contemporary cultural context, where theologians "conceptualize and articulate Christian beliefs . . . through the cognitive tools, concepts, images, symbols and thought forms—by means of which people . . . discover meaning, construct the world they inhabit, and form personal identity."[48] Grenz maintains that the theologian must, "hear," "scrutinize," and "respond" to the questions our theology raises in culture.[49] These sentiments are an echo of Lindbeck's assessment: "Thus the linguistic-cultural model is part of an outlook that stresses the degree to which human experience is shaped, molded, and in a sense constituted by cultural and linguistic forms."[50] In a final assertion, Grenz maintains the

---

45. Grenz and Franke, *Beyond Foundationalism*, 128.
46. Grenz and Franke, *Beyond Foundationalism*, 131.
47. Grenz and Franke, *Beyond Foundationalism*, 147.
48. Grenz and Franke, *Beyond Foundationalism*, 159.
49. Grenz and Franke, *Beyond Foundationalism*, 159–60.
50. Lindbeck, *Nature of Doctrine*, 34.

Holy Spirit's speaking to the community of Christ in the particularity of its historical-cultural context. He understands the "speaking of the Spirit" in the contemporary context as critical to the church's hermeneutical task, and thus "occurs in part as contemporary "knowledge"—the discoveries and insights of the various disciplines of human learning—informs our theological construction."[51] Grenz notes that Christian thinkers from the apostle Paul to Paul Tillich have drawn from this "cultural knowledge" to understand and articulate Christian truth.[52]

Grenz's careful delineation, and articulation of his approach to culture not only reflects the very best of Lindbeck's postliberal linguistic-cultural paradigm, but also carefully places it within the parameters of possible evangelical engagement. This does not mean that Grenz's appropriation is without criticism. As Knowles has noted, Kevin Vanhoozer has seriously questioned use of Lindbeck's paradigm. Vanhoozer is uncertain as to whether linguistic-cultural model is able to make truth claims about anything outside "the story world of scripture."[53] However, following Brad Kallenberg, Knowles comments, "Theology is a regulator that governs the way Christians speak about God without having to make any specifically ontological truth claims upon the statements that are made, but does not rule out that they may have an external referent."[54] In other words, evangelicals indebted to the cognitive-propositional model struggle with the flexibility, or rather, a "lack of rigidity" in the linguistic-cultural model. However, Grenz saw in Lindbeck's model the possibility of a larger cultural engagement for the sake of the church, while still holding to an understanding of truth that is compatible with essential evangelical commitments.

Some of the high points of Grenz's engagement with Lindbeck and the postliberal position resulted in an estrangement from what Grenz, after George Marsden, called, the "card-carrying evangelicals."[55] The theological faculties in the centers of traditional evangelicalism at Trinity Evangelical Divinity School and The Southern Baptist Theological Seminary brought withering criticism upon Grenz for this appropriation of non-traditional theological methodology. Grenz's calling into question of the contemporary evangelical predilection towards propositional truth, traditional evangelical doctrinal construction, and, the failure to affirm an ontologically

---

51. Lindbeck, *Nature of Doctrine*, 161.
52. Lindbeck, *Nature of Doctrine*, 161.
53. Vanhoozer, *Drama of Doctrine*, 95, in Knowles, *Beyond Evangelicalism*, 63.
54. Knowles, *Beyond Evangelicalism*, 49–63.
55. Grenz, *Renewing the Center*, 82.

independent, and inerrant scripture were at the heart of this criticism.[56] Nevertheless, for the rest of his life, Grenz followed the theological method he outlined in *Renewing the Center* and *Beyond Foundationalism*.

A Dynamic Approach to Christian, and Evangelical Theology

In summary, Lindbeck's postliberal cultural-linguistic model greatly influenced the evangelical theology of Stanley Grenz. As an evangelical, Grenz prioritized scripture in his theological construction. Thus, Lindbeck's understanding of doctrine as "second order"[57] truth claims made complete sense to Grenz. In this scheme, scripture, as the norming-norm of theology, maintained its primacy as revelation-truth[58] while simultaneously allowing for a flexibility of doctrinal construction in the local context. Of course, Lindbeck does not deny that doctrine can be a conveyor of truth claims;[59] however, cultural context coupled with the rules of grammar in a local culture change how "beliefs" embody that truth claim.[60] In this sense, "beliefs" and "truth claims" are not synonymous.

Another aspect of Lindbeck's project embraced and elaborated upon by Grenz is that of the role of the "believing community." We have already described Grenz's refinement of the "Kingdom of God" motif in traditional evangelical theology to that of "community." Lindbeck's reference to doctrine as "communally authoritative rules of discourse, attitude and action,"[61] was part of the stimulus of Grenz's full turn to community. As Grenz delineates in *Beyond Foundationalism,* the push towards the "community" motif in theology came from biblical, theological and ethical scholars over much of the last half of the twentieth century.[62] Grenz particularly drew from Robert Bellah in *Habits of the Heart*.[63] Grenz understood the community

---

56. See Erickson et al., *Reclaiming the Center*, especially the essays by A. B. Caneday and Stephen J. Wellum.

57. Lindbeck, *Nature of Doctrine*, 18, 80.

58. See Grenz's understanding of scripture as revelation in Grenz, *Theology for the Community of God*, 396.

59. Lindbeck, *Nature of Doctrine*, 80–82.

60. Lindbeck, *Nature of Doctrine*, 81.

61. Lindbeck, *Nature of Doctrine*, 18.

62. Grenz, *Beyond Foundationalism*, 203–4.

63. In his opening citation of chapter 7 in *Beyond Foundationalism*, Grenz cites Bellah: "We find ourselves not independently of other people and institutions but through them. We never get to the bottom of ourselves on our own. We discover who we are face to face and side by side with other in work, love and learning" (Bellah, *Habits of*

motif and developed it in relationship to doctrine in a fashion that had yet to be explored in evangelical theology.

Grenz's rejection of a foundationalist epistemology for evangelical theology created an assortment of problems for him. North American evangelicals had espoused a foundationalist approach to theology dating at the latest to the nineteenth century when Princeton scholars were confronted by Darwinian evolution.[64] Grenz believed that the postmodern critique of modernism had undermined and discredited foundationalist epistemology, especially in how it had been used to justify biblical authority and doctrinal "truth claims." In light of that conclusion, Grenz sought an approach to epistemology that validated scripture's primacy and created a coherence in systematic construction. Drawing off of the work of Wolfhart Pannenberg, W. V. O. Quine and Lindbeck's appreciation of Wittgenstein's "language games," Grenz was able to cobble together an epistemic theory that involved coherence, pragmatism, and, the historical nature of truth.[65] For his critics, this epistemology didn't represent a coherent epistemology at all, and was not an alternative to traditional correspondence theory.[66] This was Grenz's weakness and challenge: the need to elucidate and clearly articulate his epistemological position. The reader has to extrapolate and interpret Grenz's epistemological position from this small, and what can be a confusing section of *Renewing the Center*. This section is also where he relied upon Lindbeck's understanding of Wittgenstein's language-games to develop a theory of intertextual theology. What can we draw from this elusive attempt to recast epistemology for evangelical theology?

First, Grenz is seeking to replace what had become an incoherent foundationalist approach to epistemology in a postmodern era where the very nature of truth had become contested. He understood that the correspondence theory of truth had become contested, and in that traditional evangelical theology continued to defend varying forms of foundationalism in order to defend the nineteenth-century Princetonian construal of biblical authority, Grenz believed a new conception of epistemology must be developed in order to better fully understand and communicate the truth of the Christian faith.

Second, Grenz draws from an amalgam of sources to construct this epistemology. Turning from a pure correspondence theory, Grenz looks to

---

the Heart, 84).

64. Grenz, *Renewing the Center*, 70

65. Grenz, *Renewing the Center*, 190–99.

66. See Doug Groothuis's article, "Truth Defined and Defended," in Erickson, *Reclaiming the Center*, 59–80.

a coherence theory of truth through the writings of Quine and Murphy.[67] In this schema, a belief is determined to be valid or "truthful," in how it "coheres" with other beliefs.[68] Next, he turns to pragmatism in the work of William James and Charles S. Peirce. Pragmatism, very simply, is "what works," or, in "how the truth of any belief is measured according to its success in advancing "factual inquiry."[69] Grenz does not simply substitute coherentism, or pragmatism as a substitute for correspondence theory, but rather simply notes philosophy's own critique of correspondence theory as a valid means of ascertaining the truthfulness of a belief. This leads him to the work of Wolfhart Pannenberg and Lindbeck.

Highly influenced by Pannenberg's theological project, Grenz admired his ability to demonstrate the "internal coherence of doctrines and the external coherence of Christian doctrine with all knowledge."[70] Grenz makes an important observation in Pannenberg's work: Pannenberg rejects the scholastic concept of truth as a "constant and unchanging eternal presence behind the flow time," and instead argues that the biblical understanding of truth is essentially historical.[71] Truth shows itself throughout the movement of time, and becomes complete, or fulfilled in the end event. Christianity anticipates this end in the present—an eschatological understanding of reality, or eschatological realism. Although Pannenberg still attempted to draw from a coherentist approach to truth to construct a non-foundationalist theology, and was committed to a realist metaphysic, Grenz posited the question if it were possible to move beyond the correspondence theory and metaphysical realism as well?[72] This is where Grenz turns to Lindbeck's understanding of Wittgentstein.

After briefly outlining Lindbeck's delineation of the various approaches to doctrine—cognitive-propositionalist, experiential-expressivist, and cultural-linguistic—Grenz affirms Lindbeck's assertion that Christian doctrines "establish the ground rules for the 'game' of Christian thinking, speaking and living."[73] Lindbeck's proposal resonates with Grenz's experience of traditional evangelicalism, and seems to suggest a direction for the creation of a much more robust and meaningful Christian theology in the postmodern context.

---

67. See Quine and Ullian, *Web of Belief*; Murphy, *Beyond Liberalism and Fundamentalism*.

68. Grenz, *Renewing the Center*, 191.

69. Grenz, *Renewing the Center*, 193.

70. Grenz, *Renewing the Center*, 196.

71. Grenz, *Renewing the Center*, 196–97.

72. Grenz, *Renewing the Center*, 197–98.

73. Grenz, *Renewing the Center*, 198.

Thus, Grenz agrees with Lindbeck's pivotal assertion regarding the concept of truth as well, which places truth within the pattern (coherence) or "web" of doctrines that inform the Christian faith, and illuminates human existence.[74] In summary, Grenz, following Pannenberg, affirms an eschatological realism, where the fullness of truth is apparent only in the end, and is revealed partially over time. For Grenz, the absolute truth resides in the Trinity, whose human exemplar is found in Jesus. Human beings who "believe," experience the truth of the Trinity through the personal presence of the Holy Spirit, and participation in the community of faith.[75]

For his critics, Grenz's delineation of post-correspondence theories of truth, and the rejection of the re-orientation of metaphysical realism was unsatisfying, and simply wrong-headed.[76] Grenz understood their criticism and rejection as an unwillingness to rethink the cognitive-propositionalist commitments of the contemporary evangelical tradition. Indeed, as reviewer David Tankersley asserted, "the authors spend the entire book decrying what they believe to be the faulty theological method of the postconservative movement. Ironically, by extenuating the modern obsession with correct method, the writers may have proved the point of postconservatism."[77] This criticism did not dissuade Grenz, though it made him unwelcome in traditional evangelical circles.

Probably the most succinct example of Grenz's mature engagement and appropriation of Lindbeck's cultural-linguistic approach to doctrinal construction is found in *The Social God and the Relational Self* (2001). Although *The Social God* is the first volume in the planned six-volume "Matrix of Christian Theology" series, this first volume reveals a clear appropriation of Lindbeck's thought. A glance at the table of contents reveals a structural outline indebted to his understanding of the cultural-linguistic method with each section reflecting his use of source material and motif. "Part One: The Context: Trinitarian Theology and the Self" contains a review of historical theology and secular psychological, sociological and anthropological thought as it pertains the historic understanding of the "self."[78] Grenz is "setting the theological stage" for his reconstructive theology of the "self." "Part Two: The *Imago Dei* in Trinitarian Perspective" discusses, reviews and analyzes the biblical and theological texts relevant to Grenz's examination

---

74. Grenz, *Renewing the Center*, 199.

75. Grenz, *Renewing the Center*, 324.

76. Again, see the essays in Erickson, *Reclaiming the Center*. The title itself is aimed as a rebuke of Grenz's *Renewing the Center*.

77. Tankersley, "Review: Reclaiming the Center," 396.

78. Grenz, *Social God*, 23–140.

of the Christian understanding of the human person and self—the *imago Dei*.[79] "Part Three: The Application: The Social *IMAGO* and the Postmodern (Loss of) Self" creates, for Grenz, a biblical, theological and applicable postmodern doctrine of the self for the contemporary church. In many ways, this is Grenz's crowning achievement in the appropriation of Lindbeck's cultural-linguistic approach. It is a clear, restatement of Christian anthropology, bound up with the doctrine of the Trinity, Christology, Pneumatology, Ecclesiology and Eschatology, and a vigorous dialogue with contemporary cultural thought. It is faithful to a high, and meaningful view of scripture, with practical import of the doctrine for the contemporary church. It allows and even encourages an appropriation of the doctrine for local church contextualization and communication.

Grenz ushered in a fine example of an evangelical appropriation of Lindbeck's postliberal theological method. The withering criticism from traditional evangelical theologians initially limited a wider appropriation. Rather than embrace the method, traditional evangelicals sought to continue a path of methodological apologetic and polemic, as well as historical theological renewal, especially as it pertains to the renewal of historic Calvinism and covenantal theology. The leading lights of this type of theological construction are Michael Horton, Oliver Crisp, Fred Sanders, Stephen Wellum, Carl Trueman, John Piper and Thomas Schreiner, among others.[80] Although Lindbeck's postliberal project has been slow to make inroads in evangelical thought, it has its champions; though they might be slow to embrace the moniker, "evangelical" due to associational issues. This group is represented in the work of Willie James Jennings, Curtis Freeman, Steven Harmon, William Abraham, Paul Fiddes, and the late James W. McClendon Jr., again to name but a few.[81]

Grenz leaves an evangelical-postliberal legacy that in many ways creates a hybrid, or even a new categorization for theological construction. Younger theologians, fresh from doctoral programs, tend towards theological analysis and are not yet comfortable with construction or ecclesial application. This is changing however, and must change as the church in Western culture becomes more and more entrenched in its struggle for relevance. Grenz made his cornerstone contributions in the doctrine of

---

79. Grenz, *Social God*, 141–266.

80. For example, Gentry and Wellum, *God's Kingdom through God's Covenants*; Wellum and Parker, *Progressive Covenantalism*; Sanders and Allen, *Triune God*; Horton, *Christian Faith*; Piper, *Peculiar Glory*; Crisp, *Saving Calvinism*.

81. For example, Jennings, *Christian Imagination*; Freeman, *Contesting Catholicity*; Harmon, *Baptist Identity and the Ecumenical Future*; Abraham, *Canon and Criterion in Christian Theology*; Fiddes, *Participating in God*; McClendon Jr., *Systematic Theology*.

the Trinity, theological anthropology and eschatology. He also contributed meaningful work in the areas of cultural analysis—sexuality, postmodernism—and ethics. Many approaches to theology with the evangelical-postliberal matrix remain to be investigated. Further investigation in the areas of theological anthropology, cognition, atonement theory, ecclesiology, and epistemology come immediately to mind. Curtis Freeman recently has written a timely essay in political theology that will be valuable for the church in the future.[82] Barry Harvey has written an important monograph on Dietrich Bonhoeffer of great value to the church in postmodern culture.[83] Nevertheless, Grenz's contribution to us is a model for constructive theology in the postmodern context. He did not simply revive another theologian's work for the postmodern context, he actually created coherent teaching-doctrine for the church that utilized the "truth-as-it-is-in-the-Trinity," and made direct application to the church in its context, as well as the postmodern "self" in distress. Grenz's engagement with Lindbeck, and what was to become postliberal theological method began at least three years before other evangelicals began the conversation. It is important that Grenz's pioneering efforts continue.

Bibliography

Abraham, William J. *Canon and Criterion in Christian Theology: From the Fathers to Feminism*. New York: Oxford University Press, 2002.

Bellah, Robert N., et al. *Habits of the Heart: Individualism and Commitment in American Life*. New York: Harper & Row, 1986.

Crisp, Oliver D. *Saving Calvinism: Expanding the Reformed Tradition*. Downers Grove, IL: InterVarsity, 2016.

Erickson, Millard, et al. *Reclaiming the Center: Confronting Evangelical Accommodation in Postmodern Times*. Wheaton, IL: Crossway, 2004.

Fiddes, Paul S. *Participating in God: A Pastoral Doctrine of the Trinity*. Louisville: Westminster John Knox, 2000.

Freeman, Curtis W. *Contesting Catholicity: Theology for Other Baptists*. Waco: Baylor University Press, 2014.

———. *Undomesticated Dissent: Democracy and the Public Virtue of Religious Nonconformity*. Waco: Baylor University Press, 2017.

Gentry Peter J., and Stephen J. Wellum, *God's Kingdom through God's Covenants: A Concise Biblical Theology*. Wheaton, IL: Crossway, 2015.

Grenz, Stanley J. "Conversing in Christian Style: Toward a Baptist Theological Method for the Postmodern Context." *Baptist History and Heritage* 35.1 (2000) 82–103.

———. *Renewing the Center: Evangelical Theology in a Post-Theological World*. Grand Rapids: Baker, 2000.

82. Freeman, *Undomesticated Dissent*.
83. Harvey, *Taking Hold of the Real*.

———. *Revisioning Evangelical Theology: A Fresh Agenda for the Twenty-First Century*. Downers Grove, IL: InterVarsity, 1992.

———. *The Social God and the Relational Self: A Trinitarian Theology of the Imago Dei*. Vol. 1 of *The Matrix of Christian Theology*. Louisville: Westminster John Knox, 2001.

———. *Theology for the Community of God*. 2nd ed. Grand Rapids: Eerdmans, 2000.

Grenz, Stanley J., and Jay T. Smith, *Created for Community*. 3rd ed. Grand Rapids: Baker Academic, 2014.

Grenz, Stanley J., and John R. Franke. *Beyond Foundationalism: Shaping Theology in a Postmodern Context*. Louisville: Westminster John Knox, 2001.

Grudem, Wayne. *Systematic Theology: An Introduction to Biblical Doctrine*. Grand Rapids: Zondervan, 1994.

Harmon, Steven R. *Baptist Identity and the Ecumenical Future: Story, Tradition, and the Recovery of Community*. Waco: Baylor University Press, 2016.

Harvey, Barry. *Taking Hold of the Real: Dietrich Bonhoeffer and the Profound Worldliness of Christianity*. Eugene, OR: Cascade, 2015.

Horton, Michael S. *The Christian Faith: A Systematic Theology for Pilgrims on the Way*. Grand Rapids: Zondervan, 2011.

Jennings, Willie James. *The Christian Imagination: Theology and Origins of Race*. New Haven: Yale University Press, 2010.

Knowles, Steven N. *Beyond Evangelicalism: The Theological Methodology of Stanley J. Grenz*. Surrey: Ashgate, 2010.

Kroeber, Arthur. *Style and Civilizations*. Ithaca, NY: Cornell University Press, 1957.

Lindbeck, George A. *The Nature of Doctrine: Religion and Theology in the Postliberal Age*. London: SPCK, 1984.

McClendon, James Wm., Jr. *Systematic Theology*. 3 vols. Nashville: Abingdon, 1994–2000.

Murphy, Nancey. *Beyond Liberalism and Fundamentalism: How Modern and Postmodern Philosophy Set the Theological Agenda*. Valley Forge, PA: Trinity, 1996.

Olson, Roger E. *Reformed and Always Reforming: The Postconservative Approach to Evangelical Theology*. Grand Rapids: Baker Academic, 2007.

Pannenberg, Wolfhart. *Systematic Theology*. Translated by Geoffrey W. Bromiley. Vol. 1. Grand Rapids: Eerdmans, 1998.

Phillips, Timothy R., and Dennis L. Okholm, eds. *The Nature of Confession: Evangelicals & Postliberals in Conversation*. Downers Grove, IL: InterVarsity, 1996.

Pinnock, Clark H. *A Defense of Biblical Infallibility*. Philadelphia: Presbyterian & Reformed, 1967.

———. "Evangelicals and Inerrancy: The Current Debate." *Theology Today* 35.1 (1978) 65–69.

Pinnock, Clark H., et al. *The Openness of God: A Biblical Challenge to the Traditional Understanding of God*. Downers Grove, IL: InterVarsity, 1994.

Piper, John. *A Peculiar Glory: How the Christian Scriptures Reveal Their Complete Truthfulness*. Wheaton: Crossway, 2016.

Quine, Willard V. O., and J. S. Ullian. *The Web of Belief*. New York: Random, 1970.

Sanders, Fred, and Michael Allen. *The Triune God*. Studies in Dogmatics. Grand Rapids: Zondervan, 2016.

Sanders, John. *The God Who Risks: A Theology of Providence*. Downers Grove, IL: InterVarsity, 1994.

———. *No Other Name: An Investigation into the Destiny of the Unevangelized.* Grand Rapids: Eerdmans, 1992.
Schaeffer, Francis A. *The Great Evangelical Disaster.* Westchester: Crossway, 1984.
Tankersley, David R. "Review: Reclaiming the Center: Confronting Evangelical Accommodation in Postmodern Times." *Review and Expositor* 104.2 (2007) 396.
Taylor, Iain. *Pannenberg on the Triune God.* New York: T&T Clark/Continuum, 2007.
Tomlinson, Dave. *The Post-Evangelical.* London: SPCK, 1995.
Vanhoozer, Kevin J. *The Drama of Doctrine: A Canonical-Linguistic Approach to Christian Theology.* Louisville: Westminster John Knox, 2005.
Wells, David F. *No Place for Truth, Or Whatever Happened to Evangelical Theology.* Grand Rapids: Eerdmans, 1993.
Wellum, Stephen J., and Brent Parker, eds. *Progressive Covenantalism: Charting a Course Between Dispensational and Covenantal Theologies.* Nashville: B&H Academic, 2016.
Work, Telford. "Reformed and Always Reforming: The Postconservative Approach to Evangelical Theology." *Christianity Today* 52.2 (2008) 79–80.

Part Three

Boundary Crossings in Philosophical, Systematic, and Ethical Theology

9

David Tracy: Difference, Unity, and the Analogical Imagination

—William E. Myatt

IN THE INVITATION FOR the current volume, Paul S. Peterson describes generous orthodoxy as "a general ecumenical attitude" that maintains "the diverse expressions of the Christian faith should be in constructive conversation with one another in order to generate a positive relationship of dialogue and cooperation." For the Roman Catholic theologian David Tracy, the pursuit of generous orthodoxy is not merely expedient; it is demanded by the claims of his own faith tradition and by the very nature of Christianity's God.

A Catholic in Twentieth-Century America: Change, Upheaval, and Pluralism

David Tracy came of theological age during a time of dramatic change. As a Catholic, Tracy witnessed the events surrounding Vatican II, during which Catholics debated numerous core practices and beliefs, including the language of the mass, the role of the church in the world, the translation and application of Holy Scripture, and the give and take between theology and philosophy. When Pope John XXIII called the council to order, he famously said the church must be willing to undergo a period of *aggiornamento*, or modernization, even as it works to protect the deposit of faith which has been entrusted to it for generations. Although the time was ripe for change, there were many factions in the church wary of moving away from the traditions and teachings of the past.

Simultaneously, Tracy's early career occurred during a time of intense change in the United States. The America of the 1960s and 1970s was a place of cultural upheaval. Between the time Tracy entered graduate studies and was awarded his first teaching post, multiple civic leaders had been assassinated, the Vietnam and Korean wars were fought, and flower children were experimenting with free love and LSD. Meanwhile, in the academy, a number of hermeneutical issues were compounding such cultural factors and causing headaches for theologians. Tracy later referred to these changes with the term "historical consciousness"—a general awareness of relativity and that self-awareness that led one to conclude that their sense of truth, of time, of the possibilities of language, and even of God were constituted by factors that one could only explain as accidental. "The fact that reason has a history," Tracy would later say, "is a problem for reason."

But perhaps most problematic for the early Tracy's pursuit of the theological tasks was an exponentially increasing awareness of pluralism. The experience of pluralism confronting the theologian of the twentieth century was twofold: On the one hand, Tracy saw pluralism as a "fundamental enrichment"[1] of the theologian's situation. It enabled critical reflection, encouraged dialogue, and forced the theologian to defend her or his point of view vigorously. On the other hand, it created a confusing situation for theologians. The "dangers," Tracy said, for the discipline of theology were obvious: "the continuous diffusion of energies; the unending emergence of sects, schools, paradigms, even fads; too little real collaboration among theologians; too little mutual criticism upon agreed-upon standards, and norms for theological performance."[2] Further, when the reality of pluralism was internalized by the theologian, it created an unsettling feeling of ambiguity. The "single self" of Kierkegaard's existentialism had given way to multiplicity, with the tension of multiple publics vying for the attention of the theologian. Tracy wrote, "The fact is that theologians do not only recognize a plurality of 'publics' to which they intend to speak, but also more and more the theologians are internalizing this plurality in their own discourse. The results are often internal confusion and external chaos."[3] Any sense of cultural or existential plurality was exacerbated by observations of plurality in numerous other sources for theology: the New Testament, the Christian tradition, and the history of conflict internal to any church tradition. The challenge for the theologian, therefore, was both to utilize an "inevitably complex" methodology in fundamental theology while also being brave enough to risk interpreting systematic theological symbols.

In the midst of all these factors, David Tracy entered St. Joseph's seminary in his home state of New York and was ordained a priest in 1963.

1. Tracy, *Analogical Imagination*, xi.
2. Tracy, *Analogical Imagination*, 18.
3. Tracy, *Analogical Imagination*, 3.

Tracy's quick wit, indefatigable work ethic, and creative theological imagination eventually afforded him the opportunity to study with the internationally renowned Jesuit theologian Bernard Lonergan at the prestigious Gregorian University in Rome. Tracy was awarded a licentiate from "The Greg" in 1964, and a doctorate in 1969. His first teaching post was at the Catholic University of America in Washington, DC. Tracy left CUA after just two years, when he and twenty other faculty members disagreed openly with Pope Paul VI's encyclical *Humanae Vitae*, which prohibited all forms of artificial birth control. Tracy then took a post at the University of Chicago Divinity School, where he was eventually named Distinguished Service Professor and served on multiple prestigious committees.

We will survey Tracy's uniquely generous response to such multifaceted challenges by highlighting three themes. First, we will see how Tracy's earliest concerns were with the nature of fundamental theology. The problem for theologians was not merely the existence of diversity. Pluralism reminded the theologian of the relatively accidental nature of her location, tradition, and point of view, and it problematized the central task of theology: speaking the truth. How might the theologian engage in such a pursuit when the diversity of ideas seemed to increase exponentially with every new generation? For Tracy, the most reasonable way forward lay in outlining shared criteria of methodological adequacy in a fundamental theology that was not afraid to engage with metaphysics. But Tracy's optimism toward metaphysics did not mean he was comfortable with the status quo. Tracy's fundamental theology was revisionist, facilitating a mutually critical conversation between the Christian tradition and common human experience.

Second, we will observe Tracy engaging pluralism not by digging his proverbial heels into the ground of tradition but by illuminating the possibilities of pluralism. Instead, Tracy constructed a christology that could handle pluralism and that, indeed, looked upon pluralism as the very fulfillment of the revelation of God in the person of Jesus Christ.

Third, we will follow Tracy's lead down this christological path and see how a situation of pluralism can deeply enrich the theological conversation. Tracy's more recent writings have reflected on the form of authentically religious expression. Far from the empty aridity of scholastic theology, classic expressions of faith exploded with intense expressions of particularity, speaking against power, in love, and for hope. Retrieving the fragmentary form allows Tracy to energize the multiplying voices of liberation and resistance today.

The Early Tracy: Revisionist Theology as Search for Order in a Disordered World

Given the general sense of chaos surrounding Tracy's academic coming of age, it makes sense that he began his career searching for some sense of order in an otherwise disorderly situation. Tracy was fully Catholic, steeped in sacramental theology and thus optimistic about the possibilities of pluralism. But he was also concerned that the lazy embrace of pluralism could lead to lazy theology. Time and again in his early career, Tracy reflected on the unique role of theology: making and evaluating truth-claims. If truth were still possible in an era defined by dramatic change in the church, upheaval in society, and relativism in the academy, theologians must discover new ways of going about their craft. The old ways of doing theology simply would not work in the world of post-modernity.

Throughout his career, Tracy turned to various modes of evaluation to respond to such challenges. Guiding the search as a whole is an attempt to locate some shared space for theological evaluation. That is, if truth can be defined as that quality of being recognizably correct—a recognition that is, at least in theory, available to anyone who observes the same fact—then theological claims must be demonstrably recognizable to anyone. Failing to subject theological claims to the criteria of truth is to run the risk of slipping into an arbitrary theology, where notions like tradition or authority are alone used to determine the truth-status of a theological claim. And if there was any hope of bringing order to an increasingly chaotic theological scene, it lay in the theologian's ability to find a common framework for engaging in the theological task. The initial development of Tracy's early career reflects the desire to bring methodological order to an otherwise disorderly situation. But it would be wrong simply to see Tracy as something like a methodology policeman. His deeper concerns were explicitly theological. And later in his career, Tracy's attention shifted from method to form, from system to fragment, from religion as limit to religion as resistance, and from religious epistemology to mysticism.[4]

Tracy's first major work, *Blessed Rage for Order*, was a reflection on fundamental theology, or theological method. The purpose of this wide-ranging and creative work was to present what Tracy called simply a "revisionist" approach. For Tracy, a Roman Catholic, there were two "principal sources" for theology: Christian texts and common human experience. The most responsible theologians engaged authentically in a mutual

---

4. I am thankful to my mentor, Dr. John McCarthy, for this outline, which he presented in a graduate course on David Tracy at Loyola University Chicago in 2009.

give-and-take between these two sources. One could argue that Tracy's faith tradition opened up the possibility for engaging both sources simultaneously, in contrast to Protestants like Karl Barth or Hans Frei, who were wary of calling experience a "source" for theology. But Tracy was clear that the intellectual trajectory in which he participated was not Catholic *per se*. Tracy's concern was twofold: simply admitting that theology is dependent on one's unique experience, a hermeneutical observation, but then also engaging authentically with that experience. At the center of this latter sensitivity was a belief in the oneness of God. If indeed the God of Christianity was the singular source of truth, if God was indeed truth itself, then the theological task of naming and evaluating truth must have some universally recognizable status.

In order to locate such a status, Tracy joined an intellectual lineage of theologians who ran the theological project through publicly available criteria, theologians like Friedrich Schleiermacher who named "absolute dependence" as the universal feeling (*Gefuhl*) illustrated by faith; or Paul Tillich, who named "ultimate concern" as the existential crisis that joined his situation with others. In *Blessed Rage for Order*, Tracy called this space "the religious dimension of experience." As the theologian went about his task of engaging in a critical investigation of both Christian texts and common human experience, he or she did so by disclosing how the two sources of theology illustrated the religious dimension of experience shared by all people, from ancient people of faith to contemporary scientists disenfranchised with mystifications.

Tracy characterized the religious dimension of existence by referring to it as an experience of limit, disclosed by the universal desire to move toward and then beyond that limit. We are a limit-oriented species, and we express that orientation by always moving toward that which is more. Among the numerous human expressions that illustrate our limit-orientation, none is more profound than religion. Religions make claims about "the whole." Religious people believe these claims. They live according to them. They die for them. And they believe the very source of these claims is likewise in correlation with "the whole" itself. Tracy held that theologians would engage in a responsible theological project by determining how the two principal sources of theology illustrate that deeper orientation toward limit that is indicative of common human experience. By disclosing the religious dimension in each source, the theologian will open up a space for mutual correlation and thus for revisionist theology.

To do so, Tracy suggested engaging a relatively new philosophical approach called "phenomenology." With roots in the nineteenth- and early twentieth-century work of philosophers like Edmund Husserl and Martin

Heidegger, phenomenology worked to disclose the "phenomena" of consciousness by reflecting on the manner in which phenomena appear to the thinking subject. Drawing from the Kantian distinction between "noumena" (things in and of themselves) and "phenomena" (the manner in which things appear to us), phenomenology aimed to disclose "phenomena," objects of knowledge according to the way they are experienced. It was, in brief, philosophy from a first-person point of view.

For Tracy, it was vital to ensure two aspects of this pursuit. On the one hand, experience could not be reduced to science. Being human included subjectivity: the writing of poems, the singing of songs, laughter, telling jokes, making love, and producing art. Especially when disclosing the experience of religion, that most subjective of all human expressions, it was vital to present an account in which subjectivity was fully present. Indeed, the most authentic accounts of religious experience came from those "thick descriptions" which were themselves generated by a religious experience! The theologian's responsibility was to disclose the functionality of the religious dimension to existence, as it operated in the day-to-day lives of all people.

Simultaneously, the theologian opened up the sources of "the Christian tradition" by engaging in the hermeneutical task of analyzing texts. Yet Tracy's task was not merely textual. Borrowing from his colleague Paul Ricoeur at the University of Chicago, Tracy saw hermeneutics itself as requiring phenomenological analysis in order to account fully for the human event of understanding. Thus, as Tracy analyzed the Bible, classic Christian texts, and that set of documents Christians refer to with the tired notion of "Tradition," he did so in order to conceptualize the faith expressed by those texts as itself an expression of the religious dimension shared by all people.

Quintessentially, that expression could be found in the New Testament representation of Jesus Christ, whose memory Tracy calls a "limit-mode-of-being-in-the-world." Fundamentally illustrated in the Christian claim "Jesus Christ is Lord," a limit-mode-of-being-in-the-world discloses a concentration of that shared fundamental trust. In the person of faith, the fundamental trust in existence is concentrated densely until it bursts forth into a life of agapic love, a life lived as if in the very presence of God. The New Testament memory of Christ is thus re-presented as trust in the claims of faith unique to authentic Christian expression.

Once the theologian has completed the hermeneutical-phenomenological task of disclosing a concentrated version of the religious dimension to existence in Christian texts, she is ready to place that disclosure alongside the religious dimension to existence that is "common" to human experience in a mutually correcting dialogue of sources. Tracy argued that "an explicitly transcendental and metaphysical mode of reflection" was necessary to facilitate this mutually critical conversation. Tracy's willingness to use such loaded terminology shows a continued hope to maintain theology's most fundamental task: making and evaluating truth-claims. Given the nature of religion (faith in the whole as revealed by the power of the whole) and of religious language (claims of and about the whole), the theologian has no choice but ultimately to risk evaluating what is true (i.e., transcendental or metaphysical) about that religion and its claims.

Tracy was quick to observe that his movement toward metaphysics was indeed controversial, given the sad state of metaphysics in the postmodern era. Nevertheless, Tracy was insistent that a final evaluative process must take place in order for the Christian to display continuity with her own faith tradition. The metaphysical tools used by the theologian must be adequately conceptual and not merely symbolic. They must keep the theologian from drifting into vagueness and incoherence. The discipline must also be able to articulate the grounds for its claims, including the naming of a sufficient ground in common human experience to make its claims. In the Kantian sense of "transcendental," such reflection explored the conditions of the possibility for all understanding, while in the more contemporary sense of "metaphysical," such reflection explored the possibility of whether such limit-concepts as "God" are either affirmed or denied by the universal sensitivities disclosed by phenomenological-hermeneutical reflection.

The theological payoff for this methodological foundation is twofold: in terms of systematic theology, concepts such as God and Jesus Christ are articulated in ways that are simultaneously representative of the faith expressed in classic Christian texts and the pluralities with which any contemporary theologian is all too familiar. The Christian concept of God is opened up to reflect the dipolar nature of human existence: the pole of existence as such, which is an essentially static reality; and the pole of subjective expression, which is no less dynamic than it is for the humans Christians believe God created.

In terms of practical theology, Tracy's revisionist methodology finds its final application in the various "political theologies of *praxis*—of hope, of liberation, even of revolution,"[5] which were becoming more and more mainstream during the America of the 1960s and 1970s. The sense of optimism and possibility encouraged by Tracy's Christology found a ready corrective in the "critical social theory" that "supplemented" and "completed" the revisionist model. Critical theory allowed not merely a critique of society from a Christian-theological perspective but a critique of the critique itself. The radical faith memorialized in the Christ event demanded nothing less. The

---

5. Tracy, *Blessed Rage for Order*, 240.

role of the theologian was, therefore, to engage in both a critical analysis of culture and a hermeneutical retrieval of the forgotten stories of the Christian faith. There was no more potent disclosure of that limit-oriented nature of existence than the hidden heroes of the faith who radically lived the limit-mode-of-being-in-the-world. Retrieving their forgotten memory enabled the theologian to empower similarly radical modes of being today and, by empowering such modes of being, to engender a radical critique of society.

Analogy and Christology: Engaging Pluralism through Conversation

Having laid a methodological foundation in *Blessed Rage for Order*, Tracy endeavored in his second work to construct a systematic theology that would be consistent with the parameters defined in the first. As in *Blessed Rage for Order*, in *Analogical Imagination* Tracy exhibited an appreciation for both pluralism and critical social philosophy. Prompted by the inclusivist christology of the catholic, analogical imagination, the theologian engaged in authentically open conversation with the multiple contemporary publics constituting her situation. Indeed, Tracy's primary motivation for writing *Analogical Imagination* was the possibility of facilitating a productive conversation. Among the ways Tracy suggested facilitating this conversation was the use of Hans-Georg Gadamer's notion of "the classic" as a central idea around which systematic theological method could be construed. By approaching her tradition as a collection of religious classics, the theologian was given a ready resource for facilitating a conversation within the "self-interpretation of the religious dimension of a culture."[6] However, Tracy was also aware that the ideal of conversation often masked structures of power. Informed by a christology highlighting the Christ *event* and a twentieth-century situation highlighting the experience of "the uncanny," Tracy complemented his embrace of conversation with a suspicion informed by critical philosophy.

To facilitate an appropriate response to pluralism, it was vital that the theologian exercise explicit self-awareness. Tracy himself offered an exploration of the theologian's "social reality" by suggesting that all theologians share three "principal publics": the wider society, the academy, and the church. Although each theologian strived "for a genuine publicness and thereby implicitly address[ed] all three publics," the public setting within which a theology was constructed gave way to the determination of "distinct

---

6. Tracy, "Role of Theology in Public Life," 232.

plausibility structures" based on "clear or distinct elective affinities" between the publics and the theologian.[7]

The three models for theology—fundamental, systematic, and practical—functioned as heuristic labels according to which both contemporary and historical responses to the Christ event could be categorized. Although all three models spoke "trans-publicly," their respective publics were distinct: fundamental theologians spoke primarily to the academy and thus according to the warrants and criteria characterizing the academy; systematic theologians spoke primarily to the church and thus according to the warrants and criteria characterizing the church; and practical theologians spoke primarily to (or, perhaps "about") society and thus according to the warrants and criteria characterizing society and its needs. The overlap of these distinct theological models was clarified according to their shared tasks. Each theologian offered an interpretation of a tradition, an interpretation of the contemporary situation, and a correlation of the two.

But the theologian's responsibilities do not stop at self-awareness. The lingering temptation of a ghettoized, arbitrary, and ultimately private theology required the theologian to be aware of the multiple publics to which her work was addressed. The theologian must indeed pursue publicness as an outflow of her religious identity and as a responsible reaction to the realities of pluralism at work in twentieth-century society. The theological trajectory toward truth, the role of religion in society, and the nature of Christianity's God demanded nothing less than a demonstrably public explication of the Christian fact. The hermeneutical factors at play in the public of the academy (fundamental theology) formed a pattern that the systematic and practical theologians could follow, as they likewise moved their projects forward—not only through meaning and meaningfulness but ultimately to truth as a universally recognizable conceptualization of faith.

Publicness could be achieved as disciplinary self-awareness, and publicness included the uniquely theological vocation of risking truth-claims. Motivated by the need for self-awareness in the pursuit of conversation, the theologian engaged in a deliberate naming of the disciplinary criteria determining the relative adequacy of her project. Motivated by the theological vocation to speak truth, the theologian founded her project—regardless of the primary public to which it was addressed—on the theoretical groundwork laid by the fundamental theologian. The public of the academy thus served as the paradigmatic public informing all theologies.

The payoff for Tracy in *Analogical Imagination* came in his rather brilliant suggestion that the systematic theologian can find an analogue

7. Tracy, *Analogical Imagination*, 30–31.

for interpretation in the notion of the religious classic. Perduring as indefatigably particular intensifications of experience and thus exploding into always-elusive and ever-opening moments of appropriation, classics were "there." They existed. Classics were those beautiful and timeless expressions of singularity that exploded into multiple interpretations, spread throughout time and cultures. Classics were, in a word, public.

More specifically applicable to the concerns internal to systematic theology, religious classics embodied the public nature of classics broadly but likewise illustrated the fundamental trust in existence, or "religious dimension to existence" that Tracy had explored in *Blessed Rage for Order*. No less particular and thus no less elusive, religious classics were more specifically characterized by an experience of "the whole" disclosed as a sense of trust in the power of "the whole" and representing unique expressions of those shared fundamental questions that explode from our shared experiences of limit.

But religious classics were not mere manifestations of shared experience; they were proclamations of hope—often perceived as an in-breaking, shattering moment of intense trust in reality. The systematic theologian could secure her disciplinary status in a recognizably public manner by explicating her task as a uniquely Christian interpretation of Christian religious classics. She was a hermeneutician. Not unlike the interpreters of philosophical classics in philosophy and literary classics in literature, the interpreter of theological classics believed she could re-present disclosive and transformative truths to and in dialogue with all three publics (church, academy, society).

Even more central to her task was the interpretation of the centrally differentiating concept within Christianity, christology. The Christ-event in response to which the Christian constructed her Christology was the quintessentially classic event. Its interpreted status was never, and could never be declared, closed. As such, a chaotic plurality of interpretations remained inside Christianity and thus opened up a theological space for embracing the increasingly pluralistic situation of twentieth-century theology. Classics have somehow endured "as provocations awaiting the risk of reading," luring us "out of a privacy masked as autonomy."[8] The classics existed as claims, calls, urges toward the members of a community to enter the public realm, where what was "important and essential" was no longer denied. When the classic work of art was "actually experienced," its interpreters were "liberated from privateness into the genuine publicness of a disclosure of truth."[9]

---

8. Tracy, *Analogical Imagination*, 115.
9. Tracy, *Analogical Imagination*, 115.

This moment of intensification resulting in the production of the classic was continued in the experience of recognizing the classic as a classic. In an "actual experience of the work of art," the interpreter moved into the "back-and-forth rhythms" internal to the expression. Analogous to the discovery and disclosure of awareness that gave rise to the work, the interpreter "likewise moves between discovery and disclosure on the way to and during a recognition of truth in the classic. Within this event, the interpreter likewise moves to a sensed recognition of the essential beyond the everyday; from its hiddenness to our sensed rootedness; from its disclosure and concealment of truth to our realized experience of a transformative truth, at once revealing and concealing."[10]

The classic made a claim on the interpreter, a claim that transcended any context of pre-understanding potentially imposed upon it, a claim that could shock the interpreter with an insight into her own finitude, a claim, the authentic interpreter said, "that will interpret me even as I interpret it. I cannot control the experience, however practiced I am in techniques of manipulation. It happens, it demands, it provokes."[11]

When the classic was freed to be realized, actualized in the experience of the individual, when its truth was not confined to mediation by technical reason and "truth" thus reduced to a question of taste, it became public. Insofar as classics continued to speak, continued to resist closure, the truth they mediated was likewise recognized as permanently timely, and the meanings these expressions enabled were likewise untamed. Appropriating such classics required something like an "analogical imagination"—an ability to continue the contemporary facilitation of connections, sparks, hints, and guesses toward truth engendered by the classics' persistent confrontation with interpreters. If anything like truth remained in the increasingly pluralistic culture of the twentieth century, it could not be located by sheer acts of will—stubborn refusals to engage in authentic dialogue with the multiple voices struggling for recognition. Resurrecting retrospective utopias was not the answer; neither, however, was a lazy pluralism, a decorous defeatism—polite but, finally, reductionistic. Difference, especially religious, remained.

Conversation as Gathering Fragments

We may initiate our conclusion by suggesting a metaphor. The David Tracy of *Analogical Imagination* is like a housekeeper who moves into action, after

10. Tracy, *Analogical Imagination*, 114.
11. Tracy, *Analogical Imagination*, 119.

having heard an expensive vase shatter in an adjacent room. Upon hearing the crash, the housekeeper rushes to the scene and observes fragments scattered across the floor. He is aware that what was once pristine has now been damaged, perhaps irreparably so. The beloved vase of his employer will never be what it once was. The damage is too great. Yet, because the housekeeper knows the homeowner loves that vase—and because the housekeeper also loves it—he does not want to throw the pieces away. He begins to sweep up the scattered fragments into heaps, gathering the fragments so as to preserve what remains.

But there is much more to the illustration. Tracy indeed knew that complete and thorough reconstruction of pristine Catholicism, the "good old days" of Tridentine Christianity, was impossible. On the other hand, reconnection and conversation were not. For, the living fragments of the Catholic tradition all contained within themselves some possibility for remembering the "once whole." That "once" was not a previous era, a pre-modernity or modernity, when things were perfect. It was certainly not a new or old ideology. It was something more primordial and edenic. The living fragments contained within them a potential for recollection, which Tracy appropriated by a re-collection, a gathering of what had been shattered by "the fall." Merely to look at the clutter, the "chaotic pluralism," with sadness, disdain, or disapproval was not to recall that within the all-too-human fragments there was a fundamental connectivity. Expressed variously as a fundamental trust in existence, fleeting recollections of shalom, love, hope, community, and faith, this memory enabled a re-membering, a re-turn, an ana-theism. That memory did not provide a framework for full reconstruction, but it did provide motivation and vision. It motivated the theological housekeeper to continue sweeping, to continue the difficult task of collecting without compromising the irreducibility of each, singular fragment. Tracy engaged in this task by finding analogical connections, similarities-in-difference, that—when informed by a poetic imagination—enabled a more hopeful, manageable, ordered response to the contemporary situation than so many critical options available. Although thorough reconstruction was impossible, it was possible to keep the fragments as a memento of what once was. This tribute could be further enlivened by organizing the fragments into, say, heaps of similar colors, recognizable patterns, or certain textures differentiating the top from the bottom, the inside from the out.

Tracy's goal was much less order and systematization than it was facilitation of a conversation, a conversation that had gotten out of hand. Tracy was not a scientist; he did not have a monopoly on truth; his was not the metanarrative. But Tracy did see certain loci of overlap and difference among forms. In order to keep such forms from devolving into disparate and increasingly disconnected options, struggling against one another for more esteemed positions at the table of public discourse, Tracy became a kind of moderator, a mediator or perhaps, finally, a priest.[12] The type of "public" reflection for which he argued enabled the conversation to move forward in constructive ways without compromising the theistic and christological affirmations which differentiated this conversation from, say, the conversations engaging biologists or mathematicians or even those of other religions. Tracy's conversation was explicitly Christian and unapologetically theological; but the re-membering of his unique religious identity did not mean the conversation was sectarian or irrational. It was not "private." The conversation would become more and more navigable and the truth-options more adjudicable, the more willingly participants opened up their conversation to marginalized forms of thought and thus ensuring that their conversation was recognizably public. Such a goal was not only useful in carrying out the conversational task. It was ethical, for public modes of thought protected theologians from adopting arbitrary appropriations of traditional categories. "Publicness" was a way of encouraging responsible theological thinking. It was adverbial. Theology was done "publicly" as a uniquely contemporary instantiation of post-Enlightenment identity.

Art and Truth

In order to facilitate the task of conversation through publicness, Tracy suggested that the theologian reconsider the manner in which religious and public meaning and truth were evaluated. As a result of the kinds of questions theology asked and the reality of God upon which theology reflected, the theologian could not but develop public criteria for theological discourse. But, as we saw highlighted in *Blessed Rage for Order*, the type of discourse associated with public reasoning in modernity had been irreparably deconstructed by various postmodern thinkers. Tracy responded by reflecting on an alternative but analogous mode of reason that—like religion—had been marginalized in modernity: art. Although works of art—especially classic works of art—were obviously recognized as true, no truly appreciative

---

12. Toward the end of his summary of the disciplinary models in theology, Tracy said, "Perhaps this proposal is, finally, a futile exercise born of an irenic temperament. Yet I think not. It would be if the distinctions developed are simply invalid—ungrounded in the common drive to publicness entailed by the doctrine of God and ungrounded in their distinct relationships to society, academy, and church entailed by the doctrines of church and world" (Tracy, *Analogical Imagination*, 80). Stephen H. Webb says of his mentor, "David Tracy was an irenic and benevolent graduate school advisor who encouraged his students to follow their own paths" (Webb, "On Mentors," 237).

observer of art would want to reduce art's truth to propositions. Anyone caught up in the experience of recognition in response to a classic knew that this experience was full, embodied, human; and it was also true. Religious experience—the recognition of some truth as indicative of "the whole"—was likewise not reducible to disembodied modes of discourse.

Religion, as that quintessentially human mode of expression, was full, intense, ecstatic, fascinating, and tremendous; and religious expression was also experienced as true. By suggesting continuity between religious and artistic modes of expression, theologians could capture their experiences of truth in an adequately post-Enlightenment manner and express them in a recognizable form. If, by reflecting on truth in artistic modes of expression and reception, Tracy could locate a space where truth was both recognizable and analogical, then he could perhaps locate a space where religious pluralism did not hamstring the uniquely theological vocation of claims to truth. Such religious-as-artistic forms of expression and reception found their theological analogue in a Christology informed by the Catholic sacramental theology which was Tracy's religious heritage. But at the same time, Tracy's sensitivities were set loose by the various critics of modernity, those thinkers Paul Ricoeur famously called "masters of suspicion."[13] The imagination emerging in the late twentieth century was one informed deeply by the negations of post-Enlightenment thought, and Tracy was deeply appreciative of such insights.

By facilitating an analogical comparison between the experience of truth in classic art and the experience of theological truth mediated by tradition, Tracy was able to construct a unique approach to publicness. When such "paradigmatic expressions of human spirit"[14] were experienced as resonating with an other's experience, they manifested a claim to attention, a shock of recognition, that could not but be named "true." The truth found there "may not be adequately expressible in the propositions of objective consciousness," but when it was recognized as resonating authentically with the interpreter's experience, it was likewise recognized as "real."[15] It was these true-as-real expressions—of art, of thought, of life—that, when recognized collectively as real by members in a particular community, were elevated to classic status. And it was these classics that, when played together (sometimes sounding symphonic, sometimes cacaphonic), would create new songs of meaning.

13. See Ricoeur, "Critique of Religion," 205. Tracy referenced numerous critics, but he considered Marx, Freud, Nietzsche, and Heidegger to be especially paradigmatic.

14. Tracy, *Analogical Imagination*, 130.

15. Tracy, *Analogical Imagination*, 130.

Interrupting the Conversation

For the theologian intending to mirror the ideal of conversation in her appropriation of a tradition, the ambiguity[16] marking conversation gives way to an ambiguity marking religious traditions. Ambiguity is a dualistic idea for Tracy. On the one hand, theologians are aware that their traditions may function positively as the historical memory of a culture. The memories constituting traditions carry the "history of effects of the classic texts, persons, events, symbols, and rituals" that provide meaningfulness to a particular people.[17] A loss of these memories "can be fatal," since without them, "we cannot act."[18] On the other hand, "there are no innocent readings of the classics."[19] Tracy regularly recalls the famous saying of Walter Benjamin, "there is no document of culture that is not at the same time a document of barbarism."[20] Alongside the fanaticism attached to tradition "and its demonic history of effects" emerge "impacted memories" that remain constantly on the verge of oblivion.[21] The classics, therefore, "demand not only retrieval but critique and suspicion."[22] For Tracy, the classics themselves instantiate a uniquely disruptive form amenable to this need for critical retrieval. Although it is common for the symbols, language, and grammar of religious classics to devolve into banality, the classics themselves—those original, "intense"[23] moments of productive distanciation—perdure in a particularly interruptive and elusive manner. Of course, the responsible theologian retrieves such classics with an eye to the manner in which so many modes of Christian expression have been used to perpetuate various forms of violence.[24] Still, the classics elude easy assimilation. They are no more predictable than the plurality of interpretations to which they give rise. When retrieved and re-presented in a manner consistent with their

---

16. Tracy, *Analogical Imagination*, 49
17. Tracy, *Analogical Imagination*, 36.
18. Tracy, *Analogical Imagination*, 36.
19. Tracy, *Analogical Imagination*, 36–37,

20. Benjamin, *1938–1940*, 391. Richard Bernstein called Plurality and Ambiguity an extended reflection on this Benjaminian idea (Bernstein, "Radical Plurality," 69). Tracy himself evaluated this comment as "entirely accurate" (Tracy, "Christian Option," 119).

21. Tracy, *Plurality and Ambiguity*, 85.
22. Tracy, *Plurality and Ambiguity*, 86.

23. Tracy is appreciative of the attention to intense religious expression in William James. Tracy balances his attention to intensity with a celebration of the divine in "the everyday," or "the ordinary" (Tracy, *Plurality and Ambiguity*, 97; cf. *Analogical Imagination*, 266–68).

24. Tracy, *Plurality and Ambiguity*, 85.

"permanent timeliness," religious classics enable the resistance necessary to inform a hermeneutics of suspicion. To interpret a tradition's religious classics appropriately, one must "allow them to challenge what we presently consider possible."[25] Religious classics "entice us to hope for some other and different, yet possible, ways of thinking" and thus empower contemporary projects of resistance.[26] "Does anyone really wish," Tracy asked, "that Luther, instead of simply stating, 'Here I stand; I can do no other,' had added sotto voce, 'But if it really bothers you, I will move'?"[27]

But how might the theologian embody this resistant form in the appropriation of her own religious classics? We may make suggestions along these lines by considering Tracy's more recent reflections on the religious form, a form he no longer refers to as "classic" but as "fragment." As early as 1995, Tracy began to use the term "fragment" to suggest the form Christian theology should take in its renewed engagement with classic theological texts. In an address to the Catholic Theological Society of America, Tracy observed the "shocking silence" in most theologies of history, relative to "the evil rampant in history, the suffering of whole peoples, the destruction of nature itself."[28] After offering this appropriately Christian "confession" of his own religion's participation in the sins of history, Tracy urges his listeners to reclaim theological forms invoking the "dangerous and disruptive God of the history narrated in Exodus and in the history of Jesus."[29] Not unlike his dramatic and climactic conclusion in *Analogical Imagination*, Tracy's address to the CTSA concludes with a litany of disruptive forms—a collection of religious fragments—re-presented for the purpose of invoking hopeful resistance in the face of radical suffering.

Still utilizing a version of the transcendental-phenomenological mode of analysis that has informed so much of his theological career, Tracy calls fragments the "spiritual situation of our times."[30] Fragments inform our thinking in two ways. First, fragments embody a "negative" function, inasmuch as they "show the need to shatter any reigning totality system." Aware of the connection between totalizing frameworks and marginalization, defenders of the fragment maintain, "any form which attempts totality or closure . . .

---

25. Tracy, *Plurality and Ambiguity*, 84.

26. Tracy, *Plurality and Ambiguity*, 88.

27. Tracy, *Plurality and Ambiguity*, 91. Tracy attributes this question to Philip Blackwell in Tracy, *Plurality and Ambiguity*, 138n26.

28. Tracy, "Evil, Suffering, Hope," 29.

29. Tracy, "Evil, Suffering, Hope," 28.

30. Tracy, "Fragments," 170–84.

needs fragmentation."³¹ Second, and in contrast, fragments serve a "positive" function, inasmuch as they point to "a break out of totality into infinity" by their ability to disclose "one's own routes and one's own traditions."³² Fragments in this sense are narratival, experiential, and emotive. They function as a unitary moment of productive distanciation, where form and content are united in an explosive expression of particularity.

When such portrayals are received with sympathy, the interpreter may discern a means by which "all the others and the different" function "as possible disclosures of infinity."³³ In the fragment, the subject insists, "Do not reduce me or anyone else to your narrative."³⁴ As a "saturated phenomenon,"³⁵ religious expression may function as the "most non-reductive" means of fragmentation. In "the intense religion of the black church traditions," for example, one finds the "unassimilatable other," where "repressed, intense, saturated, and fragmentary religious forms"³⁶ break through in an explosive claim to recognition. Exemplified in the demand for liberation and justice in black theology, God is a "fragmentary, liberating God." Here, the fragment engenders not only "a shattering of any totality system" but also "the possibility of positive rediscovery of the intense presence of infinity in religious forms."³⁷ It is not accurate to assume that religion, "like the Jesuits of Voltaire's wonderful imagination . . . must always enter the rooms of modernity without warmth and leave without regret."³⁸ That, Tracy says, "is not religion."

Religion is vibrant, particularly in its most disruptive, excessive forms (gospel songs, love mystics, kabbalists, sufis, etc.); and it is indeed the recovery of these excessive forms that has energized so many recent theological, philosophical, and even sociological projects of resistance. When considered together, these various theologies represent the possibility that a fragmentary public theology should not only induce dialogue and liberation but radical critique. Embodying such forms of expression, fragments become not merely anti-totalities but "fragments of hope,"³⁹ suggestions for

31. Tracy, "Form and Fragment," 64–65.
32. Tracy, "African American Thought," 30.
33. Tracy, "African American Thought," 30.
34. Tracy, "Fragments and Forms," 124.
35. Tracy is of course borrowing from Jean-Luc Marion for the notion of a "saturated phenomenon." For Tracy on Marion, see Tracy, "Foreword," xi–xviii.
36. Tracy, "African American Thought," 30.
37. Tracy, "African American Thought," 30.
38. Tracy, "African American Thought," 33.
39. This phrase is borrowed from Ross, "Evil and Hope," 46–63. In this response to David Tracy, Ross observes that even in the profound suffering recalled in the passion

redemption that motivate believing communities toward resistance of oppressive structures. Fragmentary narratives—more typically forgotten than centralized—provide "hints and guesses of hope . . . fragmentary glimpses of light and redemption."[40] It is particularly these hope-filled narratives of religious experience that may provide an alternative "postsecular" resource for "our desiccated public realm."[41] In the "amazing theology" of slave narratives, gospel songs, and "the distinct theologies of the spirituals and the blues,"[42] one may find an especially potent corrective to the disembodied tendencies of so many fundamental rationalities.

Generous Orthodoxy and the Analogical Imagination

Any reflection on generous orthodoxy would be wise to include David Tracy among those it will survey. Tracy's deep appreciation for pluralism as a fundamental enrichment of the human situation and his persistent hope to facilitate conversation in response to pluralism qualify Tracy as exactly the type of "generous" theologian contemporary faith leaders should emulate. Yet Tracy was quite aware of the problems that tended to accompany dialogue: problems of power, of misunderstanding, of recalcitrance. In order to find motivation to continue pursuing dialogue, Tracy needed to look no further than his own faith tradition. Christianity taught the singularity of the creator God. And Christianity taught that the one God had been singularly revealed in the event of Jesus Christ. For Tracy, a Roman Catholic theologian whose intellectual genealogy ran through the likes of John of the Cross, Thomas Aquinas, and Bernard of Clairvaux, the singularity of the Christ event was anything but straightforward. The dense concentration of the religious dimension to existence, a concentration that by faith is called "the very presence of God," exploded into multiplicity. Like a timeless classic, beautifully written so as never to exhaust all possible meaning, the Christ event burst forth into multiple interpretations. Christology allowed, indeed encouraged, pluralism, even as the God to whom Christianity gave witness demanded nothing less than the timeless pursuit of truth.

---

narratives, the attentive reader may find "fragments of hope."
40. Tracy, "African American Thought," 37–38.
41. Tracy, "African American Thought," 37–38.
42. Tracy, "African American Thought," 31.

Bibliography

Benjamin, Walter. *1938–1940*. Edited by Howard Eiland and Michael W. Jennings. Vol. 4 of *Selected Writings*. Cambridge: Belknap Press of Harvard University Press, 2003.

Bernstein, Richard J. "Radical Plurality, Fearful Ambiguity, and Engaged Hope: Review of Tracy, *Plurality and Ambiguity*." *Journal of Religion* 69.1 (1989) 85–91.

Hopkins, Dwight N. *Black Faith and Public Talk: Critical Essays on James H. Cone's Black Theology and Black Power*. Maryknoll, NY: Orbis, 1999.

Marion, Jean-Luc. *God without Being*. Translated by T. Carlson. Chicago: University of Chicago Press, 2012

Ricoeur, Paul. "Critique of Religion." Translated by R. Bradley DeFord. *Union Seminary Quarterly Review* 28.3 (1973) 205–12.

Ruggieri, Giuseppe, and Miklos Tomka, eds. *The Church in Fragments: Towards What Kind of Unity*. Maryknoll, NY: Orbis, 1997.

Tracy, David. *Analogical Imagination: Christian Theology and the Culture of Pluralism*. New York: Crossroads, 1981.

———. "The Christian Option for the Poor." In *The Option for the Poor in Christian Theology*, edited by Daniel G. Groody, 119–31. Notre Dame: University of Notre Dame Press.

———. "Evil and Hope: Foundational Moral Perspectives." *CTSA Proceedings* 50 (1995) 46–63.

———. "Evil, Suffering, Hope: The Search for New Forms of Contemporary Theodicy." *CTSA Proceedings* 50 (1995) 15–36.

———. "Foreword." In *God without Being*, by Jean-Luc Marion, xi–xviii. Translated by Thomas Carlson. Chicago: University of Chicago Press, 2012.

———. "Form and Fragment: The Recovery of the Hidden and Incomprehensible God." *Reflections: Center for Theological Inquiry* 3 (1999) 62–89.

———. "Fragments: The Spiritual Situation of Our Times." In *God, the Gift, and Postmodernity*, edited by John D. Caputo and Michael J. Scanlon, 170–84. Bloomington: Indiana University Press, 1999.

———. "Fragments and Forms: Universality and Particularity Today." In *The Church in Fragments: Towards What Kind of Unity*, edited by Giuseppe Ruggieri and Miklos Tomka, 122–29. London: SCM, 1997.

———. *Plurality and Ambiguity*. Chicago: University of Chicago Press, 1996.

———. "The Role of Theology in Public Life: Some Reflections." *Word and World* 6.3 (1984) 232.

Webb, Stephen H. "On Mentors and the Making of a Useful Theology: A Retrospective on the Work of William C. Placher." *Religion and Theology* 13.2 (2006) 237–43.

10

Robert W. Jenson: God's Way and the Ways of the Church

—Christophe Chalamet

Introduction: A Lutheran and Ecumenical Theologian

ROBERT W. JENSON (1930–2017) is a signal figure in contemporary theology who embodies the perspective of a "generous orthodoxy," i.e., a theology which crosses over confessional identities and boundaries in order to retrieve the tradition, broadly construed, of the Christian Church.

His roots in North American Lutheranism are unmistakable.[1] Born in the small city of Eau Claire (Wisconsin) in 1930, where Lutheran parishes of various stripes abounded and still abound, in a time when intra-Protestant, not to mention intra-Christian dialogue, was at best burgeoning, he studied at Luther College (Decorah, Iowa) after the end of World War II, then at Luther Seminary (Saint Paul, Minnesota) starting in 1951, before returning to Luther College as a teacher (1955–1957). Until 1957 his academic career was, as it appears, mostly limited to midwestern Lutheranism.

Much changed with the years Jenson spent in Germany: he became a doctoral student at the University of Heidelberg in 1957–1958. There he met and became a friend of Wolfhart Pannenberg (1928–2014), who was only two years his senior, and who would become one of the most significant Lutheran and ecumenical thinkers in the ensuing decades. Jenson enrolled in a course Pannenberg was giving, took part in a seminar given by Hans-Georg Gadamer, and attended a daylong encounter with

---

1. I wish to thank Valérie Kim, former librarian at Bossey's Ecumenical Institute (World Council of Churches), for her help in making some of the literature used in this article available to me. For the relevant biographical literature on Robert W. Jenson, see Swain, *God of the Gospel*, 15n8. For a comprehensive bibliography of Jenson's works, see Jenson, *Theology in Outline*, 117–34.

Martin Heidegger. Jenson wrote his dissertation under the guidance of Peter Brunner (1900–1981), a former member of the Confessing Church (*Bekennende Kirche*) who, with his rather high sense of the Church as well as of the liturgy, was a singular figure in the German Protestant theological landscape of the time. Not without any incidence on ulterior commitments of his former doctoral student, in 1962, only three years after Robert W. Jenson completed his dissertation, Peter Brunner published the first part of a two-volume work titled *Pro Ecclesia*.[2] The jury of Jenson's dissertation reads like a *Who's Who* of mid-twentieth century theology: Edmund Schlink, Gerhard von Rad, Hans von Campenhausen, Günter Bornkamm. The topic of his dissertation was Karl Barth's doctrine of election. Needless to say, this topic placed Jenson in conversation with the (or at least one of the) towering figure(s) of twentieth-century Protestant theology, on one of the two theological decisions through which the Swiss theologian showed he was not interested in repristinating anything (the other decision being the unfolding, from the outset of his *Kirchliche Dogmatik*, i.e., right from the prolegomena, of the doctrine of God's triunity). Having read Jenson's dissertation, Barth praised its author, who had (in Barth's words) understood his thought, and discussed with him some of the questions the young American student raised in his critical evaluation.[3]

The richness of Jenson's formative years is, thus, clear. Ecumenical dialogues were sprouting here and there. Rome was still reluctant, in the 1950s, to join the movement and sought to restrain some of its most significant thinkers (Yves Congar, OP; Marie-Dominique Chenu, OP; Henri de Lubac, SJ), but, as we now know, it was only a matter of years until Roman Catholicism shifted its position and opened up to the ecumenical movement.

In the early 1960s, Jenson was back home, teaching at Luther College. His European training led him into some troubles with his (mostly) conservative Lutheran colleagues, who had little tolerance for critical exegesis and modern evolutionary views. They were very serious about these matters, and so, when they realized they could not get rid of their newly appointed colleague, they themselves resigned *en bloc*! After a brief sting at Oxford (1966–1968), during which he supervised Colin Gunton's doctoral dissertation, Jenson taught at the Lutheran Theological Seminary in Gettysburg, Pennsylvania. He became almost immediately involved in official ecumenical dialogues, first between Lutherans and Episcopalians, then between Lutherans and Roman Catholics. In 1988, with his last decade of teaching in view,

2. Brunner, *Pro Ecclesia*.
3. The title of the published (and drastically shortened) version of Jenson's dissertation, *Alpha and Omega*. The original title is: "Cur Deus Homo? The Election of Jesus Christ in the Theology of Karl Barth."

he moved to Northfield, Minnesota, at St. Olaf College. There he wrote his two-volume *Systematic Theology*,[4] which remains his *magnum opus*. Jenson was then invited by Wallace M. Alston Jr. to join the Center of Theological Inquiry (CTI) in Princeton as "Senior Scholar of Research."

It is impossible to write about Jenson without mentioning the name of Carl E. Braaten (born 1929), with whom Jenson organized countless conferences and published numerous volumes. They, too, met as students in Heidelberg. They co-founded two theological journals: *Dialog*, which was launched in 1961 by a small group of scholars, and *Pro Ecclesia*, in 1991, which was "their" journal, in conjunction with the Center for Catholic and Evangelical Theology, which they co-founded in 1991.[5]

Over more than six decades of theological scholarship, until his death in September 2017, Robert W. Jenson has published many significant monographs and articles, which have themselves begun to become the object of theological attention. Among his contributions, especially in his later years, one is not surprised to find reflections on creeds and canon, on the catholicity of the Protestant Reformation, on reclaiming Scripture for the Church, and, in direct relation with this last topic, biblical commentaries (on Ezekiel and the Song of Songs).[6] All of this is somehow related to his formative years, in Lutheran institutions of higher learning and especially at the University of Heidelberg, with Peter Brunner and Wolfhart Pannenberg.

God's Way

Jenson has never ceased, during his long theological existence, to consider the central theme of *theo*-logy, i.e., God. God is the alpha and omega, not just of theology, but also of Robert W. Jenson's life as a theologian. One could argue that his openness to the Christian tradition as a whole was a means to thinking anew about God, not as an object, essence, or cause, but as an event: the event of God's own life and of God's interactions with the world and with humanity. Left and right—and not simply within Lutheran or even Protestant theology—Jenson found insights, in Scripture and the Christian tradition, which compelled him to question certain philosophical and especially metaphysical underpinnings of a broad spectrum of Christian theology which have led many thinkers to conceive God's eternity as a pure *stasis*, a perfect stillness or impassibility. Even Wolfhart Pannenberg, who was among those who envisioned an eschatological ontology and so

---

4. Hereafter, *ST*.
5. See Braaten, *Because of Christ*.
6. On Jenson and Scripture, see his collected essays in Jenson, *Triune Story*.

a Christian theology in which God, as the power of the future, creates and renews the world, fell back into the metaphysical trap of conceiving God as perfectly unmoving:[7] "Aristotle's and Plato's divinity is the stillness for which moving things long; the being of Gregory [of Nyssa]'s God is that he keeps things moving. To be God is always to be open to and always to open a future, transgressing all past-imposed conditions."[8]

The Greek Fathers, and more generally Christian theologians of the first centuries, did not simply hellenize and theorize what originally was a Jewish and ethical message, as Adolf Harnack and others argued. They christianized their own hellenistic presuppositions—but they did it only up to a point, and contemporary Christian theology is called to complete this "baptism." By so doing, Christian theology and proclamation may be in a better position to convey the good news. As Jenson wrote already in 1962: "The words with which it is possible to grasp the hearts of contemporary man are the words of time, event, history. They are words like 'future' and 'purpose.' . . . We are Greeks in whom the Greek faith in the timeless has been toppled."[9]

Throughout his works, which often center on the task of *identifying* God as confessed by Christians, Jenson asserts this: God is not an essence or a substance, but the mutual relation between the Father, his Son, and the Holy Spirit.[10] Augustine led Western theology in the wrong direction with his emphasis on divine simplicity rather than, with the Cappadocians, on the mutuality of their relation as the very source of their communion and thus of God's life.[11] Of the three, the Spirit, as the drive—in God's own life as well as in creation as a whole—toward the *eschaton*, is singled out by Jenson as the very source of God's liveliness.[12] This singling out is problematic and gives unfortunate tritheistic accents to some of Jenson's assertions, such as this one: "Pentecost is the Spirit's *particular personal initiative* to delay the Parousia."[13]

These three identities, Father, Son and Spirit in their bond of unity and love, are the one personal God, the alpha and the omega. They are God's "proper name," as Jenson audaciously puts it in his book *The Triune*

---

7. *ST* 2:310n4.

8. *ST* 1:216.

9. Jenson, "Proclamation Without Metaphysics," 17.

10. Jenson's overall concern, namely "the identification of God," already governs *God After God* (1969). see, e.g., Jenson, *God After God*, 108, 123–25.

11. *ST* 1:112–13.

12. *ST* 1:157.

13. *ST* 2:178–79 (my emphasis).

Identity.[14] All three are deeply involved in, but not swallowed up by, time. As Jenson suggests in his *Systematic Theology*, in a key passage in which he makes clear his debt, on this particular point, to both Peter Brunner and Karl Barth (not, it must be noted, to Wolfhart Pannenberg):[15] "God is what happens between Jesus and his Father in their Spirit."[16] Jenson, however, immediately adds: "God is what happens to Jesus and the world."[17] Similar statements can be found from Jenson's earlier works, all the way to late publications.[18] Their implications are crucial. Before we turn to one of them, we should note that several theologians have criticized Jenson's way of identifying God with God's involvement in history. To them, Jenson's God is dependent on creation, since God's being appears to be "constituted" by history and the world.[19] This critique, which presupposes traditional views concerning divine impassibility and immutability, does not quite meet its target. It is one thing to state that God's very being is God's act, that God's being is not simply found beyond or behind God's act; it is quite another to assert that, as a consequence of this, God's being depends on God's involvement in the world. As far as I can see, Jenson maintains God's freedom to be

---

14. Jenson, *Triune Identity*, 4, 17–18, 185–86. While mostly appreciative of Jenson, R. Kendall Soulen has rightly criticized him on this point, characterizing "Father, Son, and Holy Spirit" as an appellative rather than a proper name. If "Father, Son, and Holy Spirit" were God's proper name, would we be translating them in various languages ("Père, Fils et Esprit," "Vater, Sohn und Geist," etc.)? We are usually *not* in the habit of translating proper names. For this (and other) criticism(s), see Soulen, *Divine Name(s) and the Holy Trinity*, 109.

15. See Jenson's critical review of the second volume of Pannenberg's *Systematic Theology* in Jenson, "Parting Ways?"

16. *ST* 1:221.

17. *ST* 1:221.

18. "Barth has abolished the notion of the timeless being of God by putting the historical event of Jesus' existence for his Father and his brothers in the place formerly occupied by timelessness. We are tempted to go on to say: God is what happened with Jesus of Nazareth in Israel" (Jenson, *God After God*, 132). "It is the *plot* of Jesus' history which is the plot of God's being" (Jenson, *God After God*, 106). "God is not a substance with a fixed set of attributes, but rather a *deed*. . . . It is not so much that God *is* deity, as that he *does* deity. . . . God does his godhead, his divine nature" (Jenson, *God After God*, 110). "God is an event, a happening. . . . There is not static 'essence' of God behind God's act" (Jenson, *God After God*, 125). See also Jenson, "Karl Barth on the Being of God," 47, 50; "What Kind of God Can Make a Covenant?," 7–9, where Jenson links eternity with divine faithfulness.

19. Hunsinger, "Robert Jenson's *Systematic Theology*," 176. Hart, *Beauty of the Infinite*, 157–58. McCall, *Which Trinity? Whose Monotheism?*, 128–29, 137–38. See also Swain, who writes: "I am not convinced that the way beyond Barth lies in further metaphysical revision of the church's traditional teaching about God" (Swain, *God of the Gospel*, 27).

involved in the world in the way God chooses. God never becomes a purely passive object which is determined by the world. Rather, God freely *chooses*, again and again, to have God's being partly determined by the world. It is important to see that *God* determines Godself in such a way. The world's determining of God's very being is so to speak subordinate to, included within, and governed by, God's own self-determination.

What are the implications of Jenson's views on God's act and being (or being and act)? Beyond the critique of any defense of God's ahistoricity, timelessness, and immutability, the identification of God with "what happens between Jesus and his Father in their Spirit" and with "what happens to Jesus and the world" implies that God is *personal*. On this point, in Jenson's view, the influence of German idealism, with its criticism of anthropomorphism, has obscured the scriptural witness. For all his proximity to Wolfhart Pannenberg, here too Jenson begs to differ: it simply will not do to rid theology of the notion of divine personality and to replace it with talk of a divine "field."[20] Here again Jenson sides with Karl Barth who, in idiosyncratic fashion, inverted the usual way of approaching the problem in order to suggest that we should consider human personality on the basis of God's personality, rather than the other way around,[21] and who also decided, because of modern conceptions of this term, not to speak of three divine "persons."

Stretching the Lutheran Tradition

Throughout his *Systematic Theology*, which is mainly a doctrine of God's triune being and act, Jenson proves to be a masterful theologian of "resourcement," i.e., of a retrieval of Scripture and of the theological tradition, broadly conceived, for the sake of theology's contemporary responsibility. Much more than many significant Western theologians of the twentieth century (Karl Barth, Karl Rahner, Eberhard Jüngel), he draws on insights from the Eastern tradition, just as he does not hesitate to express sharp rebukes of certain Orthodox (and Western) thinkers who, as he sees it, did not adequately ponder the liveliness of God (Vladimir Lossky and Gregory Palamas, for instance, come under Jenson's fire).[22] Jenson is, like most theologians, a practitioner of theological "cannibalism" (his own word): ancient and recent theological writings are "dismembered," for only certain bits and pieces need to be retrieved and put to use in our context.[23]

20. *ST* 1:116–17n4, 222.
21. Barth, *CD* 2/1:284–97.
22. *ST* 1:152–53.
23. Jenson, "Luther's Contemporary Theological Significance," 272.

As should be clear by now, Jenson is challenging all of Christian theology, irrespective of denominational boundaries, to consider the ways in which the Gospel compels us to think anew about God. This of course means Jenson is also challenging his own, Lutheran, tradition. One of the most obvious ways in which he "stretches" the Lutheran tradition concerns the centrality of the resurrection. This event is "the great occurrence of dramatic causality in God."[24] It is the gospel.[25] We should be careful not to overstate what, at first sight, might appear as a shift away from Good Friday in the direction of Easter Sunday. However central the resurrection may be in Jenson's theology, he also states that the cross is "the event in God that settles what sort of God he is over against fallen creation."[26] Be that as it may, the resurrection, rather than the cross, appears to be the decisive event of the Gospel in Jenson's works.

Rather than being predetermined from all eternity, the resurrection is the event which definitively and irrevocably shapes God's very being. Jenson adds, taking up the retroactive interpretation of the resurrection first articulated by Pannenberg in *Jesus—God and Man* (first published in German as *Grundzüge der Christologie* in 1964), that this event only became "an eternal certainty" in or with its occurring.[27] In the footsteps of both Wolfhart Pannenberg and Jürgen Moltmann—Barth was less helpful on this front—Jenson emphasized, since his early works, the idea that God's transcendence is God's futurity, not God's timelessness.[28] The future is "the fount of time"; it is the "prior reality."[29]

Another way in which Jenson challenges certain segments of his own tradition is found in his endorsement of the Finnish interpretation of Luther, which is known for interpreting the German reformer as teaching a version of *theosis*, or divinization.[30] Why did Jenson embrace this interpretation? Not simply, I think, out of an ecumenical concern, i.e., out of a desire to seek convergences with other Christian traditions than his own. His interest in the Finnish interpretation is related to his understanding of the very *telos* of God's way with the world, namely a real participation of all of creation in God's own communion. If this is the end of God's way, then how could

---

24. *ST* 1:160.
25. Jenson, *God After God*, 157.
26. *ST* 1:189. See Jenson, "Response to Watson and Hunsinger," 228–29.
27. *ST* 1:160.
28. Jenson, *God After God*, 171–79, 190.
29. Jenson, *God After God*, 188.
30. See, e.g., *ST* 2:290, 293–96, 311.

justification be an extraneous word which does not in any way anticipate that end for us and within us?

Jenson may challenge fellow Lutherans to a broader, more "generous" vision of Christian theology, but his own Lutheranism is in fact quite apparent in his writings, for example in his insistence on the interpretation of *logos* not as "mind," or "intelligence" to be contemplated, but rather as "word" and "speech" to be heard.[31] The importance of the notion of "promise" in his theology is also a clear link to the Lutheran tradition in which he grew up and was theologically trained.

But over the years Jenson became, as is widely acknowledged, a thinker of God's triunity. Why did he dedicate so much energy to considering the "identity" of God? A good part of the answer has to do with his views on the Church, which is "the community of a specific identification of God,"[32] the anticipation of the final inclusion in the triune God's communion,[33] as well as the very (and only) body of the risen Christ: "The Church is the risen Christ's Ego."[34] (This affirmation, alongside others, has caused alarm among Jenson's colleagues.)

Let me briefly point out the first aspect, concerning the "specific identification of God." The Church's witness is compromised when it no longer knows the reality it is called to proclaim to the world. Here is the crucial correlation between the doctrinal or dogmatic work proper, namely the quest for the identification of God's being and act, and the concern for the Church and its witness: Jenson was convinced that "insofar as that identification becomes imprecise, the church loses all ability appropriately to order its life."[35] Ecclesial disorder, on theological and ethical matters, is closely related to proper theo-logical errors. Is the Church dependent, for its existence and witness, on the triune God, or should we presume that the reality Christian communities worship is as different from the Father, the Son, and the Holy Spirit as the "energies" may be different from the "essence" which lies behind them (to use Palamite language, which Jenson, like Barth before him, rejects)? Christians do "not pray at random," but address "a specified God whose intention and character are known to us."[36] The *liturgy* is the place and time *par excellence* in which the Church listens to, and invokes, God. The Church is a gathered, visible people, not an invisible reality. "What is

31. *ST* 1:108, 165–66; 2:6–7, 156–57.
32. Jenson, "'Protestant Constructive Response' to Christian Unbelief," 63.
33. *ST* 2:220–23.
34. *ST* 2:215.
35. Jenson, "'Protestant Constructive Response' to Christian Unbelief," 63.
36. Jenson, "'Protestant Constructive Response' to Christian Unbelief," 73.

invisible is that this visible entity is in fact what she claims to be, the people of God."[37] Over the years, Jenson wrote more favorably about the Church as an institution, including as a hierarchical institution. He supported the view that having a pastor for the Church universal is necessary.[38]

Robert W. Jenson as Scriptural Theologian

Jenson is a theologian of Scripture, in the sense that his teachings about God's way, about the life and history of the triune One, oppose all metaphysical constructs which sever the being of God from the story Scripture narrates. And so, on the one hand, he seeks to overcome any speculative interpretation of the *Logos*, i.e., any *Logos*-christology which loses sight of the lived existence of Jesus of Nazareth, and on the other hand he has no interest in, and little patience for, biblical exegesis which "forgets" what biblical texts point to, namely God's way in and with the world, as well as the world's response to God. It is the duty of Christian theology to "baptize" God by thinking and proclaiming God as revealed in God's history with the world. This happens only when the authority of Scripture is acknowledged by the Church and by theologians within the Church: then only may Scripture play its role and confront us as canon.

For much of his career, Jenson was of the opinion that modern historical exegesis has impaired this use of Scripture.[39] Unlike critical exegesis, a theological interpretation of Scripture "presupposes that scripture tells the truth about God in his history with us."[40] Jenson clearly favored this approach, which he called "premodern," and which, rather than pit exegesis and doctrine *a priori* against one another, sees a "hermeneutical circle" between the two, so that exegesis enlivens and confirms doctrine, while doctrine functions as a hermeneutical guide in the study and interpretation of Scripture.[41] But he immediately added the following, which points in the direction of a more nuanced relation to modernity (and to critical thought) than one may perhaps imagine at first sight: this affinity with premodern exegesis and theological interpretation does not mean Jenson was "necessarily committed to their [the Fathers'] exact procedures or results."[42] For instance, when interpreting the Song of Songs, Jenson was not interested,

---

37. *ST* 2:174.
38. *ST* 2:242–43, 247. See also Jenson, "Church as *Communio*," 10.
39. Braaten and Jenson, "Introduction," ix–xi.
40. Jenson, *Ezekiel*, 18.
41. Jenson, "Bible and the Trinity," 339.
42. Jenson, *Ezekiel*, 23.

as were some of the ancient scholars, in the attempt to reconstruct the historical Solomon's wedding ritual. Why? Because "at the level of what the Fathers and others called the 'plain narratives' or 'historical sense' they of course did not have the heritage of modern historical criticism, and took ascriptions and references to Solomon at historical face value."[43] Moreover, the ancient interpreters, such as the Church Fathers and medieval scholars, read the Scriptures, like all readers, with certain theological, spiritual and anthropological suppositions. They were convinced that

> once the reader has made the ascent to a spiritual reading, to go back and consider bodily matters would be a relapse. Thereby the older exegesis indeed did the Song violence; there is a vital moment of truth in modernity's rebellion against it. For the poem remains, whoever affair they narrate, sensual love poetry. They are about erogenous zone and seductive aromas and lovers looking for a place to be alone and frustration and the morning after.[44]

Such comments are important. They remind us of the fact that Jenson, although not favorably inclined to embrace broad segments of modern academic exegesis ("high criticism"), was of course not untouched by the historical and critical methods. Still, one wonders whether he was sufficiently aware of the problems which arise when one seeks to overcome the limitations of the modern methods without having been trained in them—as Jenson himself was—in any serious way.

Cultural Critic

Jenson was one of the critics, in the current academic landscape, of various strands of postmodern thought. He was equally bold in his critique of what he saw as expressions of "nihilism" as he was confronting metaphysical visions of divine stillness. He wrote, for instance: "Western universities and popular forums have recently been dominated by theoretical nihilisms that are historical and conceptual siblings to Nazi ideology"![45] Nietzsche and Heidegger are objects of overly blunt and improperly argued critiques. John Milbank's relentless attack on modernity, on the other hand, is praised as "powerful."[46] With Milbank, Jenson is convinced that "from Nietzsche through Heidegger to the latest French *poseur* or American camp follower,"

43. Jenson, *Song of Songs*, 8–9.
44. Jenson, *Song of Songs*, 13.
45. *ST* 2:57.
46. *ST* 2:62n44.

the postmodern project, "whether acknowledged or not, has been 'the invention of an anti-Christianity.'"[47] In the second volume of his *Systematic Theology*, Jenson asserts that "homoeroticism is of course not a mode of sexuality at all, but an escape from it."[48] Needless to say, such polemical statements have repulsed many people, and for good reasons. But, beyond Jenson's blunt pronouncements, there is a thinker who has in fact integrated many crucial realizations of late Western modern thought. He is of course in no way naïve, for instance, about the notion that no experiential data comes to us immediately, without interpretation[49]—to the point where one wonders why and how Jenson adheres to Leopold von Ranke's famous sentence describing the aim of historical scholarship as comprehending the past "as it actually occurred" (*wie es eigentlich gewesen*).[50]

Jenson's Relevance

There are four areas, as I see it, in which Jenson's achievement is of great value for the present and future of Christian theology. Three of these four areas may stand in need, however, of adjustments and modifications.

First, let us consider Jenson's attempt to overcome all metaphysical dualisms which pit time over against eternity conceived as pure timelessness: the God of Israel and of Jesus Christ is involved, and not just with his "energies," in the world and in time. This revisioning of "standard" metaphysics is extremely important, as long as it does not reduce God to time or imprison God in time and thus loses sight of the qualitative difference between the Creator and creation (Jenson has been accused, somewhat rashly, of doing precisely that). "God is *not subject* to the march of time, but this is not because his eternity does not march."[51] The two decisive events on which the biblical narrative center, namely the exodus story and the Easter story, frontally contradict the notion of a timeless and worldless God. What I miss, in this remarkable interpretation, is the next step, which Jenson seems reluctant to make, of articulating the Church's responsibility in mirroring, however imperfectly, God's own liberating action. Why does a thinker such as Jenson, who states, following Gerhard

---

47. *ST* 2:147–48.

48. *ST* 2:93. Or consider this equally outrageous assertion: "Homoerotic acts, however occasioned or motivated, constitute desertion in the face of the threatening other sort of human, defection from the burden of co-humanity" (*ST* 2:141).

49. *ST* 2:98.

50. *ST* 1:175.

51. *ST* 1:218n61 (my emphasis).

von Rad, that "throughout Scripture, the central and historical category is 'righteousness,'"[52] not seek to connect his teaching with the insights of liberation theologies, pruning and modifying whatever appears problematic in these theologies, but also underlining what is of value? The future of Christian theology, in my opinion, lies in such a connecting. We need robust theologies of God's own life, of God's covenant with Israel and with God's creation, theologies which sustain no less robust theologies of human solidarity with the little ones, with the excluded and the voiceless. Karl Barth made more steps in this direction than Jenson.

The second major area concerns, again, the doctrine of God and has to do with Jenson's teaching on God's "futurity." Much of recent and contemporary systematic theology has underlined the "coming" (*adventus*) of God and the priority of the end over the beginning. Jenson has certainly contributed to this emphasis. There is great value in these teachings, which take seriously the eschatological dimension of Jesus' own message as well as the Gospel concerning Jesus as the crucified and risen one. The potential problem with the prioritizing of the future is, simply, that it may lead to a relative undervaluing of the past and present. Is this the case in Jenson's theology? I do not think so. On this point as well as on the first point (the overcoming of any notion of divine timelessness), some will wish to heed Barth's question to Jürgen Moltmann about the importance of reflecting on God's pre-temporality, supra-temporality and post-temporality (letter of November 17, 1964).[53] But Jenson's message, to these people, is simple: do not forget the eschatological dimension of Jesus' and of the Christian message! Do not lose sight of the fact that God is the alpha and omega "who is, who was, and who is *to come*" (Rev 1:8). And do not engage in speculative metaphysics about "a" God (which one? Is this God the God of Scripture and of the Gospel?) whose being can be studied, even for the shortest while, in abstraction from God's decision to be, in God's very being, *Immanuel*.

The third area concerns Scripture. Jenson is one of a number of theologians who remind fellow theologians, including systematic theologians, not to forget about the *primary* source of Christian theology. Scripture is where Christian theology finds its nourishment, which means that it dries up and dies when it stays away from it too long. All the most significant theologians in the history of Christianity have been expositors of Scripture, and in fact not of narrow segments of Scripture. Jenson's urgent invitation to read, study and meditate Scripture theologically is important, but it does not have to involve a rejection of modern exegetical methods. All it needs to resist is

52. ST 1:71.
53. Barth, *Letters 1961–1968*, s.v. "Letter 172."

the hegemonic intentions which, too often, accompany these methods. There is something salutary too in historical and critical exegesis, which Jenson unfortunately does not adequately acknowledge, even if, naturally, we cannot expect modern academic exegesis to embrace his view of Scripture not just as a message *about* religion and representations of the divine, but as a narration concerning someone, Christ, who, as the risen one, "can himself speak now in the church" precisely through this narration.[54]

Fourth and last: thinking theologically for the one Church Christians confess,[55] without denying our personal roots, remains a very important aim for contemporary theology. The various Christian traditions mutually enrich one another with their own specific gifts. Christian theology is, first of all, Christian, not Lutheran, Methodist or Roman Catholic, even if it is usually practiced within a particular strand of Christianity. Beyond the biographical roots of Jenson's deep-seated interest in ecumenical theology, a case could be made that Jenson's explorations of the Christian tradition, as well as his interpretation of Scripture, derive from his theology of God's liveliness: as Karl Barth already intimated, God is not a prisoner of God's own being but is intrinsically in movement, within Godself as well as towards the world. How could one remain contentedly within one's own boundaries—including one's ecclesial boundaries—after being grasped by such a realization? How could one lose sight of the universality, or catholicity, of God's action in creation and among God's people? How could one still pretend that one's own ecclesial tradition has adequately given witness to this universality? Robert W. Jenson, in the four areas surveyed here (and in others), remains a voice to be reckoned with.

Bibliography

Barth, Karl. *Letters 1961–1968*. Grand Rapids: Eerdmans, 1981.
Braaten, Carl E. *Because of Christ: Memoirs of a Lutheran Theologian*. Grand Rapids: Eerdmans, 2010.
Brunner, Peter. *Pro Ecclesia: Gesammelte Aufsätze zur dogmatischen Theologie*. Berlin: Lutherisches Verlagshaus, 1962–1966.
Hart, David Bentley. *The Beauty of the Infinite: The Aesthetic of Christian Truth*. Grand Rapids: Eerdmans, 2003.
Hunsinger, George. "Robert Jenson's *Systematic Theology*: A Review Essay." *SJT* 55.2 (2002) 161–200.

---

54. "Christ is not the content of the proclamation merely as a passive object, as that *about* which the proclamation speaks. That he is risen, and so can himself speak now in the church, is part of what is narrated" (*ST* 1:175).

55. *ST* 1:8.

Jenson, Robert W. *Alpha and Omega: A Study in the Theology of Karl Barth*. Edinburgh: Thomas Nelson, 1963.

———. "The Bible and the Trinity." *Pro Ecclesia* 11 (2002) 329–39.

———. "The Church as *Communio*." In *The Catholicity of the Reformation*, edited by Carl E. Braaten and R. Jenson, 1–12. Grand Rapids: Eerdmans, 1996.

———. "Cur Deus Homo? The Election of Jesus Christ in the Theology of Karl Barth." ThD diss., University of Heidelberg, 1959.

———. *Ezekiel*. London: SCM, 2009.

———. *God After God: The God of the Past and the God of the Future, Seen in the Work of Karl Barth*. Indianapolis: Bobbs-Merrils, 1969.

———. "Karl Barth on the Being of God." In *Thomas Aquinas and Karl Barth: An Unofficial Catholic-Protestant Dialogue*, edited by Bruce L. McCormack and Thomas Joseph White, OP, 43–51. Grand Rapids: Eerdmans, 2013.

———. "Luther's Contemporary Theological Significance." In *The Cambridge Companion to Martin Luther*, edited by Donald K. McKim, 272–88. Cambridge: Cambridge University Press, 2003.

———. "Parting Ways?" *First Things*, May 1995. 60–62. Online https://www.firstthings.com/article/1995/05/001-parting-ways.

———. "Proclamation Without Metaphysics (1962)." In *Theology as Revisionary Metaphysics: Essays on God and Creation*, edited by Stephen John Wright, 4–17. Eugene, OR: Cascade, 2014.

———. "A 'Protestant Constructive Response' to Christian Unbelief." In *American Apostasy: The Triumph of 'Other' Gospels*, edited by Richard John Neuhaus, 56–74. Grand Rapids: Eerdmans, 1989.

———. "Response to Watson and Hunsinger." *SJT* 55.2 (2002) 225–32.

———. *Song of Songs*. Louisville: John Knox, 2005.

———. *A Theology in Outline: Can These Bones Live?* Edited by Adam Eitel. Oxford: Oxford University Press, 2016.

———. *The Triune Identity: God According to the Gospel*. 1982. Reprint, Eugene, OR: Wipf and Stock, 2002.

———. *The Triune Story: Collected Essays on Scripture*. Edited by Brad East. New York: Oxford University Press, 2019.

———. *Unbaptized God: The Basic Flaw in Ecumenical Theology*. Minneapolis: Augsburg Fortress, 1992.

———. "What Kind of God Can Make a Covenant?" In *Covenant and Hope: Christian and Jewish Reflections. Essays in Constructive Theology from the Institute for Theological Inquiry*, edited by R. Jenson and Eugene B. Korn, 3–18. Grand Rapids: Eerdmans, 2012.

Jenson, Robert W., and Carl E. Braaten. "Introduction: Gospel, Church, and Scripture." In *Reclaiming the Bible for the Church*, edited by C. Braaten and R. Jenson, ix–xii. Edinburgh: T&T Clark, 1995.

McCall, Thomas H. *Which Trinity? Whose Monotheism? Philosophical and Systematic Theologians on the Metaphysics of Trinitarian Theology*. Grand Rapids: Eerdmans, 2010.

Soulen, R. Kendall. *The Divine Name(s) and the Holy Trinity: Distinguishing the Voices*. Louisville: Westminster John Knox, 2011.

Swain, Scott R. *The God of the Gospel: Robert Jenson's Trinitarian Theology*. Downers Grove, IL: IVP Academic, 2013.

11

Stanley Hauerwas: Witnessing Communities of Character

—Victoria Lorrimar

STANLEY HAUERWAS, A THEOLOGIAN with strong ecumenical tendencies, defies both systematisation and summation. Extremely prolific, Hauerwas draws on a metaphor from his childhood experiences as a bricklayer when he describes his preference for the occasional essay as doing theology "one brick at a time."[1] He is a staunch proponent of a communitarian ethic of character, considers pacifism to be a non-negotiable aspect of Christian witness and opposes the accommodation of Christianity to secular culture.

Hauerwas's audience is broad and diverse—he has achieved recognition across the separate arenas of the academy, church and the broader American public. Indeed, Hauerwas is wary of the distinction between scholarly and popular writing.[2] His work has been engaged in critical dialogue by a range of traditions, including Roman Catholicism and Anglicanism. Hauerwas himself has been shaped by many traditions—Methodist, Roman Catholic, Anabaptist and Episcopalian—and he calls himself a "high church Mennonite."[3] His lack of identification with a single tradition suggests that Hauerwas's theological contributions may also transcend denominational distinctions and have implications for the wider Christian community.

Ecclesiology is central to Hauerwas's thought, the focal point of Hauerwas's critique of Protestant accommodationism in favour of a radical alternative that challenges the traditional/conservative divide. This essay explores Hauerwas's understanding of church as incorporating the theological elements of narrative, character, kingdom and witness. It will be argued that, though Hauerwas's view of the world apart from the church is problematic

---

1. Hauerwas, *Sanctify Them in the Truth*, 9.
2. Hauerwas, *Work of Theology*, 4.
3. Hauerwas, *Hannah's Child*, 254.

at times, his ecclesiology is largely validated in a subsequent shift away from foundationalism in Christian ethics and has much to offer continued efforts toward establishing a general orthodoxy.

Background

Hauerwas provides an enormously helpful resource for understanding his context and his theology in his 2012 memoir, *Hannah's Child*. Others have written excellent critical biographies that attempt to understand Hauerwas and his theological development.[4] The reader is directed to these accounts to better understand how Hauerwas's person and work has been shaped by his personal background.

Church affiliation has been accorded similar prominence to academic affiliations in this personal history, as Hauerwas, his years in the academy not withstanding, considers himself foremost a church theologian.[5] From the kingdom emphasis of Social Gospel proponents Walter Rauschenbusch and Albrecht Ritschl, through the Christian realism of Reinhold Niebuhr and Church-world typologies offered by Ernst Troeltsch and H. Richard Niebuhr, to the deontological ethics of Paul Ramsey and James Gustafson's emphasis on character and the self, Sam Wells traces developments in Christian ethics against which Hauerwas's thought must be understood. "Like a great-grandson, he chafes at the traditions, quarrels with the rules, and distances himself from the grandees; but he can never leave the family."[6]

Overcoming Boundaries

Hauerwas sums up both what makes his theological approach one that pushes against boundaries, and what many find most challenging about his work—he manages to combine "a profound commitment to fundamental Christian convictions with a socially radical ethic."[7] *Resident Aliens*, co-authored with Methodist minister and friend Will Willimon and published in 1989, was a particularly significant work.[8] Hauerwas describes the proposal

---

4. See, for example, Cavanaugh, "Stan the Man," 17–32; Thiessen Nation, "Stanley Hauerwas," 19–36.

5. Hauerwas, *Hannah's Child*, 254.

6. Wells, *Transforming Fate into Destiny*, 2.

7. Hauerwas, *Hannah's Child*, 136.

8. Hauerwas and Willimon, *Resident Aliens*.

as "an alternative to the liberal/conservative divide in Protestant theology."[9] In *Resident Aliens*, Hauerwas and Willimon outline for a broad Christian readership the errors into which they believe American Christianity had fallen, calling for a different way of "being church" that will be explored more fully in the next section of this chapter.

Against Accommodationism

One of the specific tendencies that Hauerwas identified and challenged in prevailing Protestant theologies was their accommodation to standards of intelligibility dictated by wider spheres of discourse.[10] Much of Hauerwas's writing on the necessary distinction between church and world is bound up in a broader polemic against Constantinianism, which he describes as "the attempt to make the church safe by joining its destiny to worldly powers."[11]

During his time at Yale Divinity School, Hauerwas was already questioning the prevailing scholarly presumption that theology's task was to make faith language palatable to the world, either through subtraction or translation.[12] Hauerwas connects his early attraction to the thought of Barth and Wittgenstein with their refusal to "explain."[13] The influence of these two thinkers is clear in his rejection of what he considered to be a widespread and unhealthy relationship between Christianity and secular politics in the contemporary sphere. Later, he came to the opinion that this situation was exacerbated by the Niebuhrian endorsement of the Christian task of transforming culture, elevating pluralist ecclesiologies to the extent that a close allegiance with liberal democracy was considered the only legitimate existence for the Christian church. In the words of Hauerwas and Willimon, "the world had tamed the church."[14]

The Church as an Alternate Polis

The story of liberalism, according to Hauerwas, is that no story is necessary. Reflecting on lessons from *Watership Down*, Hauerwas draws attention to a warren in which absolute freedom appeared to reign, and the

---

9. Hauerwas, *Hannah's Child*, 193.
10. Hauerwas, "Preaching as Though We Had Enemies."
11. Hauerwas and Coles, *Christianity, Democracy, and the Radical Ordinary*, 21.
12. Hauerwas, *Hannah's Child*, 59.
13. Hauerwas, *Hannah's Child*, 60.
14. Hauerwas and Willimon, *Resident Aliens*, 41.

rabbits no longer told the stories of old.[15] In forgetting their tradition, the rabbits "had accepted a social system that required them to look after themselves first."[16] The apparent personal freedom they exalted in was in reality a ruse engineered by the farmer to keep them under his control.[17] Their loss of narrative had resulted in a loss of community and ultimately a loss of true freedom.[18]

Hauerwas too speaks of the importance of freedom, though his notion of freedom challenges the prevailing understanding in liberal democratic society. For Hauerwas, freedom depends on our being initiated into a truthful narrative.[19] Only then is true agency ensured and we can make our lives our own.[20] Moreover, this freedom only comes to us in the presence of others.[21] God's story attracts our attention through the form of another's character, challenging us toward imitation.[22] Freedom is not, therefore, the absence of a story or tradition, but in fact the converse: in choosing to be accountable to a body of people formed according to the story of Jesus we become truly free.[23]

Hauerwas therefore challenges the alliance between the Christian community and American democracy that pervades much of American Christianity.[24] The church should exist as a distinct community, not seduced by any desire or demand to be relevant to contemporary society.[25] Hauerwas is known for enigmatic statements such as "the church first serves the world by helping the world to know what it means to be the world."[26] The church provides a contrast model to the world, an alternative story and community that reveals to the world the untruthfulness of its own story.[27] For Hauerwas, the kingdom of God and the kingdom of the world are fundamentally

---

15. Hauerwas, *Community of Character*, 18, 20.
16. Hauerwas, *Community of Character*, 22.
17. Hauerwas, *Community of Character*, 21.
18. Hauerwas, *Community of Character*, 18.
19. Hauerwas, *Peaceable Kingdom*, 43.
20. Hauerwas, *Peaceable Kingdom*, 43.
21. Hauerwas, *Peaceable Kingdom*, 45.
22. Hauerwas, *Peaceable Kingdom*, 44–45.
23. Hauerwas, *Peaceable Kingdom*, 46.
24. Hauerwas, *Community of Character*, 4; *Vision and Virtue*, 241–60.
25. Hauerwas, *Vision and Virtue*, 239.
26. Hauerwas, "Jesus: The Story of the Kingdom," 50.
27. Hauerwas, "Jesus: The Story of the Kingdom," 50.

opposed, and it is only in resisting the power of the world that the world can get a "glimpse of the Kingdom of Christ."[28]

Expanding Identities

The challenge Hauerwas issues to the American church is undoubtedly of an ecumenical nature in that he criticises both conservative and liberal American churches equally for assuming a Constantinian view of how the church should exist in the world.[29] In *Resident Aliens*, Hauerwas and Willimon assert that they are neither conservative nor liberal in their political stance, for they believe that both wings of the church originate from the same false presumption that the church exists to "make a better world" by assisting the secular state.[30] Against the picture of the church so described, Hauerwas proposes an alternative vision, a way out of the "false Niebuhrian dilemma of whether to be in or out of the world."[31]

A Constructive Ecclesiology

Hauerwas's multicoloured church background might be conceived of as incongruent with a strong position concerning the role of the church. He has humorously referred to himself as a "high-church Mennonite," and more seriously as "ecclesiastically homeless."[32] Reading his autobiography, however, suggests that he is not "homeless" so much as he has been able to make a home in diverse church traditions (Methodist, Lutheran, Catholic, Episcopalian).[33] Nor does he wish his theology to be restricted to or by any particular tradition, rather it is his conviction that "no theologian should desire anything less than that his or her theology reflect the catholic character of the church."[34]

Underscoring his conviction that ethics must not be separated from theology. Hauerwas defines theology as "the kind of discourse that must, if it is to be truthful, be embedded in the practices of actual lived

---

28. Hauerwas, *Dispatches from the Front*, 112.
29. Hauerwas and Willimon, *Resident Aliens*, 15.
30. Hauerwas and Willimon, *Resident Aliens*, 156.
31. Hauerwas and Willimon, *Resident Aliens*, 39.
32. Hauerwas, *Hannah's Child*, 254.
33. Hauerwas, *Hannah's Child*, 254.
34. Hauerwas, *Peaceable Kingdom*, xxvi.

communities."[35] Theological claims are unintelligible when abstracted from church practice.[36] The "spider-web" metaphor Hauerwas favours for the task of theology is be proven apt by exploring his ecclesiology,[37] as his account of the church weaves together the elements of narrative, character, kingdom and witness in an ecclesial vision that both challenges and transcends confessional identities.

Narrative

For Hauerwas, the human response to God's revelation is the church. Christians are called to be a holy people and, as with Israel and Jesus before them, the vocation of the church is to imitate God.[38] By attending to the narrative of Jesus' life we learn perfection from him, a learning process that Hauerwas argues can only be done as part of a community that practises virtues.[39] To imitate Jesus is to join with him in a journey by which the people of God are trained to be citizens of the kingdom of God proclaimed in the story of Jesus' life, death and resurrection.[40]

The domain in which the faith narrative is to be explored and lived out is the church—this narrative is "unintelligible extracted from an ecclesial context."[41] Thus, Hauerwas is suspicious of attempts by theologians to develop general hermeneutical theories.[42] For Hauerwas, the church is the only valid interpreter of Scripture. He rejects literal and historical-critical approaches to understanding Scripture, arguing that these methods of textual criticism rely on the false assumption that Scripture is self-interpreting.[43] Rather, he contends that Scripture cannot possibly be understood without the moral and spiritual transformation that comes from participation in the church.[44]

35. Hauerwas, *Sanctify Them in the Truth*, 157.
36. Hauerwas, *Sanctify Them in the Truth*, 22.
37. Hauerwas, *Sanctify Them in the Truth*, 2.
38. Hauerwas, "Jesus: The Presence," 76–86.
39. Hauerwas, "Jesus: The Presence," 76.
40. Hauerwas, "Jesus: The Presence," 76, 83.
41. Hauerwas, "Jesus: The Presence," 153.
42. Hauerwas, *Unleashing the Scripture*, 21.
43. Hauerwas, *Unleashing the Scripture*, 21.
44. Hauerwas, *Unleashing the Scripture*, 28.

Character

Hauerwas's focus on character ethics developed out of a rejection of quandary ethics, which concentrates on the decision involved in any given moral dilemma and assumes a choice that can be universally agreed upon as correct. In particular, his early work engaged the situation ethics of Joseph Fletcher and drew on the works of Julius Kovesi and Ludwig Wittgenstein as he challenged the emphasis on casuistry.[45]

The emphasis on character in Hauerwas's ethics owes much to the writings of Aristotle and Aquinas. While Hauerwas certainly holds their accounts of morality in high esteem, he argues that their emphasis on the prior unity of virtues for moral formation is circular. What is required in order to improve their account of moral growth is the inclusion of a truthful narrative by which morals must be formed.[46] In this respect, Hauerwas subscribes more to the virtue ethics of MacIntyre, who also recognised the need for a narrative context in which virtues could develop.[47]

Bound up with the narrative that guides the acquisition of virtues is the context in which moral development must take place—the church. Hauerwas often draws on the metaphor of apprenticeship in order to describe the role of community in forming character.[48] It is from the masters that we learn the skills necessary to live faithfully to the Christian narrative.[49] We see here the particular influence of Iris Murdoch, as Hauerwas connects truthful living with the need to see the world rightly.[50]

Hauerwas's ecclesiology also constitutes a recovery of the ordinary practices of the church, imbuing the gestures of church life such as the act of kneeling to pray with significance in their own right.[51] Worship orients us toward the proper direction for ethical "seeing."[52] Liturgy shapes Christians to live the story of God correctly.[53] Furthermore, these practices contribute to the notion that the church is countercultural, opposing the prevailing worldly practices. This is all a part of what Nicholas Healy terms a "turn to the concrete," a tendency he identifies in postliberal

---

45. Hauerwas, "Situation Ethics," 11–29.
46. Hauerwas, *Community of Character*, 136.
47. MacIntyre, *After Virtue*, 176.
48. Hauerwas, *Community of Character*, 126.
49. Hauerwas, *Community of Character*, 160.
50. Hauerwas, *Vision and Virtue*, 30–47.
51. Hauerwas, *Christian Existence Today*, 106.
52. Hauerwas and Willimon, *Resident Aliens*, 95.
53. Hauerwas, *Christian Existence Today*, 107.

ecclesiologies.[54] It is through the concrete practices of the Christian community that the Hauerwasian church makes it possible for the world to hear the story by which they are formed—the story of God's calling of Israel and Jesus.[55] Hence Hauerwas's well known dictum: "The church does not *have* a social ethic, but *is* a social ethic."[56]

Kingdom

In discussing Jesus as he is portrayed in the gospels, Hauerwas points out that he was far less concerned with his own status than with proclaiming the kingdom of God.[57] The early Christians acknowledged this and recognised that the kingdom proclaimed by Jesus could only be understood by paying attention to how the attributes of that kingdom were exemplified in his life.[58]

The narrative of Jesus and the kingdom of God is fundamentally different to any other human narrative by which we could live—it reconfigures time itself by orienting the church toward the *eschaton*. Hauerwas is largely in agreement with H. Richard Niebuhr that many of us are "fated" to be Christian in the same way we belong to a particular ethnic group. However, he argues that God's story enables us to "turn our fate into destiny"—to make our lives our own—in a way that other stories cannot.[59]

This kingdom is associated with character in Hauerwas's work. Morals depend upon vision, which in turn is determined by the social context we inhabit.[60] For the Christian community, the kingdom of God is the vision that guides moral formation. As Wells puts it, "the church's vision of the world from an eschatological point of view is what enables it, through narrative, to form its character by claiming its actions as its own."[61]

---

54. Healy, "Practices and the New Ecclesiology," 287.
55. Hauerwas, *Christian Existence Today*, 101.
56. Hauerwas, "Gesture of a Truthful Story," 319.
57. Hauerwas, "Jesus: The Presence," 73.
58. Hauerwas, "Jesus: The Presence," 74.
59. Hauerwas, *Christian Existence Today*, 43.
60. Hauerwas, *Vision and Virtue*, 14, 34.
61. Wells, *Transforming Fate into Destiny*, 30.

Witness

The church is at once storyteller of and character in the narrative of how creation is ordered by God to his own good purposes.[62] By telling the story of God's work for us in Israel, Jesus and today, and by living as part of that story ourselves, the church acts as a witness.[63]

Hauerwas has written much about the "peaceable kingdom," which he identifies as the nonviolent witness of the Christian community.[64] This centrality of peace derives from considering the cross to be the summary of Jesus' life—the circumstances of his death embodied a kingdom of peace and forgiveness that believers may inhabit in the present.[65] The cross is understood to be the inevitable consequence of living peaceably in a violent world.[66]

The courage for the church to live peaceably in a world that is often violent comes from the reality of Christ and the eschatological nature of the kingdom he proclaimed.[67] The resurrection testifies to the victory of the peace, renunciation and humility displayed by Christ on the cross. With the vindication of such a death brought by the resurrection, this peaceful way of life is affirmed as the means of ongoing witness to the reign of God. Hauerwas represents this commitment to nonviolence as countercultural—the church refuses to accommodate itself to secular political agendas by trusting that God will ultimately dispense justice, even if he does not intervene in the present.[68]

The Church and Truth

For Hauerwas, the truth claims of theological affirmations such as "Jesus is Lord" are not grounded in notions of philosophical certainty, which dominated the modern period, but rather are verified through the witness of actual lives lived according to these claims.[69] Hauerwas is in agreement with Bruce Marshall that the holding of Christian beliefs as true necessitates a changed life—if the life remains unchanged then these beliefs are not genuinely held

---

62. Hauerwas, "Church as God's New Language," 160.
63. Hauerwas, *Community of Character*, 249–50.
64. Hauerwas, *Peaceable Kingdom*, 102.
65. Hauerwas, *Peaceable Kingdom*, 85.
66. Thomson, *Ecclesiology of Stanley Hauerwas*, 11.
67. Hauerwas, *Against the Nations*, 59.
68. Hauerwas, *Against the Nations*, 59; Wells, *Transforming Fate into Destiny*, 125.
69. Hauerwas, *In Good Company*, 49.

to be true.[70] He expresses this point with the question, "what could it possibly mean to 'believe' that Jesus had been raised from the dead if a people do not exist who continue to 'eat and drink' with their Lord?"[71]

Hauerwas recognises that the world is changing. While rational objectivity still holds forth in some circles, many subscribe to a world that is relativistic and pluralistic.[72] Hauerwas cites Yoder's call to speak about the truth of the church and its belief within the language of this new world, to use the biblical phrases of "witness" and "proclamation" in place of the modern "truth claims."[73] Hauerwas takes issue with the modernist preoccupation with metaphysical arguments for truth, arguing instead that narrative is a more basic epistemological category than explanation or understanding.[74] The truthfulness of a story cannot be established through appealing to a prior universal norm, rather its truth is attested by how it illuminates and compels people's lives by its vision.[75] For the church to be faithful to God's story and witness to its truth through changed lives, it must progress beyond the subversion to secular culture that has characterised much of its existence from the Enlightenment until now.[76]

Outlook

This final section offers an assessment of Hauerwas's ecclesiology, first considering several shortcomings as well as its positive influence on subsequent Christian ethics and potential for ecumenical progress. Hauerwas's ecclesiology has attracted various criticisms that ought to be addressed. The understanding of the church as sole witness potentially undermines the sufficiency of Jesus as portrayed in the gospels for apologetic appeal. Similarly, Scripture is not afforded authority on the basis of divine inspiration or revealed morality, but rather on the basis of the community that is shaped by its narrative.[77] Richard McCormick and Mark Gingerich contend reasonably that positioning the church as a politic apart from the world precludes any conversation between the church and secular society.[78] Nigel Biggar argues

70. Hauerwas, *Sanctify Them in the Truth*, 5; cf. Marshall, "What Is Truth," 423.
71. Hauerwas, *Sanctify Them in the Truth*, 5.
72. Partridge, "Disenchantment and Re-Enchantment of the West," 235.
73. Yoder, *Priestly Kingdom*, 56.
74. Hauerwas, *With the Grain of the Universe*, 206.
75. Hauerwas, *Community of Character*, 149.
76. Olson, *Journey of Modern Theology*, 675.
77. Hauerwas, *Community of Character*, 63.
78. McCormick, *Notes on Moral Theology*, 25; Gingerich, "Church as Kingdom," 140.

that Hauerwas's "lack of ecclesial humility" necessitates an unreasonably low view of the world.[79] Certainly Hauerwas does not seem to allow the possibility that kingdom work might be done by those not a part of the church, that God might be present and working in the good actions of non-believers or adherents to other faiths, an oversight indeed. A common criticism concerns whether it is even possible for the church to exist empirically as Hauerwas describes it,[80] though Hauerwas counters such criticisms adequately by arguing that the church is holy regardless of how accommodated it may be, and asserts that "we too often lack the vision to see the miracle that is the church."[81] Acknowledging these shortcomings, let us move on to what we may learn from Hauerwas's extensive corpus.

Hauerwas's critique of the Christian social ethics tradition he inherited is perhaps vindicated in the strong turn away from foundationalist ethics today. The extent of Hauerwas's direct influence is difficult to discern, yet we may reasonably say that virtue ethics enjoys far greater prominence today than prior to the publication of *A Community of Character* in 1981. James Fodor contends that postliberal theology "has contributed enormously to the reinvigoration of Christian ethics," reinjecting the language of "virtue," "character" and "narrative" into a field "that for the last several hundred years has been thoroughly dominated by utilitarian and deontological outlooks."[82]

Wells identifies the rehabilitation of pacifism as a central concern for theologians to be another constructive outcome of Hauerwas's work. He brought Yoder's theological ethics to a much larger audience, and has prompted both critical conversation with just war theory and consideration of how Christians might reflect a peaceable witness to the world.[83]

Reflecting on his approach to theology, Hauerwas thinks of his writings as letters to the church.[84] As a theologian, he views his great contribution to a generous orthodoxy and the promotion of ecumenism as "thinking through the loss of Christendom."[85] Hauerwas expresses the hope that his "ecclesial homelessness" will be in service to Christian unity;[86] examining

---

79. Biggar, *Behaving in Public*, 95.
80. Healy, *Hauerwas*, 98.
81. Hauerwas, *Sanctify Them in the Truth*, 10–11.
82. Fodor, "Postliberal Theology," 243.
83. Werpehowski, "Talking the Walk," 240–41.
84. Hauerwas, *Work of Theology*, 24.
85. Hauerwas, "Which Church? What Unity?," 119.
86. Hauerwas, *Hannah's Child*, 254–55.

the impact of such a diverse background on his thought suggests this may be so. He is indeed a "living ecumenical movement."[87]

We can take much also from Hauerwas's ability to see denominational boundaries as porous, and his refusal to prioritise distinct affiliations over Christian unity. He jokes that in his present Episcopalian ecclesial context, he is "bringing Methodism home" to its roots in the Church of England— this ability to both emphasise commonalities and contextualise historically the differences between traditions is of enormous value if generous orthodoxy as a whole is to flourish.[88]

Hauerwas is often provocative in his views on church unity. He chose the occasion of Reformation Sunday to preach a sermon effectively denouncing the Reformation for the disunity it wrought in the church.[89] He takes the pre-Constantinian, pre-denominational church as a model for how virtue-forming Christian communities might look.[90] For Hauerwas, church unity is not simply an acknowledgement that many reasons for past divisions are no longer relevant, but an admission that each church needs connections with churches across the world to guard against distorting the gospel.[91]

At the least, Hauerwas blurs the distinctions between Christian traditions. Gerald Schlabach provides the astute summary: "Hauerwas wants Catholics to be more Anabaptist, and Anabaptists to be more Catholic, and Protestants to be both, and the only way he can put this together in terms of his own ecclesial location is to be a 'Catholic' Methodist in roughly the way that some Episcopalians are Anglo-Catholic."[92] While Hauerwas accepts this picture of himself, he is less concerned with the labels. He recently summarised his own theological project as follows: "I have tried to show that fundamental theological convictions about the Father, the Son, and the Holy Spirit are inseparable from the work they do for the formation of a people set loose in and for the world."[93] An extensive body of work is expressed thus in a simple and remarkably consistent objective. The Hauerwasian church upholds traditional theological commitments, yet demands a radically countercultural relationship to the broader society. In

---

87. Hauerwas, "Which Church? What Unity?," 99.

88. Hauerwas, *Hannah's Child*, 279.

89. The text of the sermon, which was preached in 1995, is published in Hauerwas, "Reformation Is Sin," 241–44.

90. Hauerwas, *Peaceable Kingdom*, 73.

91. Hauerwas, "End of Protestantism," 96.

92. Schlabach cited in Hauerwas, *After Christendom*, 9–10.

93. Hauerwas, *Work of Theology*, 23.

underscoring the solid boundary between church and world, the demarcations between church and church are absorbed into a larger community of Christians practising the virtues embodied in the life, death and resurrection of Jesus—an ecumenical ecclesiology that will reward further critical engagement and efforts toward a generous orthodoxy.

Bibliography

Biggar, Nigel. *Behaving in Public: How to Do Christian Ethics*. Grand Rapids: Eerdmans, 2011.

Cavanaugh, William. "Stan the Man: A Thoroughly Biased Account of a Completely Unobjective Person." In *The Hauerwas Reader*, edited by John Berkman and Michael Cartwright, 17–32. Durham: Duke University Press, 2001.

Fodor, James. "Postliberal Theology." In *The Modern Theologians: An Introduction to Christian Theology Since 1918*, edited by David Ford, 229–48. Oxford: Blackwell, 2005.

Gingerich, Mark. "The Church as Kingdom: The Kingdom of God in the Writings of Stanley Hauerwas and John Howard Yoder." *Didaskalia* 19.1 (2008) 129–43.

Hauerwas, Stanley. *After Christendom: How the Church Is to Behave If Freedom, Justice, and a Christian Nation are Bad Ideas*. Nashville: Abingdon, 1991.

———. *Against the Nations: War and Survival in a Liberal Society*. Minneapolis: Winston Seabury, 1985.

———. *Christian Existence Today: Essays on Church, World, and Living In Between*. Durham: Labyrinth, 1988.

———. "The Church as God's New Language." In *The Hauerwas Reader*, edited by John Berkman and Michael Cartwright, 142–64. Durham: Duke University Press, 2001.

———. *A Community of Character: Toward a Constructive Christian Social Ethic*. Notre Dame: University of Notre Dame Press, 2005.

———. *Dispatches from the Front: Theological Engagements with the Secular*. Durham: Duke University Press, 1994.

———. "The End of Protestantism." In *Approaching the End: Eschatological Reflections on Church, Politics, and Life*, 87–97. London: SCM, 2014.

———. "The Gesture of a Truthful Story: The Church and 'Religious Education.'" *Encounter* 43.4 (1982) 319–29.

———. *Hannah's Child: A Theologian's Memoir*. Grand Rapids: Eerdmans, 2012.

———. *In Good Company: The Church as Polis*. Durham: Duke University Press, 1994.

———. "The Interpretation of Scripture: Why Discipleship Is Required." In *The Hauerwas Reader*, edited by John Berkman and Michael Cartwright, 255–66. Durham: Duke University Press, 2001.

———. "Jesus: The Presence of the Peaceable Kingdom." In *The Peaceable Kingdom: A Primer in Christian Ethics*, 72–95. Notre Dame: University of Notre Dame Press, 1983.

———. "Jesus: The Story of the Kingdom." In *A Community of Character: Toward a Constructive Christian Social Ethic*, 36–52. Notre Dame: University of Notre Dame Press, 2005.

———. *The Peaceable Kingdom: A Primer in Christian Ethics*. Notre Dame: University of Notre Dame Press, 1983.

———. "Preaching as Though We Had Enemies." *First Things*, May 1995. Online. https://www.firstthings.com/article/1995/05/003-preaching-as-though-we-had-enemies.

———. "Reformation Is Sin." In *Sanctify Them in the Truth: Holiness Exemplified*, by Stanley Hauerwas, 241–44. Edinburgh: T&T Clark, 1998.

———. *Sanctify Them in the Truth: Holiness Exemplified*. Edinburgh: T&T Clark, 1998.

———. "The Significance of Vision: Toward an Aesthetic Ethic." In *Vision and Virtue: Essays in Christian Ethical Reflection*, by Stanley Hauerwas, 30–47. Notre Dame: University of Notre Dame Press, 1981.

———. "Situation Ethics, Moral Notions, and Moral Theology." In *Vision and Virtue: Essays in Christian Ethical Reflection*, by Stanley Hauerwas, 11–29. Notre Dame: University of Notre Dame Press, 1981.

———. *Truthfulness and Tragedy*. Notre Dame: University of Notre Dame Press, 1977.

———. *Unleashing the Scripture: Freeing the Bible from Captivity to America*. Nashville: Abingdon, 1993.

———. *Vision and Virtue: Essays in Christian Ethical Reflection*. South Bend, IN: University of Notre Dame Press, 1981.

———. "Which Church? What Unity? Or, An Attempt to Say What I May Think about the Future of Christian Unity." In *Approaching the End: Eschatological Reflections on Church, Politics, and Life*, by Stanley Hauerwas, 98–119. London: SCM, 2014.

———. *Wilderness Wanderings*. London: SCM, 1997.

———. *With the Grain of the Universe: The Church's Witness and Natural Theology*. Grand Rapids: Brazos, 2001.

———. *The Work of Theology*. Grand Rapids: Eerdmans, 2015.

Hauerwas, Stanley, and Roman Coles. *Christianity, Democracy, and the Radical Ordinary: Conversations between a Radical Democrat and a Christian*. Cambridge: Lutterworth, 2010.

Hauerwas, Stanley, and William H. Willimon. *Resident Aliens*. Nashville: Abingdon, 1989.

———. "What About the Church? A Response." *The Christian Century* 106.4 (1989) 111–28.

Healy, Nicholas. *Hauerwas: A (Very) Critical Introduction*. Grand Rapids: Eerdmans, 2014.

———. "Practices and the New Ecclesiology: Misplaced Concreteness?" *International Journal of Systematic Theology* 5.3 (2003) 287–308.

John Paul II. "Redemptor Hominis." In *The Encyclicals of John Paul II*, edited by J. Michael Miller. Huntington: Our Sunday Visitor, 1996.

MacIntyre, Alasdair. *After Virtue: A Study in Moral Theology*. Notre Dame: University of Notre Dame Press, 1984.

Marshall, Bruce D. "What Is Truth." *Pro Ecclesia* 4.4 (1995) 404–30.

McCormick, Richard A. *Notes on Moral Theology: 1981–1984*. Lanham: University Press of America, 1984.

Olson, Roger E. *The Journey of Modern Theology: From Reconstruction to Deconstruction*. Downers Grove, IL: IVP Academic, 2013.

Partridge, Christopher. "The Disenchantment and Re-enchantment of the West: The Religio-Cultural Context of Contemporary Western Christianity." *Evangelical Quarterly* 74 (2002) 235–56.

Thiessen Nation, Mark. "Stanley Hauerwas: Where Would We Be Without Him?" In *Faithfulness and Fortitude: In Conversation with the Theological Ethics of Stanley Hauerwas*, edited by Mark Thiessen Nation and Samuel Wells, 19–36. Edinburgh: T&T Clark, 2012.

Thomson, John. *The Ecclesiology of Stanley Hauerwas: A Christian Theology of Liberation*. Aldershot: Ashgate, 2003.

Wells, Samuel. *Transforming Fate into Destiny: The Theological Ethics of Stanley Hauerwas*. Carlisle, Cumbria, UK: Paternoster, 1998.

Werpehowski, William. "Talking the Walk and Walking the Talk: Stanley Hauerwas's Contribution to Theological Ethics." *Journal of Religious Ethics* 40.2 (2012) 228–49.

Yoder, John Howard. *The Original Revolution*. Scottdale: Herald, 1971.

———. *The Priestly Kingdom: Social Ethics as Gospel*. Notre Dame: University of Notre Dame Press, 1984.

12

Marilyn McCord Adams: Philosophy, Theology, and Prayer

—Christine M. Helmer

MARILYN MCCORD ADAMS WOULD have rejected the word "orthodox" as a descriptor for her philosophical and theological work.[1] She was well aware that for centuries, theologians with ecclesial and academic power have wielded this word as a means of enforcing normativity and stifling creativity. Her approach to theology, on the other hand, was one of rigorous and questioning inquiry into truth, which demanded honesty and openness. How McCord Adams probed orthodoxy's central doctrines—sin and Christ, evil and God—and revised them in intellectually compelling and ethically serious ways is the theme of this essay.

Philosophy in Theology?

Marilyn McCord Adams had just been appointed Horace Tracy Pitkin Professor of Historical Theology at Yale Divinity School in 1993. The work for which she was known was a two-volume study of William of Ockham, the fourteenth-century nominalist philosopher.[2] This work changed the way that philosophers understood Ockham's innovations. It would also change the way that theologians at Yale and beyond would regard the importance of philosophy for theology. Since the late nineteenth century, Protestant theologians had policed the boundary between philosophy and theology. "No metaphysics, no mysticism in theology," the German theologian Albrecht Ritschl had pronounced. For one hundred years, theologians

---

1. I am grateful to the *Anglican Theological Review* for granting permission to publish this revised reprint of my article, "Marilyn McCord Adams: How a Theologian Works."

2. McCord Adams, *William Ockham*.

insisted on protecting theology from philosophical danger. Theology's truths were based on revelation and scripture. Philosophy was based on human reason. Any encroachment by philosophy onto theological terrain called theology into question. Marilyn McCord Adams introduced medieval philosophy into Protestant theology. The results were transformative for her students and for the field.

When McCord Adams arrived at Yale, she had been recently ordained an Episcopal priest. Her office was at Seabury, the dormitory at YDS for female divinity students. It was in that context, as a graduate student in Yale's Department of Religious Studies, that I first got to know her. At our first meeting she told me that she had been lecturing on Luther and Calvin as part of the history of theology sequence. This sequence was innovative in Protestant theological education because it connected medieval theology to the early modern reformers in one course. Adams showed me her copy of Dillenberger's anthology of Martin Luther's works, which included an excerpt of Luther's 1525 text, *De servo arbitrio* ("On the Unfree Will"). "Luther's philosophy," she said, "is incoherent. I don't appreciate this about Luther, but am willing to learn more about him." My research question at the time had been how to connect Luther to Ockham. Luther as a student at the University of Erfurt had been educated in the *via moderna*, or modern way of philosophy innovated by Ockham. Philip Melanchthon, Luther's colleague in Wittenberg, once reported that Luther could cite passages from Ockham verbatim. Luther scholars, however, particularly those trained in Germany, had taken Albrecht Ritschl's prohibition against philosophy in theology at face value. According to German Luther scholars, Luther was to be regarded as a Protestant theologian who had vigorously resisted any philosophical tainting of Christian faith. Either simple faith in Christ or the slippery philosophical slope into false and dangerous teaching.

My perception of Luther changed through those tutorials with Professor McCord Adams. Seeing Luther through her eyes, the magisterial reformer was transformed into a late medieval Catholic theologian, who made constructive use of philosophical-theological categories to better understand the mysteries of Christian faith. Luther was a preacher of the word, yet he was also a theological dialectician. He had some of the deepest insights of any theologian in the history of Christianity into the divine mercy on the cross, yet was also remarkably sophisticated in his use of logic in trinitarian and christological syllogisms. Luther insisted that every doctor of theology continue to steep herself in the basic truths of faith and preoccupy herself with obeying the Ten Commandments; yet he was also a philosophical theologian who, in spite of some flamboyant rhetoric against Aristotle and sophistries, perceived with great acumen the necessity for adapting philosophical tools of language and metaphysics in order to make truth claims about the Trinity, the incarnation, and the real presence of Christ in the eucharist.

A new picture of a philosophically astute Luther emerged from those tutorials in Seabury Hall. From early modern anti-philosophical reformer Luther became a philosophically fascinating figure, one who stood in a long line of medieval theologians who made use of philosophy to inquire into the truth of Christian doctrine. Luther's discussions of doctrine and Bible began to appear in a new light that illumined underlying philosophical commitments. Luther, like Ockham before him, appropriated and transformed inherited philosophical categories and logic. Sometimes Luther stretched them to the point of rupture, as only this remarkable reformer could, but did so by remaining true to medieval inheritances regarding the dialectical pursuit of truth, the recognition of authorities in this inquiry, and in negotiating philosophy to best suit the theological subject matter.

McCord Adams taught Protestant theologians that philosophy is an ally, not an enemy. Philosophy can help theologians make better arguments. Protestants trained in the continental-theological tradition of German Idealism can benefit from medieval doctrinal insights and paradigms. Anselm of Canterbury should be consulted alongside the seminary's required readings in Hegel and Moltmann. Theologians must be honest about the philosophical commitments they inadvertently smuggle into their theological work. Even if he could not admit it, Barth made use of philosophical resources from Hegel's metaphysics and Kierkegaard's existentialism. Philosophy has always been part of the theologian's métier. Why not reflect seriously on this inevitable connection?

Who Is Responsible?

Philosophy is the handmaiden, not enemy, of theology. This presupposition informed McCord Adams's theological work. While on the surface it could seem as if her scholarly interest was historical theology, her intention was to work out a generative theology for today. She focused her constructive theology on two themes that were Luther's as well: evil and the cross, or in other words, sin and grace. Her theological analysis of the world began where Luther's did too: the incapacity of free will to achieve its salvation.

Can free will explain evil? This question strikes at the heart of the "problem of evil" that has been a philosophical topic since Leibniz articulated it in the early eighteenth century. The question concerns how to reconcile God's will for maximal goodness in creation with the empirical dominance of evil. If God wills the good for creation, why does evil appear to have the upper hand?

Free will has been promoted in recent philosophical discussion. God created humans with free will to exercise in moral decision making. Humans have the freedom to choose to obey the moral law, or not. Freedom is God's wonderful gift to human creatures. Free will sets humans apart from animals, distinguishing them from other created beings who do not have the freedom to choose the good. Humans are free to disobey the divine prohibition. If they do, they are accountable for this decision. Unfortunately at their origins and in all successive generations of the human race, persons have chosen evil over the good. Given the divine respect for the created good of free will, God does not intervene to rescue humans from their bad choices. Yet God watches as humans struggle with the consequences of disobedience. Humans are guilty, and thus must endure punishment (*poena* in Latin) for sin. Punishment is both personal, as the bearing of the consequences of individual bad choices, and corporate, as the unleashing of evil in a broader social and environmental context. The term *horrendous evils* would become McCord Adams's phrase analyzing the human condition.

McCord Adams had experienced evil first hand. As an ordained priest McCord Adams ministered to young people dying of AIDS: suddenly, alone, rejected. In Los Angeles in the 1980s, persons with AIDS were denounced by homophobic Christian preaching. McCord Adams discerned her ministry of advocacy on behalf of LGBTQ people there in LA, a commitment that endured throughout her life.

Amid the dying, McCord Adams's critique of free will was born. How could individual free will explain the preponderance of evil in the world? She describes the evil in the world as inexplicable, cruel, and tragic, listing examples that are so "horrendous" that they exert a visceral shock when reading them: rape, torture, incest, death by starvation, and the Nazi death camps.[3] The focus of her concern is evil that destroys personhood; her interest lies with the individual. Evil works its way into the individual psyche so that a person no longer can regard his or her life as a good to him or her. While the philosophical argument here is more complex, the main point is that evil is not an abstract category that affects the masses, but it is deeply personal; it destroys the individual. McCord Adams is concerned with the cause—the fact that individuals who perpetuate evil on others cannot in most cases fathom the extent of suffering they inflict on others. She is also concerned with the effect—that the magnitude of suffering in many cases

---

3. McCord Adams, *Horrendous Evils and the Goodness of God*, 26–27.

exceeds the personal capacity to integrate the trauma into psychic coherence. Sometimes no meaning can be assigned to suffering.

If human free will cannot explain why horrendous evils exist, then who is responsible? When posed in this way, there is only one answer: the one who created this world, God. In the Christian theological tradition, a few theologians have dared to assign responsibility to God by arguing against free will. Luther, with his idea of double predestination, assigned responsibility of both damnation and salvation to the divine eternal will. Friedrich Schleiermacher too insisted on the claim that God is responsible for sin. While this runs the risk of misunderstanding God as capricious or cruel, this claim has a deeper theological point that McCord Adams makes clear for today. God does not watch as humans take their own lives in acts of desperation. Rather, the God who created a world in which horrendous evils exist is ultimately the one who must "make good" on creation. This argument is Anselm of Canterbury's, one of McCord Adams's beloved medievals, who claimed that God is obligated to see the divine project succeed. God is responsible for creating a world "such as this"; God who is greater than anything that can be conceived—another of Anselm's phrases—is the hope for individuals and world.

Who Can Save?

The problem of evil is much worse than what free will can explain. On this point McCord Adams is part of a chorus of theologians who insist that free will is too thin a reed to bear responsibility for personal blessedness, let alone the world's. Luther too contested free will's capacity to make a decision about eternal destiny. If the soul is made for eternity, then its salvation is ultimately God's business.

A major building block in McCord Adams's account of salvation is philosophical. The question "how can God save?" presupposes the question, "what does God save?" Her response is to explain the metaphysical structure of reality, specifically human reality. The "stuff" of which humans are made is the same "stuff" that God saves. The relation between matter and spirit makes up the structure of reality. The human condition is a function of this relation. In this regard McCord Adams reveals her commitment to an ancient philosophical account about the relation between soul and body that informs medieval theology. The Greek philosopher Aristotle thought that the soul informs matter, or in other words, souls exist as embodied individuals. Precisely this relation between soul and body is "non-optimal" as McCord Adams claims.[4] Humans are vulnerable to horrors because soul and body are joined in an unstable relation. This instability is best illustrated in psychological terms. Healthy psychological development requires specific steps, from a mother's nurturing love to social relations that convey the mutual recognition necessary for the healthy integration of life events into a unified consciousness. Yet life events are not optimally engineered for psychic well-being. Families and societies inflict trauma on individuals that disrupt and harm development. When evil becomes too much for integration, then psychic collapse ensues.

What is set up as the human condition is what God has to do something about. McCord Adams constructs a specific theological order to a theology of salvation: first the job description, then the one who fits the job description. If human vulnerability to horrors is a function of the mismatch between body and soul, then the divine promise of salvation requires a person, uniting body and soul, in a way that both succumbs to the human condition and reconstitutes it in a new way. Medieval theology inspires McCord Adams's commitment to a particular Christology. Christ is the one who bridges both sides of the divide, spirit and matter, divinity and humanity. Christ is composed of two natures, divine and human, that are fitted together in one person. McCord Adams uses historical sources in her constructive theological ideas about Christ's person as participating in the mismatch between soul and body and reorienting it. The reorientation occurs by virtue of divinity working in the person of Christ. God in Christ orders body and soul in such a way as to heal and save, and finally to overcome horrors forever in the life to come.

There are three stages of what McCord Adams calls "horror defeat" by Christ. The first stage is the incarnation, God's personal way of uniting the divine self to humanity in Jesus. McCord Adams is committed to historical reality here, attested in the Bible and subject of Christian preaching. The second stage is the way in which Christ becomes present to individuals in order to reshape individual personhood. The goal is psychic harmony between body and soul and integration of life events into a coherent consciousness. McCord Adams insists that Christ's real presence has this contagious effect. Communicating Christ's presence is the task of the church. Through its ministry of the care of souls and distribution of the body of Christ for eating, the church makes Christ present. The third stage of horror defeat is eschatological. In the new creation, there will be no tears.

McCord Adams directs her theological attention to the individual and God who in Christ follows the human path of embodiment's susceptibility

---

4. McCord Adams, *Christ and Horrors*, 18.

to horrors. With this interest in the individual, she takes up Luther's insistence that the gospel is intensely personal. The gift of Christ is *pro te*, for you. Both the created reality of the individual and the christological claim about the person of Christ have to do with the concern for the individual. Here McCord Adams turns the individual into a bearer of a theological truth. The individual is "infinitely valuable" in both a created and a redemptive sense. Christ's defeat of horrors begins with the cross. It ends with the redemption of all creation.

The constructive theology that McCord Adams articulates is remarkably in line with Luther's. Luther maximizes sin in order to maximize grace. When theological description takes human and cosmic lostness seriously, then there is only one who can take up the challenge to save. McCord Adams, like Luther, looks squarely at the reality of the human condition, and dares to believe that God is greater and more generous, capacious, merciful, and just than can be conceived. The God who is responsible will do what it takes to realize the final cause of goodness for all. The creation project will succeed because God has underwritten it with the divine life.

How Do Theologians Work?

Academic work requires a subject matter. A subject becomes an object of study when it is measured, categorized, and interpreted. Whether a chemical reaction or a text, a subject becomes an object to be investigated. Content has to do with what is studied. How content is approached is the question of knowledge. Academic inquiry has to do with both aspects, subject matter and form. How one comes to know something about an object of inquiry is related to the question of what is actually studied.

Of all the disciplines in the academic universe (university!), theology in the contemporary era poses a distinctive challenge. Theology's subject matter is God; the Greek terms, *theos* for God, and *logos* for rationality make up the neologism *theology*. The resulting term *theology*, the study of God, expresses both content and approach: God is the content of this academic discipline, and rational inquiry is the way in which God is rendered as subject of study.

This minimal circumscription of theology, however, is merely the beginning of a centuries-long discussion regarding the special nature of theology in view of its distinctive subject matter. God cannot be studied as an object alongside other finite objects. God is the *ens realissimum*, the most real being, the ground and creator of beings. As creator of all that exists, God transcends human categorization. How then can God be studied?

McCord Adams insists on theology as a necessary discipline in the contemporary university. If the different disciplines in the university are designed to study the realities that make up the world, then theology must take up its rightful place among the disciplines. God as most real being must be studied in relation to the other realities, material and spiritual, that make up the world. The metaphysical question regarding what kind of being God has is one that philosophers can ask. Even if philosophy has its location in a secular institution, such as the departments McCord Adams taught in throughout her career, including UCLA, the University of North Carolina/Chapel Hill, and Rutgers University, this discipline cannot bracket the study of God. The history of western philosophy is inextricably interwoven with metaphysical and theological questions about the ground of being. The hermeneutical question regarding God concerns the biblical and textual study that is part of a theological curriculum. Words have referents; stories are about characters. The Bible is about God in relation to particular characters who have warts and character flaws. God too has character development along plot lines. The diversity of texts might not add up to a completely coherent view; in fact diversity of texts is a bonus—more material for different preaching. Yet these texts refer in partial and fragmentary ways to a reality that exists outside the text. Their study requires hermeneutics, the application of historical, grammatical, and literary tools to better understand how divine reality enters the world and people's lives.

Philosophical analysis and hermeneutical study are necessary to theology, even more so if theology is to be taken seriously as an academic discipline in the contemporary university. Theology was the "queen of the sciences" in the Middle Ages. Today, however, theology's academic legitimacy is contested. Suspicions abound regarding theology's alleged confessional tainting of knowledge, its universalizing of Christian categories for the study of religion, and its emphasis on faith that precludes intellectual integrity. Academic theologians today are united in their efforts to clarify the academic commitments of their discipline. As one of the oldest fields of study in the West, having informed education in the West for almost a millennium, theology is currently on the defensive. Arguments on behalf of theology's legitimacy insist on its academic responsibility to adhere to standards befitting all disciplines in the university. Intellectual rigor, historical awareness, and argumentative clarity are the rules that theologians, just like any academic, assent to following.

Yet theologians cannot be restricted by these rules, particularly if the rules have become metaphysically narrow-minded and methodologically flat. McCord Adams was never satisfied with a defensive posture. Rather, she affirmed that theology today can contribute a unique perspective to academic study because it has God as its subject matter. While defense of theology's legitimacy is important, arguments for theology's contributions to the academy are perhaps even more so. Human reason has specific modes of analysis and reflection. Yet McCord Adams insists that epistemological tools are too limited, in her words "too small" to approach the God who is infinitely bigger than that which a puny and finite mind can conceive. Not only are academic theologians committed to the intellectual rigor prescribed by participation in the university, but they can offer new ways of appreciating and approaching aspects of reality that are occluded or even prohibited by academic methodologies taken as consensus. Her work on eleventh-century theologian Anselm of Canterbury is an example of this position. The proof for God's existence that Anselm provides in his *Proslogion* is not merely an exercise in human reason. This proof requires additional support, that of prayer. Anselm begins his argument with a prayer addressed to the subject outside of human reason. Prayer is the first step in theological method. One cannot speak about God in the third person without first being in communication with God. First to second person speech is integral to theological method. A human person cannot say anything about God without divine assistance. The study of God presupposes an invitation that God first draw near.

In an essay on prayer published in the *Anglican Theological Review* in 2016, McCord Adams reflects on prayer as constitutive of theological method.[5] She knows that theology's presence in the secular academy is contested. Yet theology, like other academic disciplines, presupposes subjective acknowledgment that one's subject matter is worthy of study. Yet theology is unlike other disciplines because its subject matter outclasses all other objects; theologians inquire into divinity, the cause and source of all that exists. Because this research subject transcends the human capacity to know, it requires a special approach. Mind and soul must be attuned by a distinctive subjective disposition to this particular reality. Prayer is this approach.[6]

The *discipline* of theology requires the *discipline* of prayer. Third-person discourse about God presupposes first-to-second person speech that constitutes a relation. McCord Adams notes the relational dimension of prayer. Prayer sets person and community into relation with a God whose companionship never fails, a relationship that goes through bumps and crises and questioning, and a connection that effects change in the personality of the one praying. Theological method includes a salvific dimension. As the person who prays grows and develops in relation to the ground and goal of

5. McCord Adams, "Prayer as the 'Lifeline of Theology.'"
6. See McCord Adams's collection of prayers, *Opening to God*.

her being, she experiences the effects of the God who draws near in prayer. God's presence in prayer is the promise of holding together individual fragmented and disjointed parts and knitting them together as unfolding of the divine plan for the soul's harmony. Prayer expands a common academic notion that objective study of one's subject matter precludes experience of it. With prayer, relationship is part of the method. Theologians speak and write about their subject matter because they are already wrestling with and grasping ideas in the life of prayer.[7]

A theologian is a "participant observer," to use anthropologist Clifford Geertz's term. Theology is constructed from a life with God. Theologians, McCord Adams writes, "accept God's invitation to turn their very selves into laboratories where God is at work."[8] Theology is also observation. Theologians are aware that a life with God informs the perspectives of theologians in the past. Anselm's ontological proof for God's existence cannot be understood without taking his prayer into account as constitutive of his claims. An adequate hermeneutic is sensitive to strategies that theologians in the past have used to approach their subject matter. Their ideas cannot be abstracted from their religious practices, lives, and historical communities. In this regard, the theological insight on being a "participant observer" can contribute an imaginative perspective to discussions of method in the university. Philosophers have for some time paid attention to the inevitable subjective shaping of research. While Kant developed a modern epistemology based on the categories for perceiving the world of appearances, contemporary feminist philosophers insist that bias, ideology, experience, and culture play significant roles in how a subject matter is viewed and studied. Participant observers are asked to be aware of their subjective positions, while leaving open theoretical spaces for observation and analysis. As scholars continue to reflect on their epistemologies, they should be inspired by theologians who have been honest about their participative observations for centuries.

Theological practices are necessary for the life of a theologian. Theology's content demands this. McCord Adams takes God seriously as theology's subject, the divine promise of wholeness in a world characterized by fragments, including those in the theologian's own soul. Doctrinal themes of evil and grace, cross and redemption emerge from one's existence. The theologian's existence attests to doctrine's truth about sin and evil. Brokenness as the result of acts by others, the incapacity to hear and respond, and one's own inability to be attuned to divine presence are entanglements of

---

7. The word *wrestling* alludes to the title of McCord Adams's collection of sermons, *Wrestling for Blessing*. This title refers to the story of Jacob wrestling with the angel in Genesis 32:22–31.

8. McCord Adams, "Prayer as the 'Lifeline of Theology,'" 280.

the human created condition. Proximity to the holy, as McCord Adams insists, heals, integrates, and facilitates attunement. Salvation begins in the soul, the result of divine presence communicated in the church. Feeding on the body of Christ, hearing the gospel, and praying for peace are ways the society of Christians shares the light of the gospel that edifies the soul. McCord Adams was particularly fascinated by the doctrine of the real presence of Christ. Her monograph on the metaphysics of the eucharist attests to the intellectual wrestling with the philosophical commitments attuned to make sense of the redemptive effects of flesh and blood in bread and wine.[9] Holiness is catching; redemption is contagious. Getting as close to the real thing as possible, even by taking it up into one's own digestive system, is a theological practice that sustains body, soul, and mind.

How Is Theology Constructed?

The theological project preoccupying Marilyn McCord Adams was to build stronger connections between academic and ecclesial institutions. She was aware of the challenges of academic legitimacy facing theology in secular institutions. She was committed to the idea that Christian divinity schools needed to improve their intellectual game in order to be taken seriously in the university. She knew that the churches need robust theologies in order to communicate the gospel with intellectual and spiritual integrity as well as to make more just church-political decisions.

As she worked to connect philosophy and theology, academy and church, McCord Adams's theological aim was constructive. She based her constructive theology on the central Christian doctrines of sin and grace, focusing them on the contemporary reality of horrendous evils and the theological reality of Christ's work in overcoming them. Her theological focus was on God, whose act of creating material reality obliges God to guarantee its success. Humans can catch glimpses of divinity carrying out this plan by participation in prayer and the eucharist. They can participate in the ongoing wrestling with God for answers by seeking to formulate better questions. Her constructive theology attests to these commitments, seeking and questioning, articulating and preaching, all the while holding onto the hope that God will make good on all that God has made.

---

9. McCord Adams, *Some Later Medieval Theories of the Eucharist*.

Outlook

The revisionist orthodoxy that McCord Adams worked out in her publications reveals her commitment to systematicity. How a theologian conceives one doctrine has to do with the way that doctrine is related to others. If sin is conceived in the terms of horrendous evils, as McCord Adams does, then the One who is assigned the task of making good on creation must both identify with the horrors and overcome them in ways that are individually significant and cosmically relevant. McCord Adams built her work on the Reformation principle that maximal sin is related to maximal grace and she connected the doctrinal correlation of sin/grace to the divine nature. Christ gives his body and blood as offer of intimate presence while God accomplishes the divine work of redemption.

Yet McCord Adams knew that the hope of redemption is compromised by horrors and traumas so great that responsibility for them could not be assigned to individual choice or integrated into personal consciousness. Cosmic evils threaten divine goodness. Following this line of questioning led her away from Augustine towards Anselm of Canterbury, who helped her conceptualize a theology of the divine obligation to creation and the metaphysic of a God-man who both identified with human trauma and overcome its horrors on the cross. She based her theological commitment to the materiality of creation on Aristotle's hylomorphism and took up Rudolf Otto's image of the nonrational God in order to make the claim concerning the metaphysical size gap between God and humans. God is much larger than what human morality presupposes, and humans much more vulnerable to horrors than free choice allows. This led her, finally, to relate creation to eschatology. The end must ultimately attest to the divine good reason for having created a world of embodied creatures in the first place.

McCord Adams paved a new way for connecting metaphysics with Christian doctrine. Contemporary Protestant theologians need no longer be indebted to German Idealism for their philosophical foundations. McCord Adams liberated them from the historicist model to probe reality, whether human or divine, with tools from medieval philosophy, using medieval sources to articulate an eyes-wide-open theological account of the world in which we live and of the God in Christ who is concerned with this particular world. She understood it to be theology's responsibility to probe the reality of what it means to be human, in all its created diversity and vulnerability to horrors. And it was theology's responsibility to express the Christian hope in the God in Christ who demonstrates divine compassion by uniting with human vulnerabilities and overcoming them in his body, both in the resurrection and in the world to come.

No consideration of McCord Adams thought can ignore the commitments of her life. She lived the pathway of her questions. Her ethics were generous and inclusive—and tough-minded. She enlarged the meanings of orthodoxy to include ecclesial and political justice for LGBTQIA people. The God who could not be bound by the rules of mere reason was the One who created a diversity of sexual orientations. McCord Adams challenged those in ecclesial power who would reproduce structures of sadism, of exclusion, and oppression, and in doing so gave us a theology for the ages that is also an urgent voice in our time.

Bibliography

Helmer, Christine. "Marilyn McCord Adams: How a Theologian Works." *Anglican Theological Review* 100.2 (2018) 327–38.

McCord Adams, Marilyn. *Christ and Horrors: The Coherence of Christology*. Cambridge: Cambridge University Press, 2006.

———. *Horrendous Evils and the Goodness of God*. Ithaca, NY: Cornell University Press, 1999.

———. *Opening to God: Childlike Prayers for Adults*. Louisville: Westminster John Knox, 2008.

———. "Prayer as the 'Lifeline of Theology.'" *Anglican Theological Review* 98.2 (2016) 271–83.

———. *Some Later Medieval Theories of the Eucharist: Thomas Aquinas, Giles of Rome, Duns Scotus, and William Ockham*. Oxford: Oxford University Press, 2010.

———. *William Ockham*. 2 vols. Publications in Medieval Studies. South Bend, IN: University of Notre Dame Press, 1987.

———. *Wrestling for Blessing*. London: Darton Longman & Todd, 2005.

Part Four
Ecumenical Theology Today

13

Pentecostalism and Christian Orthodoxy: Revision, Revival, and Renewal

—Wolfgang Vondey

PENTECOSTALISM EMERGED AS A worldwide Christian movement in response to social, cultural, economic, moral, and theological concerns of the late nineteenth and early twentieth century.[1] The movement became readily associated with these concerns because it responded to them in unusual ways often critical of and criticized by the established traditions. Orthodox patterns of thought and praxis were made responsible by Pentecostals for an intellectualized theology, a stagnation of the faith, the rise of creedal Christianity, lack of participation by the laity, ignorance of biblical teaching, neglect of preaching the gospel, corruption of church government, empty rituals, institutionalization, low church attendance, and other problems.[2] In turn, Pentecostals were often ostracized and even persecuted by the established churches as heretical, un-orthodox, and anti-ecumenical.[3] The ensuing confrontation was the result of both the seemingly unorthodox Pentecostal response to the persistent problems heralding the end of Christendom and the resistance of the Christian establishment to the emerging Pentecostal tradition.

Amidst this complex history, a commitment to revising Christian orthodoxy has emerged among Pentecostals in two main forms: (1) the notion of revival, dominant since the pioneering days and responsible for identifying Pentecostal and charismatic Christianity widely as revival movements and (2) the more recent idea of renewal, which has broadened the nomenclature of Pentecostal and charismatic movements to the prominent notion of Renewal Christianity. This essay traces both ideas as

1. See Anderson, *To the Ends of the Earth*; *Introduction to Pentecostalism*.
2. See Vondey, *Beyond Pentecostalism*.
3. See Vondey, *Continuing and Building Relationships*, 1–31.

expressions of the ethos of Pentecostal ecumenism and brings them into dialogue with contemporary notions of revising Christian orthodoxy. I suggest that the notion of renewal is not simply a correlate of revival but a fundamentally different approach to the Christian world. The so-called Renewal Christianity, which has emerged from the confrontation between Pentecostalism and the established ecumenical traditions, is orthodox in a radical and generous sense by extending the boundaries of orthodoxy from the center of the Christian establishment to the margins of the ecumenical world and back again.

Pentecostalism as Revival of Christian Orthodoxy

Revival has consistently been seen as the trademark of Pentecostals. The term "revival" has been applied to Pentecostalism as a whole in the sense that the Pentecostal movement in its essence is perceived as bringing to life again the biblical event of Pentecost, the gift of the Holy Spirit and the accompanying charismatic manifestations.[4] Revival functions as an umbrella term for the events that together comprise the historical origins of classical Pentecostalism in North America, such as the Holiness revivals of the nineteenth century, the revival at Camp Creek (1886), the revival at Topeka (1901), and the Azusa Street revival (1906).[5] The origins of global Pentecostalism can be attributed to corresponding Indian, Korean, Welsh and other similar revival events worldwide.[6] Revival clearly identifies a self-perception among Pentecostals and represents a generally adopted term to classify Pentecostalism in the broader Christian landscape.

Responsible for this terminology has been the strong emphasis on evangelization and mission and the influence of rural camp meeting revivals on classical Pentecostals.[7] In the North American transition of Pentecostalism to the urban environment of the early twentieth century, a mixture of the camp meeting revivalism and African American worship was transformed into new ritual practices radically dissimilar from the established Anglo-European structures.[8] In contrast to the structural liturgy of Christian orthodoxy with its conceptually fixed, written, priest-centered, and performance-oriented framework of sacramental celebration,

---

4. Hocken, "Pentecostal-Charismatic Movement as Revival and Renewal." See, for example, Frodsham, *With Signs Following*.

5. See, for example, Hollenweger, *Pentecostals*, 21–26.

6. Anderson, *To the Ends of the Earth*, 11–36.

7. Eslinger, *Citizens of Zion*.

8. Vondey, "Making of a Black Liturgy."

the Pentecostal revivals emerged as open, flexible, oral, and participation-centered arrangements of worship, prayer, and praise. This contrast to traditional liturgical patterns was nourished by dominant restorationist ideas and an underlying romanticized image of the apostolic age.[9] Pentecostals sought the restoration of "the old time religion, camp meetings, revivals, missions, street and prison work and Christian Unity everywhere."[10] The contemporary Pentecostal movement was seen as a revision and reform of the Christian establishment—in radical opposition to the traditional churches but in line with the commitments of Christian orthodoxy.

> We believe with all our hearts in the "Apostolic Movement" not as a name for a church, but as a religious "reform movement" composed of all clean people who will join in our battle cry and reform slogan of "Back to Christ and the apostles!" . . . But this is only a "reform movement," not a church, not the church, not the churches of God. As many churches as like can belong to this reform movement, as many do; but it is not a church, the church nor the churches; and it is a mistake we ought to get out of to call a Bible congregation of believers set in divine order by any sort of sector nickname.[11]

Pentecostals identified their own revivals with a return to Pentecost and used the terms "Apostolic Movement" or "Latter Rain Movement" to indicate that "the first Pentecost started the church, the body of Christ, and this, the second Pentecost, unites and perfects the church into the coming of the Lord."[12] At the same time, Pentecostals adamantly proclaimed that they were "not fighting men or churches, but seeking to displace dead forms and creeds or wild fanaticisms with living, practical Christianity."[13] The Pentecostal revival was both a return to and reform of Christian orthodoxy seen in its purest and unadulterated form in the times of the apostles.

Similar forms of revivalism can be observed throughout Christianity, typically understood with reference to an unusual demonstration of God's presence and power and as manifesting a significant stage in God's overall redemptive plan.[14] In this sense, the history of Christianity is comprised of a continuing series of the revival and reform of orthodoxy, each significant

---

9. Blumhofer, "Restoration as Revival"; Wacker, "Playing for Keeps."
10. Apostolic Faith Mission, "Apostolic Faith," 2.
11. "Not Missions, but Churches of God," 2.
12. Myland, *Latter Rain Covenant*, 101; Dayton, *Theological Roots of Pentecostalism*, 26–28.
13. Apostolic Faith Mission, "Apostolic Faith," 2.
14. See Gray, "Anatomy of Revival," 255–63.

for the stage it represents yet always remaining a partial manifestation that anticipates the more universal realization of God's redemptive activity.[15] Revival is different from reform, yet this distinction is "a difference in degree, not in kind."[16] In its historical advancement, as in the case of classical Pentecostalism, the deployment of revival is subject to the ideology of revivalism—the use of techniques in order to perform and sustain the manifestations of revival.[17] From this perspective, revivalism is primarily an instrument of evangelism and tool of Christian mission and, like reform, often with unforeseen separatist tendencies.[18] The immediate goal of revivalism is the conversion of the individual and the growth of the revivalist group with little immediate concerns for the broader theological agenda. Revivals are concentrated on theological and religious issues that may initiate ecclesiastical and social reform or even cultural change.[19] Revivalism, however, does not possess the scope, vision, structure, and methods to engage Christian orthodoxy on a global scale.

The problems of revivalism can be clearly observed in classical Pentecostalism where a selective use of glossolalia as forced measurement for the success of the early movement led to the institutionalization of revivals buttressed by doctrinal (rather than experiential) demands for the praxis of Spirit baptism and the solidification of Pentecostal denominations through the pressures of socialization.[20] The lesson from the history of Pentecostalism is that revivals do not function as permanent replacements or long-term equivalents of reformed orthodox patterns of theology and praxis. Revival is not a theological tradition but a temporary stage of performative activity, often functioning as the origin for subsequent stages and thereby demanding new forms of orthodoxy and further revival. For an understanding of the origin of Pentecostalism and its emergence from and distinction to Christian orthodoxy, the notion of revival is indispensable. However, for an understanding of Pentecostalism as a continuing and stable Christian movement and theological tradition, the notion of revival is insufficient.

The growing awareness of the continuing expansion of the Pentecostal revivals worldwide has led to the realization that the confrontation with

---

15. See Vondey, "Full Gospel or Pure Gospel."
16. Murray, *Revival and Revivalism*, 23; Gray, "Anatomy of Revival," 263.
17. See Gray, "Anatomy of Revival"; Richery, "Revivalism."
18. Goen, *Revivalism and Separatism*, 36–114; Sweet, *Revivalism in America*, 140–61.
19. For examples, see Thomas, *Revivalism and Cultural Change*; Smith, *Revivalism and Social Reform*; Hammond, *Politics of Benevolence*; McLoughlin, *Revivals, Awakenings, and Reform*.
20. Vondey, *Beyond Pentecostalism*, 182–91.

Christian orthodoxy and the broad changes of identity, cultural values, social behaviours, and religious practices that are characteristic of the changing global face of Christianity are more extensive than the notion of "revival" indicates.[21] Instead, a new terminology has emerged to document the expansive changes in religious life, institutions, structures, liturgy, catechesis, worship, preaching, ecumenical relations, and theological parlance of Pentecostals worldwide: the notion of "renewal."[22]

Pentecostalism as Renewal of Christian Orthodoxy

The significance of renewal in place of the dominant notion of revival lies in the different functional quality of each practice. The term "renewal" exceeds the temporary performative aspects, scope, and theological focus of revival towards the self-understanding of an established religious tradition. Roman Catholic historian and theologian of the charismatic movement, Peter Hocken, was one of the first to reflect extensively on this distinction between revival and renewal.[23] As an important characteristic of the history of Pentecostalism, he suggested that the change of language from revival to renewal is much more significant than the widely known adjustment from Pentecostal to charismatic. Renewal encompasses a more expansive "network of trends and convictions"[24] than conveyed by either "Pentecostal" or "charismatic" terminology. The idea of the renewal of orthodoxy focuses on what is essential and foundational to maintaining the worldwide effectiveness of the gospel.[25] The Pentecostal and charismatic movements are intended to renew Christianity permanently, not to stimulate a temporary revival of neglected orthodox teachings and practices. Hocken identified revival as an essential but transitional component of the larger phenomenon of renewal, for which there exists no single theological model. In other words, it is difficult to institutionalize renewal or to infer its practical applications from particular techniques and functions from Pentecostal and charismatic practices alone. Hocken's reflections identify a certain irreducible but persistent character of renewal that ties the notion to the manifestations of Pentecostalism but that also exceeds the movement. If the purpose of revival is to bring to life again

---

21. See Ryan, "'Life in the Spirit.'"
22. Pew Forum on Religion and Public Life, *Spirit and Power*.
23. See Hocken, "Revival and Renewal"; *Streams of Renewal*; "Pentecostal-Charismatic Movement as Revival and Renewal"; *Strategy of the Spirit?*
24. Hocken, "Pentecostal-Charismatic Movement," 42.
25. Hocken, "Pentecostal-Charismatic Movement," 44.

what was dead, the purpose of renewal is the permanent availability of this new life for the sake of transforming the whole of Christianity.

However, it is somewhat misleading to speak of the "purpose" of renewal, since there exists no objectively quantifiable reality that would express that purpose: orthodoxy is not defined by what is the "new" (*neos*) but by what is the "correct" (*orthos*) teaching of the faith. If Pentecostals ascertain the purpose of renewal in terms of a constant newness of the correct teaching (a perpetual "neo-orthodoxy"), this purpose in turn must become subject to the mechanisms of that renewal.[26] To paraphrase the ancient dictum: *ecclesia semper renovata est*. Although the emphasis on purpose highlights that renewal can function in the performative and institutionalized environments of the established traditions, renewal employed as an instrument of a revivalist mentality is likely sustained only until the intended purpose has been reached or it risks to become a perpetual instrument and thus performative part of the establishment. The perpetual instrumental use of renewal is limited to an imagination dictated by the normative patterns and expectations of a Christian orthodoxy accustomed to a calculated risk but unwilling to sacrifice itself. On the other hand, if renewal is to resist this purpose, as Pentecostalism suggests, then Christian orthodoxy must open up the theological imagination to unlimited—and therefore potentially unorthodox—trajectories, methods, and possibilities. Orthodoxy itself is always subject to renewal.

Pentecostalism illustrates the resistance of renewal to its instrumentalization at the hands of Christian orthodoxy through a multiplicity of practices including the speaking with tongues, prophecies, healing, dreams, and visions, patterned after scriptural practices, on the one hand, and the indigenous, spiritual beliefs and practices that seem to border on syncretism, on the other.[27] Pentecostals are hesitant to accept the predominantly negative understanding of exceptional patterns and practices and emphasize, instead, that a "theologically responsible syncretism"[28] is an acceptable revision of Christian orthodoxy in the unavoidable and messy encounter between the different communities, cultures, disciplines, thoughts, and imaginations of global Christianity.[29] It is precisely this tension of normative and exceptional patterns that characterizes Pentecostals as a "movement in transition," a community "at a crossroads," a "religion made to travel," and a

---

26. See Cartledge, "*Theological Renewal* (1975–1983)"; Stibbe, "Theology of Renewal and the Renewal of Theology."

27. Ma, *When the Spirit Meets the Spirits*; "Santuala"; Droogers, "Normalization of Religious Experience."

28. Hollenweger, *Pentecostalism*, 132–41.

29. See Vondey, *Pentecostalism*.

"global culture" always on the way to the full renewal of Christianity.[30] This character of Renewal Christianity represents God's whole-hearted involvement in all of life, and it is the insistence on the renewing work of God's Spirit into all dimensions of creation that constitutes much of the attraction, relevance, and challenge of global Pentecostalism.

The Place of Renewal in Christian Orthodoxy

The rise and growth of Renewal Christianity has led to distinctions between its orthodox and unorthodox character and discussions about its location at the center or the margins of Christian orthodoxy. Christianity, by virtue of its mission, is always oriented toward the margins of the world (see Acts 1:8) and initial assessments frequently located Pentecostalism not at the center but at the margins of Christendom.[31] Broadly speaking, these margins include any area, state, condition, teaching, and praxis outside the mainstream of the established and normative traditions. Predominant boundaries identify the margins not only at the longstanding geographical and cultural differences that characterized the global map of Christendom but also at the thresholds of the widespread distinctions between priesthood and laity, theology and spirituality, the dialogue among the religions, the reconciliation of the churches, or the dichotomy between church and academy. Renewal occurs at these margins wherever we encounter a "creative re-visioning"[32] of what is considered acceptable, normative, or orthodox. Pentecostalism is shaped by these margins and moves them forward in the attempt to change the face of global Christianity.[33]

From a Pentecostal perspective, the margins of Christian orthodoxy are the playground of renewal because they constitute a place of risk, tension, and uncertainty less prone to the domination of the theological agendas, doctrinal articulations, and expected methodologies developed at the center of orthodoxy. In this sense, global theology depends on the voices from the margins in order to remain grounded in the realities of the Christian life across the global diversity of cultures, languages, ethnicities, and traditions. Nonetheless, in the same sense, a global Renewal Christianity cannot

---

30. See Anderson and Hollenweger, *Pentecostals after a Century*; Dempster et al., *Globalization of Pentecostalism*; Petersen, *Not by Might nor by Power*; Solivan, *Spirit, Pathos, and Liberation*.

31. Anderson, *Vision of the Disinherited*.

32. Sugirtharajah, *Voices from the Margin*, 1–8.

33. See the volumes in the "Christianity and Renewal—Interdisciplinary Studies" series, edited by Wolfgang Vondey and Amos Yong.

be an exclusive "journey at the margins"—still a dominant perception in a variety of theological contexts, among them Asian American theology, Latino/a theologies, liberation theology, and even classical Pentecostalism.[34] The particularities of these "marginalized" perspectives are not interchangeable with one another or with the agenda of global renewal. A renewal movement that listens to the margins can escape the narrow identity of the margins only if it reaches out to the whole of the Christian world. The same vision must also account for a renewal of the center.

During the twentieth century it was common to identify Christian orthodoxy with a theology of the center, what Fernando F. Segovia calls the "traditional Eurocentric perspective."[35] Global theology, in this sense, has been "a movement away from the longstanding control of theological production by European and Euro-American voices and perspectives toward the retrieval and revalorization of the full multiplicity of voices and perspectives at the margins."[36] This ethos of multiplicity resonates with global Pentecostalism, and today Pentecostals are found both at the margins and the center of orthodoxy, to maintain the image. Yet, Pentecostals do not forsake the center in favor of the margins. Rather, the shift of Renewal Christianity toward the east and the southern hemisphere retrieves the voices from the margins only if those voices speak to the center. At the same time, this move from the margins to the center is plausible only if the center has been transformed by the public witness and missionary presence of those on the margins.[37] Renewal Christianity issues a call forward from the margins to the center and back again![38] This traversing of boundaries constitutes the greatest challenge of renewal.

The contemporary renewal of Christian orthodoxy from either the margins or the center is the activity of a movement, not yet a state of being. Pentecostalism as a renewal movement within Christianity is governed by the desire for balance between what is considered central and what appears marginal to a static orthodox worldview. However, as the range of a renewed orthodoxy shifts and expands, so does the distance between the center and the margins of renewal. As a result, the margins of Christian orthodoxy do not stay the same: new margins emerge as old margins are widened, dissolved, or rearranged. Those who remain at the old margins inevitably

---

34. See Rieger, *Opting for the Margins*; Phan and Lee, *Journeys at the Margin*; Blumhofer et al., *Pentecostal Currents in American Protestantism*.

35. Segovia, *Decolonizing Biblical Studies*, 85.

36. Segovia, *Decolonizing Biblical Studies*, 123.

37. Johns, "From the Margins to the Center."

38. See Ackermann, "Forward from the Margins"; Ronan, "From the Margins to the Universe," 102–10.

position themselves neither at the center nor at the margins of the current world, that is, still in the purview of renewal but not actively participating in the revisioning of Christian orthodoxy. The margins must not be romanticized: suffering, oppression, and persecution of the marginalized are real, and need to be abolished. Holding on to the margins stifles theological imagination, creativity, and hope, and solidifies the insider/outsider status that the renewal of Christianity seeks to overcome. The dominant theological response during the twentieth century has been to shift away from the "unstable" margins to the renewal of the center instead. The difficulties of this task are well illustrated in the recent debate among Evangelicals about the "renewing" or "reclaiming" of the center as a means of revisioning Christian orthodoxy. Two alternatives of theological renewal have emerged that may be evaluated from the perspective of global Pentecostalism, known by the monikers "generous orthodoxy" and "radical orthodoxy."

Renewal as Generous Orthodoxy

Similar to Pentecostalism, and partially because of it, contemporary Evangelicalism has become a movement in transition.[39] In reaction to the challenges of postmodernism, Stanley J. Grenz has called Evangelicals to embrace Hans Frei's vision of a "generous orthodoxy."[40] Grenz understood Frei's idea as a theological program that demands and evokes "the renewal of a 'generous orthodoxy' that is as 'orthodox' as it is 'generous.'"[41] What Grenz envisioned was a renewed center of Evangelical orthodoxy that would overcome the dominant "conservative/liberal" rhetoric of the twentieth century and thus would better meet the challenges of the postmodern world.[42] This renewal of orthodoxy would result in ending the dichotomy between the margins and the center and providing a stable and generous identity to the tradition. For Grenz, "the crucial importance of this balance between center and margin" has become evident in the theological "task of serving as a renewal movement within and toward the church as a whole."[43] Pentecostals are a significant manifestation of this renewal: the voices from the margins, Grenz points out, "above all Pentecostal and charismatic contributions . . . are now shaping

---

39. For a wider discussion, see Vondey, *Beyond Pentecostalism*, 191–201.
40. Grenz, *Renewing the Center*, 333–59.
41. Grenz, *Renewing the Center*, 334.
42. See Jacobsen and Trollinger Jr., *Re-forming the Center*.
43. Grenz, *Renewing the Center*, 344.

evangelicalism."[44] The vision of a generous orthodoxy brings Pentecostalism to the heart of the renewal of the Christian world.

The call for a generous orthodoxy has received sharp criticism from the Evangelical conservative orthodoxy. The contested nature of renewal is highlighted above all by the critical responses that demand a "reclaiming" rather than "renewing" of the center.[45] Grenz's critics find generous orthodoxy not as forsaking the center/margin dichotomy but as steering between the two, thus forming inevitably a new center with a new set of dichotomies. The opposition views the future of Evangelical orthodoxy instead in a new conservative theology.[46] In contrast to a generous theological programme, the new conservative agenda is generous only in reaction to theological shifts by conserving and reclaiming the orthodox tradition as it was perceived before the shift and not as the result of a deliberate pursuit of renewal in response to the changes.[47] While both sides emphasize the importance of the center to identify Evangelical orthodoxy, a reclaiming of the center is less "generous" in its departure from historic orthodox teachings and practices than the renewal theology envisioned by Grenz, whose proposal the conservative camp views as accommodating postmodern tendencies and destroying the foundations of the orthodox Evangelical tradition. This critique solidifies the current situation as the most far-reaching impasse in the further revisioning of Protestant Christian orthodoxy. Pentecostalism is allowed as part of Evangelicalism if it participates in the reclaiming of the center; as a renewal movement, however, Pentecostalism is excluded from the conservative agenda.

Renewal as Radical Orthodoxy

The impasse among Evangelicals raises questions about the significance attributed to the center of orthodoxy with regard to the role of both the renewal of Christianity, in general, and confessional renewal movements, Pentecostal or charismatic, in particular. The dilemma is concentrated in a debate about the limits and possibilities of historical Christian orthodoxy. The situation is therefore not unique to Pentecostals and Evangelicals. Since the late 1990s a largely Catholic and Anglican theological movement has called with similar fervour for a so-called "Radical Orthodoxy."[48] Where generous

44. Grenz, *Renewing the Center*, 187.
45. Erickson et al., *Reclaiming the Center*.
46. Erickson et al., *Reclaiming the Center*, 323–49.
47. Erickson et al., *Reclaiming the Center*, 328.
48. See Milbank et al., *Radical Orthodoxy*; Hemming, *Radical Orthodoxy?*; Smith, *Introducing Radical Orthodoxy*.

orthodoxy calls for a critical appropriation of postmodern sensitivities, and its conservative opponents speak of the certain demise of the postmodern, Radical Orthodoxy intends to walk both paths, albeit with a different goal. While the movement attempts, similar to a generous orthodoxy, to overcome the modern dilemma, Radical Orthodoxy (much like classical Pentecostalism) turns not to the postmodern but the pre-modern. At the same time, while Radical Orthodoxy rejects the nihilistic absurdity of postmodernism (similar to the opponents of a generous orthodoxy), the "radical" programme often deliberately speaks in the language of the postmodern (much like global Pentecostalism). In other words, Radical Orthodoxy is more radical than generous orthodoxy precisely in its insistence on the broadness of the boundaries which constitute Christianity and which make it possible to speak of Christian orthodoxies in the plural.[49] If Radical Orthodoxy is a renewal movement, then it must be understood apart from the false binary of the center and margins of Christian orthodoxy.

While the impasse in contemporary Evangelicalism evolves primarily around the center and margin dichtomy, Radical Orthodoxy also engages the renewal of the social, cultural, anthropological, historical, political, and metaphysical realms of the Christian world. If the goal of a generous orthodoxy can be described as "turning around the center,"[50] and that of conservative orthodoxy as "turning back to the center," then the focus of Radical Orthodoxy lies beyond concerns about a particular orthodox mainline altogether. In this sense, the concepts advanced by Radical Orthodoxy further illustrate the broader dimensions of renewal beyond the constraints of locating orthodox thought and praxis in a particular location, form, or content of the Christian teachings.

Typically seen as a manifesto for the agenda of Radical Orthodoxy, John Milbank's *Theology and Social Theory* criticizes the roots of modernity's "secular, scientific" convictions.[51] For Milbank, secular modernity has posited its own confessional reality rooted in a pretentious rejection of Christian orthodoxy yet remaining indebted to essentially religious and fundamentally theological positions so that modernity "is actually *constituted* in its secularity by 'heresy' in relation to orthodox Christianity."[52] Hence, Radical Orthodoxy, in response to the secular rejection of Christian orthodoxy, understands itself as a post-secular critique and renewal of Christian faith and

---

49. Ward, "Radical Orthodoxy and/as Cultural Politics," in Hemming, *Radical Orthodoxy?*, 106.
50. Oden, *Turning around the Mainline*.
51. Milbank, *Theology and Social Theory*.
52. Milbank, *Theology and Social Theory*, 3.

the church. This renewal of orthodoxy is "radical" in the sense that it seeks to thoroughly retrieve and rethink the "roots" (*radix*) of Christian orthodoxy and their significance for the Christian life today by focusing on (1) a critique of modernity and liberalism, (2) a quest for the post-secular, (3) an emphasis on participation and embodiment, (4) a renewed appreciation of sacramentality, liturgy, and aesthetics, and (5) the pursuit of a constructive critique and transformation of culture.[53] In this broad field of interests, some have suggested that global Pentecostalism offers a particular appropriation of the sensitivities underlying a radical orthodox agenda.

James K. A. Smith argues that Radical Orthodoxy and global Pentecostalism pursue similar theological interests by sharing a rejection of modernity, modern dualism, the myth of secularity, and pure reason, and offering in their place an alternative to postmodernism in the form of an unapologetically confessional theology.[54] Global Pentecostalism, he suggests, is perhaps better equipped to develop the cultural criticism envisioned by proponents of Radical Orthodoxy.[55] Support for this assessment may be found in Pentecostal spirituality and theology, which pushes beyond the pre-modern resources envisioned by Radical Orthodoxy to the roots of Christianity in the New Testament, to a prophetic appraisal of reality in light of the event of Pentecost, and to the spiritual discernment of the Christian life in light of the example of the apostolic church.[56] Pentecostalism has many similarities with the postmodern worldview.[57] Nonetheless, its radical commitment to the sovereign and transforming presence of God as manifested on the day of Pentecost is neither modern nor postmodern. Some have seen the agenda of the Pentecostal movement as radical because of its pre-modern commitments and restorationist tendencies, while others have identified Pentecostal motivations with a recovery of primal Christian speech, hope, and piety.[58] Although Pentecostalism and Radical Orthodoxy are not formally associated, a renewal of Christian orthodoxy developed through an encounter with Pentecostalism has all the sensitivities of a radical renewal project. In this sense, one might answer positively to Smith's inquiry whether Pentecostals are not "more radical than the radically orthodox."[59]

53. Smith, *Introducing Radical Orthodoxy*, 70–80.
54. Smith, "What Hath Cambridge to Do with Azusa Street?"
55. Johns, "Pentecostalism," 112.
56. Smith, "What Hath Cambridge to Do with Azusa Street?," 101, 112.
57. See Johns, "Pentecostalism and the Postmodern Worldview."
58. Cox, *Fire from Heaven*, 81–122; Wacker, *Heaven Below*.
59. Smith, "What Hath Cambridge to Do with Azusa Street?," 101.

Conclusion

Whether conservative, central, marginal, generous, or radical, Pentecostalism is inextricably involved in the theological shaping and revisioning of Christian orthodoxy today. The preceding conversation with dominant Pentecostal views on revising Christian orthodoxy suggests that it is misleading to separate the ideas of a "generous" and "radical" orthodoxy in the context of renewal. Global Pentecostalism tends toward remaining grounded in the rules of conservative orthodoxy while experimenting with the radical extension of those rules for the sake of renewing the whole world. Paradoxically, Pentecostalism is radical precisely in its insistence on orthodoxy—not its departure from it. Put differently, Renewal Christianity is radically orthodox in its generous understanding of what constitutes the boundaries of orthodoxy. Pentecostal faith and practices extend those boundaries because renewal expands not only from the center but from the margins of the world. In this sense, a Pentecostal perspective is oriented towards the renewal of orthodoxy because of its familiarity with both the center and the margins, which allow Pentecostal sensitivities to traverse global Christian faith and practices in their entirety.

Global Pentecostalism offers a multiplicity of resources to understand and engage in the revising of Christian orthodoxy. Because Pentecostal history, theology, spirituality, and praxis are interwoven in the challenges and opportunities, we might say that Pentecostalism manifests the character of a generous, radical orthodoxy in a way that makes Pentecostalism an exemplary movement of renewal. Nonetheless, the end of renewal is not a Pentecostal orthodoxy. The courage and curiosity of renewal ultimately lead also beyond Pentecostalism. Those who dare look beyond the Pentecostal movement will find that the renewal of Christianity is not situated in one particular form of activity, theological locus, or doctrine. Its method proceeds from a theological imagination not bound to existent questions, concerns, and rules but directed in eschatological expectation towards the newness of the kingdom of God. The renewal of orthodoxy serves as the inherent method of a dynamic movement that pushes the boundaries of orthodoxy outward and forward throughout all theological and non-theological dimensions to the "end" of life and creation which is the "new." At the end of the renewal of Christian orthodoxy, Pentecostals find not an endless striving towards the "new" but an eternal rest in the newness of all creation.

Bibliography

Ackermann, Denise M. "Forward from the Margins: Feminist Theology for Life." *Journal of Theology for South Africa* 99 (1997) 63–67.

Anderson, Allan H. *An Introduction to Pentecostalism: Global Charismatic Christianity.* Cambridge: Cambridge University Press, 2004.

———. *To the Ends of the Earth: Pentecostalism and the Transformation of World Christianity.* New York: Oxford University Press, 2013.

Anderson, Allan H., and Walter J. Hollenweger, eds. *Pentecostals after a Century: Global Perspectives on a Movement in Transition.* Sheffield: Sheffield Academic, 1999.

Anderson, Robert Mapes. *Vision of the Disinherited: The Making of American Pentecostalism.* New York: Oxford University Press, 1979.

Apostolic Faith Mission. "The Apostolic Faith." *The Apostolic Faith* 1.1 (1906) 2.

Blumhofer, Edith. "Restoration as Revival: Early American Pentecostalism." In *Modern Christian Revivals*, edited by Edith L. Blumhofer and Randall A. Balmer, 145–61. Urbana: University of Illinois Press, 1993.

Blumhofer, Edith L., et al., eds. *Pentecostal Currents in American Protestantism.* Chicago: University of Illinois Press, 1999.

Cartledge, Mark J. "*Theological Renewal* (1975–1983): Listening to an Editor's Agenda for Church and Academy." *Pneuma: The Journal of the Society for Pentecostal Studies* 30.1 (2008) 83–107.

Cox, Harvey. *Fire from Heaven: The Rise of Pentecostal Spirituality and the Reshaping of Religion in the Twenty-First Century.* Cambridge, MA: Da Capo, 1995.

Dayton, Donald W. *Theological Roots of Pentecostalism.* Metuchen: Hendrickson, 2000.

Dempster, Murray W., et al., eds., *The Globalization of Pentecostalism: A Religion Made to Travel.* Oxford: Regnum, 1999.

Droogers, André. "The Normalization of Religious Experience: Healing, Prophecy, Dreams, and Visions." In *Charismatic Christianity as a Global Culture*, edited by Karla Poewe, 33–49. Columbia: University of South Carolina Press, 1994.

Erickson, Millard J., et al. *Reclaiming the Center: Confronting Evangelical Accommodation in Postmodern Times.* Wheaton: Crossway, 2004.

Eslinger, Ellen. *Citizens of Zion: The Social Origins of Camp Meeting Revivalism.* Knoxville: University of Tennessee Press, 1999.

Frodsham, Stanley H. *With Signs Following: The Story of the Pentecostal Revival in the Twentieth Century.* Springfield: Gospel, 1946.

Goen, C. C. *Revivalism and Separatism in New England, 1740–1800: Strict Congregationalists and Separate Baptists in the Great Awakening.* New Haven: Yale University Press, 1962.

Gray, Tony. "An Anatomy of Revival." *Evangelical Quarterly* 72.3 (2000) 249–70.

Grenz, Stanley J. *Renewing the Center: Evangelical Theology in a Post-Theological Era.* 2nd ed. Grand Rapids: Baker Academic, 2006.

Hammond, John L. *The Politics of Benevolence: Revival Religion and American Voting Behavior.* Norwood: Ablex, 1979.

Hemming, Laurence Paul, ed. *Radical Orthodoxy?—A Catholic Enquiry.* Aldershot: Ashgate, 2000.

Hocken, Peter. "The Pentecostal-Charismatic Movement as Revival and Renewal." *Pneuma: The Journal of the Society for Pentecostal Studies* 3.1 (1981) 31–47.

———. "Revival and Renewal." *Journal of the European Pentecostal Theological Association* 18 (1998) 49–63.

———. *The Strategy of the Spirit? Worldwide Renewal and Revival in the Established Church and Modern Movements*. Guildford, Surrey: Eagle, 1966.

———. *Streams of Renewal: The Origins and Early Development of the Charismatic Movement in Great Britain*. Exeter, Devon: Paternoster, 1986.

Hollenweger, Walter J. *Pentecostalism: Origins and Developments Worldwide*. Peabody: Hendrickson: 1997.

———. *The Pentecostals: The Charismatic Movement in the Churches*. Minneapolis: Augsburg, 1972.

Jacobsen, Douglas, and William Vance Trollinger Jr., eds. *Re-forming the Center: American Protestantism, 1900 to the Present*. Grand Rapids: Eerdmans, 1998.

Johns, Cheryl Bridges. "From the Margins to the Center: Exploring the Seminary's Leadership Role in Developing the Public Presence of Pentecostalism." *Theological Education* 38.1 (2001) 33–46.

Johns, Jackie David. "Pentecostalism and the Postmodern Worldview." *Journal of Pentecostal Theology* 7 (1995) 73–96.

Ma, Julie C. "Santuala: A Case of Pentecostal Syncretism." *Asian Journal of Pentecostal Studies* 3.1 (2000) 61–82.

———. *When the Spirit Meets the Spirits: Pentecostal Ministry among the Kankan-ey Tribe in the Philippines*. Berlin: Peter Lang, 2001.

McLoughlin, William G. *Revivals, Awakenings, and Reform*. Chicago: University of Chicago Press, 1970.

Milbank, John. *Theology and Social Theory: Beyond Secular Reason*. 2nd ed. Oxford: Blackwell, 2006.

Milbank, John, et al., eds. *Radical Orthodoxy: A New Theology*. New York: Routledge, 1999.

Myland, D. Wesley. *The Latter Rain Covenant and Pentecostal Power*. Chicago: Evangel, 1910.

"Not Missions, but Churches of God in Christ." *Word and Witness* 8.6 (1912) 2.

Oden, Thomas C. *Turning around the Mainline: How Renewal Movements Are Changing the Church*. Grand Rapids: Baker Academic, 2006.

Petersen, Doug. *Not by Might nor by Power: A Pentecostal Theology of Social Concern in Latin America*. Oxford: Regnum, 1996.

Pew Forum on Religion and Public Life. *Spirit and Power: A 10-Country Survey of Pentecostals*. Washington, DC: Pew Research Center, 2006. Online. http://pewforum.org/Christian/Evangelical-Protestant-Churches/Spirit-and-Power.aspx.

Phan, Peter C., and Jung Young Lee, eds. *Journeys at the Margin: Towards an Autobiographical Theology in American-Asian Perspective*. Collegeville, MN: Order of Saint Benedict, 1999.

Richery, Russel E. "Revivalism: In Search of a Definition." *Wesleyan Theological Journal* 28.1–2 (1993) 165–75.

Rieger, Jeorg, ed. *Opting for the Margins: Postmodernity and Liberation in Christian Theology*. AAR Reflection and Theory in the Study of Religion. Oxford: Oxford University Press, 2003.

Ronan, Marian. "From the Margins to the Universe." *Cross Currents* 42.1 (1992) 102–10.

Ryan, Joseph Michael. "'Life in the Spirit': Cultural Values and Identity Changes among Catholic Pentecostals." PhD diss., University of Pennsylvania, 1978.

Segovia, Fernando F. *Decolonizing Biblical Studies: A View from the Margins*. Maryknoll, NY: Orbis, 2000.

Smith, James K. A. *Introducing Radical Orthodoxy: Mapping a Post-Secular Theology*. Grand Rapids: Baker Academic, 2004.

———. "What Hath Cambridge to Do with Azusa Street? Radical Orthodoxy and Pentecostal Theology in Conversation." *Pneuma: The Journal of the Society for Pentecostal Studies* 23.1 (2003) 97–114.

Smith, Timothy L. *Revivalism and Social Reform: American Protestantism on the Eve of the Civil War*. Baltimore: Johns Hopkins University Press, 1980.

Solivan, Samuel. *The Spirit, Pathos, and Liberation: Toward an Hispanic Pentecostal Theology*. Sheffield: Sheffield Academic, 1998.

Stibbe, Mark. "The Theology of Renewal and the Renewal of Theology." *Journal of Pentecostal Theology* 3 (1993) 71–90.

Sugirtharajah, S. F., ed., *Voices from the Margin: Interpreting the Bible in the Third World*. Maryknoll, NY: Orbis, 2004.

Sweet, William Warren. *Revivalism in America*. Nashville: Abingdon, 1944.

Thomas, George M. *Revivalism and Cultural Change: Christianity, Nation Building, and the Market in the Nineteenth-Century United States*. Chicago: University of Chicago Press, 1989.

Vondey, Wolfgang. *Beyond Pentecostalism: The Crisis of Global Christianity and the Renewal of the Theological Agenda*. Grand Rapids: Eerdmans, 2010.

———, ed. *Continuing and Building Relationships*. Vol. 2 of *Pentecostalism and Christian Unity*. Eugene, OR: Pickwick, 2013.

———. "Full Gospel or Pure Gospel: Principles of Lutheran and Pentecostal Theology." *Dialog: A Journal of Theology* 55.4 (2016) 11–23.

———. "The Making of a Black Liturgy: Pentecostal Worship and Spirituality from African Slave Narratives to Urban City Scapes." *Black Theology* 10.2 (2012) 147–68.

———. *Pentecostalism: A Guide for the Perplexed*. London: Bloomsbury, 2013.

Wacker, Grant. *Heaven Below: Early Pentecostals and American Culture*. Cambridge, MA: Harvard University Press, 2003.

———. "Playing for Keeps: The Primitivist Impulse in Early Pentecostalism." In *The American Quest for the Primitive Church*, edited by Richard T. Hughes, 196–219. Urbana: University of Illinois Press, 1988.

14

Shifting Paradigms—Future Ecumenical Challenges

—Johanna Rahner

The Hermeneutical Shift

From Unity to Diversity

TWO TRENDS APPLY TO the ecumenical question with regard to the future. The first is the process of secularization, that is, the segmentation within society that demands that churches redefine their place[1]—faith being just one option among many. The second is a growing awareness of the global dimension of church and the political challenges that come with it.[2]

Both trends mean that the classic paradigm of the ecumenical movement and its crucial elements are stretched to their limits. Konrad Raiser describes these elements as a "Christocentric orientation," "a concentration on the church" (that is, ecclesiology as the central topic), and a kind of "universal outlook."[3] He also states that "this approach cannot work in societies that are very differentiated functionally, and it becomes an illusion in societies without one normative tradition, where the faith of individuals is increasingly a matter of individual choice."[4] That means that the classic paradigm has no relevance because developing a strategy for dealing with plurality and diversity becomes the litmus test of ecumenism.

Two things become increasingly important. First, a paradigm with universal aspirations cannot be conceived of without being accused of a hidden agenda of domination. How do we deal with this reality? Second,

1. See Raiser, "Ethik und Ekklesiologie," 416.
2. See Raiser, "Ethik und Ekklesiologie," 417.
3. See Raiser, *Ökumene im Übergang*, 69. For an analysis of the individual elements, see Raiser, *Ökumene im Übergang*, 69–76.
4. Aargaard, "Ecclesiology and Ethics," 161.

from where does a "global model" even derive its criteria when everyone is talking about inculturation, diversity, and so on? A fundamental theological problem seems to be unsolvable: How does the underlying strict Christocentrism of the classic paradigm relate to the plurality of religions—the new paradigm that has emerged in the last few decades?[5]

Given this perspective, the limits of the classic ecumenical paradigm and therefore the need to supplement it become more and more urgent. This problem particularly concerns what Raiser calls the "centerpiece" of ecumenism, ecclesiology.[6] One observation is crucial. Ecumenical hermeneutics has changed from eliminating differences—by searching for a growing consensus in different ecclesiological issues—to an explicit recognition and appreciation of differences. "Although the previous paradigm was blatantly vertical when it talked about the church [that is, only one true church, one true tradition, one true approach for all things], we now find a horizontal understanding of unity in the sense of mediation between different traditions and positions."[7] Plurality now is to be understood not as an acceptable evil, but as a good that needs to be preserved. This approach fits well with the late-modern *zeitgeist* and its "praise for diversity." The consequences are obvious. "Reconciling or balancing the differences between various church traditions becomes the highest form of ecumenical unity that realistically can be achieved."[8] Consequently, "this shift in focus means that talking about the unity of the church has become questionable in itself."[9] No wonder everyone now prefers unity in reconciled diversity as the promising future model. But a closer look reveals that the model of a unity in reconciled diversity also dulls every critical denominational characteristic. Because, as Bruce D. Marshall reminds his fellow ecumenists, the strategy of reconciled diversity "apparently allows only limited possibilities for ecclesial repentance." Amicable relations between churches seem to assume the integrity of each community's doctrines, which in turn means that they assume the absence of any qualitative defects in the doctrines and

---

5. See Aargaard, "Ecclesiology and Ethics," 161. Raiser addresses this question, see Raiser, *Ökumene im Übergang*, 91.

6. See Raiser, *Ökumene im Übergang*, 112.

7. Raiser, *Ökumene im Übergang*, 119–20.

8. Raiser, *Ökumene im Übergang*, 119–20. Raiser addresses the fact that in the history of the church people who thought differently about the faith were often times excluded from the church or even persecuted. This was often done because of an overemphasis on the idea of church unity. He thus asks whether this idea itself of ecclesial unity should be abandoned, as that it has so often been misunderstood.

9. Raiser, *Ökumene im Übergang*, 120.

sees them as adequate for Christian communal life.[10] No changes needed? Business as usual for every denomination? What about the idea that conversion is at the heart of ecumenism?

At this point, even ecumenical experts start to feel uncomfortable. Thou shalt not dismiss the question of truth! That is the eleventh commandment, but what then is the truth? Does distinguishing between true plurality and a false pluralism help? On closer examination, a closer look at distinguishing between legitimate and illegitimate diversity to define the degree of reconciliation leads nowhere. Such a distinction would "at best become trivial—in light of the tensions and contradictions in the life of the churches. In the worst case, it would turn into an instrument of power to suppress diversity."[11] But what is the alternative?

Even if it is a necessary feature of a modern church to allow for the coexistence and plurality of churches, and even if every denomination is obliged to reflect upon that reality—what does it mean to be only one of many churches? This question cannot simply stop with the plurality of churches. Plurality and differences make sense only if we can deal with them. Talking about the plurality of the churches requires an answer to the question about our acceptance of diversity, because we can only talk about differences where the other is seen as and is taken as seriously as the other. But how do we deal with this question properly?

Although the internal differentiation in every denomination today has, through a process of centuries of learning, become a nonnegotiable characteristic of their identity, it still seems to be a challenging question for the ecumenical journey. Interestingly, both issues are deeply intertwined. In other words, the more you can accept differences within your own denomination, the better prepared you are to accept them as an ecumenical necessity. Accepting plurality in your own community gives you a kind of master plan for dealing with interdenominational differences constructively. If you think about your denomination as a monolith, you cannot accept a different way of thinking outside of it.

Is there a useful technique for a successful future diversity management? An observation made by Ottmar Fuchs gives us some direction. He notes that ecumenism or interreligious dialogue cannot work unless it dares to engage in the controversy "whether one's own tradition (solution or way of thinking) is, in part or overall, *more truthful* or *better*"[12] than the other. Only the idea of a wholesome contradiction, which starts

---

10. See Aargaard, "Ecclesiology and Ethics," 171.
11. See Raiser, *Ökumene im Übergang*, 117.
12. Fuchs, "Dialog im 'Martyrium' der Wahrheit," 357–58.

the struggle for better solutions, makes sense of diversity. I can change my mind only when I truly care how you see the world. Only an open exchange of arguments, challenging one another, and discussing the potential rivalries of truth produce positive momentum. Thus, a culture of controversy and debate must be developed, taking the claims to be better seriously and integrating them into ecumenical work productively. Only those fundamentally willing to question their own approach and argue about the truth can ultimately understand themselves as reconciled in differences. Then we can get down to the brass tacks.

Yet, what is the reality in our ecumenical committees and dialogues? Some time ago the Swiss ecumenical theologian Eva-Maria Faber rightly asked if anyone engaged in ecumenical committees and dialogues reckons with new insights and new propositions that leave the well-trodden paths of ecumenical dialog and sets out on the adventure of new ways. Are we not simply reading the results already sure that we will not hear anything fundamentally new?[13] That is a shame! And it is far from the reality that in ecumenical dialogue we must struggle with one another to learn from each other. Because without struggling about the truth, we will not advance the question of what reconciliation really means when we are talking about the unity of the churches as a unity in *reconciled* diversity.

From Doctrine to Ethics

A second shift in ecumenical hermeneutics has become apparent in the last decade, confronting the ecumenical movement with the experience of a new kind of insoluble problem. The dominant perspective in the ecumenical dialogue has changed from structural and doctrinal questions about the nature and essence of the church (a kind of ontology of the Church) to a new and different perspective. Here one looks at the identity of the church that is tied to its function in the ethical and political realms.[14] A new paradigm of a functional ecclesiology has become apparent. It understands acting in the world as a process of the church coming into its own. The world is being renewed, but the church is also renewing itself through its acting.[15] With the idea of church as developed in the 1970s and 1980s, it is now possible to build bridges to Orthodox ecclesiology and to a Roman Catholic

---

13. See Faber, "Umkehr und Veränderungsbereitschaft."

14. And thus the dichotomy of essential and functional ecclesiology is subverted. As Raiser argues, a new situation has emerged which is strongly influenced by secularization and new ethical issues related to globalization. See Raiser, *Ethik*, 415.

15. See Raiser, *Ökumene im Übergang*, 130.

Church that renewed itself in the Second Vatican Council by moving from a self-definition as the Church of Christ to being church in the modern world. This development made the 1970s a golden era of the ecumenical movement[16] and made ecumenism, with its political and ethical questions, an attractive issue in many parts of the world. The primary image of any ecclesiology was the church in action. But the halcyon days of ecumenism have come to an end. This "political approach to social ethics, as it has been developed within the WCC, is a project of modern *Western* thinking. But the shared assumptions of the good life on which this approach was based disappeared in the 1980s and 1990s into the particular agendas of different cultures, subcultures, and ethnic groups, and there has been increasing conflict between the many participants with their differing scenarios about what changes are needed."[17]

As a result, the increasing awareness of the fundamentally ethical dimension of ecclesiology, and thus of the relevance of ethical questions for ecclesiology, leads to a fundamental shift in the ecumenical agenda.[18] Ethical questions can ultimately divide churches. Two problem areas now appear. First, how do we escape the temptation to short-circuit the question ethically about what it truly means to be a church? If we fail, we will find ourselves between the Scylla of ecclesial Donatism (church as community of the pure, the true believers) and the Charybdis of ethical institutionalism (the sacred magisterium that tells what true Christian behavior is). Here we would need a reassurance of those ecclesiological core beliefs that help prevent such a short circuit. The second problem is that we must realistically assume that traditional ecumenical hermeneutics is not really prepared for new challenges and the cultural and political shifts in late modern times. How do we solve this problem?

We must recognize that ethical questions about the highly controversial relationship between individual and community cannot be answered solely on the basis of a common theological anthropology. If we link them to anthropology only, the focus immediately shifts toward problems of individual ethics, but that narrows our perspective. The question of how communities, individuals, and ethics come together must be open to an appropriate definition of the relationship between individual and community. At the same time, questions about the possibility of pluralization in ethical questions within denominations become apparent along with the problem of how ethical dissent within a faith community—understood as faithful and loyal dissenting

16. See Raiser, *Ökumene im Übergang*, 85.
17. Aargaard, "Ecclesiology and Ethics," 160.
18. See Gibaut, "Die Auferbauung des Leibes Christi," 424–25.

opinion—is possible. How can an individual think and act differently and yet remain a full member of one community of believers?

In particular, churches are not seen solely as moral communities—institutions representing a set of ethical and moral orientations and providing resources of meaning and learning. Rather, the ecclesiological wish list of each denominational ecclesiology comes to the fore.[19] This is not a big surprise. We can easily identify all the classic problems of ecclesiology: Questions about authority in the church, representative structures, organization and management, participation, the hermeneutics of scripture and tradition, and so on. Furthermore, in light of related issues like individualization, pluralization, and credibility, the ability of the respective ecclesial concepts to adapt to modernity and democracy are other issues to be addressed.

The Sociological Shift: Being Catholic or Protestant in the Age of Authenticity

We are living in an "age of authenticity."[20] "The faith of the individuals is increasingly a matter of individual choice."[21] Even denominational priorities seem to have shifted fundamentally: My own lifestyle is not determined by my religious or denominational orientation. Instead, I search for a form of spirituality that fits my lifestyle. I measure my faith practices by how much I benefit from them. "The religious life or practice that I become part of must not only be my choice, but it must speak to me, it must make sense in terms of my spiritual development as I understand this. But if the focus is going now to be on my spiritual path ... my placing in the broader 'church' may not be that relevant for me."[22] In this observation, we find another limiting factor for the classic paradigm of the ecumenical movement.

Belonging to a church or a denomination today says more about one's individual preferences than about a denominational identity or system of belief and its idea of God, church, redemption, and so on. What matters is that I "discover my route to wholeness and spiritual depth. The focus is on

---

19. Raiser draws attention to different ecclesiologies and the associated ethical implications. In his view, the Catholic and Orthodox ecclesiologies, which emphasize the church as the body of Christ, the ethical conceptions are often won in a sacramental view of the world. Protestant conceptions of the church remain skeptical, however, regarding ecclesiologically conceptualized ethics. However, many free churches are an exception in this regard, as they tend to emphasize an ethics of Christian discipleship. See Raiser, *Ethik*, 419.

20. See Taylor, *Secular Age*, esp. 473–505.

21. Aargaard, "Ecclesiology and Ethics," 161.

22. Taylor, *Secular Age*, 486–87.

the individual, and on his/her experience. Spirituality must speak to this experience. The basic mode of spiritual life is thus the quest,"[23] and religious existence is a kind of pilgrimage through the whole of life. Churches react to this changing demand with a pluralization and flexibilization of their offers. "Churches have gone along with this global tendency of pluralization and individualization by deconstructing to some degree their all-embracing traditions and adapting them to the preferences and shopping habits of contemporary individuals. The monolithic religious institutions and traditions have lost ground as standards and landmarks of religiosity, and the ideals of authenticity and self-spirituality have taken their place."[24]

As Taylor argues, "For many people today, to set aside their own path in order to conform to some external authority just doesn't seem comprehensible as a form of spiritual life. The injunction is, in the words of a speaker at a New Age festival: 'Only accept what rings true to your own inner Self.'"[25] It is only logical that this "kind of search is often called by its practitioners 'spirituality,' and is opposed to 'religion.' This contrast reflects the rejection of 'institutional religion,' that is, the authority claims made by churches which see it as their mandate to preempt the search, or to maintain it within certain definite limits, and above all to dictate a certain code of behavior."[26] What does this fundamental shift mean for our own religious environment here in Europe? In this sense, the actual question about the "future of the North Atlantic religions" is if there is a connection "between modes of quest and centers of traditional religious authority, between what Wuthnow calls dwellers and seekers?"[27] But the future of the faith in the crucial territory of Latin Christianity remains unclear: "The fading contact of many with the traditional languages of faith seems to presage a declining future. But the very intensity of the search for adequate forms of spiritual life that this loss occasions may be full of promise."[28]

---

23. Taylor, *Secular Age*, 507–8. "Moreover, the seekers in this case are the heirs of the expressive revolution, with its roots in the reactions of the Romantic period against the disciplined, instrumental self connected to the modern moral order. This means . . . also that they are seeking a kind of unity and wholeness of the self, a reclaiming of the place of feeling, against the one-sided pre-eminence of reason, and a reclaiming of the body and its pleasures from the inferior and often guilt-ridden place it has been allowed in the disciplined, instrumental identity. The stress is on unity, integrity, holism, individuality; their language often invokes 'harmony, balance, flow, integrations, being at one, centred'" (Taylor, *Secular Age*, 507).

24. Jonkers, "Are There Any Good Reasons," 207.

25. Taylor, *Secular Age*, 489.

26. Taylor, *Secular Age*, 508.

27. Taylor, *Secular Age*, 532–33.

28. Taylor, *Secular Age*, 533.

To describe this future, Charles Taylor refers to Mikhail Epstein's term "minimal religion,"[29] which Epstein introduced for "postatheistic" Russia and whose premises, for good reason, bear resemblance to Karl Rahner's concept of a "third confession," which he introduced in the 1970s. Taylor talks about a spirituality of people that emerged in a militant atheistic regime that kept all confessional options (which were equally unknown) at an equal distance. "'Minimal religion' is a spirituality lived in one's immediate circle, with family and friends, rather than in churches, one especially aware of the particular, both in individual human beings, and in the places and things which surround us. But because this religion was born outside of any confessional structures, it has its own kind of universalism, a sort of spontaneous and unreflective ecumenism, in which the coexistence of plural forms of spirituality and worship is taken for granted. Even when people who start with this kind of spirituality end up joining a church, as many of them do, they retain something of their original outlook."[30]

Karl Rahner summed up the phenomenon of a third confession in the 1970s. "Above and beyond a mere human relatedness and tolerance, it allows for and requires everything that already happens today in ecumenical closeness and common ecumenical acting. What unifies the third confession . . . is what God gave all Christian churches in Jesus Christ and which all accepted, from which they all lived, and which became the living seed from which a full unity can eventually blossom."[31] However, we still have to find criteria for the description of that which is shared by all and for the quest for common answers to the questions of the time. In light of the changes in the way we talk and preach to a secular, pluralistic, and atheistic world, Karl Rahner saw this criteria as the yardstick for a future ecumenical confession.

But frankly, I'm doubtful that all these fundamental changes will end in an enlightened, religiously and culturally pluralistic humanism as a core belief, or future mainstream Christianity. The abandonment of tradition in our time (particularly characteristic of Christianity in the secularized and highly developed societies of the North) and pluralism (that for sociopolitical reasons alone has become irreversible) mean that postdenominational religious identities are now constructed from a *mélange* of sociological, political, and cultural convictions, but not from theological criteria. This situation creates two additional risks. First, post- or transdenominational identities simply mirror the fractured mentalities and non-simultaneities

---

29. See Taylor, *Secular Age*, 533–35.
30. Taylor, *Secular Age*, 534.
31. Rahner, "Dritte Konfession?," 145.

of their surrounding societies and stabilize them instead of critically challenging them. Such differences, resting on sociological grounds, are much more difficult to handle than the traditional differences in theological teaching. How and on what basis can we legitimize the criteria on which we judge others? Second, we find that post- or transdenominational identities define their beliefs almost through exclusion, by interpreting the differences they experience not with a view toward unity, but toward dissociation. They feel the need to declare the differences, to assert the crucial marks of distinction. Every attempt at relativizing such differences attacks the root of their identity and is therefore excluded from the start. Every different view of how things are necessarily stands outside the common foundation. The boundary between right and wrong threatens to become more and more apodictic. A crucial tendency thus becomes obvious: A shift toward fundamentalism. "For the foreseeable future . . . the dominant theological tone of emerging world Christianity is traditionalist, orthodox, and supernatural. This would be an ironic reversal of most Western perceptions about the future of religion."[32]

The Global Shift: "It's the Economy, Stupid!" and Pentecostalization as a Marketing Strategy

From the perspective of a religious customer, the plurality of churches is undoubtedly much more sensible as a successful marketing strategy of Christianity than the ecumenical project of a unity of the churches or the idea of only one, holy, catholic, and apostolic church. Because only "competing churches can offer all Christian products"[33], the denominational variety can cater much better to the needs of an economized and globalized late modernity with its specific rationalities of supply orientation, competition, sales opportunities, trademark marketing, value of brand recognition, and acceptance by the customer. But one thing should make us a little skeptical. The market always prefers a monopoly of products that have been designed with only consumption in mind. Moreover, to be recognized in the market one needs to be unambiguous. Therefore, the range of different denominations is reduced to the significant and unambiguous ones. Simultaneously, the market meets the very needs that it itself produced.

From this perspective, the ecclesial productivity of the Christian communities of the South and their charismatic-Pentecostal self-staging is unsettling. In this case, very different types of Christian denominations

---

32. Jenkins, *Next Christendom*, 9.
33. Graf, "Ökumenische Selbstaufhebung des Protestantismus?," 206.

act like selling companies in an unlimited, free-floating religious market. For all churches in this market, only one rational counter strategy often exists, namely sharpening the profile of their "brand" with view to local demand.[34] Their religious offers are designed for maximum recognition, and their placement in the market is a mirror of a commercialized, consumer-oriented profile marketing. Religious identity trusts in exclusivity and, with that, in the mechanisms of exclusion. Authenticity means being different, and what is true is what sells. "Questions of religious truth are being interpreted as mere questions of identity and questions of identity are being interpreted as questions about a market profile."[35] A "culturally hegemonic capitalism" is on its way to becoming the dominant religious culture in the Global South. This "culturally hegemonic capitalism . . . takes control over our hopes and desires, our fears and needs. It forms the joys and the hopes, the grievances, and the anxieties of people today only to satisfy them tomorrow. It provides languages and pictures for this and it provides fulfillment: Concrete and palpable."[36]

Looking at the churches of the South, we can see that competition in the religious market is powerful and that the pressure to succeed is enormous. We cannot underestimate the dangers.

First, in the market of possibilities, whoever practices denominational identity by successful branding has an advantage. This approach, however, strengthens those practices within the denominations that do not bear the label of religious enlightenment or even enlightened Christianity. Forced competition in the market of denominations, which in the end produces only consumer-oriented and thus increasingly theologically haphazard ecclesial products, can be won only by adjusting the product portfolio. Who then cares if the longing for a supernatural experience, for a miracle (springing either from social misery, pre-enlightened mentality, or a rediscovery of the emotionality and wholeness or bodylines of the religious[37]) is satisfied by the Holy Spirit (for Pentecostals) or by the Virgin Mary (for Catholics)? In both cases, we use a theology of revelation

---

34. In Germany, the EKD tried to label itself the "church of freedom," which stylizes our longing for freedom and individuality as the late-modern signature of being a Protestant. In this understanding, Roman Catholicism is left with the strategy of pretentious piety, which might be attractive for the media but is nothing more than a colorfully masked event-culture behind which lurk heteronomy and clericalism.

35. Schärtl, "Amerikanisierter Katholizismus?," 464.

36. Bucher, "Auf ihm bestehen," 4.

37. See Schüßler, "Gott erleben und gerettet werden?"

that creates an immediate, eventful, and spectacular shortcut between the experience of God and God's reality.[38]

Second, the societal context also leads to an extensively cultivated and powerful mixture of religious community-building and politico-economic lobbyism or tribalism. It leads to a Gospel of Prosperity designed according to the principles of economic liberalism that, with its health-and-wealth message, mistakes relationships of dependence and utility based on tribe and bribe, which are strengthened by the religious communities themselves, as divine predestination. "Global South Christians retain a very strong supernatural orientation and are by and large more interested in personal salvation than in radical politics."[39]

Consequently, one becomes immune to the need for change in the global economic system, which, and not just according to Pope Francis, presents one of the greatest challenges for all churches today for theological and social-ethical reasons. A Gospel of Prosperity is not just counter-indicative, it also stabilizes the system. Such immunization is also dangerous on an economic level. In an almost paradoxically concrete application of Max Weber's thesis on Calvinism, Evangelical Pentecostals do not see striving for riches and the acquisition of wealth through one's own accomplishments as a structural sin that needs to be criticized, but as something worth striving for. In the Pentecostal communities, even the common people can rise in status, become pastors, and thus make money. Pentecostal churches are for people who want to climb the social ladder.

One can justly doubt whether the true future of Christianity can be found here. The churches might be packed and the communities might be vibrant, but the question remains: Under what conditions? Thus, the triumph of the Pentecostalization of the denominations raises the question whether the decisive difference in the future will be between an enlightened and a fundamentalist version of Christianity. This situation would, in my opinion, shipwreck the project of ecumenism.

The European Ecumenical Heritage in a Changing World

Despite all the cries of naysayers, no shortage of theological challenges for ecumenism will exist. In the last few years, the political and societal relevance of religion and faith has re-entered the public consciousness even in societies that define themselves as secular. At a time when homeland

---

38. See Schüßler, "Gott erleben und gerettet werden?"
39. Jenkins, *Next Christendom*, 8.

becomes plural and cultures meet in an unfamiliarity that seems to be irreconcilable at first glance, the shaping of a peaceful coexistence is one of, if not *the* most decisive challenges. "Deep, true, and lasting peace between humans, that is not built on the sacrifice of others and exists without a polarization towards enemies, is hard to obtain. It even goes beyond human powers. But when it becomes reality then it is a true sign that God (the Holy Spirit) is at work in humans."[40] Only where we are able to testify to that sign in bringing together the other, the foreign, and our own in a struggle for truth as a unity in difference can we develop a new hermeneutical model that establishes the idea coming together, not only coexisting but also accepting each other, learning from each other, inspiring each other, and yet remaining different. Such a model would not solely be a viable option for the future coexistence of the denominations. For that model, the denominational history of Europe is a paradigmatic place where we can learn about the other and from the other. This approach has been shown in analyses of the Reformation jubilee of 2017.

After all, the historical conflicts (2018 marks the 400th anniversary of the beginning of the Thirty Years' War) there can be little doubt, that, first of all, only the coexistence of a plurality of confessions and denominations that is guaranteed by the constitutional law of a secular state marks the beginning of modern Europe. However, in the same root we also find the values of tolerance and of freedom of religion, faith and conscience—for which religious minorities fought for in the wake of the Reformation. The various denominations did not simply remain in a state of confessional opposition. Indeed, they opposed—on the grounds of their religious convictions—the political instrumentalization of their religious differences. Step by step, they then learned to leave their defensive apologetic positions and began to encounter one another, not in a derogatory, but in an appreciative way. They learned to respect other positions, started a dialogue, and began to transform themselves. This work led them to understand that they can enrich each other, an understanding that in itself promotes peace and tolerance. But such an insight could only come about as the result of a religious learning process unparalleled in human history. In this learning process, a method was developed that deals productively with different claims regarding the truth. It not only respects the point of departure of the other but also understands the position of each partner in dialog as mutually enriched by a joint witnessing. It is this constructive cooperation, and not an unconnected plurality of denominations, that is the legacy of the Reformation, which to

---

40. Schwager and Niewiadomski, "Dramatische Theologie als Forschungsprogramm," 64.

this day fundamentally shapes European, and in all likelihood German, identity. Thus, whoever talks about tolerance, freedom of faith, and freedom of conscience stands on a foundation that would not exist were it not for the unique and ecumenical impact of the history of the Reformation. This history is both a common gift and a common obligation. And it is the inviolable heritage of good old Europe for the rest of the world.

Translated by Christian Henkel

Bibliography

Aargaard, Anna Marie. "Ecclesiology and Ethics." *Studia Theologica* 55 (2001) 157–74.
Bucher, Rainer. "Auf ihm bestehen, nicht ihm verfallen. Die katholische Kirche auf dem religiösen Markt." *Euangel* 2 (2017) 4. Online. https://www.euangel.de/ausgabe-2-2017/werkzeuge-auf-dem-pastoralen-markt/auf-ihm-bestehen-nicht-ihm-verfallen.
Faber, Eva Maria. "Umkehr und Veränderungsbereitschaft als konstitutive Elemente des ökumenischen Weges." *Stimmen der Zeit* 230 (2012) 723–34.
Fuchs, Ottmar. "Dialog im 'Martyrium' der Wahrheit." In *Die Dokumente des Zweiten Vatikanischen Konzils: theologische Zusammenschau und Perspektiven*, edited by Peter Hünermann and Bernd Jochen Hilberath, 357–71. Vol. 5 of *Herders Theologischer Kommentar zum Zweiten Vatikanischen Konzil*. Freiburg: Herder, 2006.
Gibaut, John. "Die Auferbauung des Leibes Christi: Überlegungen zu Ekklesiologie und Ethik im Dialog von Glauben und Kirchenverfassung." *Ökumenische Rundschau* 60 (2011) 411–25.
Graf, Friedrich Wilhelm. "Ökumenische Selbstaufhebung des Protestantismus?" *Jenseits der Einheit: Protestantische Ansichten der Ökumene*, edited by Friedrich Wilhelm Graf and Dietrich Korsch, 181–207. Hannover: Lutherisches, 2001.
Jenkins, Philip. *The Next Christendom: The Coming of Global Christianity*. Oxford: Oxford University Press, 2007.
Jonkers, Peter. "Are There Any Good Reasons for Our Attachment to Religious Traditions?" In *The Catholic Church and Modernity in Europe*, edited by Pancratius Beentjes, 205–24. Münster: LIT, 2009.
Rahner, Karl. "Dritte Konfession?" In vol. 27 of *Sämtliche Werke*, edited by Karl-Rahner-Stiftung, 135–45. Düsseldorf: Benziger, 2002.
Raiser, Konrad. "Ethik und Ekklesiologie." *Ökumenische Rundschau* 44 (1995) 411–21.
———. *Ökumene im Übergang. Paradigmenwechsel in der ökumenischen Bewegung*. München: Kaiser, 1989.
Schärtl, Thomas. "Amerikanisierter Katholizismus? Ein Blick aus den USA zurück nach Deutschland." *Stimmen der Zeit* 137 (2012) 459–71.
Schüßler, Michael. "Gott erleben und gerettet werden? Praktiken und Affektstrukturen des pentekostalen Christentums in europäisch-theologischer Perspektive." In *Gerettet durch Begeisterung? Anfragen und Veränderungspotential durch pentekostal-charismatische Religiosität*, edited by Gunda Werner. Freiburg: Herder, 2018.

Schwager, Raymund, and Józef Niewiadomski. "Dramatische Theologie als Forschungsprogramm." In *Religion erzeugt Gewalt—Einspruch!*, edited by Raymund Schwager and Józef Niewiadomski, 39–77. Münster: LIT, 2003.

Taylor, Charles. *A Secular Age*. Cambridge, MA: Belknap Press of Harvard University Press, 2007.

15

Theology Today in India: Ecumenical or Interreligious?

—Michael Amaladoss, SJ

IN THE MOVEMENTS OF theologizing in the Western world, which often tend to identify itself with the "World" as such, we Indians are outsiders. The movements of Western theology are closely conditioned by the movements of Western philosophies. Theology is still largely understood as "Faith seeking understanding" and the seeking is conditioned by various philosophical trends. Creative theology may be done more in the universities than in the Churches. The official theology of the bigger Churches seeks to hold on to tradition, though they do seek to dialogue with modern trends. "Official" theology is done or taught in the Third World, more in seminaries than in universities and in this way they are conditioned by their Western patrons in open and subtle ways. But this has not stopped a group of Asian theologians, sometimes supported by the local Churches, as, for instance, the Federation of the Asian Bishops' Conferences, from doing what we call Asian contextual theology. These contextual theologies dialogue, not with local or global philosophical trends, but with the living realities of Asia: the many poor and their lives, the rich cultures and the living religions. As a matter of fact, all the major world religions were born in Asia. Big ecumenical questions are discussed by the mother Churches in Euro-America. The Asian local Churches were more busy with the dialogue of the Gospel with the local Asian realities. They sought to show that Christianity came as the fulfilment of the Hindu quest for God. For example, J. N. Farquhar wrote *The Crown of Hinduism* (1913), referring, of course, to Christianity. Pierre Johanns wrote four small booklets *To Christ through the Vedanta* (1944), showing how the philosophies of Samkara, Ramanuja, Vallaba and Chaitanya[1] can find fulfilment in the Christian philosophy of St. Thomas Aquinas. A. J. Appasamy

---

1. These were well known Indian (Hindu) theologians.

showed *Christianity as Bhakthi Marga* (1928). There may be no ecumenical dialogue among these and other writers in India.

The Beginnings of Indian Theology

After the Second Vatican Council, the Catholic Church in India organized a series of theological research seminars: (1) *On Religion and Development* (1973); (2) *Can We Consider the Non-Biblical Scriptures as Inspired?* (1974); (3) *Ministries in the Church* (1976); (4) *The Indian Church in the Struggle for a New Society* (1981); and (5) *Sharing Worship: Communicatio in Sacris* (1988). What is significant about these seminars was that, though they were organized by the Roman Catholic Church, the members of other Churches fully participated, not only in the theological discussions, but also in worship, including the Eucharist. I would like to note a number of things here. The group engaged in research and reflection was ecumenical. But it was not discussing what could be called strictly ecumenical or inter-ecclesial questions. It was discussing, what are often considered as, pastoral questions. They were dialoguing, not with each other, but with the world, with their life in the world and its many realities, experiences, problems and questions and with the many believers who share their life and also their experiences and questioning. Here was a sort of common ground for the Christians of different Churches. As a matter of fact, theological groups in the West did not consider these as worthy of their attention because they were considered pastoral and not strictly theological questions. For the Westerners theology had to dialogue with European philosophy. This was a narrow minded approach, of course. But I shall let it pass, though I know Asian theologians who resented this. The deeper questions are: What is theology? Who theologizes? Only the professionals or also the People of God? Does theologizing need to be philosophical? When focusing on the questions of life in the world does it/should it take into account also other human and social sciences like sociology, cultural anthropology and psychology? I know that this is not the place to discuss these questions. But it is good to keep them in mind. The final and the most important question is: If theology is talk about God, which God do we talk about: our God, the Christian God or the God of all peoples and religions? What is interesting is that we seem to be moving towards a situation that in India we can think of theology as an interreligious project. I shall try to explain the slow emergence of this.

A Positive View of Other Religions

The first step is having a positive attitude to the other religions. In the missionary tradition inherited from Europe we had been taught to look at other religions as false and inadequate to promote salvific divine-human encounter. But as we have seen above, when the missionaries came to India and the more intelligent and open ones encountered Hindus and read their scriptures, namely the Vedas and the Upanishads, heard their devotional hymns in the various Indian languages, south and north, and studied the philosophical discussions of the Buddha, Shankara, Ramanuja and a host of others, they discovered treasures of great devotion to God in various forms and theological reflections of a very high order. They also experienced the detached lives of the sannyasis and the fervour of popular religious practices. They found that God had been at work here among these people. But convinced of their own superiority they evolved a framework of preparation-fulfilment in the divine plan of salvation for humanity. Christianity comes to fulfil the religious yearnings prepared by these religio-philosophical-devotional texts. This represents a first phase of dialogue. Members of the different Churches engaged in this.

This positive appreciation of the other religions was expressed, for example, by an Assembly of the Federation Asian Bishops' Conferences (FABC) in 1974, meeting in Taipei, Taiwan. It said:

> In Asia especially this (evangelization) involves a dialogue with the great religious traditions of our peoples. In this dialogue we accept them as significant and positive elements in the economy of God's design of salvation. In them we recognize and respect profound spiritual and ethical meanings and values. Over many centuries they have been the treasury of the religious experience of our ancestors, from which our contemporaries do not cease to draw light and strength. They have been (and continue to be) the authentic expression of the noblest longings of their hearts, and the home of their contemplation and prayer. They have helped to give shape to the histories and cultures of our nations. How then can we not give them reverence and honour? And how can we not acknowledge that God has drawn our peoples to Himself through them?[2]

In a second assembly of the same group of Bishops four years later on the theme of prayer they said: "Sustained and reflective dialogue with them in prayer (as shall be found possible, helpful and wise in different situations) will

2. Rosales and Arevalo, *For All the Peoples of Asia*, 1:14.

reveal to us what the Holy Spirit has taught others to express in a marvellous variety of ways. These are different perhaps from our own, but through them we too may hear His voice, calling us to lift our hearts to the Father."[3]

Here we see them taking a step further. Their positive recognition of the other religions leads them to pray together with them, of course, when and where and how it is possible under the circumstances. Theologically such an interreligious relationship is placed in the context of the Kingdom of God that embraces all religions. The FABC has an *Office of Theological Concerns*, which is made up theologians from the different Asian countries, meets periodically and publishes theological statements on various topics. Its very first statement was *Theses on Interreligious Dialogue*. There were seven theses with an accompanying commentary. In that document, they say, referring to their own positive appreciation of other religions:

> This positive appreciation is further rooted in the conviction of faith that God's plan of salvation for humanity is one and reaches out to all peoples: it is the kingdom of God through which he seeks to reconcile all things with himself in Jesus Christ. The Church is a sacrament of this mystery—a symbolic realization that is on mission towards its fulfilment (*LG* 1:5; cf. BIRA IV/2). It is an integral part of this mission to discern the action of God in peoples in order to lead them to fulfilment. Dialogue is the only way in which this can be done, respectful both of God's presence and action and of the freedom of conscience of the believers of other religions (cf. *LG* 10–12; *Ecclesiae Sanctae* 41–42; RH 11–12)[4]

Religions and the Kingdom of God

Here we see a new image of the network of the various world religions in Asia. The goal of God's mission is the Kingdom of God. All the various religions are reaching out in their own ways to this Kingdom. The Church is also on its way to this Kingdom. But it sees itself as its "sacrament" or "symbol and servant" facilitating the movement of the other religions towards the Kingdom of God. Obviously we have moved a step further in the process of experience and reflection. Earlier, in a framework of "preparation—fulfilment," the Church saw itself as the fulfilment of the other religions. Now the point of fulfilment is the Kingdom of God in the future. The Church, as also

---

3. Rosales and Arevalo, *For All the Peoples of Asia*, 1:35.
4. See Gnanapiragasam and Wilfred, *Being Church in Asia*, 13.

the other religions, is on its way towards the Kingdom. But it feels called to serve others on their way to the Kingdom.

On the occasion of a special Synod of Bishops in Asia, the Indian Bishops said:

> As God's Spirit called the Churches of the East to conversion and mission witness (see Rev 2–3), we too hear this same Spirit bidding us to be truly catholic, open and collaborating with the Word who is actively present in the great religious traditions of Asia today. Confident trust and discernment, not anxiety and over-caution, must regulate our relations with these many brothers and sisters. For together with them we form one community, stemming from the one stock which God created to people the entire earth. We share with them a common destiny and providence. Walking together we are called to travel the same paschal pilgrimage with Christ to the one Father of us all (see Luke 24:13ff; NA 1; GS 22).[5]

So here we see the Church, in the company of other religions, being on a pilgrimage towards God, "the one Father of us all." In other words all the religions are common pilgrims towards the Kingdom of God. Bishops from other countries repeat the same image.[6]

Theology as Dialogical, Interreligious Reflection

Once we realize that we, together with the members of other religions, are common pilgrims towards the Kingdom of God, then theological reflection on our life in the world, especially in the context of the many Asian religions, also becomes a dialogical, interreligious reflection. This has happened in Asia. The FABC had a special section called *Office of Ecumenical and Interreligious Dialogue* (OEIA). It conducted a series of meetings called *Bishops Institute for Interreligious Affairs* (BIRA). These had representative bishops and theologians from the different Asian countries. For their meetings they also invited as participants Buddhists, Muslims, Hindus and Scholars of Confucian and Taoist Traditions. They had five meetings between 1992 and 1996 on the theme "Working Together for Harmony in God's World" leading to statements.[7] This is one way of conducting an interreligious theological reflection.

---

5. See Phan, *Asian Synod,* 21.
6. Phan, *Asian Synod,* 22–48.
7. See Eilers, *For All the Peoples of Asia,* 2:141–78.

Parallel to this effort, another section of the FABC called *Office of Theological Concerns* (OTC) also developed a "theology of harmony." They did not invite experts from other religions. But they did take into account their perspectives in developing their own theology of harmony.[8] What this shows is that theological reflection can be interreligious without the group doing it being itself interreligious, provided it is open to take into account the perspectives of various religions in the course of its own reflection. As a matter of fact this particular group was doing this also when it explored other themes in theology.

Hindu-Christian Theologians

This process can go deeper still. A particular theologian can feel that s/he her/himself is Hindu-Christian. Obviously one cannot belong to two religious institutions for simple sociological reasons. But at a theological and spiritual level one can feel Hindu-Christian. S/he may have been born and brought up as a Christian. But at some stage of her/his life s/he feels that his/her ancestors were Hindus and s/he has also inherited their religious and spiritual riches. S/he then tries consciously to carry on an inner spiritual and theological Hindu-Christian dialogue.

Raimon Panikkar is a good example. He explained his double identity himself in an interview in 2000. He said:

> I was brought up in the Catholic religion by my Spanish mother, but I never stopped trying to be united with the tolerant and generous religion of my father and of my Hindu ancestors. This does not make me a cultural or religious "half-caste," however. Christ was not half man and half God, but fully man and fully God. In the same way, I consider myself 100 percent Hindu and Indian, and 100 percent Catholic and Spanish. How is this possible? By living religion as an experience rather than as an ideology.[9]

It is sufficient to read the numerous books of Raimon Panikkar to understand what a "Hindu-Christian" theology could be.

I myself feel that I am Hindu—Christian. Brought up as a Catholic and a Jesuit, at some stage of my personal and theological development I have discovered my roots in my Hindu ancestors. My family has been

---

8. See Theological Advisory Commission of the Federation of Asian Bishops' Conferences, *Asian Christians Perspectives on Harmony*.

9. Panikkar, "Interview," 834–36. For other examples of "Hindu-Christians," see my chapter, "Hindu and Christian—Conflict or Challenge?"

Christian only for four generations. Today I do not feel the need to abandon my Hindu roots. Rather I seek to nourish myself from them by going back to Hindu spiritual texts and devotional poems. I do not make artificial efforts to integrate the two traditions. But there is an ongoing dialogue within, which corrects exaggerations on either side and promotes an integration in the way I look at God, the humans and the universe. My God is non-dual or *advaitic*. Jesus Christ is for me an Asian. My theologizing seeks to make space for other religions and their perspectives, particularly Hinduism. My spirituality is Hindu-Christian. My way of thinking is not Greek rational and dichotomic, but Indian, non-dual and symbolic.[10]

Interreligious theology, therefore, need not necessarily be done by an interreligious community. This remains possible. But it can also be done by an interreligious person. Certainly it is not only an academic, intellectual effort, but also a personal commitment. Becoming such a person may not always be easy, though it might come naturally to some. The personal diary of Swami Abhisiktananda shows how difficult it can be.[11]

Conclusion

Theology is talk about God. I think that it is time that we went back to the One God of All in the place of the many Gods that the various religions have shaped up. The pluralism of the many religions have pluralized God so to speak, setting one God against the others. The image of the One God can certainly be enriched, but never exhausted, by the many names that the different religions give God. Once we identify God with one of the names, then the true God disappears. The many gods with their many names fight for the place of the one God without in the least deserving it.

Talking about God must be the expression of our own particular experience of God. But unfortunately, we tend to absolutize the language of our experience, darkening the experience itself in the process. Our language, culture and philosophy seek to condition and limit our experience, conflicting with other experiences. Pluralism, instead of being richness, becomes a problem. The true God, the Absolute, disappears in the process.

When we focus on the One God of All and accept also the multiplicity of expressions we will be faced with a kaleidoscope that is ever rich and ever changing—but always beautiful.

---

10. Please see the many chapters in my book referred to in the previous footnote. See also my other books, like *Asian Jesus*; *Quest for God*; *Experiencing God in India*; *Dancing Cosmos*.

11. See Abhishiktananda, *Ascent to the Depth of the Heart*.

Bibliography

Abhishiktananda, Swami. *Ascent to the Depth of the Heart*. Delhi: ISPCK, 1998.
Amaladoss, Michael. *The Asian Jesus*. Maryknoll, NY: Orbis, 2006.
———. *The Dancing Cosmos: A Way to Harmony*. Anand: Gujarat Sahitya Prakash, 2003.
———. *Experiencing God in India*. Anand: Gujarat Sahitya Prakash, 2016.
———. "Hindu and Christian—Conflict or Challenge?" In *Interreligious Encounters: Opportunities and Challenges*, edited by Jonathan Y. Tan and Michael Amaladoss, 173–92. Maryknoll, NY: Orbis, 2017.
———. *Quest for God: Doing Theology in India*. Anand: Gujarat Sahitya Prakash, 2013.
Amalorpvadass, D. S., ed. *Can We Consider the Non-Biblical Scriptures as Inspired?* Bengaluru: National Biblical Catechetical and Liturgical Centre, 1974.
———, ed. *The Indian Church in the Struggle for a New Society*. Bengaluru: National Biblical Catechetical and Liturgical Centre, 1981.
———, ed. *Ministries in the Church*. Bengaluru: National Biblical Catechetical and Liturgical Centre, 1976.
———, ed. *On Religion and Development*. Bengaluru: National Biblical Catechetical and Liturgical Centre, 1973.
Appasamy, A. J. *Christianity as Bhakthi Marga*. Madras: Christian Literature Society, 1928.
Eilers, Franz-Josef, SVD, ed. *For All the Peoples of Asia*. Vol. 2. Manila: Claretian, 1997.
Farquhar, John N. *The Crown of Hinduism*. London: Oxford University Press, 1913.
Gnanapiragasam, J., and Felix Wilfred, eds. *Being Church in Asia*. Manila: Claretian, 1994.
Johanns, Pierre. *To Christ through the Vedânta*. Ranchi: Catholic, 1944.
Panikkar, Raimon. "Interview." *Christian Century* 117 (2000) 834–36.
Phan, Peter C., ed. *The Asian Synod: Texts and Commentaries*. Maryknoll, NY: Orbis, 2002.
Puthanangady, Paul. *Sharing Worship: Communicatio in Sacris*. Bengaluru: National Biblical Catechetical and Liturgical Centre, 1988.
Rosales, Gaudencio B., and C. G. Arevalo, eds. *For All the Peoples of Asia*. Vol. 1. Manila: Claretian, 1997.
Theological Advisory Commission of the Federation of Asian Bishops' Conferences. *Asian Christians Perspectives on Harmony*. FABC Papers 75. Hong Kong: FABC, 1996.

16

Next Steps—and Visions? Lutheran Perspectives on Doctrinal Ecumenism

—Bernd Oberdorfer

The Death of "Doctrinal Ecumenism"—Adjourned

CRITICS OF THE SO-CALLED "Consensus Ecumenism" (*Konsensökumene*, or *Lehrkonsensökumene*) often argue that this model of ecumenical dialogue, if not mistaken in itself, in any case has exceeded its peak and should therefore not be continued. The arguments are various: Some claim that these dialogues have the inappropriate form of political negotiations and only result in formula compromises (*Formelkompromisse*) which do not represent a real consensus. Others criticize that, for example, the 1999 "Joint Declaration on the Doctrine of Justification" (JDDJ) between the Lutheran World Federation and the Pontifical Council for Promoting Christian Unity had no concrete consequences, that it did not even make Eucharistic hospitality possible. Others say that a consensus of doctrine only is of no use if it does not emerge from and is not embedded in experiences of shared communion in liturgical and diaconal life.

However, although it is true that isolated expert discourses on the controversial topics of sixteenth-century theology cannot produce church communion, the consensus *de doctrina evangelii*, according to article 7 of the Augsburg Confession, is a necessary element of church unity. Thus, from a Lutheran perspective, doctrinal dialogues are indispensable if the promotion and expression of communion between churches is required at all. Moreover, although JDDJ did not cause a more inclusive communion between the Lutheran Church and the Roman Catholic Church, it nevertheless did not actually lack ecumenical consequences: First, the "differentiated consensus" on the doctrine of justification was officially affirmed by the World Methodist Council in 2006 and the World Communion of Reformed Churches in 2017, and in the same year the Anglican Communion declared its agreement to the content of JDDJ without formally signing it.[1] So there is a broad ecumenical "consensus in basic truths" with reference to justification now which does not oblige to neglect remaining differences but implies that these differences need not any longer be regarded as church-dividing. Second, although not changing the legal position of the Roman Catholic Church, JDDJ influenced the ecumenical atmosphere between Lutherans and Roman Catholics producing a spirit of mutual trust which enabled both churches to find ways of common commemoration of the 500th anniversary of the Reformation. Thus, based on the common study "From Conflict to Communion,"[2] the ecumenical events in Lund and Malmö on October 31, 2016, when the heads of LWF and leading representatives of the Roman Catholic Church, among them Pope Francis, joined in commemorating Reformation, are fruits of the ecumenical dynamics JDDJ has initiated.[3]

But exactly *because* the history of the reception of JDDJ can be labelled a "success story"[4], the evident stagnation in some crucial matters of ecclesial communion must remain a matter of serious concern. Particularly, the fact that the Roman Catholic church officially does not allow Protestants—not even the non-Catholic partner in bi-confessional marriages—to receive Eucharist communion continuously challenges ecumenical efforts to overcome the theological impediments. Obviously, this includes theological dialogues in order to find a consensus which allows at least for Eucharist hospitality. Therefore, the model of "consensus ecumenism" has not become outdated.

Eucharist/Holy Supper: A Consensus in Basic Truths?

Recent theological research has shown that a "consensus in basic truths" of the doctrine of the Eucharist or Lord's Supper is within reach if the concept of "*differentiated* consensus" is taken seriously. This concept, as already mentioned, only requires that the divergent doctrine (and practice) of the respective other church no longer needs to be regarded as church-dividing. Then, if a basic consensus with regard to the gift of Christ's presence within the sacramental elements of bread and wine can be affirmed, Lutherans can accept as doctrine and practice of a particular sister church that (1) the Roman Catholic Church understands the mass as a sacrifice—if (and because)

---

1. See Schuegraf, "Was Sie getan haben."
2. See LRCCU, *From Conflict to Communion*; cf. Oberdorfer, "Feiern? Gedenken? Büßen?," 3–8.
3. See Oberdorfer, "Gruppenbild in Albe."
4. See Schuegraf, "Was Sie getan haben"; Oberdorfer, "Auf dem Weg."

it is made clear that this sacrifice only represents (*vergegenwärtigt*) Christ's sacrifice on the cross and neither *repeats* nor even *complements* it; (2) the Roman Catholic Church regularly practices the *communio sub una*, i.e., offers the participants only the consecrated wafer and not the wine—if it is made clear that the full form of Eucharist is the *communio sub utraque* and the congregations are encouraged to celebrate the full form as regular as possible; (3) the Roman Catholic Church interprets the way of Christ's presence within bread and wine in term of "transubstantiation"—if it is made clear that this conception is not compulsory and does not exclude other conceptions like the Lutheran "consubstantiation"; (4) for the Roman Catholic Church the consecrated wafers retain their changed "substance" after the Eucharist and thus can be used sacramentally outside the mass setting (*extra usum*)—if it is made clear that this expanded use is nothing but an extension of the mass as a celebration of the *congregatio sanctorum* and not a substitute for it;[5] (5) the Roman Catholic Church celebrates the feast of *Corpus Christi*—if it is made clear that by revering the consecrated wafer the Church worships the gift of Christ's presence and not its own competence to consecrate. Conversely, Catholics can accept that (1) the Lutheran understanding of the Holy Supper preserves crucial characteristics of the Catholic conception of the Eucharist; (2) the Lutheran conception of Christ's presence "within, together with and among" bread and wine does not safeguard the *unio sacramentalis* less strongly than the Catholic concept of "transsubstantiation"; (3) divergent liturgical practices in the Lutheran Holy Supper do not mark a church-dividing difference.

Thus, a "Joint Declaration on the Doctrine of Eucharist/Holy Supper" seems to be easy to achieve. However, both sides agree that such a declaration would not support but rather damage the ecumenical progress. It would not result in Eucharist communion, not even in mutual Eucharist hospitality, because, from a Catholic perspective, the church-dividing issue is not the understanding of the Eucharist itself but its ecclesial embedding. To say it more concretely: The problem is not *what happens* in the Holy Supper but rather *who acts*. Thus, an isolated consensus on the Eucharist would raise hopes which would have to be frustrated. Therefore, if a consensus which includes concrete consequences is aimed at, this consensus must refer to the

---

5. The same goes for the even more problematic fact that the Roman Catholic Church still allows priests to celebrate the mass individually, without participation of other members of the Christian congregation. From a Lutheran perspective, this practice is irregular and can only be tolerated and regarded not to be church-dividing if it is clearly marked as exceptional because the mass in its core realizes the *communio sanctorum* as both the communion *with* the body of Christ and the communion *of* the Body of Christ, i.e., the congregation of the Church.

understanding of the Church and Ordained Ministry as well because of the ecclesial relevance of the Holy Supper. Church officials like Kurt Cardinal Koch, then, suggested initiating a dialogue in order to develop a "Common Declaration on Church, Ordained Ministry and Eucharist."

Towards a "Common Declaration on Church, Ordained Ministry and Eucharist/Lord's Supper"? First Evaluations

In recent years, two joint Lutheran–Roman Catholic working groups published extended studies which introduce themselves as first steps towards a differentiated consensus on these three topics: the US-American "Declaration on the Way"[6] and the Finnish "Communion in Growth."[7] Both claim to have achieved substantial progress in a common understanding of church, sacraments and ordained ministry.[8]

The US declaration[9] formulates thirty-two "agreements" which it recommends to worldwide reception. In the particularly sensitive matter of ordained ministry, the Lutherans affirm that it does not derive from the "common priesthood of all believers" but rather has its own status. They therefore reject the idea that the ordained ministry has its authority through mere "delegation" by the congregation. The distinction between pastors/priests and bishops, according to the Declaration, does not only result from sociological needs but is a work of the Holy Spirit. That is, the Lutherans accept—without further explanation—that bishops are theologically necessary. They even observe in the Lutheran communion a growing awareness of the need for a ministry of the universal unity of the church and hope that the way the "papal leadership" is exercised in present time (that is, presumably, by Pope Francis) offers a historic chance for open and fruitful ecumenical dialogues about an adequate form of papacy.

The thirty-two agreements are followed by fifteen "remaining differences" which—according to this arrangement—are supposed to be analyzed in the light of the agreements. Indeed, in this light, some of them prove to have lost church-dividing relevance. As to the ordination of women, however, the Declaration raises doubts. It only argues that Lutheran churches by

---

6. See Committee on Ecumenical and Interreligious Affairs, et al., *Declaration on the Way*.

7. See LCDCF, *Communion in Growth*.

8. For a more extended interpretation of both studies, see Oberdorfer, "Der Weg ist (nicht?) das Ziel."

9. See Ecumenical Studies Committee. "On the American Document."

ordaining women do not change their theology of ordination and therefore the differentiated ecumenical consensus concerning ordination is not addressed. But given the strict Roman Catholic exclusion of the mere possibility of female priests, the understanding of ordained ministry might dissent more deeply than the Declaration suggests.

The Finnish study states an even more profound consensus. Methodically, it adapts the concept of differentiated consensus. In the respective chapters, both churches first "formulate the common understanding of Church, Eucharist, and Ministry together" "in uniformly accepted language."[10] Based on this "common statement," "the doctrinal statements traditionally seen as in conflict are examined to establish if they still exclude each other or if they are simply different expressions of the same basic truth."[11] Here "a consensus in form and language on every imaginable doctrinal question" is not necessary.[12]

The study claims a basic ecclesiological consensus with reference to the "communio" ecclesiology of Vatican II. Lutherans, moreover, could adopt the idea of the essentially sacramental character of the church. Embracing the possibility of a wider concept of "sacrament," Lutherans could also accept the Catholic practice of seven sacraments, including marriage. As to Holy Supper, neither the *communio sub una* nor the sacramental use of the consecrated wafers *extra usum* is seen as a substantial problem; the Finnish Lutherans are even willing to confirm Eucharist as a sacrifice. Both churches state together (i.e., "in uniformly accepted language") that "the common priesthood of the faithful and the ministerial or hierarchical [!] priesthood" "differ from one another in essence and not only in degree"[13] which actually is a formula used in *Lumen Gentium*. Not surprisingly, both churches agree that the "development of the threefold ministry can be seen as an expression of the guidance of the Holy Spirit, and is more than a matter of arbitrary human choice."[14] So, the ministry of bishops is held to be necessary. Other forms of *episcope* (e.g., synods) are hardly mentioned. Even the "efforts to promote unity, witness, and service" which are ascribed to the "Petrine Ministry" are unanimously regarded "as willed by God."[15] Because JDDJ declared a consensus in basic truths of justification, according to the study "the most important obstacle to a renewed understanding

---

10. LCDCF, *Communion in Growth*, 12.
11. LCDCF, *Communion in Growth*, 12.
12. LCDCF, *Communion in Growth*, 12.
13. LCDCF, *Communion in Growth*, 197.
14. LCDCF, *Communion in Growth*, 212.
15. LCDCF, *Communion in Growth*, 260; cf. 262.

of the ministry of the pope has been overcome."[16] The Finnish Lutherans are even willing to affirm papal ministry as an institution *iure divino*. The Reformers' "rejection of the *ius divinum* claim" is regarded to be "neither fundamental nor categorical."[17] Luther's strong critique of the papal ministry is qualified as "historically conditioned";[18] according to the study, it therefore "cannot be taken as a constructive ecumenical basis for dialogue on the Petrine Ministry."[19] The Lutherans even express sympathy for the purpose of the papal infallibility "to protect the freedom of the Gospel and the fundamental truths of Christian faith" (chapter 5.5., headline) and compare it to the Lutheran concept of "*status confessionis.*"[20]

The Finnish study gives an extremely one-sided picture of Lutheran ecclesiology. Its reading of Lutheran confessions more than once reverses their meaning into the opposite. It clearly shows the intention to make the Lutheran doctrine converge as closely as possible to the Roman Catholic doctrine. There are hardly any traces of an effort to insert Lutheran inputs into the dialogue.

The US-*Declaration on the Way* gives a more complete, more differentiated, more adequate picture of the Lutheran doctrine of Church, sacraments and ordained ministry and therefore is a more useful tool for the ecumenical dialogues to come. However, not unlike the Finnish study, it lacks a balance between the concepts of ordained ministry (including bishops) and common priesthood of all believers and, because of that, between episcopal and synodal *episcope*. Due to its focus on episcopacy, it primarily represents the "High Church" strand of the Lutheran tradition. Yet characteristic of German Lutheranism, for example, is a complex combination of "High Church" and "Low Church" elements. In Lutheran ecclesiology, there has always existed a "delegation" model of ordained ministry meaning that a Christian congregation—by will of God, *iure divino*—has to elect ("delegate") someone for the permanent function of preaching the Gospel in public and administering the Sacraments. The ordained ministry, then, according to this model, is a (necessary!) specific form of realizing the common priesthood of all believers, rather than being something essentially different. It is not helpful to conceal (or even discredit) this model in the ecumenical dialogues in order to achieve consensus more easily.

---

16. LCDCF, *Communion in Growth*, 264.
17. LCDCF, *Communion in Growth*, 261.
18. LCDCF, *Communion in Growth*, 186.
19. LCDCF, *Communion in Growth*, 186.
20. LCDCF, *Communion in Growth*, 272.

To conclude: From a Lutheran perspective, I would think, the ecumenical dialogue with the Roman Catholic Church referring to ordained ministry cannot limit itself to proving that the Lutheran understanding of ordained ministry complies with all Roman Catholic requisites and thus there is no *defectus ordinis* (which, more or less, both studies do). Sometimes it even seems that the Lutherans try to justify the ordination of women as an exception rather than an implication of their doctrine of ordained ministry. But if the Lutheran Churches affirm that their understanding of the common priesthood of all baptized believers does not allow excluding baptized women from being ordained, they *ipso facto* affirm that for them the ordination of women is an *essential element* of ordained ministry. Then the Roman Catholic exclusion of women would mark a *defectus ordinis* (although not devaluating the status of the ordained male priests)—of which the Lutherans would have to decide whether they regard it as Church-dividing or not. This, by the way, has consequences for the idea of a Lutheran recognition of the "Petrine Ministry": If the Pope were not only the leader of a sister Church but the head of the universal Church, and if the Lutherans recognized that the Pope performs this function as ordained minister according to Lutheran doctrine, why should they accept then that this specific function could only be exercised by men?

Unity? What Unity? A Final Remark

Although there is a widespread conviction that the churches should strive for "visible unity" or "full visible unity,"[21] there are no realistic scenarios of concrete forms for this unity. Of course, the Protestant churches have developed a broad spectrum of "communions," even "unions"—but it can be doubted whether these models are applicable to a "unity" which includes the Roman Catholic Church. Actually, the Roman Catholic Church established forms of "union" which allow the Unified Oriental Churches a lot of autonomy with respect to Church order (such as the marriage of priests) or liturgical practice. But would this model work for Protestant churches, too? Would the Roman Catholic Church, for example, be willing to accept female pastors and bishops, or the practice of divorce and re-marriage in a "unified" Lutheran Church although it interdicts this in its own legislation? If not—and if the Lutheran Churches cannot be convinced to change their practice in order to "return" to the "Una Sancta"—are there any alternative models of "visible unity" which comply with the ecclesiological

21. See Oberdorfer and Schuegraf, *Sichtbare Einheit der Kirche in lutherischer Perspektive*.

standards of *both* Churches? In my opinion, there is an urgent need for further investigation.

Bibliography

The Committee on Ecumenical and Interreligious Affairs, et al., eds. *Declaration on the Way: Church, Ministry, and Eucharist.* Minneapolis: Fortress, 2015.

Ecumenical Studies Committee. "On the American Document *Declaration on the Way: Church, Ministry, and Eucharist.*" *Deutsche Nationalkomitee des Lutherischen Weltbundes*, November 24, 2017. Translated by Timothy J. Wengert. Online. https://www.dnk-lwb.de/de/content/position-paper-ecumenical-studies-committee-american-document-declaration-way-church.

Lutheran-Catholic Dialogue Commission for Finland (LCDCF), ed. *Communion in Growth: Declaration on the Church, Eucharist, and Ministry.* Helsinki: Evangelical Lutheran Church of Finland; Catholic Church in Finland, 2017.

Lutheran-Roman Catholic Commission on Unity (LRCCU). *From Conflict to Communion: Lutheran-Catholic Common Commemoration of the Reformation in 2017.* Leipzig: Evangelische Verlangsanstalt, 2013.

Oberdorfer, Bernd. "Auf dem Weg—wohin? Ökumenische Perspektiven: Eine lutherische Sicht." In *Auf dem Weg zur Gemeinschaft. 50 Jahre internationaler evangelisch-lutherisch/römisch-katholischer Dialog*, edited by André Birmelé and Wolfgang Thönissen, 352–68. Leipzig: Evangelische Verlagsanstalt, 2018.

———. "Der Weg ist (nicht?) das Ziel. Was folgt auf die 'Gemeinsame Erklärung zur Rechtfertigungslehre'?" *Una Sancta* 73 (2018) 227–41.

———. "Feiern? Gedenken? Büßen? Ökumenische Perspektiven auf das Reformationsjubiläum: Zur lutherisch-katholischen Studie 'Vom Konflikt zur Gemeinschaft.'" *Materialdienst des Konfessionskundlichen Instituts Bensheim* 64.1 (2014) 3–8.

———. "Gruppenbild in Albe. Wie Lutheraner und Katholiken in Lund gemeinsam das Reformationsjubiläum begingen." *Evangelische Theologie* 77 (2017) 75–80.

Oberdorfer, Bernd, and Oliver Schuegraf, eds. *Sichtbare Einheit der Kirche in lutherischer Perspektive. Eine Studie des Ökumenischen Studienausschusses/Visible Unity of the Church from a Lutheran Perspective. A Study by the Ecumenical Study Committee.* Leipzig: Evangelische Verlangsanstalt, 2017.

Schuegraf, Oliver. "'Was Sie getan haben, haben Sie für uns alle getan': Zur jüngsten Erfolgsgeschichte der Gemeinsamen Erklärung zur Rechtfertigungslehre." *Una Sancta* 73 (2018) 191–204.

www.ingramcontent.com/pod-product-compliance
Lightning Source LLC
Chambersburg PA
CBHW071238230426
43668CB00011B/1488